Managing Without Profit

Leadership, management and governance of third sector organisations

Mike Hudson

Third edition

DIRECTORY OF SOCIAL CHANGE

'Managing Without Profit *contains much wise counsel, born of extensive experience in the third sector and acute insight into how managers manage and leaders lead.*'
Dawn Austwick, Chief Executive, Esmee Fairbairn Foundation

'*It's never too late to learn something new – this book can teach us all a lot about the art of managing and leading values-based, mission-led organisations.*'
Jackie Ballard, Chief Executive, Royal National Institute for Deaf People

'*One of the critical elements of an effective charity is excellent management;* Managing Without Profit *provides a comprehensive map of what constitutes excellent management. Its focus on clear strategic thinking, planning and measuring social impact is absolutely what's needed for high performing charities today.*'
Martin Brookes, Chief Executive, New Philanthropy Capital

'*A growing third sector, with more power and influence, needs exceptional management and it needs management learning: that's the value of the Hudson book.*'
Stephen Bubb, Chief Executive, ACEVO

'*A book about social enterprise without a single wasted word – just clear, concise and comprehensive guidance on how to manage without profit.*'
Greg Clark MP, Shadow Secretary of State for Energy and Climage Change and former Shadow Minister for Charities, Social Enterprise and Volunteering

'Managing Without Profit *has been for many years the pre-eminent book for everyone concerned with non-profit organisation governance. It does both theory and practical application with equal brilliance, so this new, updated version is particularly welcome.*'
Michael Day, Chief Executive, Historic Royal Palaces

'Managing Without Profit *has become the most significant contribution to the management and leadership of organisations within civil society. In this new edition Mike Hudson has once again demonstrated his grasp of the issues. A must-have book for all those concerned with non profits.*'
Stuart Etherington, Chief Executive, NCVO

'*Essential reading for anyone who manages or governs nonprofit organisations.*'
Phil Hope MP, Minister of State for Care Services and former Minister for the Third Sector

'*An invaluable resource for anyone wanting to get to grips with management in today's growing third sector.*'
John Low, Chief Executive, Charities Aid Foundation

'Managing Without Profit *is a vital book for both senior management and board members of leading charities. At Christian Aid we have used and shared this book widely. Mike provides an excellent resource for managing in a competitive and challenging environment.*'
Daleep Mukarji, Chief Executive, Christian Aid

'*As the third sector develops in a changing world,* Managing Without Profit *is a valuable guide for the busy manager who needs up-to-date guidance quickly and easily.*'
David Nussbaum, Chief Executive, WWF-UK

Published by
Directory of Social Change
24 Stephenson Way
London NW1 2DP
Tel: 0845 077 7707; Fax: 020 7391 4804
Email: publications@dsc.org.uk
www.dsc.org.uk
from whom further copies and a full publications list are available.

First edition published 1995 by Penguin
Second edition published 1999 by Penguin
Reprints 2002, 2004, 2005 and 2006 published by the Directory of Social Change

Third edition published 2009 by the Directory of Social Change

ISBN 978 1 903991 99 2

British Library Cataloguing in Publication Data

A catalogue record for this book is available from the British Library

Typeset by Marlinzo Services, Somerset
Printed and bound by Page Bros, Norwich
Cover and text designed by Kate Bass

All Directory of Social Change departments in London:
0845 077 7707

Directory of Social Change Northern Office
Research: 0151 708 0136

Contents

About the author

Mike Hudson is the Director of Compass Partnership, a group of management consultants which works exclusively with nonprofit organisations. He studied Engineering Science at Durham University and then pursued his interest in protecting the environment by working for Friends of the Earth, latterly as Administrative Director. After graduating with an MBA from London Business School, he worked for an international firm of consultants helping multinational firms in the UK and the USA resolve strategic management problems.

He has provided consultancy services to the nonprofit sector for 25 years in the course of which he has worked with a wide cross-section of organisations, infrastructure bodies and their funders (some of which are listed in Appendix 1). He has also worked on policy development for the sector with the Home Office and more recently with the Office of the Third Sector. His overseas assignments have included work for organisations in Bangladesh, the Czech Republic, Nepal, Poland, South Africa, Switzerland, Uganda and Zimbabwe.

Mike has been a Visiting Fellow at the London School of Economics and is currently a Visiting Fellow at Cass Business School, City University, in London.

He is a member of the Board of the Leadership Foundation for Higher Education and a member of the Editorial Board of *Governance* magazine. He is also the author of *Managing at the Leading Edge* (DSC, 2003), a book on the latest developments in leading, managing and governing nonprofit organisations in the USA.

He is married to Diana, has four children and lives near Marlow. He is a Fellow of the Royal Society of Arts.

Preface

Much has changed since the second edition of this book was published in 1999. The seeds of the future of the third sector were laid in the mid-1990s and were just beginning to come to fruition when that edition was published. Labour had recently won a landslide general election victory and was committed to supporting an expanded role for the sector. Many senior people from the sector took positions in the government and many ministers had direct experience of working in the sector.

This coincided with growing interest in the political philosophy of the 'Third Way'. This philosophy reflected a move away from the traditional 'left' and 'right' analysis and argued that a mixture of market economics and state intervention was needed to achieve greater social justice. As a result, commitment to delivering public services in partnership with third-sector organisations grew and the third sector was increasingly seen as a crucial partner in developing and delivering public policy.

There has also been dramatic growth in the profile achieved by advocacy and campaigning; Make Poverty History and Stop Climate Change being two of many examples. Today most public policy is developed in close consultation with representative nonprofit organisations and the media makes extensive use of commentary from the sector.

Since the last edition was published there have also been significant changes in the regulatory context. The Charities Act 2006 has been passed, and the principle of public benefit has been established. Two new organisation forms have become available (Charitable Incorporate Organisations and Community Interest Companies), and the Compact between the government and the voluntary sector is, slowly, becoming accepted as the basis for good relationships.

There have also been major changes in the expectations placed on third-sector organisations. Accountability requirements have increased with the adoption of more rigorous accounting standards (known as SORP 2005), and organisations are expected to be more transparent in reporting what they do, how they spend their money and what they achieve.

The art of managing strategic performance has also moved ahead significantly as organisations have striven to get a much tighter grip on measuring and understanding the difference they make to people's lives both at the individual and organisation-wide levels.

The governance of many organisations has been reviewed, streamlined, re-structured and modernised both to add greater value and to meet new demands for greater accountability. The Code of Governance has been widely accepted as the standard for good governance.

The shape and nature of the sector has changed. There has been significant growth in the establishment of strategic partnerships across organisation boundaries and in mergers between organisations of all sizes. Increased contracting-out of services has led to greater competition between organisations and the need for more businesslike skills.

The sector has continued to grow. New developments have included an unprecedented growth in social enterprise. There are now over 55,000 of these businesses with a social purpose, including well-known names such as The Eden Project, Cafedirect, and *The Big Issue*. Cooperatives and mutual societies have also increasingly come to be seen as part of a more widely defined sector, which includes all 'civil society' organisations.

Today, the third sector is poised for further expansion. There is growing recognition that organisations which are independent from government are best placed to address some of the most intractable social problems society faces. They have the combination of entrepreneurial skills and social consciences to provide the services that best meet people's needs. The prospects for the sector look even better than when I wrote the second edition.

All this means that major revisions were needed to this book:

- The governance chapters have been re-organised and substantially re-written to reflect the new expectations on governance and to include new and updated material on assemblies and advisory boards, group structures, choosing chairs and conducting reviews of the performance of boards and of individual board members.
- The strategy chapters have had sections added on 'scorecards' to track corporate performance, managing knowledge and capturing and promoting information about the real differences organisations make to people's lives.
- There are new sections on competitive strategy and how to build an organisation's capacity to win work from public-sector purchasers.
- There is an entirely new chapter on how to gather information and tell stakeholders about the difference organisations make to people's lives.
- The management structures chapter has a new section on the many types of deputy chief executive roles that have become increasingly popular in recent years and another on integrating meetings and management structures.
- There is a new chapter on managing strategic partnerships, setting out the different types of partnerships that can be established and how they can be created and managed. There is also a new section on mergers.

- The leadership chapter includes a new section on trust and integrity.
- All the other chapters have been updated, tightened up and refreshed with new case examples.
- The further reading appendix has been moved to the knowledge section of the Compass Partnership website, so it can be kept much more up to date (www.compasspartnership.co.uk).

The fundamental objective remains, nevertheless, unchanged – to give busy managers easily accessible advice that can both be read from cover to cover or dipped into when you need a fresh perspective or new ideas.

To guide readers around the book, left hand page 'headers' are chapter titles and right hand page 'headers' are section titles.

I hope you find that this edition meets your needs, and I urge you to continue writing to me (mhudson@compassnet.co.uk) with your comments and suggestions for future editions.

Mike Hudson
June 2008

Foreword

The historical perspective that opens this book is fascinating in reminding us that management in philanthropic organisations has a long history, and that many of the dilemmas which face us today also confounded our predecessors.

However, those who, with me, have spent a long career in what we now call the 'Third Sector' can be in no doubt that the challenges are more complex than any which faced those predecessors.

Few people have as much experience of developing strategies for overcoming those problems as Mike Hudson and that experience is put to extremely good use in this comprehensive guide to managing in the Third Sector.

The significant changes which have happened in recent years make this new edition very timely. The boundaries between the private, public and charitable sectors are certainly not always clear cut but there remains a strong case that managing in the Third Sector *is* different from the other two because these organisations 'have the extraordinary freedom to determine what is needed, what they do in response, how they do it and whether it has any real impact. This challenge lies at the heart of the strategic management of these organisations' (p. 16). It is a challenge indeed and this book will be of enormous importance in helping Boards, chief executives and senior managers meet it. How I wish it had been to hand when I was managing a merger, a newly created organisation, or trying to drive through changes!

The clear chapter headings, summaries and suggestions for further reading create an accessible format. Many theories of management are well set out and summarised but most useful of all are the case studies, drawn from a huge variety of organisations, usually identified but sometimes tactfully anonymous.

I am confident that *Managing Without Profit* will remain the much quoted text book for all those whose vision is to achieve excellence in the Third Sector.

Baroness Pitkeathley

Jill Pitkeathley was Chief Executive of Carers UK before being made a life peer. She is Chair of the Cabinet Office Third Sector Advisory Body and of the Children and Family Court Advisory and Support Service (CAFCASS).

Jill was a founding member of ACEVO, the Association of Chief Executives of Voluntary Organisations.

Acknowledgements

This third edition of Managing Without Profit is the result of a continuing collaboration with a large number of people who have provided me with immense support and guidance.

My thinking has been informed by British and American academics and authors who write about business management and increasingly about the management of third-sector organisations. They are too many to mention by name, but they deserve acknowledgement because their work continues to make a significant contribution to mine.

Particular thanks are due to all the clients of Compass Partnership who have invited my colleagues and me into their organisations and provided the crucial practical experience without which it would not have been possible to write a book that attempts to combine theory and practice.

Many readers of the first edition found the case studies to be among the most instructive parts of the book. Special thanks therefore go to everyone who has updated case studies or allowed me to use their organisations as new case studies for this edition.

I would like to repeat my thanks to all the trustees, chief executives and managers who assisted with the first two editions. You laid the foundations upon which this third edition has been built and I continue to be deeply grateful for your contributions. I would also like to express my gratitude to past and present colleagues at Compass Partnership. Your ideas, opinions and wisdom have all contributed to the content of this book.

Thanks are due to people who contributed to the text and case studies: Joe Saxton of nfpSynergy for research into organograms, Rebecca Packwood for the NSPCC case study and Robert Davies of Dundas & Wilson LLP for legal advice.

My colleague Melinda Letts deserves very special thanks for working meticulously through both the previous edition and this one and making a large number of constructive and insightful comments.

I am also most grateful to Lynne Berry, Chief Executive of WRVS, and Allison Aldred, then South Asia Regional Director of Oxfam and now an Associate with Compass Partnership. Both worked rigorously and systematically through the final draft and gave many insightful comments that have been incorporated into this edition.

Rosie Clay edited *Managing at the Leading Edge* and agreed to edit this edition of *Managing Without Profit*. She deserves thanks for working scrupulously through the manuscript, correcting errors and making many improvements.

The whole team at the Directory of Social Change, including John Martin, Lucy Muir-Smith, Claire Milburn and Kate Bass who deserve grateful thanks for going the extra mile with this book.

Debbie Emerson once again deserves particular thanks. She has provided the highest possible quality of administrative support for the creation of all three editions of this book.

Finally, my most grateful thanks are due to my wife Diana, who once again backed me throughout this venture, and to our children Jennifer, Timothy, Jessica and Katherine for providing loving support from the start to the finish of this project.

Introduction

Not-for-profit organisations exist throughout the world.

They prosper in industrialised economies and they are also a central part of the social fabric in developing economies. They thrive in free democratic societies and they play an important role in less democratic regimes. They flourish in urban areas and are equally important in rural areas. Not-for-profit organisations exist everywhere because of a human quality that brings people together to provide services for themselves and others and to campaign against abuse of fellow human beings, animals and the environment. People want health, welfare, educational, humanitarian, environmental and cultural services to improve the world we live in. They expect the organisations that provide them to be 'not-for-profit' because all depend, to some extent, on voluntary donations of money and time.

This book is about leading, managing and governing not-for-profit organisations. It describes how to improve the performance of organisations that are part of what is often called the 'third sector'.

DEFINING THE THIRD SECTOR

This sector consists of organisations whose primary objectives are social rather than economic. The core of the sector includes charities, religious organisations, arts organisations, community organisations, campaigning organisations, trade unions and other not-for-profit organisations.

The term 'third sector' distinguishes these organisations from the 'private sector' and the 'public sector'. The ethos that all these organisations share is that they are driven by a cause. They are established and managed by people who believe that changes are needed and who want to do something about it themselves. These organisations share two common characteristics. Unlike private-sector organisations, they do not distribute profits to their owners; and, unlike public-sector organisations, they are not subject to direct political control. These organisations have the independence to determine their own futures.

Around the periphery of these third-sector organisations there is a growing number of bodies that are semi-independent from the public sector. Examples include social housing organisations, education colleges, non-departmental public bodies, foundation schools and hospital trusts. There is also a group of organisations such as social enterprises, cooperatives, friendly and provident societies and independent schools which occupy a position that overlaps with the private sector. Together the organisations at the core and periphery of the third sector are known as 'civil society' organisations and are analysed more fully in section 1.2. Whilst this book is primarily about the third sector, many of the theories and practices also apply to wider civil society organisations.

Scope of the third sector

Until relatively recently it was thought that these diverse organisations had little in common. All were seen as separate strands of social life, each with its unique history and role in society. Increasingly, these organisations are seen as part of one sector because they have a common heritage and the same motivation and desire to improve the world in which we live.

They are coalescing because they recognise that they have much more in common with each other than with organisations in the public or private sectors. The process began in the USA some thirty years ago when organisations began to be seen as part of the 'nonprofit' sector. In America the sector is much larger because many hospitals, colleges and universities have always been independent, nonprofit organisations. Their desire to keep government small led to much more widespread contracting-out of the provision of public services.

In the UK many social welfare and healthcare organisations were independent until the twentieth century, when they increasingly became part of the welfare state. Significant numbers of organisations and services are now moving back into the third sector as government policy encourages 'choice' for users of these services and 'contestability' as a way of securing efficiencies and value for money.

The third sector is enormously influential. Many of the greatest social changes and innovations have been brought to fruition through the creation of a third-sector organisation. Hospital services, education, services for disadvantaged groups and people with disabilities, research into disease, spiritual development, benevolent funds for industry employees, social services, international development and, more recently, environmental protection and human rights campaigns all emanated from third-sector organisations.

This sector is currently growing in confidence. At a time when many public-sector organisations are perceived to be inadequate at dealing efficiently with the social problems of today, the third sector sees itself as having the potential to play a greatly expanded role.

The marriage of mission and management

These organisations are driven by a desire to improve the world in which we live. Most of the people who lead, manage, govern, work and volunteer for them believe in the creation of a fairer, more caring, better-educated and more healthy world.

The mission often pervades all aspects of these organisations. Board members volunteer their time because they support the mission; staff often work long hours for no extra financial reward; and funders give money to demonstrate their solidarity with the mission.

Management is equally important to the success of these organisations. Until the middle of the 1970s management was not a word many people used when talking about third-sector organisations. Management was seen to be part of the culture of business and was not felt to be appropriate in the nonprofit world.

The dramatic growth and the increasingly professional and skilled approach of these organisations have completely changed that view. Nowadays management is being colonised for third-sector organisations and its language and concepts trip off people's tongues as easily as eloquent speeches about the cause.

But leadership, management and governance cannot be imported unchanged and imposed on third-sector organisations. They require subtle and critical adjustments to reflect the different ethos that underlies these organisations. All too often people from both the private and public sectors believe or make the implicit assumption that their management theories should be applied to third-sector organisations to make them more effective. 'If only this charity were more businesslike' is a common sentiment. However, while general management theories bring great benefits, they are of limited value unless they are tailored to address the critical cultural and organisational features of third-sector organisations.

This book is an overview of the leadership, management and governance of third-sector organisations. It sets out the essential elements of each that are needed to make organisations more successful. It is based on a series of propositions, which in summary are that:

- Boards need to take responsibility for 'governing' organisations. They need to delegate 'management' to chief executives and their paid staff.
- The process of strategic management is a powerful way of focusing the diverse constituencies of these organisations on to their purpose.
- Managing performance is a critical ingredient of effective third-sector organisations.
- Management structures need to be flexible, responding with frequent adjustments of roles to reflect changing circumstances.
- Strategic partnerships with third-sector, private and public-sector organisations increase the reach and impact of these organisations.
- Improvements in management skills at all levels of organisations are critical to enable organisations to grow and develop.

- Chief executives have both to manage their organisations and provide them with leadership – creating a sense of mission, inspiring people and focusing the organisation on the achievement of ambitious objectives.
- Managers have to manage their boss, work as part of a team, and learn the subtle skills of delegating work and empowering people.
- Organisations need to use every available opportunity to maximise learning.

In schematic form the chapters have been grouped together as follows:

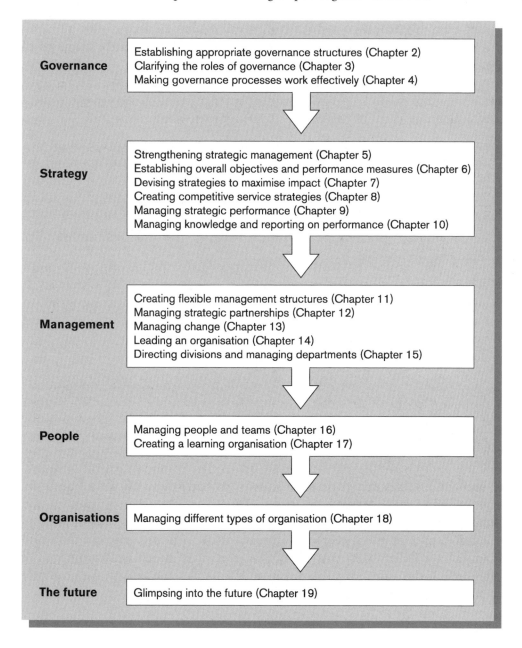

Governance
Establishing appropriate governance structures (Chapter 2)
Clarifying the roles of governance (Chapter 3)
Making governance processes work effectively (Chapter 4)

Strategy
Strengthening strategic management (Chapter 5)
Establishing overall objectives and performance measures (Chapter 6)
Devising strategies to maximise impact (Chapter 7)
Creating competitive service strategies (Chapter 8)
Managing strategic performance (Chapter 9)
Managing knowledge and reporting on performance (Chapter 10)

Management
Creating flexible management structures (Chapter 11)
Managing strategic partnerships (Chapter 12)
Managing change (Chapter 13)
Leading an organisation (Chapter 14)
Directing divisions and managing departments (Chapter 15)

People
Managing people and teams (Chapter 16)
Creating a learning organisation (Chapter 17)

Organisations
Managing different types of organisation (Chapter 18)

The future
Glimpsing into the future (Chapter 19)

The book is prescriptive. It demonstrates ways to improve leadership, management and governance. It is, however, based on the premise that third-sector organisations are full of contradictions and ambiguities. There are no right or wrong prescriptions for many situations. These organisations are complex and messy. They have many stakeholders with different values and they attract an extraordinarily diverse range of people as volunteers, managers and board members.

Consequently, advice that is appropriate in one set of circumstances may be totally inappropriate in another. Understanding the context of any situation requiring attention is absolutely crucial to making an appropriate diagnosis of leadership, management and governance issues and deciding what should be done. It is so easy to take a successful experience from one situation and apply it to another, failing to recognise that small but significant changes in the context can render that previous experience completely irrelevant.

Having a deep and rounded view of a situation is vital to understanding how improvements can be made. Sometimes people are too quick to jump on the latest management bandwagon, so planned improvements achieve less than their instigators intended. Research into organisational change in nonprofit organisations in the USA shows that most change efforts fail to achieve the desired results (*Investing in Capacity Building*, Barbara Blumenthal, The Foundation Center, 2003).

So this book offers guidance based on the experience that my colleagues at Compass Partnership and I have gained over 25 years of consulting with civil society organisations. This has included over 1,000 assignments typically lasting from three to six months with organisations of almost every type and size, a selection of which is included in Appendix 1.

It also builds on extensive research I have undertaken in the UK, the USA and Australia. The aim of the book, therefore, is to explain what currently appear to be 'best' management practices by marrying research evidence with 'hands-on' experience of what works well in particular circumstances and what is reported not to work so well.

The book assumes that these organisations do not survive on good leadership, management and governance alone. They all need flair, creativity and imagination to succeed. They do not exist to make profits, but they do need to be driven by prophets – people who have a vision of how to improve the world in which we all live. The book assumes that the values, beliefs and imagination of the people who work for these organisations are as important as the quality of leadership, management and governance.

The book is aimed primarily at medium-sized and larger organisations, including those with more than a handful of staff and those with national or international scope. It is relevant to single-site and multi-site organisations, those with local branches and those without, and those undertaking one activity as well as those offering many services. Many of the ideas are also relevant to the thousands of smaller organisations in this sector.

The book was written for people who want a thorough briefing on the leadership, management and governance of third-sector organisations. It should be of particular interest to:

- board members, committee members, chief executives, managers and staff;
- government departments, local authorities, health authorities and companies working with third-sector organisations;
- foundations, governments and companies providing funding;
- academics and students studying management and social policy.

The book can be read from cover to cover, but it has been organised to allow easy access and reference to specific issues that readers will face. Readers of previous editions have said that they reach for it when they want to put a problem into a broader context. The book will therefore have achieved its objective if a dog-eared copy can found in your briefcase or shoulder bag.

I could have written many books from the mountain of material I have collected through my consultancy work and the literature I have gathered from the UK, the USA and Australia in my research for this book. However, my aim was to distil it all down into a practical overview for busy managers who need to learn a lot in a short space of time.

Finally, this is the third edition. Previous editions encouraged readers to send me comments, feedback and examples of good practice. Many people wrote to me, and some of their experiences and cases have been included in this edition. Continuing that spirit of cooperation and the desire to do better that pervades the sector, further comments and cases would be most welcome. They should be sent to me at: Compass Partnership, Greenbanks, New Road, Bourne End, Bucks, SL8 5BZ (Tel.: +44 (0) 1628 529750; e-mail: mhudson@compassnet.co.uk).

Glossary

The diverse histories of third-sector organisations mean that different organisations often use very different language to describe the same idea. To maintain clarity and avoid repetition, the following terms are used consistently throughout the book.

The board The body that is legally responsible and accountable for governing and controlling the organisation, sometimes called council, management committee, board of directors, board of trustees, executive or governing body.

Board members People who sit on the board and are legally accountable for all the organisation's work and are usually unpaid. Sometimes called council members, management committee members, trustees, directors, or members of a governing board.

Branches Field outposts of the organisation, including national branches of international organisations, local groups and church dioceses, and autonomous branches of federal organisations that have come together as part of a movement.

Chief executive The senior paid member of staff who reports to the board. Sometimes called the director, the head, the principal, the general secretary, the director general and other similar terms.

Committees Small groups who are delegated responsibilities by the board.

Department In smaller organisations, the level of organisation below the leadership team. It might be called a region, a team or a project. In larger organisations departments report to divisions.

Division The level of management (in large organisations) between the chief executive and the managers of services. Examples of divisions include operations, services, finance, fundraising, marketing and communications.

Divisional directors The paid managers (usually in large organisations) who report to the chief executive and who have managers of departments reporting to them.

HR The human resources function of an organisation.

ICT The information and communications technology function of an organisation.

Leadership team   The chief executive and the divisional directors or senior managers who together have overall responsibility for the day-to-day management of the organisation. Often called the senior management team, sometimes called the executive directors, the term stresses the leadership function of this group.

Officers   People who are elected to specific positions on the board and are usually unpaid (including the chair, vice-chair, treasurer and secretary to the board).

Organisation   The body that is providing services or organising campaigns, whether it be a voluntary body, a charity, a trust, a cooperative, a trade union, a housing association, a professional institution, a school, a college, etc.

Service   The benefit the service user receives, irrespective of whether it is a conventional service, a performance, an education, spiritual development, some information or another desired benefit.

Service delivery unit   The lowest level of the organisation at which human and financial resources are brought together by a manager to deliver a service with specific objectives, a budget and performance measures (see section 8.2, Defining services and campaigns, for a full description).

Service users   The people who benefit from a service provided by a third-sector organisation, whether students, trade union members, patients, clients, people with disabilities, church-goers or members of an audience. Although somewhat prosaic, this term is better than 'beneficiary', which some see as condescending, or 'customer', which implies that people pay for the service.

Stakeholders   People or other organisations who have an acknowledged interest in the organisation, including members, funders, purchasers, service users, board and committee members, managers, staff, volunteers and branches.

1 The re-discovered sector

1.1 A HISTORICAL PERSPECTIVE

The central philosophy that permeates virtually every part of the third sector is the human desire to assist other people without gaining personal benefit. Most people think of it in terms of charity and assume that it is a modern phenomenon. Some suggest it goes back to Elizabethan times or, at most, to Roman times. Indeed, fear of voluntary associations as a locus for political dissent is well documented in imperial Rome; for example, Trajan refused a provincial governor's request to form a fire brigade, saying it would become a political pressure group.

In fact the word 'charity' has Greek origins – χαρις – which originally meant grace and subsequently came to mean favour, kindness and goodwill towards another. A related meaning in Greek was thankfulness or gratitude. The word 'philanthropy' also has a Greek origin – meaning love of people.

However, the philosophy of charity goes back much further. People say, 'Charity begins at home' – and so it did. From earliest times it was the extended family that looked after its young, sick, disabled, elderly, widowed and orphaned members. With the growth of the first towns and cities and the movement of people away from their families, new forms of social provision were needed. Early Egyptian civilisations developed a strong moral code founded on social justice. This code encouraged people to help others in relation to their need, for example, by ferrying a poor person across a river without charging. The Pharaoh himself contributed by giving shelter, bread and clothing to the poor almost 5,000 years ago.

In ancient India, the Buddhist Emperor Asoka (c. 274–232 BC) provided medical facilities, ordered wells to be dug and, in an early environmental initiative, planted trees for people's enjoyment. In early Greek society, wayfarers were either given food and shelter in the houses of wealthy people or they would share the hospitality of peasants. The Jewish prophets were the forerunners of the modern campaigning organisation. They worked tirelessly for social, economic and political justice and put pressure on their governments to change both policies and administrative practices. The idea of alms-giving was also widely recognised.

In Roman times the right to free or cheap corn was dependent on citizenship and was hereditary – passing from father to son. Trusts also date back to Roman times, as people established schemes to maintain control over the fate of an economic asset after their death. A good example of self-help that originated in Imperial Rome was the establishment of burial societies, which were created to ensure that people of modest means received a decent burial. They ran as cooperatives, required a monthly payment and were also a focus for social events.

Throughout history, charity has also been closely interwoven with the growth of religious organisations. Jewish teaching promoted the view that the poor had rights and the rich had duties. Early Christian churches established funds to support widows, orphans, the sick, the infirm, the poor, the disabled and prisoners. Church-goers were expected to bring gifts which were laid on the Lord's table so the recipients obtained them from the hands of God. The first legacies were authorised by Emperor Constantine I in AD 231 enabling endowments to be established for charity.

In the Islamic world, philanthropy was used to establish many great hospitals. Early examples of 'hardship funds' also come from Islam, when indigent patients were given five pieces of gold on their discharge. In short, the charitable sector has been around for a long time, always playing a significant role.

Management problems have a long history

Management of these organisations also has a long history. Many of the dilemmas which perplex organisations today also confounded their predecessors. Medieval monasteries in Britain tended to be indiscriminate in their alms-giving. They consequently fostered a class of professional beggars which in time contributed to the breakdown of this system of relief. Similar problems occurred when hospitals, designed for use by the poor, were placed at the service of rich people. The issue of payment for services clearly concerned these organisations as much as it troubles modern charities.

Arguments about the conflicting roles of the public and charitable sectors raged during the sixteenth century when Henry VIII and Edward VI confiscated hospital and guild property. During this time, the Reformation undermined the church-centred welfare system and the gap was filled by greater state intervention funded by increased taxes. This included money given to almshouses, hospitals and university colleges, loan schemes to help people start businesses, and for capital works such as building bridges and repairing roads. Indeed, the boundary with the state was just as much an issue then as it is today. For example, in 1572 Elizabeth I passed a law that allowed parishes to levy a poor rate to pay for the upkeep of almshouses and workhouses, effectively subsidising charitable provision with state money.

Abuse by charities is also an old phenomenon. In 1601 Elizabeth I passed the Charitable Uses Act, which gave the Chancellor power to investigate the misuse of charitable funds. The Act provides an interesting perspective on the history of the third sector. Charitable endowments could only be given for:

> relief of aged, impotent and poor people, maintenance of sick and maimed soldiers and mariners, schools of learning, free schools and scholars in universities, repair of bridges, ports, havens, causeways, churches, sea banks and highways, education and preferment of orphans, relief, stock or maintenance of houses for correction, marriages of poor maids, supportation, aid and help of young tradesmen, handicraftsmen and persons decayed, relief or redemption of prisoners or captives and aid or ease of poor inhabitants concerning payment of taxes.

The beginning of a more strategic approach

For much of the period up to the middle of the nineteenth century, charity in Britain was characterised by a large number of often jealous organisations pursuing activities without any real understanding of the extent or of the underlying causes of poverty. Organisations worked with little knowledge of what others were doing and with little examination of the circumstances of individual beneficiaries. However, during the second half of the nineteenth century, charities began adopting a more coherent approach. The Poor Law Amendment Act of 1834 had drastically reduced relief for the poor. Paralleling this government action, charities wanted to distinguish between the poorest people with no resources and less deserving people who could rely on workhouses.

The emerging sector took a great leap forward with the formation of the Charity Organisation Society in 1869. It is an example of how many of the great innovations in human welfare have led to the creation of third-sector organisations and have subsequently become an accepted part of civil society. Founded after Henry Solly read a paper to the Society of Arts, it aimed to encourage responsible spending on the poor and avoid welfare dependency. Henry Solly became its first General Secretary and remained in that position for forty years. This organisation, today called Family Action, was among the first to put into place what would now be called a strategic approach to meeting people's needs. It strove to:

- prevent indiscriminate giving of relief;
- promote careful enquiries into individual cases;
- discover the causes of an individual's distress;
- remove the causes of distress;
- coordinate charitable activities to prevent excessive help being given to particular people.

In addition to taking a more strategic approach, which is now a central part of managing third-sector organisations, Family Action also combined service delivery with a sharp and effective campaigning role. It fought against the state and against voluntary organisations because it believed both approached welfare in ways that encouraged dependency.

Governments of the time also engaged with the sector in more strategic ways. For example, contracts were used extensively in the early part of the twentieth century when the Liberal Government of 1905 funded friendly societies and councils for voluntary service to deliver its reforms.

WHEN WERE THEY ESTABLISHED?

Providing housing, hospital care, services for disabled people, protecting the environment and campaigning for social change all had or have a venerable history, illustrated by the establishment of the following organisations:

1123   St Bartholomew's Hospital
1215   St Thomas's Hospital
1697   Oxford Hospital, Ampthill
1698   Society for Promoting Christian Knowledge
1702   Hospital for Fishermen, Yarmouth
1707   Almshouses at Abingdon
1823   Anti-Slavery International
1824   Royal National Lifeboat Institution
1824   Royal Society for the Prevention of Cruelty to Animals
1830   Society for the Improvement of the Condition of the Labouring Classes
1854   Oxford Economic and Sanitary Association
1862   Peabody Trust
1865   Salvation Army
1866   Barnardo's
1868   Royal National Institute of Blind People
1869   Family Action
1870   British Red Cross
1881   Children's Society
1884   National Society for the Prevention of Cruelty to Children
1886   Octavia Hill Housing Trust
1889   The Guinness Trust

1895	The National Trust
1902	Cancer Research UK
1908	Scout Association
1910	Guide Association
1918	National Council for One Parent Families
1919	Save The Children Fund
1921	Royal British Legion
1924	Wellcome Trust
1930	Youth Hostels Association
1931	Guide Dogs for the Blind Association
1937	Nuffield College, Oxford
1942	Age Concern
1942	Oxfam
1946	Mencap
1948	Leonard Cheshire Disability
1950	Queen Elizabeth's Hospital, Bristol
1953	Samaritans
1956	Abbeyfield Society
1958	VSO
1961	National Institute for Social Work
1966	Shelter
1967	St Christopher's Hospice
1971	Greenpeace
1976	Parents for Children
1979	Victim Support
1981	Business in the Community
1983	Terrence Higgins Trust
1984	Comic Relief
1985	Muslim Aid
1991	The Halo Trust
1994	The Big Lottery Fund
2000	Smile Train
2002	New Philanthropy Capital
2005	Stop Climate Chaos
2007	Help for Heroes
2008	Ethnic Health Foundation
2009	The British Asian Trust

Organisations are referred to by their latest name.

State intervention increases

The trend towards a more strategic approach occurred at the same time as increased state intervention in social affairs. As a result, many of the innovative schemes for meeting people's needs that were established by the third sector over the last 150 years have gradually been adopted by government. This started when government began playing a greater role in education in the 1840s. The basic principles of services provided by the state, including universal provision and minimum standards, were established and later extended to other services, including pensions, school meals, unemployment and health insurance.

Until 1948 voluntary and charitable organisations remained major providers of direct services. Voluntary hospitals were part of the third sector, and services for children and people with disabilities relied heavily on voluntary organisations. Voluntary providers were at the same time increasingly criticised for rivalry among themselves and for their inability to deliver universal services without payment at the point of delivery. As state provision expanded, the role of the voluntary sector was seen as supplementary to state provision and not as the parallel system that had existed earlier.

In the period immediately after the Second World War, the role of the voluntary sector was further reduced as the state took over hospitals and other services and offered more comprehensive provision through local social services departments. For a period the third sector played second fiddle.

Revival of the sector

However, from the beginning of the 1960s the voluntary sector began to re-exert its influence as new needs were identified and new means of raising income were established. It has not looked back since that date. In particular:

- **service-providing organisations** began to deliver a wide range of services that were previously provided by the state;
- **specialist organisations** were established for almost every conceivable cause (the National Council for Voluntary Organisations' directory currently lists almost 2,000 voluntary organisations with a nationwide remit);
- **government and local authority funding** for charities grew to the extent that it now exceeds their voluntary income.

Most significantly, the separation of purchasers from providers of services has presented new opportunities for third-sector organisations. Many are now returning to their previous role as mainstream providers of services. They are competing with one another, and more recently with private and public sector providers for the growing number of contracts that government, local and health authorities are putting out to tender.

The pace of growth and revival has continued in recent years:

- There are now 164,000 general charities with a total income of over £31 billion (*The UK Civil Society Almanac*, NCVO, 2008).
- There are estimated to be 865,000 civil society organisations with an income of £109 billion (*The UK Civil Society Almanac*, NCVO, 2008).
- Over 55,000 social enterprises have been established in the UK with a combined income of £27 billion (Social Enterprises Coalition).
- The Compact between the government and the voluntary sector, agreed in 1998, has established the ground rules for effective contracting relationships. It also established the right of organisations to deliver public services and campaign for social and environmental improvements.
- The Charities Act 2006 has created a new definition of charity based on public benefit and new descriptions of charitable purposes.
- Two new legal forms for nonprofit organisations have been established – community interest companies and charitable incorporated organisations.

NEW DESCRIPTIONS OF CHARITABLE PURPOSES

The Charities Act 2006 defines a charity as a body or trust which is for a charitable purpose, and is for the public benefit.

It includes descriptions of the main purposes which are charitable:

- prevention or relief of poverty
- advancement of education
- advancement of religion
- advancement of health or the saving of lives
- advancement of citizenship or community development
- advancement of the arts, culture, heritage or science
- advancement of amateur sport
- advancement of human rights, conflict resolution or reconciliation or the promotion of religious or racial harmony or equality and diversity
- advancement of environmental protection or improvement
- relief of those in need by reason of youth, age, ill-health, disability, financial hardship or other disadvantage
- advancement of animal welfare
- promotion of the efficiency of the armed forces of the Crown; or the efficiency of the police, fire and rescue services or ambulance services
- other purposes charitable in law

Civil society is now widely viewed as the glue that is needed to hold neighbourhoods together and to enable communities to overcome problems of drug abuse, crime and decay. Whilst the state clearly has a role to play, it is increasingly clear that state intervention alone is not sufficient to enable regeneration of communities and the establishment of community cohesion.

Growing state funding has been augmented by significant new funding from the new philanthropists. These successful entrepreneurs want to use their wealth and often their skills to improve society. Unlike previous generations who gave away their fortunes as legacies after they died, the new philanthropists want to see the impact of their beneficence during their lifetimes. They also want to ensure that the money is effectively used and expect recipient organisations to track their performance and report on their results.

Today, the civil society sector is poised for further growth and development, more than anything, because the values it holds enable it to command the respect and confidence of both decision makers and the wider general public.

1.2 BOUNDARIES OF THE SECTOR

The sector consists of an extraordinarily diverse range of organisations: some are charitable (Oxfam), some are not (Greenpeace), some are based on vast membership (the National Trust), some are not (English National Ballet), some are primarily government-funded (Victim Support), some eschew government funding (Amnesty International), some are politically left of centre (Unite), some right (the Adam Smith Institute), some are large (The Wellcome Trust) and many are small (the British Hedgehog Preservation Society).

There are many names which broadly cover the notion of this sector. Each establishes increasingly broad boundaries:

- The **charitable sector** includes all organisations which meet the conditions required for charity registration.
- The **voluntary sector** includes charities and many other organisations with social and political aims that have not registered as charities or do not meet the criteria.
- The **NGO sector** (an acronym for non-governmental organisations that is widely used in the international development field) refers to voluntary or charitable organisations.
- The **nonprofit sector** is a wider term which emanates from the USA and includes independent not-for-profit universities and hospitals, trade unions, professional associations and other organisations which can make profits but do not distribute them.
- **Civil society organisations** is a term used to refer to all the nonprofit institutions that exist in modern democratic societies. This term has become more common following the re-emergence of voluntary organisations in Eastern Europe and the greater independence of organisations that used to be part of the state in the UK.

- **Economie sociale** is the widest term and is used in the European Union; it includes civil society organisations and many business-type organisations such as mutual insurance companies, savings banks, cooperatives and agricultural marketing organisations whose profits are used to benefit their members or customers.

None of these definitions suits the purposes of this book. The charitable and voluntary sectors are too narrow; many of the propositions about management have much wider application. The nonprofit sector is a negative definition which emphasises the intention not to make profits – when in practice many of these organisations need to make a financial surplus to replace their capital and to fund new activities. The *économie sociale* is a little too wide. Many of the additional organisations captured in this definition have a better fit with private-sector management theories.

This book therefore adopts the term **third sector** and includes within it all organisations that:

- exist primarily for a **social purpose** rather than having a profit-making objective;
- are **independent of the state** because they are governed by an independent group of people and are not part of a government department or a local or health authority;
- **re-invest their financial surpluses** in the services they offer or the organisation itself.

The boundaries are fuzzy

The boundaries between the private, public and third sectors are not clear-cut. Some organisations are widely agreed to be at the heart of the sector; other organisations sit on its periphery. Many share the values of the sector but also have characteristics in common with either the public or the private sector.

A useful way to think of the third sector is as a core of pure third-sector organisations and peripheries which overlap with both the private and public sectors. Many of these, such as museums, housing associations and education colleges, can use third-sector management skills but are ultimately subject to some control by government.

THE BOUNDARIES BETWEEN THE SECTORS

Civil society

Third-sector

- Voluntary organisations
- Campaigning organisations
- Self-help organisations
- Community organisations
- Political parties

- Churches
- Trade unions
- Clubs
- Aid agencies
- Housing associations

Public sector
Boundary

- Foundation hospitals
- Academies
- Foundation schools
- Further and higher education colleges
- Non-departmental public bodies
- Museums
- Universities

Private sector
Boundary

- Social enterprise
- Cooperatives
- Trade associations
- Professional associations
- Friendly societies
- Provident associations
- Mutual assurance societies
- Independent schools

Mainstream

- Central government
- Local government
- Health authorities
- Police authorities
- Fire services

Mainstream

- Listed companies
- Private companies
- Partnerships
- Sole traders

Organisations move across the boundaries

Over the years there has been considerable movement of organisations across the boundaries of the sectors. Movement across the third–private boundary has been mainly one-way. Building societies and mutual societies all began life as social enterprises but are now more closely related to the private sector, operating in competition with profit-distributing businesses. The Abbey National, for example, began when twelve building workers formed a society to save money for purchasing houses. It gradually grew into a huge institution that had to operate in a competitive market, lost its third-sector roots and eventually became a private company that is now owned by a Spanish bank.

Whilst few companies have become third-sector organisations, there are now extensive collaborations between the sectors as both recognise that neither economic nor social development can happen in isolation. This is reflected in the growth of 'corporate social responsibility' and a range of increasingly sophisticated partnerships between companies and third sector organisations (described in section 12.3, Partnerships with the private and public sectors).

Historically, movement across the third–public boundary has been dominated by the state taking responsibility for services that are needed by the majority of people. Starting with the maintenance of bridges (a common charitable purpose of monastic foundations), through the care of prisoners (originally a charitable activity) to the case of hospitals taken over to create the NHS in 1948, the movement used to be towards the public sector.

That trend has now been reversed. The perceived limitations of the public sector as an efficient supplier of services have persuaded governments around the world to delegate responsibility for the management of services. Schools, hospitals, colleges, youth and other services are increasingly being required to operate more like independent non-profit-distributing organisations than under the rules of public service. These organisations are finding that they have to compete against one another for funds and service users and have to diversify their funding sources to top up their government grants. When this happens they begin to behave like independent not-for-profit organisations and consequently fit more appropriately into the third sector.

This flood of organisations from the public to the periphery of the third sector is being driven by:

- **a political philosophy** that believes state-run organisations are seldom efficient or responsive to people's changing needs, and consequently it is better to separate the functions of the *purchaser* (to specify standards, and desired outcomes) and the *provider* (to deliver services efficiently and effectively, responding quickly to changes in the external environment);
- the drive to give **local managers greater control** over the management of their organisations;
- a belief that **competition between suppliers** can lead to efficiency gains, even though the notion of competition in the provision of basic services can be deeply uncomfortable, particularly to professionals in these services;
- a desire by **citizens to participate** in society and have choice.

This trend is likely to continue because the political philosophy that favours independence from the state has become well established. Indeed, as providers are given greater independence, they are becoming more sophisticated managerially, require less support from centralised bureaucracies and place increasing value on their independence.

In summary, even before these new organisations joined the third sector, it was a significant part of the social fabric in the UK and many other countries. Today it is becoming increasingly responsible for the provision of a huge range of essential services.

1.3 THE SECTOR IS SIGNIFICANT AND GROWING

The scope and scale of the third sector is now so huge that it affects virtually everyone. People volunteer, they join professional associations, attend college or an artistic event, worship, join a trade union, support a campaign, donate to charity or join a club or society. They are all engaging in civil society.

In the UK, six out of ten adults benefit from charities every month (CAF, 2008). Many of our lives are touched by the sector more than once a week and some more than once a day, as we:

- seek advice from a Citizens' Advice Bureau (nearly two million people do every year);
- volunteer (21 million people do every year);
- visit a sports club (there are 150,000 in the UK);
- call a charity help line (60,000 people do every day);
- join an organisation (The National Trust has 3.5 million members);
- read the *Guardian* or the *Observer* (they are both owned by the not-for-profit Scott Trust and have a readership of over 1.3 million);
- attend a community meeting.

The sector is not only diverse, it is also very influential. In 1948 William Beveridge wrote, 'the strength of voluntary action is the distinguishing mark of a free society'. More recently, Professor Ken Young has argued that the voluntary sector makes three crucial contributions to society:

1. **Representation.** Voluntary action in today's changed circumstances has a wider role – and is of greater social and political significance – than that of an adjunct provider of social services alongside mainstream state provision. It contributes to the representative process, to the development of public policy and to the processes of social integration and cohesion.
2. **Innovation.** The creativity of voluntary bodies is a source of innovation. Governments today address issues that are often formulated and shaped by those outside the central departments. The history of social policy in Britain is largely one in which the agenda for action has been set by voluntary bodies turning hitherto tolerated conditions into problems and claims to action.
3. **Citizenship.** The effectiveness of voluntary bodies as advocates of change owes much to their informal nature. Whether or not people are excluded from effective citizenship rests in no small measure upon the strength of the local voluntary sector.

(*Meeting the Needs of Strangers,* Gresham College, 1991)

Today, the third sector is a major influence on the way we see and think about society, and no significant governmental decision is usually taken in a sophisticated democracy without many third-sector interest groups being consulted or making their case.

THE THIRD SECTOR AFFECTS EVERY STAGE OF OUR LIVES

Before conception	**During pregnancy and birth**	**Early childhood**	**During education**
Sex Education Forum	National Childbirth Trust	Pre-school Learning Alliance	Nuffield Foundation
Family Planning Association	Baby Life Support Systems	National Association of Toy and Leisure Libraries	Barnardo's
	Active Birth Centre	Child Accident Prevention Trust	The Scouts and Guides

In adolescence	**In further education**	**In employment**	**In leisure**
ChildLine	London Business School	Confederation of British Industry	The National Trust
Action for Children	Workers Educational Association	UNISON	The Royal Opera House
YWCA			

In sport	**In housing**	**In campaigning**	**In sickness**
British Olympic Association	Anchor Housing	Amnesty International	The Stroke Association
British Blind Sport	Abbeyfield Society	Greenpeace	Asthma UK
	The Guinness Trust	Shelter	Mind

In health	**In relationships**	**In disability**	**In emergencies**
Royal Society for Public Health	Relate	RNID	RNLI
	WPF Therapy	Leonard Cheshire Disability	WRVS
		MENCAP	British Red Cross
			Victim Support

In research	**In giving**	**In poverty**	**In retirement**
Cancer Research UK	Charities Aid Foundation	Family Action	REACH
University of Cambridge	Time Bank	Salvation Army	Pensioners Link
British Heart Foundation	New Philanthropy Capital		U3A (University of the Third Age)

In old age	**At death**	**After death**
Age Concern	Dignity in Dying	Cruse Bereavement Care
Help the Aged	Natural Death Centre	The Compassionate Friends
	St Christopher's Hospice	The Stillbirth and Neonatal Death Society

13

1.4 **MANAGING THIRD-SECTOR ORGANISATIONS**

There are many similarities in the leadership, management and governance of organisations in all sectors of the economy. All rely on skilled people who need to have objectives, control resources, work in teams, have professional development and be praised and criticised. The third sector has particular parallels with the private sector because organisations which sell services, sometimes at subsidised prices, need some of the theories of the market place. Likewise, many organisations are providing public services in situations where there is little connection between the recipient of the service and payment for that service. This can lead to insatiable demand which has to be managed by setting the right criteria for assistance, limiting the availability of the service and accepting waiting times.

Indeed, it is fair to say that the **similarities between all sectors are growing**. Many public sector organisations have been given greater independence and are expected to operate as Executive Agencies working like businesses but delivering public services. Businesses now have corporate social responsibility departments and track their social and environmental performance as well as financial results. Third-sector organisations frequently compete for contracts often against private and public sector providers.

Partnerships between organisations across the sectors are also increasing as public and private organisations discover that each have different attributes that can be combined to great effect. They have discovered that working together can be a very effective way of tackling some of the most intractable social problems that society faces (see section 12.3, Partnerships with the private and public sectors, for examples).

The crucial differences between the sectors

Nevertheless, a central theme of this book is the proposition that managing third-sector organisations is subtly different from managing in the private or public sectors.

In the private sector there is a relatively straightforward relationship between suppliers and customers. Suppliers offer goods and services to customers, and in return customers pay a market price. In the public sector, government and local authorities supply public services, and in return the voters choose the government which they believe offers the most appropriate programme of taxation and public services or which is most competent in delivering its responsibilities.

In the third sector a **different model of transactions** applies because the connections between provision and payment for services is weak or non-existent.

The most straightforward cases are of organisations funded purely by donors, where money is given and used to fund projects, supply services or carry out research. Oxfam, the Royal National Lifeboat Institution and Cancer Research UK are typical examples. Here there is no connection between the funders and the users. Donors trust the organisation to spend their money as effectively as possible. This is the pure third-sector model.

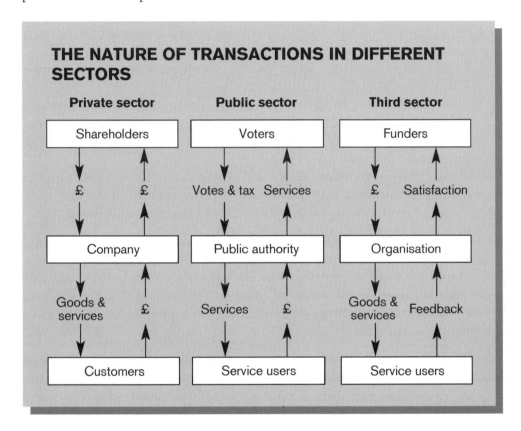

THE NATURE OF TRANSACTIONS IN DIFFERENT SECTORS

A variation of the third-sector model occurs where the funding comes from contracts. Although these are often won on competitive tender and there is still no direct connection between the user and the funder, the contractor acts as a proxy for users and requires performance measures to demonstrate that the services have been delivered to the required standard.

In some bodies, such as arts and leisure organisations, services are funded by a mixture of sources, so organisations are working in 'muted' markets, where there are signals from users and there is competition. In all these cases, the key difference between the third and the other two sectors is that there is only a weak link between the service users and the funders of the service.

This crucial difference in the nature of transactions means organisations have to manage:

- **The different expectations of funders and users.** Funders want value for money, users want quality services and managers have to make the trade-offs to satisfy both.
- **The balance between supply and demand.** For popular services that are free to users, such as advice, social services, health and disability services and international aid, managers face the constant challenge of managing demand, because supply is limited. Managers have to make decisions because the invisible hand of the market, which regulates supply and demand in the private sector, is not making those decisions for them.
- **The need to be highly responsive to service users.** In social care and health, children's services and disability groups it is now expected that organisations will listen to and be highly responsive to the service users' needs and expectations.
- **The need to seek continuous feedback.** The feedback which companies get automatically from their customers (or lack of them) and which the public sector gets from the ballot box is much weaker in the third sector so managers actively have to seek it and supply it to funders.

These management challenges are even more complicated when donors, volunteers or service users are elected to the board or appointed to the staff. This may mean managers and board members are better informed, but it also creates more relationships requiring active management to maintain everyone's commitment and morale.

So a crucial difference between third sector and other organisations is that they have to **bridge the gap between funders and service users.** The market does this in the private sector and political processes do it in the public sector. It is only third-sector organisations that have the extraordinary freedom to determine what is needed, what they do in response, how they do it and whether it has a real impact. This challenge lies at the heart of the strategic management of these organisations.

Defining characteristics of third sector organisations

In addition to the different nature of the transactions, there are eight other characteristics of third-sector organisations which, although not exclusive to the sector, combine to make management a challenging occupation:

- **It is easy to have vague objectives.** Social, health, educational, environmental and spiritual objectives are particularly difficult to specify precisely. Third-sector organisations do have to specify strategic objectives, as we shall see in later chapters, but, when they do, it quickly becomes clear that:

– the harder one tries to pin them down to specifics, the more difficult it is to capture exactly what the organisation wants to achieve in quantitative terms;

– different constituencies in the organisation place different emphasis on different objectives; it is consequently tempting to adopt a large number of broad statements of good intentions that satisfy different interests. This allows people to pick and choose the objectives they prioritise, thus defeating the point of having a limited number of specific objectives.

- **Impact is hard to measure.** Because it is difficult to specify objectives precisely, it is also difficult to measure the impact of organisations, services, campaigns or individuals. How effective was the counselling service? Did our work contribute to reduced teenage pregnancies? Was the measured improvement the result of our service or was it caused by the efforts of other organisations? Are citizens getting better advice? These types of questions are not easy to answer. Furthermore, because measuring performance is difficult, it is easy to forget to celebrate success. Achievements are seldom as clear-cut as meeting sales, financial or service-quality targets.

- **Third-sector organisations are accountable in different ways to many stakeholders.** Members, service users, funding bodies, individual donors, staff and volunteers all have different claims on a third-sector organisation. They are often in a position to have a powerful influence on the future of the organisation, yet they invariably have different views of priorities and sometimes on the style and culture of the organisation as well.

- **Management structures are intricate.** The need to keep the interests of different stakeholders in a delicate balance results in complex structures of governing bodies, committees, user-groups and funder-groups, each of which has a legitimate position in the structure. Taken together, this requirement creates a complex machine which has to be consulted, coordinated and managed in order to get things done. However streamlined, third-sector organisations tend to have far more intricate structures than organisations of equivalent size in the private or public sectors.

- **Voluntarism is an essential ingredient.** The majority of third-sector organisations have unpaid voluntary governing boards whose members may or may not have governance experience. Many rely on voluntary labour and the 'voluntary' commitment of employees, giving extra time for no financial reward. This coalition of voluntary interests has to be held together with few financial incentives. In return for their voluntary commitment people often expect to have their views listened to and managers feel they have a duty to consider them.

- **The mission has a powerful impact on approaches to management.** The ideology that lies behind the organisation can strongly influence people's assumptions about the way the organisation should be managed. For example, people in campaigning organisations tend to take a highly political approach to management; they build coalitions among people with common views rather than using formal decision-making structures; they lobby decision-makers and challenge authority. In contrast people in therapeutic organisations tend to take very conciliatory approaches to management; they see all sides of an issue and find it difficult to reach decisions quickly.

- **Values have to be cherished.** Third-sector organisations are at their most effective when the people involved share common values and assumptions about the organisation's purpose and its style of operation. Insensitivity towards cherished values quickly results in de-motivation and lengthy argument. The point is not that organisations in other sectors do not have values, but that people contributing to third-sector organisations are motivated by values that are inextricably linked with the organisation's aims and are therefore important to everyone.
- **The financial 'bottom line' is not the main determinant of priorities.** Third-sector managers can only use a financial bottom line of profit to guide their choice of future priorities and investments when there is a financial crisis. In other circumstances these organisations have to rely more heavily on complex negotiation to agree priorities. There is no standard methodology or template for this. Every organisation has to develop its own criteria for allocating resources that suit its circumstances at a particular time.

People have multiple motives

Beyond these explicit characteristics, there is a human perspective that needs to be understood in order to gain a complete picture of the challenges of leading, managing and governing these organisations. This issue is seldom discussed openly but nevertheless is central to an understanding of their management.

Virtually everyone who contributes time and effort to these organisations has well-founded motives. These may be based on deeply felt desires to create a fairer and more just world, a wish to be altruistic and genuinely philanthropic motives. Without these values the sector could not exist. However, people often have other – more self-serving – motives for contributing to these organisations:

- They join governing boards, particularly of larger and more prestigious organisations, because of the recognition, esteem and status that are attached to board membership. Such membership frequently leads to contacts with other people in powerful positions, to increased influence and to a greater sense of self-worth.
- Some donors give money in order to gain recognition, for public-relations benefits, to salve their consciences and (sometimes) to gain greater influence over the organisation's affairs.
- Some volunteers give their time because of their need for friendship and social activity, to gain useful skills, to enhance their employment prospects and to give them a role in the broader community.

Some people seek employment in third-sector organisations because they would not be comfortable working within the ideology of the private sector or the constraints of the public sector.

● Some managers' egos can grow to the point where their own status and influence is put before the interests of their organisations or its service users.

This is not to argue that altruism does not exist. It does and it is present in most third-sector organisations. But people have multiple motives, and the hidden ones have a significant impact on leadership, management and governance. At their most extreme, these motives can combine to make the future of organisations a greater priority than the services they give to users. Meeting the needs of volunteers can become more important than the services they provide, giving roles to board members can create unnecessary committees, and keeping staff employed can be more important than reducing costs.

Fortunately, not all these explicit and implicit characteristics apply to all organisations simultaneously! However, they do create a special set of circumstances, and this explains why leading, managing and governing these organisations needs to be based on an understanding of their special nature. They illustrate why the tools and techniques that work in other sectors are only partially applicable to this sector. Finally, they explain why theories about leadership, management and governance need to start from a set of propositions that are derived specifically to help people who run third-sector organisations.

1.5 DECIDING WHERE TO START MAKING IMPROVEMENTS

This book sets out the elements of leadership, management and governance that are required for organisations to be effective. There are, however, prior questions about where to start making improvements and how much attention to give them.

One of the most nebulous issues that chairs, boards, chief executives and senior managers of organisations face is determining which aspects of leadership, management and governance most require attention. There will always be opportunities for improving all of them, but **choices have to be made** to ensure that the organisation makes the greatest improvements for the effort expended.

Governance structures and processes may need modernising, top management may need to be re-structured to suit new circumstances, organisation or service strategy may need to be refreshed, people management systems may require improvement, new partnerships may be required or learning may need to be better embedded into the way the organisation works.

Judgements have to be made about **where to expend effort**. This is not an easy decision because it requires a deep understanding of the organisation. Responsibility for prioritising improvements in leadership, management and governance falls to the chair and chief executive, guided by the board and the leadership team. They will need to have an overview of the organisation and insights into its strengths and weaknesses. Their judgement should be informed by other managers and staff, who will often have insightful perspectives on what needs to change to make the organisation more effective.

This process of 'organisational analysis' is particularly important for new chairs and chief executives, as they determine their priorities. It is equally important for incumbent chairs and chief executives, as they need to be continuously assessing the overall strengths and weaknesses of the organisation.

The ultimate aim of organisational analysis is to determine the best ways of increasing the organisation's impact – the extent to which it is making a significant difference to people, animals or the environment. This might be about the efficiency and effectiveness of governance and management, it might be about innovation and the creativity of the organisation, it might be about its ability to focus on what it does best or it might be about the commitment, motivation and morale of its people.

Making improvements to the leadership, management and governance of organisations also **requires careful sequencing**. Sometimes a weak team may need to be strengthened before a new strategy can be developed. In other circumstances, a new strategy may be needed before it is possible to decide upon the future shape of the management team. Sometimes governance needs to be strengthened before it has the authority and power to catalyse necessary changes in top management. In other circumstances a new chief executive may be required to give the organisation the capacity to strengthen its governance.

Crucial judgements also have to be made about the **capacity of the organisation to manage change**. The introduction of too many management initiatives can lead to all of them taking longer than planned and, at worst, none becoming fully embedded. The 'real work' of the organisation always has to continue in parallel with making improvements, so capacity for change is always constrained. It is easy for people at the top to see what needs to be done, but getting everyone affected to share their assessment and then to deal with the many consequences of change often takes much more time and effort than anticipated.

It also depends on **winning 'hearts and minds'**. People need to be convinced that changes are necessary and willing to give their energy and commitment. We are all good at seeing what other people should do differently, and usually less good at accepting changes proposed by others.

Once all these judgements have been made, boards and senior managers need to **decide how much effort and resources** should be devoted to improvements. Some investments in organisation capacity can be crucial to increasing their effectiveness. Other investments can waste precious and hard-earned resources. Chairs and chief executives need to be convinced that the benefits of these investments will greatly exceed the costs. Guided by their boards and management teams, they have to perform a 'high-level' organisational analysis and make the really important judgements about where to start, how long things should take, what sequence should be chosen and how much resource to expend to achieve maximum benefit.

These decisions usually require a combination of rigorous analysis and experienced judgement. The Compass Partnership organisation development diagnostic tool is provided at Appendix 2 to help readers begin the process of organisational analysis. A more finely tuned and sophisticated diagnostic tool has been prepared by McKinsey & Co as part of their report on *Capacity Building in Nonprofit Organisations* in the USA and can be downloaded from www.vppartners.org.

SUMMARY OF KEY POINTS

Historical perspective

- The history of the third sector goes back to the earliest civilisations
- The special problems of managing these organisations have an equally long history
- Following rapid growth in the nineteenth and early twentieth centuries, the sector in Britain was eclipsed by the welfare state
- It has re-emerged with the entrepreneurial skills and social conscience needed to address many of today's pressing social, educational and environmental problems

Boundaries of the sector

- The third sector includes organisations that:
  - exist primarily for a social purpose
  - are independent of the state
  - re-invest financial surpluses in their services
- The boundaries with the public and private sectors are not clear-cut and over time, organisations move across the boundaries

The sector is significant and growing

- The number and size of organisations are both growing
- The crucial contributions of the sector are its ability to represent people's views, to innovate and to provide people with a sense of citizenship

Managing third-sector organisations

- The central difference between the third and the other sectors is that there is only a weak link between providers of funds and service users
- The eight distinguishing factors that make leadership, management and governance challenging are that:
  - it is easy to have multiple and vague objectives
  - impact is hard to measure
  - organisations are accountable to many stakeholders
  - management structures are intricate
  - voluntarism is an essential ingredient
  - the mission has a powerful impact on approaches to management
  - values have to be cherished
  - the financial 'bottom line' is not the main determinant of priorities
- Management is complicated by the fact that people who contribute to third-sector organisations have a pot-pourri of motives which may be both philanthropic and self-serving

Deciding where to start making improvements

- One of the most nebulous issues that chairs, boards, chief executives and senior managers face is determining which aspects of leadership, management and governance most require attention
- Judgements have to be made about where to expend effort and how much resource should be used
- The ultimate aim of organisational analysis is to determine the best ways of increasing the organisation's impact
- Making improvements to the leadership, management and governance of organisations also requires careful sequencing
- Crucial judgements also have to be made about the capacity of the organisation to manage change
- These decisions usually require a combination of rigorous analysis and experienced judgement

FURTHER READING

Nonprofit Organisations – Theory, Management and Policy, Helmut Anheier, Routledge, 2005

The UK Civil Society Almanac, National Council for Voluntary Organisations, published annually

On Being Nonprofit – A Conceptual and Policy Primer, Peter Frumkin, Harvard University Press, 2002

More and recent books and reports can be found at www.compasspartnership.co.uk.

2 Establishing appropriate governance structures

2.1 NEW EXPECTATIONS OF GOVERNANCE

A textbook on leadership, management and governance could start from many different places; theories about why these organisations exist, the perspectives of people being governed and managed or a description of the challenges board members and managers face. This book starts by looking at governance. Governance is the provision of oversight and accountability of an organisation's work. The term embraces the structures and processes of the governing body and its committees and the functions that chief executives and managers perform to support governance.

The first of the three chapters on governance explores the structures of governance because they are the foundations on which organisations are built. Governance structures determine how board members and the chair are chosen, who chooses them and how long they serve. This group of people ultimately decides the organisation's mission, objectives and strategy and appoints the chief executive.

Whilst it is important to establish an appropriate governance structure, it should be noted that the structure itself is unlikely to be a major determinant of successful governance or indeed of an organisation's performance. The skills of board members, and their ability to work as a team and appoint an effective chief executive are likely to be a much greater influence on effective governance.

But, having governance structures that do not fit the organisation's circumstances can be a significant impediment to effectiveness. Inappropriate structures consume excessive management time, are frustrating for members and managers and can cost more than the value they add. And a weak structure becomes a serious problem when an organisation faces a crisis.

The expectations of governance have changed dramatically over recent years. Following a series of failures of governance in the corporate sector and a number of charity commission investigations into organisations with major problems, the third sector realised that its governance was not 'fit for purpose'.

These failures were followed by many investigations into the roles and delivery of governance in the corporate, public and third sectors. In the corporate sector a series of reviews (know as the Cadbury, Hampel, Greenbury, Turnbull, Smith and Higgs reviews) were eventually brought together to create a Combined Code for the governance of private sector companies.

In the public sector the Committee on Standards in Public Life produced the Seven Principles of Public Life, the Treasury produced guidance on the governance of public sector organisations and the Independent Commission for Good Governance in Public Services produced the Good Governance Standard for Public Services.

Similar developments followed in the third sector, with the National Council of Voluntary Organisations (NCVO) producing a review called *On Trust*, (1992), the (former) Housing Corporation establishing new expectations in *Modernising Governance: An Enabling Approach*, (2001) and a welter of advice being produced on the governance of schools, hospitals, universities, further education colleges and cooperatives. This resulted in the many initiatives to improve governance practices including the creation of a series of Codes of Governance for different types of organisations. These established standards that governance should meet, and have been followed by assessment tools that organisations can use to determine whether they adhere to the standards.

Modernising governance in the third sector has had five central themes:

- **Increasing the effectiveness of boards.** It has aimed to ensure that boards added significant value to the organisation, that they contributed to the development of the organisation's objectives and strategy and that they provided proper support for chief executives.
- **Providing better accountability for organisations.** It has set out to ensure that stakeholders and regulators had a better understanding of what organisations were achieving and were confident that proper controls were in place.
- **Recognising skills and expertise of governance.** It has acknowledged that governance requires skills that could be taught and learned through experience and that there was an art to being an effective board member.
- **Understanding and responding to stakeholders.** It has sought to establish mechanisms to ensure that boards acted on members', users' and other stakeholders' views.
- **Building and maintaining public trust**. It recognised that ultimately public trust in institutions depended on having transparent and accountable governance arrangements.

Together, these various initiatives have brought about a transformation in the standards expected of governance. It is now quite clear what good governance means and how it should be delivered. Furthermore it is accepted that as organisations grow and develop they have to review, develop and enhance their governance arrangements and at the same time ensure that they are proportionate to the organisation's circumstances.

This chapter describes:

- different types of board structures;
- the functions of assemblies and advisory boards;
- factors that determine the appropriate size of boards;
- the special case of federal structures;
- the design of committee structures;
- different methods for choosing the chair and other officers.

It does not address the legal issues that board members will have to consider (for example whether to register as a company limited by guarantee, a community interest company or a charitable incorporated organisation and whether to seek charitable status), since these are matters requiring legal advice.

2.2 DIFFERENT TYPES OF BOARD STRUCTURES

Before describing types of board structures, the distinction between members of the organisation (people who join the organisation and get a vote at its annual meeting) and members of the board (people who are elected to take on governance responsibilities) should be noted. Confusion occurs because both are called 'members'.

There are three main types of board. These types are determined by the arrangements and procedures for choosing board members.

1. **The elected and representative board**

   In this arrangement, the board is chosen by the organisation's membership, which elects from among itself individuals to serve on the board. Many membership organisations, mutual support organisations, cooperatives, churches, professional and employers' organisations have this model. This structure enables boards to take direct account of members' views.

   A variant on this arrangement is a 'two-tier' model in which the organisation's members choose a wider council and this body in turn elects or appoints members of the board. The National Trust has this arrangement.

   A further variation within this model occurs where a small group of people, usually fewer than a hundred people, who are the members of the organisation, elects members of the board. These 'guardians' may be past board members or individuals who have made a significant contribution to the organisation. They meet once a year to elect the board and perform other legal duties. Some arts organisations, some national charities and some housing associations have this type of governance arrangement because they do not have a wider membership and do not want a self-selecting board.

GOVERNANCE STRUCTURE OF THE NATIONAL TRUST

The National Trust works to preserve and protect the coastline, countryside and buildings of England, Wales and Northern Ireland. It is one of the largest charities in the UK, with 3.5 million members and an annual income of over £335 million.

It is governed by the board of between 9 and 15 trustees who are appointed by a council of 52 people. The council consists of 26 people who are elected by the members of the National Trust and 26 who are appointed by organisations whose interests coincide with those of the Trust.

Four committees report to the board of trustees, all focusing on governance matters. The Trust also has eight expert panels whose role is to advise staff and the board of trustees. These include panels for archaeology, architecture, arts, gardens and parks, land use, learning, commercial and nature conservation.

The chair, deputy chair and the senior member are elected by the council. The senior member cannot be a trustee.

The appointments committee recommends suitable candidates for chairs of country and regional committees and chairs of advisory panels to the board. The nominations committees assist the council in the selection or election of the chair and deputy chair, members of the board of trustees, external members of council and elected members of the council.

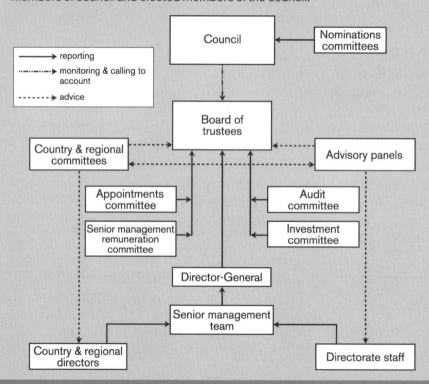

In this arrangement membership of the organisation is not open to the public. The members of the organisation either choose new members themselves or they are appointed by the board. This results in an intriguing structure in which the members elect the board and the board chooses the members. The Woodland Trust has this type of structure.

Another variant involves particular sub-groups (for example people from different nations, regions or branches) nominating or electing people to a pre-determined number of board positions (for example a member from each region). This is designed to allow views from different geographic areas to be represented on the board. The Youth Hostels Association has this arrangement.

2. **The self-selecting board**

In this arrangement, board members themselves are responsible for choosing new members. Board members are therefore also the legal 'members' of the organisation. This type of board is common in service delivery voluntary organisations, housing associations and independent schools. Appointments to the board are likely to be based on specific skills identified by the board, previous governance experience and connections with important stakeholder groups. The Woodland Trust and Shelter have this arrangement.

THE GOVERNANCE OF SHELTER

Shelter, the National Campaign for Homeless People, receives income of £49 million per annum. Its services, including Housing Aid Centres and projects, a free housing advice helpline and e-mail advice, help 170,000 people in housing need each year.

Shelter has a board of 13 members, who are collectively responsible for the strategic management of the charity. The board meets approximately seven times per year, and some activities are delegated to three sub-committees: audit, risk and finance, remuneration and nominations.

Membership of the board is advertised externally, and the nominations committee interviews candidates and recommends new members based on relevant skills, competencies and experience.

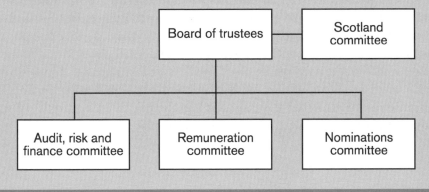

3. **The appointed board**

On these boards a third party, such as the organisation which established the body or a government minister, appoints members. This model is common in intermediary or 'umbrella' bodies that represent the interests of other organisations and in non-departmental public bodies (NDPBs). These third parties appoint their representatives to the boards of such organisations.

Each type of governance structure seeks to resolve the tension between having a board that **represents** the interests of the organisation's stakeholders and one that has the right balance of **skills and experience** required to provide top-quality governance. This does not imply that representatives are not skilled, but that elections may not produce an appropriate range and balance of experience.

Over recent years there has been a clear trend towards establishing skill-based boards, reflecting the growing demands on governance and the increasing size and complexity of organisations.

Methods for choosing board members

The two methods of choosing board members are **nominations** that lead to elections, and **selection** that leads to appointment. In an election people are nominated by a member or they nominate themselves, and an agreed electorate receives details about the experience of people who wish to stand, sometimes with a description of their aspirations for the organisation. The members vote using an agreed voting system and the election is decided by the number of votes gained by each candidate.

In a selection system, the board establishes the skills and experiences that it requires, produces a role description, conducts a search for candidates and chooses those people who best fit the requirements. Increasingly, members of the board or its nominations committee will expect candidates to complete an application form and attend an interview as part of the selection process.

The distinction between the two systems is not as clear-cut as it might at first sight appear, because even in an electoral system elections are not always fought in practice. Often people have to be persuaded to put their names forward, and boards have to work at finding candidates. They may then come up with precisely the number of people required to fill the available positions. This is not to suggest that the arrangements are 'rigged'; it is just the way things work in practice for many organisations, where elections are held only when more people put themselves forward than there are seats on the board. So in practice, a skills-based board can be created from an electoral system by putting forward a balanced slate of candidates that fits the required skills and the number of places available.

Another way of accommodating the need for both representation and skills is to use a 'pre-selection' process where members who wish to stand for election meet a selection panel to discuss their skills, commitment and experience. This can be a two-way exploration of mutual expectations that leads selection panels to encourage people to stand and sometimes results in people withdrawing their applications.

Boards may also offer guidance to the electorate by briefing them about particular skills and experience the board needs, and encouraging them to take this into account when voting.

After an election, further steps can be taken to balance representation, skills and experience by giving the board the power to appoint additional members (known as co-opting).

Unitary boards

The overwhelming majority of boards and (paid) leadership teams in third-sector organisations have completely separate memberships. A few, however, have modelled their structure on corporate-sector boards where board members are a mix of executive directors and non-executive directors, who work together to provide both governance and management, with the non-executives having a series of specific responsibilities (such as setting remuneration).

GOVERNANCE OF CfBT EDUCATION TRUST

CfBT Education Trust is a leading education consultancy and service organisation which provides education for public benefit both in the UK and internationally. It has an annual turnover exceeding £100 million and employs more than 2,000 people worldwide who support educational reform, teach, advise, research and train.

The organisation has a board of 10 trustees who are elected by the membership. The board delegates many of its responsibilities to an operations committee consisting of eight executive and four non-executive members. The non-executive members are chosen by an appointments committee and they each have specific responsibilities (for example to chair the education committee).

The operations committee meets monthly and operates as a unitary board combining the functions of governance and management. The non-executives are remunerated to reflect the higher expectations placed on these paid trustees. Their performance is appraised by the elected trustees.

A few large third-sector organisations have adopted this structure. Those with charitable status have to get approval from the Charity Commission. Others emulate this structure by inviting all members of the leadership team to attend board meetings and contribute, but not allowing them to vote.

2.3 ASSEMBLIES AND ADVISORY BOARDS

An alternative way of overcoming the need for governance to be representative and skills based is to establish a separate body whose primary function is to represent the views of particular stakeholder groups. This body is often called an assembly or advisory board. Sometimes this body has the power to appoint the board (see boards elected by a small membership described in section 2.2, Different types of board structures).

Members of the assembly can be appointed by the board and or they can be elected by the wider membership of the organisation. Some assemblies consist of the organisation's 'elder statesmen' and other people on whose experience and expertise the organisation wishes to draw on a regular basis. In this case, appointments are made by the board, and it is perceived as an honour to be invited to join such a group.

Some assemblies have a specific role to represent members' views to the board and some act more as consultative fora. In either case, their role is to listen systematically and closely to the views of the members and other stakeholders and to ensure that the board is kept continuously abreast of these opinions. Typically, assemblies might meet once or twice a year and provide advice, from stakeholders' perspectives, on matters such as strategic plans, the organisation's performance, policy issues and major decisions. Effective two-way communication between the board and the assembly is essential to ensure each understands the deliberations and decisions of the other.

This kind of structure is particularly applicable to membership organisations that make complex demands on their board and also require a high level of representation. Trying to combine the two functions can make boards large, unwieldy, and not necessarily composed of people with the skills needed for strong and effective governance. Splitting the functions is a way of letting boards and assemblies focus sharply on the tasks that each is best placed to deliver. Representatives concentrate on the job of listening to members of their constituencies and reporting views systematically to the board. Board members can then devote their skills and expertise to delivering top-quality governance.

Assemblies are more prevalent that might be expected. A survey of 71 organisations identified that 28% had an assembly or advisory board. They were more common amongst organisations concerned with sports and recreation, international development, training and education and umbrella organisations.

Most had had them for over 10 years. One-third of these bodies had less than 50 members and two thirds had less than 100 members (*BoardsCount*™, John Tierney, Governance Hub, 2007).

Whilst the role of assemblies is clear in theory, many members report that they are sceptical about their value. Chairs and chief executives report that there is a real challenge in ensuring that they make a significant and continuing contribution to the governance of the organisation.

2.4 **FEDERAL STRUCTURES**

Some organisations have a somewhat different type of governance structure from the 'linear' arrangements described so far. These structures are created either:

- when a group of organisations come together to form a 'central' body and cede some powers to it, or
- when organisations decide that the best way to grow is to establish semi-independent organisations in other countries or other parts of their own country. These national organisations or local branches are called 'the field' in this book.

'Federal' organisations are 'circular' in nature, because the member organisations both deliver services and campaigns and have a degree of control over the central organisation.

Well-known examples of federal organisations with branches include the Samaritans, Relate, Groundwork and Citizens Advice. International organisations with federal structures include Greenpeace International, International Planned Parenthood Federation, Amnesty International and WWF International.

A key determinant of these structures is the balance of power between the 'centre' and the 'field'. At one end of the spectrum the field elects or appoints the board from amongst their members and controls everything the centre does. The centre and the field organisations share the same name and there will be agreements over use of the name, standards of work and policy positions. At the other end of the spectrum, a looser federation comes together to coordinate strategy but members exert little further control over one another. They are in effect an 'umbrella' body.

Federal structures are appropriate when:

- Member organisations raise a significant proportion of their own income and wish to have control over how it is spent.
- Member organisations are highly dependent on volunteers to deliver their services and those volunteers want to have some control over how their branch or national organisation works.

Federal structures have the advantage of allowing their semi-independent field organisations the freedom to manage themselves in ways that suit local circumstances. However, large federal structures are cumbersome to manage and, because major changes have to be agreed by a majority of members, these organisations do not always respond quickly to changes in their environment. The centre has to devote significant resources to consulting and gaining a consensus on major issues. Consequently, some federal organisations have changed to 'line' structures, including the British Red Cross, Victim Support and the Alzheimer's Society. They wanted to make their organisations more responsive to changing external circumstances and to put more resources into services and less into the management of the organisation.

2.5 GROUP STRUCTURES

Group structures are established when an organisation wishes to make a clear legal distinction between itself and one or more subsidiary organisations. Group structures have a group-level board and separate legally constituted boards for each subsidiary. The simplest group structure has a parent and one subsidiary. Many charities have subsidiary trading companies that run a business to make profits which are passed up to the group. Scope Central Trading Limited, for example, raises millions of pounds each year from trading activities such as Scope shops. More complex structures may have a number of subsidiaries undertaking different activities.

Group structures need to be established when the subsidiaries have a different legal status from the parent or when the parent wishes a subsidiary with the same legal status to be able to operate with a degree of independence. Group structures are sometimes established when organisations merge, so the merging organisations retain their own boards, identities and legal responsibilities, but are owned by a parent that retains key functions such as appointing subsidiary board members, approving strategy and budgets and monitoring performance.

GOVERNANCE OF SWAN HOUSING GROUP

The Swan Housing Group manages over 7,600 homes in Essex, Suffolk and East London.

The Group consists of three registered social landlords, all of which are charitable organisations, and three private companies.

- Swan Housing Association is the 'parent' association for the Group.
- Swan (Essex) holds general needs properties, mainly in the Basildon area.
- Swan (London) is a specialist housing association providing supported housing services.

The three private companies carry out a range of supporting activities:

- Pike Housing Services Limited is a wholly owned subsidiary company of Swan (Essex) Housing Association providing market rented accommodation.
- Swan Commercial Services is a wholly owned commercial company which supports the work of the Swan Housing Group in achieving its objectives across a range of activities, including acquisition and development.
- Swan New Homes is a wholly owned subsidiary company that provides new homes for sale.

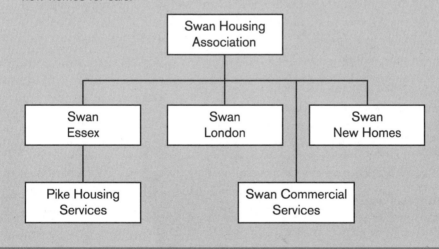

The establishment of a group structure can be used to make a clear distinction between the strategic functions of the parent and the operational roles of the subsidiaries. The parent can be responsible for determining the organisations it establishes or takes over and the functions it will deliver at group level, such as finance, ICT and HR. These are generally areas where there are economies of scale. The subsidiaries can then focus on the delivery of agreed services to approved standards in fixed geographic areas.

Many housing associations have successfully merged into groups, with subsidiaries operating in different parts of the country or providing different types of housing (for example family housing and special needs housing).

The types of subsidiaries that groups can encompass include charities, trading and other for-profit companies, community interest companies, social enterprises and grant-giving trusts. Some organisations, particularly in the USA, have separated out the provision of back office services (finance, HR, facilities and ICT) into separate 'management service organisations' (see section 12.2, Selecting partnership type to suit circumstances) and these too can be subsidiaries.

The advantages of group structures are that they:
- allow diverse organisations to work together;
- provide the subsidiary with the security and support offered by the parent;
- enable subsidiaries to be more tightly controlled than if they were only accountable to themselves;
- encourage exploitation of economies of scale.

Potential disadvantages include:
- greater management overheads;
- more complex governance arrangements;
- fuzzy boundaries between parent and subsidiary responsibilities.

The last four sections have demonstrated that there is no ideal board structure. They have also shown that the governance structure has to be related closely to the functions it is designed to perform. This relationship has been clearly described in the academic literature on governance.

THEORETICAL PERSPECTIVES ON GOVERNANCE

There are six theories about the fundamentally different functions that boards deliver and the ways in which board members of each should be chosen:

1. In the **agency theory** governance is a way of ensuring that management acts in the best interest of stakeholders. The main job of the board is to control managers and see that they strive to achieve the organisation's objectives. Board members should be chosen on the basis of their independence.

2. In the **stakeholder theory** governance represents a wide range of people and groups with an interest in the organisation and negotiates and resolves conflicts between them. Board members should be chosen to reflect the relevant interests.

3. In the **stewardship theory** governance works in partnership with management to improve organisation performance by adding value to big decisions on objectives and strategies. Board members should therefore be chosen on the basis of their expertise.

4. In the **resource theory** governance creates and maintains links with key external stakeholders to ensure that resources flow to the organisation and that it responds to external change. Board members should therefore be chosen on the basis of their links and contacts.

5. In the **democratic theory** governance represents the views of the organisation's members or constituencies that it serves. Board members should elected by their constituents.

6. In the **managerial theory** boards leave power with the professional management. They are chosen by the organisation's 'owners' and only get involved when the organisation faces crises.

In practice, many boards deliver a mixture of these functions. No single theory accurately reflects the complexity and sophistication of the sector or the different tensions that board members experience.

Summarised from: *The Governance of Public and Non-Profit Organisations,* Ed. Chris Cornforth, Routledge, 2003

2.6 BOARD SIZE AND MEETING FREQUENCY

The size of the board is an important consideration in the design of a governance structure. In recent years organisations with large boards (for example more than twenty people) have been reducing their size whilst those with smaller boards (for example fewer than five people) have been increasing their size.

Boards want to have a range of different perspectives to enable them to make good judgements on a wide range of issues. Some also want to represent different stakeholders' views, so there are pressures to increase board size. However, as boards grow larger it becomes harder to get agreement, each member has less 'air time' and greater effort has to be invested in preparing and managing meetings.

Organisations that face the greatest pressure on size are those that wish to have geographic representation on the board. This happens when representation from regions of the world, nations of the UK or regions of England is required alongside a range of specialist skills.

So the appropriate size for a board depends on circumstances. But the size of the board also determines the roles it can perform. A board with between seven and twelve members can be **hands-on**, whilst still sticking to a governance role. It can meet frequently, and may not need to delegate much to committees. As the number of members grows beyond twelve boards become increasingly cumbersome to manage and members each feel less personally responsible for governance decisions.

When boards grow into the upper teens and into the twenties, they are likely to have a much more **representative** role. A wide range of views can be presented but meetings have to concentrate on fewer critical issues so taking decisions is less efficient. Boards at the larger end of this range are more likely to appoint an executive committee to perform some of the hands-on functions of governance. This size is suitable in situations where representation of many different constituencies is a paramount priority.

When a board has more than 25 members its primary role is likely to be **policy-making**. It functions as the organisation's parliament, debating broad policy issues but remaining distanced from month-by-month decisions. These boards meet less frequently, and are likely to delegate decision-making and most of the practical functions of governance to an executive committee.

A survey of over 500 organisations found that 43% had boards of six to ten members and 33% had eleven to fifteen members. Larger organisations (with incomes of £5 million per year or more) tended to have larger boards; 47% had boards of eleven to fifteen members and 19% had boards of sixteen to twenty people. Almost a third of the smallest organisations (with incomes of less than £100,000 per year) had boards of two to five people (*Review and Development of the Code of Good Governance*, nfp Synergy, 2008).

Whilst the current orthodoxy is that the most appropriate number of board members is somewhere between nine and fifteen members, size is not the only determinant of effectiveness. Large, well managed boards can add more value than small, poorly managed ones. Nine of the twelve boards in a study of great nonprofits in the USA (*Forces for Good*, Crutchfield and McLeod Grant, Jossey-Bass, 2007) had boards of more than 20 people and the largest had 42 members.

Although US boards are different because members are generally expected to fundraise, the research suggests that effectively managed organisations can be supported by larger boards. Nevertheless, as three well-known American governance gurus say, 'we have seen boards of all sizes that are effective and ineffective, engaged and disengaged, incredibly valuable or nearly worthless' (*Governance as Leadership*, Chait, Ryan and Taylor, Wiley, 2005).

Despite this research, my experience is that small boards:

- find it easier to hold management tightly to account;
- feel a stronger sense of personal responsibility for the organisation;
- find it easier to make significant progress at meetings;
- can function with slightly less preparation and 'stage management' of meetings.

Board size is also closely related to meeting frequency; smaller boards can meet more often whilst larger boards meet less frequently and delegate more work to committees. A survey found that most boards meet between five and eleven times per year, and 39% of the boards of the largest organisations (with incomes of £5 million or more per year) meet four times a year. The boards of smaller organisations meet more frequently, with 12–19% meeting monthly. (*Review and Development of the Code of Good Governance*, nfp Synergy, 2008).

2.7 DESIGNING COMMITTEE STRUCTURES

When organisations grow beyond a certain size or degree of complexity, most boards find they need to create sub-groups to take responsibility for some of the board's work.

Three types of sub-groups are established. **Committees** are permanent groups to which specific, ongoing functions are delegated. Committees can take decisions on behalf of the board and are accountable to the board for their actions.

Advisory panels are established to advise the board on an ongoing basis. They have no decision-making power, though in some cases, such as medical research advisory panels, they can be very influential. **Task groups** are established to carry out specific jobs in a given timescale and then report back to the board. The task may require either actions (e.g. to coordinate preparation of the strategic plan) or investigation (e.g. to propose improvements to governance procedures).

The key to the success of all these sub-groups is to ensure that they perform only governance tasks that are delegated to them by the board. All three types are generally supported and serviced by management, but they have to be careful not to stray into management, because that confuses the accountability roles of governance with the delivery roles of management.

If managers require groups of people to assist with their work they can appoint management task groups. Board members can join these groups, particularly if they have relevant expertise, but they attend as independent people volunteering their skills and expertise, not as board members.

There are many reasons for establishing sub-groups of the board. Sometimes boards have limited time and simply need to delegate some of their responsibilities. Sometimes they need specialist advice from people with particular expertise. They may recruit such people without requiring them to sit on the board.

The number of committees organisations have varies widely. The best data suggests that the average organisation has three committees. Organisations with an income of less than £1 million per year have, on average, two, and those with an income of more than £10 million typically have between four and six. On average these committees have six members and meet three times per year. (*BoardsCount*™, John Tierney, Governance Hub, 2007). In addition these organisations may also have task groups and advisory panels.

Problems arise when an organisation fails to keep a tight grip on the structure and roles of groups contributing to governance:

- the total number grows, because there are always reasons to establish them and cutting them may imply criticism of the members' work;
- they expand beyond their stated remit and cause confusion about who is responsible for what;
- they can blur the direct line of accountability of staff to chief executive to board.

So, organisations need to ensure that board and members of sub-groups are crystal clear about the roles of each group and the methods by which they are accountable to the board. Furthermore, every sub-group should be expected to add value to the organisation. Each needs to make a unique contribution to the enterprise and ensure that the benefits they generate significantly outweigh the costs of establishing and servicing them.

Functions to delegate to committees

Boards have to decide whether to delegate any governance functions to committees and, if so, which ones. In the past there was a tendency to create many committees, in some cases organised to mirror the structure of management (e.g. committees for services, fundraising, finance and communications). These days, boards are being stricter and only establish committees that are required to support governance.

Boards can delegate a variety of functions to permanent committees:

- **Finance committees** can be given responsibility for overseeing the preparation of an annual budget, reviewing performance against budget and scrutinising major capital expenditures.
- **Investment committees** (in organisations with significant financial assets) can be given responsibility for appointing and overseeing investment advisors and advising on investment strategy.
- **Audit committees** (particularly in larger organisations where finance and audit need to be clearly separated) can be given responsibility for overseeing the annual audit, ensuring that appropriate financial controls are in place and overseeing risk management.
- **Remuneration committees** can advise the board on remuneration of the chief executive and sometimes the leadership team as well. They may also advise on organisations' overall remuneration policies.
- **Nominations committees** can take responsibility for planning board and committee succession, managing the process of seeking and selecting new members, overseeing the election process, and guiding induction, training and professional development of board and committee members.
- **Governance committees** can take responsibility for overseeing board performance reviews and changes to governance structures and processes. They can also be responsible for all the nominations functions listed above.
- **Compliance committees** can be established in federal organisations to ensure that members comply with agreed standards and to deal with any breaches.
- **Service and research committees** can provide the board with specialist or professional advice on issues relating to the main areas of organisations' services or research.
- **Fundraising committees** can oversee fundraising strategy and contribute ideas and contacts and provide governance oversight of the fundraising function.
- **HR committees** can provide governance oversight of employment policy and procedures and can also be the body that hears grievance and disciplinary appeals. These functions can sometimes be combined with those of the remuneration committee.

Executive committees

Some large boards that meet relatively infrequently appoint an **executive committee** (sometimes known as the management committee or by the rather quaint and old fashioned term, 'finance and general purposes committee'). The board delegates specified responsibilities to this group to govern the organisation in between its meetings.

Where this arrangement exists, the board needs to clarify:

- whether both groups should have a common chair (two chairs can lead to confusion and misunderstanding, but doing both jobs is a time-consuming task for one person and limits the number of people who will stand for the job);
- whether all the members of the executive committee should be members of the board (common membership simplifies matters, but it limits the opportunity for the executive committee to co-opt people with the required skills);
- whether the chief executive reports to the board or to the executive committee (it is usually a mixture of both, but it is worth clarifying where the buck stops to avoid problems);
- whether other sub-groups report to the board or to the executive committee (so they are crystal clear about lines of accountability).

Advisory panels

Advisory panels are essentially committees without decision-making powers. They are useful when a board needs expert advice but does not wish to delegate responsibility for taking final decisions. Examples include medical research panels which advise boards on spending research funds, and standards panels which advise on professional or technical standards.

Advisory panels are generally a permanent part of a structure, so they are appropriate when the board needs ongoing advice over a period of years from a group that builds its experience over time. Boards and senior management need to be seen to listen closely to their advisory panels. Members give their time voluntarily and have no real power in the organisation; they need to know that they are a valued part of the decision-making process and they should be given top-quality support from management.

Task groups

Task groups are teams of people established to resolve well-defined problems within a given time-frame. They are most effective at resolving specific governance problems. The board can establish the group, agree a brief and a timescale, determine its membership and delegate the problem. Examples of responsibilities delegated in this way include purchasing new property, forming a strategic alliance with another organisation, recruiting a new chief executive and overseeing a governance consultancy.

Task groups have the great advantage of flexibility. They can be created when required and disbanded when they have completed their work. Members are motivated by having a clearly specified task to undertake within an agreed time-frame. They get the satisfaction of completing their commitments.

Board member portfolios

One further elaboration of the governance structure is to give individual board members responsibility for providing oversight of specific issues or management functions on behalf of the whole board. These board members take a particular interest in their area of responsibility, build a closer relationship with the relevant manager and inform board deliberations on the issue. Examples of portfolio responsibilities include particular services or campaigns, public relations, high-profile events, communications, property, legal matters and risk.

This arrangement does not absolve other board members from responsibilities for these functions, but it does mean that they look to the portfolio holder to give close thought and attention to that area. This helps to make more effective use of board members' time. The role has to be delivered particularly carefully to avoid the board member unintentionally colluding with management or transgressing the boundary between governance and management. There are dangers both of getting too involved in detail and of pursuing personal hobby horses. The role has to focus on providing governance accountability.

2.8 CHOOSING THE CHAIR AND OTHER OFFICERS

The way the chair is chosen is an important part of the governance structure. There are a number of ways of doing it, though the boundaries between them can be fuzzy as described earlier in relation to the election and selection of board members.

1. **Election by the full membership of the organisation**
    This is more common in organisations with a large membership where the chair may play a high-profile role representing the organisation's cause and its interests. This arrangement has the advantage of being democratic, but it may not always produce a chair with the range of skills and experience needed to lead the governance of the organisation. Some organisations with an electoral system therefore establish a pre-selection system to ensure that all the candidates have the necessary skills. However, there is a danger that this could appear to be a manipulation of a democratic process.

2. **Election by the board from amongst board members**
    This is more common in organisations with self-selecting boards. In practice the process is often informal, with a vice chair or the chair of the nominations committee taking soundings amongst members about their interest in the post and their views on other possible candidates.

3. **Selection by a panel and approval by the board or the membership of the organisation**
    This method attempts to combine the advantages of a skill-based selection process with democratic approval of the preferred candidate. It gives the board or the membership the opportunity to reject the chosen candidate if they wish.

Where there is an element of selection, it makes sense to involve the chief executive in the process, as the relationship between him or her and the chair is crucial in ensuring that the board and management work effectively together.

Whether chairs are selected or elected, there should be a detailed description of the roles that they are expected to perform and a specification of the required skills and experience. There should be a term of office and a limit to the number of terms the chair can serve.

Many boards do not plan chair succession very effectively. The benchmarking of voluntary sector governance (*BoardsCount*™, John Tierney, Governance Hub, 2007) identified that only a quarter of organisations surveyed had a succession plan. Boards, and in particular the incumbent chair, need to think a year or more into the future. They should identify if there are potential candidates on the board and if not begin the process of attracting people to the post, allowing time to induct a new chair and for an orderly handover of responsibilities.

Choosing other officers

Governance structures sometimes include positions of vice chairs, treasurers and secretaries. **Vice chairs** can play important roles supporting and standing in for the chair, sharing the work of leading governance, providing a sounding board for the chair, giving feedback from performance reviews and being a conduit for informal feedback from board members. This position is sometimes elected and sometimes selected from members of the board.

Treasurers take particular responsibility on behalf of the whole board for providing governance oversight of organisations' finances. They usually chair the finance committee, if there is one, and can be a useful sounding board or source of advice for the finance director. Finding the requisite financial skills within an existing board is often difficult, so the post sometimes has to be appointed from outside the organisation.

Secretaries tend to be the minute taker in small organisations and the company secretary in organisations with limited company status. In larger organisations these roles are performed by staff. In smaller organisations this position is sometimes filled by election of the members. As there is seldom competition for the role, appointment by the board is more common.

The benchmarking of voluntary sector governance found that three-quarters of boards had a vice chair and 61% had a treasurer (*BoardsCount*™, John Tierney, Governance Hub, 2007).

SUMMARY OF KEY POINTS

New expectations of governance

- Organisations need to have an appropriate governance structure
- The structure itself is unlikely to be a major determinant of an organisation's performance. Board member skills and team-working skills will be much more significant
- The expectations of governance have changed dramatically over recent years
- Modernising governance has aimed to increase board effectiveness, provide better accountability, recognise the skills of governance, respond to stakeholders and maintain public trust

Different types of boards

- The three types of boards are determined by who chooses board members and how they are chosen. They are:
  - elected and representative boards
  - self-selecting boards
  - appointed boards
- Each type of structure seeks to resolve a tension between having a board that represents the interests of stakeholders and one that has the right balance of skills and experience
- The two methods of choosing board members are election and selection, but the boundaries between them are fuzzy in practice

Assemblies and advisory boards

- Some organisations have assemblies or advisory boards
- They are used for a variety of functions including representing members' views, reviewing policy and strategy, and appointing the board

Federal structures

- In federal structures, members' organisations both deliver services and campaigns and have a degree of control over the central organisation
- A key determinant of how these structures are governed is the balance of power between the 'centre' and the 'field'
- Federal structures have the advantage of allowing independent field organisations the freedom to manage themselves and also be part of a wider movement
- However, they are cumbersome and find it difficult to respond quickly to changes in their environment
- The additional tasks of governing federal organisations can include: setting standards for members, establishing federation-wide policy and controlling use of the brand

Group structures

- Group structures are established when an organisation wishes to make a clear legal distinction between itself and one or more subsidiary organisations
- A group structure can be used to separate the strategic functions of the parent and the operational roles of the subsidiaries
- Group structures allow diverse organisations to work together; provide the subsidiary with the security and support offered by the parent; enable subsidiaries to be more tightly controlled than if they were only accountable to themselves; and encourage exploitation of economies of scale
- They can lead to greater management overheads, more complex governance arrangements and fuzzy boundaries between parent and subsidiary responsibilities

Board size and meeting frequency

- There is no ideal size for a board. The appropriate size is determined by circumstances
- Boards need to be large enough to provide different perspectives on a wide range of issues and not so large that governance becomes inefficient
- Different-sized boards perform different roles. Smaller boards can be more hands-on, medium-sized boards can have more of a representative role and larger ones have to restrict themselves to establishing high-level policy

Designing committee structures

- Boards establish committees so that they can delegate board work
- Committees should only perform governance tasks
- Committees, advisory panels and task groups each have different roles
- Governance functions that can be delegated include: finance, investment, audit, remuneration, nominations, governance review, compliance and professional advice on the organisation's main services or research

Choosing the chair and other officers

- Chairs can be chosen by election from the full membership, by election from the board and by selection using a panel
- Other officers including vice chairs and treasurers are usually appointed from within the board, or, in the case of treasurers, recruited specifically to this role

FURTHER READING

Boards that Work, David Fishel, DSC, 2003

The Governance of Public and Non-Profit Organisations, ed. Chris Cornforth, Routledge, 2003

Governance as Leadership, Reframing the Work of Nonprofit Boards, Richard Chait, William Ryan and Barbara Taylor, Wiley, 2005

More and recent books and reports can be found at www.compasspartnership.co.uk.

3 Clarifying the roles of governance

3.1 BOARDS NEED PRECISELY DEFINED ROLES

Boards of third-sector organisations are a coalition of people, often from different backgrounds and with different motives, who join together to provide organisations with governance. They have to work as a team to deliver the special roles that only a board can provide.

Boards have to perform a leadership function. They have to add value to the organisation by steering, anticipating and providing wisdom and good judgement. They have to concern themselves with the vision of the organisation, its values and culture and its achievements. They have to pay close attention to the systematic development of a strong board that not only plans succession but strives to increase the calibre of the people it attracts. Effective boards understand the essential contribution that they have to make in the limited time that members give to the organisation. To do this they have to be totally clear about their roles and the boundaries on those roles.

Effective board members recognise that the task of running a board is a complex and subtle activity. The simple description that boards set policy and strategy and staff implement it does not explain what boards do in practice.

Boards have to fulfil the very different functions of:
- determining mission, policy, strategy;
- establishing and maintaining values;
- providing representation;
- ensuring financial viability;
- ensuring accountability;
- providing insight, wisdom and judgement to management;
- resolving conflicting interests;
- managing governance;
- appointing and developing the chief executive;
- setting risk policy and taking legal responsibility.

These functions align directly with the six theories about roles described in the previous chapter. In addition boards have to take legal responsibility for the organisation's work.

This chapter sets out fundamental concepts about the roles of boards. It describes:

- the life cycle of boards;
- the fundamental roles of governance;
- the distinctive roles of governance and management;
- the roles of high-performance boards;
- the roles boards play in delivering key governance functions;
- the standards boards should meet;
- the key roles of the chair.

This chapter focuses on the roles of good governance. The next chapter describes the processes that are needed to create highly effective boards. Both assume that there is no simple 'correct' role for a board. All organisations have to define their roles according to their circumstances.

3.2 THE LIFE CYCLE OF BOARDS

The development of many boards follows a common pattern which can be described as a life cycle. The detail of the cycle varies from one organisation to the next, but it provides an overview that can help boards to understand the way their roles evolve in line with the development of the organisation.

The founding phase

Many organisations are established by a charismatic founder who has the vision and personality to define a social, cultural or environmental problem and to create an organisation to address it. The founder gathers together a group of people who share the same views, and an organisation is created. The founder is sometimes the first chief executive or chair and may hold on to that position when other staff are hired.

The appointment of the first member of staff is a significant development with many implications for individuals' roles. Board members find that their role as both doers and deciders begins to change. Further staff may be appointed, and the organisation may reach the point where it needs a 'head'. This person may be called the director (because the term chief executive sounds too grand for a small organisation). At this point, the board has to go through its first transformation and to distinguish its role more clearly from that of the staff. This may be the first time that the board has had to discuss its roles and to change its behaviours and methods of working in a significant way. It may coincide with the departure of the founder and can be a traumatic period in an organisation's life.

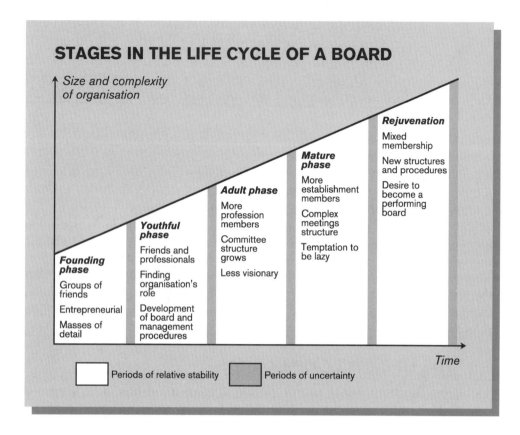

The youthful phase

When new roles are agreed, the board settles down into the second stage of the cycle. The organisation grows, more staff are appointed and soon the chief executive has a leadership team who take responsibility for most of the day-to-day work of the organisation.

As time passes, the board begins to take a back seat. There is a danger that meetings become more routine, attendance may fall and the staff's respect for the board may decline. A crisis may jerk the board out of its complacency; perhaps because the organisation has outgrown the capabilities of its chief executive, or there has been a dispute with staff or a difference of opinion over a policy issue. Whatever the cause, it is likely that when the immediate situation is resolved the board will find that it needs to reassess its role and review its structure.

The adult phase

When the board reassesses its role, it may conclude that it needs people with a different range of skills. Once found, these people generally bring new assumptions and, after a period of time, some of the longer-standing members may leave or be gently persuaded to move on with honour and dignity. The organisation settles into the third stage of the cycle. The new board may bring a new mindset that prioritises the establishment of clearer objectives, better monitoring of performance and tighter management of the budget. There is a risk, however, of losing the sense of mission that inspired the organisation in the first place.

After a while changing circumstances or another crisis may precipitate a review. Committees may be streamlined, some may be replaced with task groups and advisory panels, new operating procedures may be written and the role of the board is transformed again. Members heave a sigh of relief, and may start to meet less frequently and give the staff greater freedom within agreed boundaries.

The mature phase

As the years pass, the board takes a more hands-off role. The well-established organisation finds it easier to recruit new members, who may be leading figures in their own fields with less time to devote to the board. Some attract 'big names', who are willing to lend the respect that goes with their name but unwilling to get involved in the detail of the organisation's work. There is the danger of meetings becoming ritualised and boards concentrating on maintenance of the organisation rather than driving it to have greater social impact. Ultimately, a lazy board risks slipping back into a previous stage of development.

The stylised and slightly colourful life cycle just described will vary widely from one organisation to another, with some organisations remaining at one stage for many years. However, the pattern can help boards to describe their circumstances and understand why sometimes governance feels comparatively easy and sometimes it feels as if everything needs to change at the same time. Having a picture of a previous stage and a new one can help board members and managers understand the context of change, recognise the issues requiring attention and move organisations forward into the next stage of development.

Some boards are created to take responsibility for existing organisations (for example, after a merger) or well-funded start-up organisations (for example, new government-funded bodies). They have to skip rapidly through all the stages. Members find that they have to put significant effort into understanding one another, the leadership team and an organisation, often under considerable time pressures.

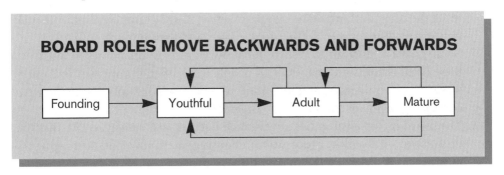

3.3 THE FUNDAMENTAL ROLES OF GOVERNANCE

Boards have many functions:

1. They have to be aware of the changing external environment and ensure that the organisation is geared up to respond to new circumstances. They have overall responsibility for deciding the **mission, objectives and strategies** of the organisation. They are responsible for agreeing the policies that the organisation adopts. They also have to monitor its performance against the agreed plans.

2. The board is ultimately responsible for establishing and upholding the **values** of the organisation. It sets the standards of behaviour that it expects from everyone else in terms of openness, transparency, clarity of communications and so on. It should model these in its own ways of working.

3. Boards have a **representation and listening** function. Board members have to pay attention to the voices of all the organisation's stakeholders, including users, funders, staff and the general public. They have to tune in to stakeholders' concerns and take decisions that reflect their interests. Many boards are elected by a membership. These board members also have to listen to the views of the people who elected them. They have to keep themselves informed about members' ambitions for the organisation and their concerns about the way it is run. Their continuing involvement with other members will be critical to discharging this function. This does not mean that they should see their role as being delegates of a particular group or as being mandated to take a particular viewpoint. Board members must always act independently and in the best interests of the organisation they are governing.

4. The board is ultimately responsible for the **economic viability** of the organisation and ensuring its long-term financial security.

5. The board is ultimately **accountable** for the organisation. It is responsible for overseeing all the organisation's work, for ensuring that the necessary reporting procedures are established and that it knows and understands what the organisation is doing. Depending on the nature of the organisation, it may be directly accountable to members, funders, regulatory bodies and the general public.

6. The board has to **support management** with advice, insight, wisdom and good judgement. Board members bring experience from other walks of life that helps to set the organisation's work into perspective, so they can play a valuable role in bringing different perceptions to decisions and their implications.

7. Boards have a function to **resolve tensions** within the organisation. Since these organisations are coalitions of people with different interests, including service users, funders, staff and volunteers, the board has to arbitrate between competing demands placed on the organisation.

8. The board has to ensure that **governance itself is well managed** and that the organisation has robust processes for choosing board members, managing meetings and reviewing the quality of governance.

9. The board is responsible for **appointing and supporting a chief executive.**
10. Boards have to **establish their appetite for risk** and agree an overall approach to managing and mitigating risk. Boards are also **legally responsible for the organisation's work.** These are significant responsibilities, and will weigh heavily on board members' minds particularly when organisations are taking major decisions and when they face financial difficulties.

In the limited time that board members devote to the organisation they have to focus their efforts sharply on these crucial functions that no one else can discharge.

THE FIVE Ss OF GOVERNANCE

The roles of governance have been neatly summarised into five 'modes' in which boards operate. Boards need to ask different types of questions when working in different modes.

In the **support mode** boards encourage management and provide advice. They ask:

- Have you got what you need to do that?
- Should we celebrate that?

In the **stretch mode** the board challenges management to make improvements. They ask:

- Can't we do better than that?
- Can we work with other organisations to achieve that?

In the **scrutiny mode** they examine propositions and hold management to account. They ask:

- Have you really made the case for that?
- What are the implications of doing that?

In the **stewardship mode** boards guard the organisation's assets, its reputation and its long-term future. They ask:

- Will we have sufficient reserves in the future?
- Is the reputational risk too great?

In the **strategy mode** they consult widely and make the big decisions that affect future direction. They ask:

- How will external trends affect that?
- What are the opportunities in this area?

Julia Unwin argues that successful boards are aware of the different modes and when they are operating in each. She also points to the dangers of operating in the wrong mode, for example offering support when they should be in scrutiny mode.

Source: 'The five S's in governance', Julia Unwin, *Governance*, March 2006

3.4 DISTINGUISHING GOVERNANCE FROM MANAGEMENT

There is no completely clear-cut distinction between governance and management. Unfortunately, the roles of the board and of paid management cannot be neatly separated. But neither do they need to overlap significantly. They need to be distinct but complementary. The key functions of the board are different from the tasks of management *and* they will vary in different circumstances.

Governance is the board's responsibility and it is delivered with support from management. Governance is about ensuring that the organisation has a clear mission and strategy, but not necessarily about developing it. It is about ensuring that stakeholders' views are heard but not about managing all communication with different stakeholder groups. It is about ensuring organisations' economic viability but not about raising all the required resources. It is about giving guidance on the overall allocation of resources, but is less concerned with the precise numbers. Governance is about ensuring organisations are accountable but not about managing the performance-reporting system. Governance is concerned with providing insight, wisdom and good judgement. It is about ensuring that organisations are well managed, but not about managing them.

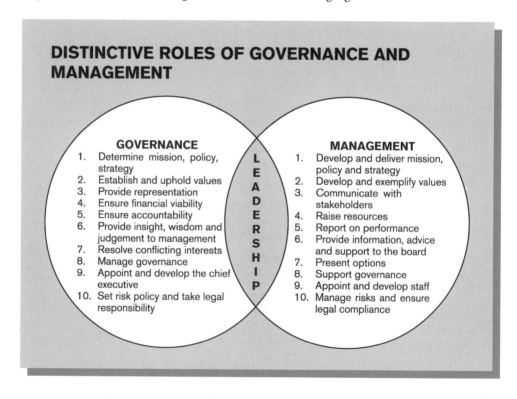

DISTINCTIVE ROLES OF GOVERNANCE AND MANAGEMENT

GOVERNANCE
1. Determine mission, policy, strategy
2. Establish and uphold values
3. Provide representation
4. Ensure financial viability
5. Ensure accountability
6. Provide insight, wisdom and judgement to management
7. Resolve conflicting interests
8. Manage governance
9. Appoint and develop the chief executive
10. Set risk policy and take legal responsibility

LEADERSHIP

MANAGEMENT
1. Develop and deliver mission, policy and strategy
2. Develop and exemplify values
3. Communicate with stakeholders
4. Raise resources
5. Report on performance
6. Provide information, advice and support to the board
7. Present options
8. Support governance
9. Appoint and develop staff
10. Manage risks and ensure legal compliance

Management is responsible for developing strategy and for implementing it once it is agreed by the board. Managers are responsible for turning the board's intentions into action and for managing the systems and procedures needed to get results. Managers crucially influence the organisation's values, by the way they work and the signals they give to staff and volunteers. They are responsible for maintaining close contact with stakeholders, for raising funds and ensuring that they are spent effectively. They report on performance and take action to address under-achievement. They support governance by ensuring that the necessary processes and mechanics are in place and run smoothly, and they appoint and manage the rest of the staff.

Extent of separation of governance and management

Governance and management have separate but overlapping functions. The extent of separation needs to be appropriate for the circumstances. When board members and managers have a high level of trust in one another there will be a greater degree of separation between the roles each performs.

When objectives and strategies are not clear, when management is not taking full account of stakeholder views, when the organisation is not economically viable, then it is appropriate that boards become more involved. Their first reaction should be to hold management to account for poor quality work and then they should also provide advice and support.

Great care needs to be taken to avoid falling into the trap of doing management's work, because this will make management less likely to own the outcomes and more likely to blame the board when things don't work out as planned. There is a very fine line between providing advice and starting to perform management's roles.

Similarly when the board is not providing strategic advice, is meddling in detailed management issues and is not properly managing the governance of the organisation, management has judiciously to take appropriate actions to remind the board of its strategic roles and help the chair in particular to maintain that role.

In addition to establishing and appropriate degree of separation, board members and managers need to have realistic expectations of one another. People are fallible; everyone has other lives, and not everyone can perform perfectly on every occasion. Unrealistic expectations lead to disappointment and loss of morale on the part of both board members and managers. They do not serve the organisation well. Experienced board members and managers make realistic judgements about people's abilities, provide a little bit of stretch, but refrain from having unrealistic ambitions about one another.

SEPARATION OF GOVERNANCE AND MANAGEMENT

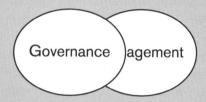

Governance can extend too far into management. This may need to happen when management is weak, but there is a danger that the board starts doing management's work. If management does not have the skills to deliver agreed plans, then it may be better for the board to make changes to management rather than taking over management responsibilities.

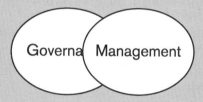

Management can extend too far into governance. This may need to happen when governance is weak. Managers then have a disproportionate influence over policy and strategy, and may not be subjected to rigorous challenge. In the longer term, staff interests start to predominate over those of other stakeholder groups, leaving the organisation less fit to achieve its primary purpose. Management may need to help the board to regain its appropriate role.

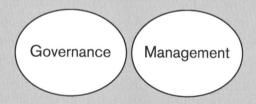

Governance and management sometimes operate almost as if they are separate entities. This happens when communications and relationships are poor. There is a danger that management will not be held properly to account and that relationships will deteriorate.

The extent to which board members and managers have the skills and experience needed to manage their organisation also determines the appropriate separation of the roles of governance and management. Organisations with more skilled boards and with high-calibre management can have greater separation of the roles.

Organisations with boards and management that face challenges beyond their abilities risk getting into serious difficulty if neither group has the skills to resolve the issues. These organisations are in danger of entering a spiral which starts with a declining reputation, leads to difficulty in attracting effective staff and board members, and culminates in deteriorating services and a further fall in reputation. It will need the dedication of a few people over an extended period to start the process of building a new board, carving out a governance role and creating a stronger team of staff. The appointment of a highly competent chief executive, a strong and dedicated chair and sometimes outside consultants as well is likely to be an essential part of rebuilding the organisation.

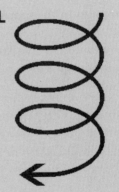

THE DANGEROUS DOWNWARD SPIRAL

Weak governance and poor appointments to the chief executive and senior management leads to governance being less well supported and makes the organisation less attractive to new board members.

Recruitment of less effective board members perpetuates the downward spiral of the organisation.

To avoid this situation, boards should ensure that organisations **do not take on responsibilities, commitments and plans that are more demanding than their ability to deliver.** There may be pressing social, environmental or cultural problems that require attention, but that does not mean organisations should take on more complexity than they are capable of managing. The most effective boards make good judgements about the fit between the organisation's ambitions and its capacity to deliver them with confidence.

3.5 **ROLES OF HIGH-PERFORMANCE BOARDS**

Moving beyond the essential roles, the best boards anticipate and shape the future, they add continuous value and they ensure that their governance arrangements are exemplary.

Effective boards usually take few decisions; they have a much more sophisticated role. The critical ingredient of an effective board is to **anticipate decisions.** Boards that anticipate are in command of the organisation's affairs. Boards that fail to anticipate find that events run out of control and they are driven by circumstances into crisis management. In these circumstances the board finds itself repeating the work of the staff, dragged into the detail and unable to raise itself into a more strategic role.

When a board has a commanding view of what it is trying to do and how it is going about the task, it actively anticipates:
- changes in the external environment;
- changes in the size and needs of the user group or campaign priorities;
- opportunities to deliver new services and campaigns or to refresh existing ones;
- opportunities for new partnerships;
- changes in the funding;
- succession of the chair;
- review of the chief executive's performance;
- processes for determining new strategies and monitoring overall performance.

With good anticipation, an effective board finds that **shaping decisions** is just as important as taking them. It creates the context within which the organisation functions. It influences the organisation by asking the right questions at the right time. It guides with wisdom and good judgement rather than by making decisions on matters of detail.

When boards are anticipating and shaping they **add value** to the organisation. They can look back over the previous year and know what has changed as a result of the board's work. A good question boards ask themselves is 'what would have been different if we hadn't met last year?'

These are the defining characteristics of mature boards that are maintaining a tight grasp on governance.

GENERATIVE GOVERNANCE

Three American nonprofit governance gurus argue that boards should work in different modes:

- The **fiduciary mode** where boards are concerned with stewardship of the organisation's assets
- The **strategic mode** where boards work in strategic partnership with management
- The **generative mode** where boards provide a crucial source of leadership for the organisation

They point out that, as a result of focusing more sharply on the oversight and functional roles of governance, some boards have ceded too much of the interesting work of envisioning the future, re-framing the organisation's goals and spotting new opportunities to management.

They argue that this work should be done in partnership, and that to do it board members need to spend time out of the boardroom visiting projects, meeting with other boards and interacting with stakeholders so they have the experiences needed to work in a generative mode.

They encourage boards to spend more time considering catalytic questions such as:

- What do you hope will be most strikingly different about this organisation in five years' time?
- Five years from today, what will this organisation's key constituents consider the most important legacy of the current board?
- If we could successfully take over another organisation, which one would we choose and why?
- What headline would we most/least like to see about this organisation?
- What is the biggest gap between what the organisation claims it is and what it actually is?

These actions help boards to operate in a generative mode.

Source: *Governance as Leadership*, Richard Chait, William Ryan and Barbara Taylor, Wiley, 2005

High-performance boards also invest time in ensuring that the organisation's overall governance arrangements are tailored to suit future needs.

This investment pays handsome dividends, so when difficult issues arise there is a framework for discussing and resolving them. It takes time to agree roles and procedures but, once this has been done, meetings run more smoothly and decision-taking is easier.

Defining the board's role is an ongoing task. Over time external circumstances will change, new members will join the board, and a new chief executive will bring different assumptions. These changes will require the board to spend more time redefining its own role and its expectations of management.

ROLE OF THE LEADERSHIP FOUNDATION BOARD

When I joined the board of the Leadership Foundation for Higher Education I observed that:

- The chair and chief executive had a shared conception of the role of the board
- The board focused on current performance, policy developments and new initiatives
- The chair helped to keep board discussions at a strategic level by asking particularly pertinent questions
- The chair sometimes directed a question at a specific member (keeping them on their toes!)
- Board members brought high value by coming from a range of different backgrounds
- The board challenged management in a constructive but authoritative way
- New board members need time to understand the context of the organisation, its programmes and its culture

3.6 DELIVERING GOVERNANCE OF KEY FUNCTIONS

Boards play specific roles in the delivery of certain organisational functions including strategic planning (section 7.5, Developing strategic plans), managing corporate performance (Chapter 9), policy-making, managing risk and regulatory compliance. Some of these are described more fully elsewhere in this book. In each of these functions board members and managers play distinct and complementary roles.

Strategic planning

The board's role in planning depends on its size, the competencies of its chief executive and leadership team, and the organisation's experience in planning.

In a well-developed organisation the board's role in planning is likely to include:

- confirming the planning process;
- considering the results of a strategic review and the resulting identification of key strategic issues;
- challenging proposed outcomes, performance indicators and strategies for achieving them;

- confirming revisions to the mission and values and the broad financial envelope;
- reviewing key risks and mitigating actions;
- approving the resulting plan.

In organisations with less experience of planning, the roles of the board, a board committee or a board member might include additionally:

- helping with the development or re-development of a planning process;
- contributing to the strategic review;
- attending consultation events for stakeholders;
- contributing to the development of proposed outcomes and strategies.

Boards that are striving to operate in a more generative role (see box) will want the whole board to be working in partnership with management on key aspects of the strategic planning process.

Managing corporate performance

Boards have to hold management accountable for corporate performance. They are responsible for ensuring that the organisation has a robust process for gathering information and reporting on its overall performance. They should move into 'scrutiny' mode when considering performance against plans, and be prepared to ask tough questions. Boards are sometimes too polite and forgiving when assessing performance, when they should instead be expecting explanations and proposals for improving areas of under-performance as well as praising achievements.

Policy making

Organisations have policies on many topics including service quality, fundraising methods, employment, financial reserves, equal opportunities, confidentiality, whistle blowing, abuse and many other matters.

The board's primary responsibility in relation to policy is to approve it. The extent to which it participates in policy development will depend on the organisation's size and circumstances and on the nature of the policies under consideration. Board members may also monitor implementation of important policies, but are less likely to be involved in functional or operational policy. Implementation of policy should always be a management responsibility.

COUNCIL POLICIES AT THE GIRLS' DAY SCHOOL TRUST

Organisations can have policies on a wide range of issues. These are the policies that have been agreed by the council of the Girls' Day School Trust, a charity that runs 29 schools and two academies:

- accessibility
- admissions
- appointment of heads
- audit and budget framework
- bursaries and scholarships
- complaints
- curriculum
- drugs
- equal opportunities
- exclusion
- health and safety
- local governing bodies
- minimum accommodation standards
- pay
- parent contract/fees
- performance review
- pupil–teacher ratio
- risk management
- safeguarding
- strategic planning

Managing risk

The board is responsible for considering the major strategic risks that the organisation takes. Risk management should:

- identify key risks;
- estimate the likelihood of the risk occurring;
- estimate the likely impact if it does occur;
- describe actions taken to transfer, control or manage the risk;
- identify who is responsible for managing the risk;
- report on further actions required.

The board should be involved in agreeing its appetite for risk, approving the risk management system and in monitoring the risk register. Development and management of the register and taking actions to minimise risk should be a management responsibility.

Compliance

The board is responsible for ensuring that the organisation complies with legal and regulatory requirements. It needs to have a list of compliance requirements and to confirm periodically that they are being met.

Management needs to record breaches of compliance requirements and actions taken. It needs to ensure that staff are aware of compliance requirements, and to inform the appropriate authorities when they have not been met.

3.7 STANDARDS BOARD MEMBERS SHOULD MEET

These days there are high expectations of everyone who is involved in public life. The public wants individuals and organisations to be worthy of their trust and to adopt the highest standards of behaviour. The seven principles of public life created by the Committee on Standards in Public Life have been interpreted for third-sector organisations and provide a good foundation for the standards that should be expected of individual board members.

THE PRINCIPLES OF PUBLIC LIFE

These principles have been adapted for the voluntary sector by the National Council for Voluntary Organisations. They provide a useful starting point for defining the behaviours of board members.

Selflessness
Board members have a duty to act in the best interest of the organisation as a whole. They should not do so in order to gain financial or other material benefits for themselves, their family, their friends or the organisations they come from or represent.

Integrity
Board members should not place themselves under any financial or other obligation to outside individuals or organisations that might influence them in the performance of their duties.

Objectivity
In carrying out their duties, including making appointments, awarding contracts, or recommending individuals for rewards and benefits, board members should make choices on merit.

Accountability
Board members are accountable for their decisions and actions to the public, funders and service users. They must submit themselves to whatever scrutiny is appropriate to their role.

Openness
Board members should be as open as possible about all decisions and actions they take. They should give reasons for their decisions and restrict information only when the wider interest clearly demands.

Honesty
Board members have a duty to declare any interests relating to their role and to take steps to resolve any conflicts arising in favour of their trustee role.

Leadership
Board members should promote and support these principles by leadership and example.

EXAMPLE NATIONAL OCCUPATIONAL STANDARD
Determine the strategy and structure of the voluntary or community organisation

When determining the strategy and structure of the organisation, as trustees **you are responsible for:**

1. ensuring the organisation sets aims or legal objects that reflect its values and mission, that look positively to the future and that enable the organisation's current mission to be achieved

2. where an organisation employs staff, working with them to produce a strategic plan that meets the organisation's agreed aims and intended outcomes

3. ensuring the organisation has an appropriate structure incorporating legal and governance frameworks

4. ensuring a programme of activities which continually builds upon, and makes good use of, the organisation's resources

5. regularly reviewing and updating the strategic plan to keep it fit for purpose

In order to be able to carry out these responsibilities fully, as trustees **you need to know and understand:**

a. the advantages, disadvantages, and implications for trustees, of the different types of legal structures for an organisation, as appropriate

b. the requirements of the governing documents

c. the day-to-day nature of work carried out by the organisation

d. your organisation's governance, management and operational structure, and why it is appropriate to the organisation

e. the importance of financial planning, budgets and of monitoring income and expenditure, outputs and outcomes

f. how to evaluate current and recent performance and what has or hasn't worked

In order to determine the strategy and structure of the organisation **you need to have read,** where applicable:

i the organisation's annual budget

ii the organisation's strategic plan

iii the organisation's business plan

iv the organisation's annual report

Source: *Trustee and Management Committee National Occupational Standards,* NCVO, 2006

Competencies required of board members depend on the size, complexity and stage of development of the organisations they are governing. Providing top quality governance of a complex multi-million pound, geographically dispersed service-providing and campaigning organisation clearly requires a wider range of skills than governing a small single site, single service organisation.

In the voluntary sector, National Occupational Standards set out the competencies that board members need to discharge their responsibilities effectively. They are organised under four headings:

1 Safeguard and promote the values and mission of the voluntary or community organisation
2 Determine the strategy and structure of the voluntary or community organisation
3 Ensure the voluntary or community organisation operates in an effective, responsible and accountable manner
4 Ensure the effective functioning of the voluntary or community organisation's board of trustees.

Each standard sets out what a board member is responsible for, what they need to know to carry out these responsibilities, and what documents they need to have read. The standards also set out qualities that board members should draw upon when discharging their responsibilities.

Lists of standards and competencies provide useful check lists, but they do not of themselves get to the heart of really effective board membership. This requires skills such as:

- preparing thoroughly for meetings and prioritising points to be made;
- knowing how and when to make interventions in meetings;
- being succinct and making maximum use of board members' valuable time;
- recognising when to pursue an issue and when to accept the majority view;
- being able to support a board position, even when it does not accord entirely with a personal view;
- using emotional intelligence to read people's feelings;
- listening carefully to other members' points of view;
- clarifying points of detail outside meetings;
- maintaining contact with other board members between meetings;
- keeping in touch with the organisation's work without interfering with management responsibilities.

BOARD COMPETENCIES

Research by Richard Chait, a well-known American guru on nonprofit board performance, has correlated the competencies of boards with the effectiveness of the nonprofit organisations they manage. These are described in six dimensions.

Competency	Definition
1. Contextual dimension	The board understands and takes into account the values and beliefs of the organisation it governs.
2. Educational dimension	The board ensures that board members are well informed about the organisation, the relevant profession and the board's role, responsibilities and performance.
3. Inter-personal dimension	The board nurtures the development of members as a group and fosters a sense of cohesiveness.
4. Analytical dimension	The board recognises complexities in the issues it faces, and draws upon different perspectives to find appropriate solutions.
5. Political dimension	The board accepts the need to develop healthy relationships with key constituencies.
6. Strategic dimension	The board helps ensure a strategic approach to the organisation's future.

His research concluded that organisations which had boards that exhibited all six competencies performed significantly better than those lacking one or more of these competencies.

Source: *The Effective Board of Trustees,* Richard Chait *et al.,* Oryx Press, 1991

Conflicts of interest and loyalty

In discharging their responsibilities board members have to be particularly aware of the dangers of **conflicts of interest.** Conflicts of interest arise where an individual's personal or family interests conflict with those of the organisation. Conflicts can:

- inhibit free discussion;
- result in decisions or actions that are not in the interests of the organisation;
- risk creating the impression that the organisation has acted improperly;
- harm the organisation's reputation.

Avoiding conflicts of interest is one of the seven principles of public life and a supporting principle in the Code of Governance for the Voluntary and Community Sector.

It is therefore important to avoid the appearance of impropriety, **anticipate** the issue and decide how it should be handled before it arises in practice.

Examples of potential conflicts of interest include agreeing contracts where a family member has an interest, having a connection with someone being recruited, or sharing sensitive information that would benefit a family member.

Well-governed organisations:
- have a conflict of interest policy;
- establish and maintain a register of interests;
- require board members with conflicts to withdraw from decisions;
- record details of discussions and decisions from which those with conflicts have withdrawn.

Conflicts of interest are different from **conflicts of loyalty.** A conflict of loyalty occurs when people find themselves representing the interests of two different organisations and a decision by one would significantly affect the other. This can happen in partnerships and intermediary organisations when taking decisions that will benefit some but not all of the partners. It can also happen when someone is a member of the board of a funding body and of an organisation that it funds, or is an officer of or a candidate for a political party. These issues are sometimes wrongly seen as conflicts of interest, which they are not unless there is an issue of personal or family gain.

Legally, in board meetings, members must act in the best interests of that organisation. When members feel they face a conflict of loyalty the most honest approach is to inform the board of that conflict and disclose any pertinent information. This helps everyone to understand the context of the conflicted person. In many cases this may be sufficient. Sometimes it might be appropriate to abstain from a discussion or decision, recognising that the majority view has to prevail.

Sometimes the conflict of loyalty is significant. The hard reality in these circumstances is that board members ultimately have to decide whether they will live with a decision they did not support, or leave the board.

Some boards find it is valuable to codify the behaviour expected of board members into a form of contract. A code can help to establish greater clarity about expectations. It can cover matters such as conflicts of interest and loyalty as well as broader requirements about not acting for personal gain, behaviour in board meetings and arrangements for leaving the board. (NCVO publishes a model code called *Best Behaviour*, NCVO, 2004.)

Role of the board in establishing culture and values

Beyond their formal roles, boards are a significant determinant of the culture and values of the organisation. The way board members behave as individuals, their diligence, their creativity and their willingness to listen will rub off on the rest of the organisation and indicate desirable ways of working.

Their ability to work as a team, to work in different modes, to bring different points of view and to share responsibility for agreed decisions will all be noticed and will set the tone for the leadership team and other parts of the organisation.

The board should embody the values of the organisation. This is not just about agreeing a 'values statement'. It is also about ensuring that the board holds true to those values both in what it decides and in how it goes about its work.

3.8 THE KEY ROLES OF THE CHAIR

Chairs of third-sector organisations have a unique and special role. Discharging the role effectively is a critical ingredient in the long-term success of the organisation.

There are six roles for which chairs should see themselves accountable:

1. **Chairs are responsible for the performance of all aspects of governance**
   Their role is to ensure that the very many factors that combine to produce good governance are working to the highest standard. This includes clarity of structures and roles and the effectiveness of all processes of governance.
2. **The chair is the chief executive's line manager**
   Chairs have to operate on a number of different levels in this role. They have to:
   - hold the chief executive firmly to account for implementation of the organisation's strategy and plans and of specific board decisions;
   - work closely together to deliver top-quality governance;
   - act as a sounding board for the chief executive's dilemmas and early thoughts;
   - be personally supportive during difficult times.
   Chairs sometimes face the difficult circumstances of a chief executive who is not performing to the standard expected. When evidence of poor performance begins to emerge, it is crucial that the chair continues to express to all stakeholders, except the board, his or her full confidence in the chief executive until the moment when it is decided that the chief executive should be dismissed. Any indication of lack of confidence can be very undermining for the chief executive, so performance issues should be treated as highly

confidential, though the chair can discuss in private board sessions the performance issues that have been raised. Legal advice should be sought when poor performance begins to emerge to ensure compliance with employment law.

3. **Chairs manage the boundary between governance and management**
The chair is responsible for keeping board members focused on their governance role, and for avoiding incremental slippage into the management role. The chair therefore has a duty to protect staff from over-enthusiastic board members who become too involved in detailed managerial issues. While this boundary is never clear-cut, and management may require assistance from board members with special skills and experience, the chair should act swiftly when any board member begins to interfere in management issues. Chairs should remind board members that their job is to hold management accountable for the organisation's work and that they must resist any temptation to do the work of management.

4. **Chairs are responsible for succession planning**
The chair is responsible for ensuring that board member succession is planned well in advance of anticipated departures and that people with the necessary skills are selected or put forward for election.
They have a particular responsibility for developing people with the potential to succeed them in the chair. The best way to ensure that all the work that chairs put in during their time in office is continued into the future is to leave the organisation in the hands of someone who can take the organisation on to its next stage of development. This can require effort over an extended period of time. It may involve other board members and the chief executive, but ultimately it is the responsibility of the chair.

5. **The chair can be the figurehead**
The chair can represent the organisation on key public occasions. This is a sensitive issue because the figurehead roles of the chair and chief executive overlap. The precise boundary will depend on the two individuals, and this needs to be discussed and agreed. (This is described more fully in section 4.6, Ensuring effective chair–chief executive relationships).

6. **The chair is responsible for getting the best possible performance from the board**
The preparation, authority and emotional intelligence of the chair will all help to ensure that every member contributes at their highest standards and that the contribution of the board as a team is maximised.

WHAT THE CODE OF GOVERNANCE SAYS ABOUT THE ROLE OF THE CHAIR

The chair should ensure:

- the efficient conduct of business at the organisation's board and general meetings
- that the organisation's business is efficiently and accountably conducted between board meetings
- that the organisation complies generally with the sector's Code of Good Governance
- that the appraisal and remuneration of the organisation's chief executive are properly overseen
- that the employment of the chief executive complies with employment legislation and good practice, and
- that the appraisal of board and board member performance is properly conducted

Source: *Good Governance – A Code for the Voluntary and Community Sector,* ACEVO, Charity Trustee Networks, ICSA, NCVO, 2005

SUMMARY OF KEY POINTS

Boards need precisely defined roles

- Boards have to add value to the organisation by steering, anticipating and providing good judgement
- Board members have to work as a team to deliver those roles that only the board can provide

The life cycle of boards

- Boards go through phases of development that can be characterised as founding, youthful, adult, maturity and rejuvenation. They can slip back into previous stages of development
- Different ways of working are needed for each stage of development

The fundamental roles of governance

- The key roles of the board are to:
  - agree the mission, objectives, strategies and policies
  - establish and uphold the organisation's values
  - provide representation
  - ensure the organisation's viability
  - ensure accountability of the organisation
  - provide wisdom, insight and judgement to management

- resolve conflicting interests between different stakeholder groups
- ensure governance is well managed
- appoint and support the chief executive
- set risk policy and take legal responsibility for the organisation

Distinguishing governance from management

- There is no clear-cut distinction between the roles of governance and management. They need to be separate but complementary
- At its simplest, governance is about ensuring and guiding, whilst management is about doing
- The degree of separation of governance and management depends on circumstances, but boards should not encroach into management and management should not have too great an influence on governance

Roles of high-performance boards

- Effective boards have a commanding view of the organisation and its environment so they can anticipate decisions
- With anticipation boards shape decisions by asking the right questions
- The best boards know the difference they have made

Delivering governance of key functions

- Boards play specific roles in the delivery of certain functions including strategic planning, managing corporate performance, policy making, managing risk and regulatory compliance
- Each has to be delivered in partnership with management, which plays a different role in relation to these functions

Standards board members should meet

- The principles of public life are a foundation for standards of governance
- National Occupational Standards indicate some of the knowledge board members need to have
- Meeting the highest standards is ultimately about a series of behaviours that can be learned with experience
- Conflicts of interests arise where an individual's personal or family interests or loyalties conflict with those of the organisation
- Conflicts of loyalty occur when people find themselves representing the interests of two different organisations and a decision by one would significantly affect the other
- Boards need to be aware that the way they work rubs off on the rest of the organisation

The key roles of the chair

- Chairs are responsible for the performance of governance, line managing the chief executive, managing the boundary between governance and management, planning succession and sometimes being a figurehead

FURTHER READING

A CEO's Guide to Board Development, ACEVO, 2007

Chief Executives on Governance, ACEVO Commission of Enquiry, 2007

Your Chair and Board – A Survival Guide and Toolkit for CEOs, ACEVO, 2008

Governance, Bi-monthly magazine, Plaza Publishing Ltd

Good Governance – The Chair's Role, Dorothy Dalton, NCVO, 2006

Governance as Leadership, Reframing the Work of Nonprofit Boards, Richard Chait, William Ryan and Barbara Taylor, Wiley, 2005

The Dynamic Board – Lessons from High Performing Nonprofits, McKinsey & Company, 2003

More and recent books and reports can be found at www.compasspartnership.co.uk.

4 Making governance processes work effectively

4.1 GOVERNANCE REQUIRES METICULOUS MANAGEMENT

It might seem odd for a book that describes the subtle distinctions between governance and management to start talking about the management of governance. But governance is a demanding role and even when the structures (Chapter 2) and the roles (Chapter 3) are clear, it is essential that the processes of governance are scrupulously managed.

These start with finding, appointing and inducting board members who, between them, have a wide range of skills and the necessary level of governance experience to meet the organisation's expectations. Organisations also need to have rigorous processes for selecting, appointing, inducting, supporting and appraising the chief executive. They need to establish open and trusting relationships with him or her, and to find ways of working that suit both parties. The chair in particular has to form a close working relationship with the chief executive, and develop it as circumstances change.

At a more mundane – but extremely important – level, all the elements for productive meetings need to be organised to the highest standard.

Another key requirement is a tightly managed process for reviewing the performance of governance arrangements. Some boards, particularly those responsible for medium-sized and larger organisations should also have a process for reviewing the performance and contribution of each member.

These are all pre-requisites for effective governance. But above all, governance requires people on the board and in committees who work together as high-performing teams to further the organisation's mission. The board and the management need to establish the circumstances in which everyone involved is highly motivated, cares deeply about the future of the organisation and can work together to provide that subtle mix of accountability, strategic insight, emotional intelligence and wise judgement that leads to effective governance.

This chapter sets out how to establish effective governance processes and to give board and committee members some common models of how governance works. It describes how to:

- recruit, induct and develop board members;
- manage board meetings;
- increase committee effectiveness;
- appoint and appraise chief executives;
- establish good relationships between the chair and the chief executive;
- create shared assumptions about governance;
- manage the development of the board's effectiveness.

These are the seven essential processes that are needed to deliver effective governance.

4.2 RECRUITING AND INDUCTING BOARD MEMBERS

Boards need to attract people who can make a real contribution to the present needs and future development of their organisations. This section explains good practices in:

- finding and recruiting board members;
- recruiting people to different types of board;
- involving service users on boards;
- developing board member skills.

There is a 'market' for board members, although it is not generally viewed in this way. Organisations are competing to attract potential board members to their cause. Talented people, particularly those with governance skills, are a scarce resource. They are in a position to choose which organisations they wish to help. This choice will depend on whether the organisation can satisfy their particular motives for joining a board. These are likely to include their desire to:

- see the organisation succeed (sometimes born out of personal convictions or circumstances);
- 'put something back' into the community;
- put their skills and experience to good use;
- make new contacts or friends;

- have the prestige that is attached to board membership;
- put the organisation's name on their CV;
- develop skills and enhance their career prospects;
- find an additional role in their life.

The art of successfully recruiting members therefore requires boards to understand the types of people they are likely to attract and how they can be persuaded to join the board.

It is important to have realistic expectations and to see the relationship as a trade wherein individuals give their time and energy in return for rewards that meet their needs.

Finding board members

In the past, finding and recruiting board members may have involved a discreet word with a single candidate. The informal approach can be an effective way of capturing the interest of people who might not have considered joining a particular board and should not be under-valued.

Nevertheless, these days the best boards use a range of recruitment methods to create diverse boards and recruit the most talented people. Boards are strengthened when they take a systematic and energetic approach to recruiting new members. If little effort is put into searching for good candidates, boards risk reducing the quality of their governance. The recruitment, selection and election processes should be just as professional as those used to appoint staff. Recruiting a new chair should be a particularly rigorous process.

A series of steps can be taken to recruit new members. How they are pursued depends on the type of board (elected, self-selecting or appointed) but the principles are similar for all types. Effective boards:

- agree the grid of skills and representation required (see p. 75);
- actively seek to create boards with diverse membership (see p. 77);
- prepare job descriptions setting out what the board expects of members;
- prepare a person specification setting out the broad characteristics required of board members (e.g. previous governance experience, knowledge of the third sector, an ability to understand a high-level overview of an organisation's finances, experience of a similar size organisation)
- require the appropriate people (e.g. chair, nominations committee, staff, board members of nominating organisations) to make a concerted effort to seek people with the requisite skills and motivation;

- seek members from within their own organisations, for example from their members, supporters and branches;
- advertise for members when it is important to be completely transparent or when an injection of different types of people is needed;
- use trustee brokerage services to find people who have already volunteered to be trustees;
- use recruitment agencies to expand the pool of candidates;
- attend 'speed dating' events organised by infrastructure organisations;
- expect people who stand for election to meet the criteria set out in the job description.

Many boards report that they find it difficult to recruit new members. The main reason for this is that they put insufficient resources into attracting people to these positions. Organisations are often willing to spend thousands of pounds recruiting a new member of staff but feel it is inappropriate to spend money recruiting board members. This is clearly a matter of judgement for the board, but the consequence of under-investment can be vacancies on the board and weaker governance.

Boards that are really keen to attract new members invest in a range of recruitment techniques, and most report that when they make sufficient efforts they are successful in recruiting new people.

Skill and experience grids

Whichever method is used to choose board members, organisations recognise that they need a mix of skills and experience to provide the highest standards of governance. One helpful tool is a skills and experience grid that shows, on two axes, the skills and experience required and those that board members possess.

Given that the types of skills and experience required usually exceed the number of board positions, some members will be expected to offer a range of different skills.

EXAMPLE SKILLS GRID FOR A CONSERVATION CHARITY

Skills are rated as follows: 1 = substantial skill and experience
2 = some knowledge
3 = no relevant experience

	Ann	John	Kate	Ravi	Tracy	Victor
Technical skills						
Business	2	1	1	2	1	1
Corporate planning	1	2	1	1	1	1
Performance management	1	3	3	3	3	3
Charity leadership	1	3	1	3	2	2
Finance	2	2	1	3	1	2
Audit	3	3	1	3	2	3
Conservation	3	3	3	2	3	3
Personnel	2	2	2	3	1	3
Public relations	2	3	2	3	3	2
Marketing	2	3	3	3	1	1
Public affairs	1	3	2	2	2	2
Investments	3	3	2	3	3	3
Fundraising	1	2	3	2	2	1
Legal	3	3	3	3	2	3
Forestry	2	3	2	1	2	3
ICT	2	3	2	2	3	2
Property management	2	3	3	2	3	3
General skills						
Chair a committee	No	Yes	No	Yes	Yes	No
Represent the organisation	Yes	Yes	Yes	Yes	Yes	Yes
Speak at events	Yes	Yes	Yes	Yes	Yes	Yes
Profile						
Gender (M/F)	F	M	F	M	F	M
Age at December 2009	46	53	42	37	45	55
Location	London	Perth	Bedford	Surrey	London	Cardiff
Disability			Yes			
Retirement date	2010	2013	2013	2010	2015	2011

These grids can be extended to include an element of representation, for example by seeking members from different parts of the country. They can also be used to manage the diversity of the board by identifying characteristics such as gender, age and race.

A further development of the grid is to map out expected and required retirement dates for board members and identify skill and experience gaps that will need to be filled in the future.

INUNDATED WITH VOLUNTEERS FOR BOARD MEMBERSHIP

Many organisations complain of the difficulty of finding new board members. The 79-year-old YWCA Canberra, Australia, a AU$9.6 million social service provider, is a shining example of how to ensure quality people queue up to join a demanding board.

They use a wide range of approaches, starting with their 'Women as Decision Makers' open training programme, consisting of three two-and-a half-hour workshops. This attracts potential members who can apply to join their system of apprentice board members who shadow the board for up to 12 months. The self-funded and hugely popular training programme provides a professional development opportunity for women who want to become involved in community boards.

They also have a breakfast on World YWCA day to promote board membership and they use advertisements and an e-mail network to gain access to a large pool of potential board members. Other public events through the year profile the organisation and provide opportunities to recruit new members and engender interest in the organisation.

People who are seriously interested in joining the YWCA board can apply to become one of four trainee members. These trainees attend board meetings and make an increasing contribution during their 12-month apprenticeship. There can be 12 or more applications for these coveted positions.

The organisation makes high demands of its board members. The board of 12 people meets 11 times a year, expects all new members to attend an orientation programme and keeps its discussion at a highly strategic level.

In addition it has an annual planning day shortly after new members have been elected to ensure everyone is focused on the same priorities. Board members are expected to keep up to date on governance by reading the Australian publication *Board Matters*. There are also a number of members who have been able to participate in the Australian Institute of Company Directors' respected course for company directors through a scholarship programme provided by government.

The result of these arrangements, according to their executive director, is that whenever a place becomes available there are always four people trained up to take the spot. This is particularly important as Canberra has a transient population of government employees moving between state and federal jobs. It also creates opportunities for younger people who may not usually volunteer for these types of positions to become involved.

Having a pool of people to choose from means the board has plenty of scope to determine its composition. The YWCA's approach proves the point that an organisation which sets high standards can have good people queuing up to join their board.

Ensuring diversity

There is a great deal of evidence showing that diverse teams are more effective than homogeneous ones. Yet there are still many boards that could be characterised as being 'male, pale and stale'.

Diversity is concerned with gender, age, race, disability, faith and sexual orientation. The boards of organisations working to effect social change should reflect the diversity of their stakeholders and of the wider communities in which they work.

Achieving diversity requires effort and commitment. This begins by having an explicit objective of creating a diverse board that is discussed and agreed by the board. It also requires time and resources needed to establish diversity. Actions to encourage diversity can include:
- advertising in media that reach particular groups of people;
- paying for child care to allow attendance at meetings;
- holding meetings in accessible venues and at times that suit people from different groups;
- making documents available in large print, Braille, tape and providing sign language interpreters;
- being prepared to contribute to reasonable 'loss of earnings' where it can be discussed openly and where it will not cause divisions within the board.

Achieving diversity does not come from the tokenism of simply putting someone from a minority community on the board. It should be part of a broader initiative to ensure diversity in all aspects of the organisation's work.

It should lead to more creative boards, better able to anticipate the future demands of the organisation and to see new opportunities that would not have been spotted by existing members.

Recruiting board members

The way board members are recruited sends important messages to candidates about the seriousness the organisation attaches to the role.

All three types of board (see section 2.2, Different types of board structures) can have a recruitment process that requires candidates to review a job description and complete an application form. This ensures that potential candidates have **clear expectations of the duties of board members** and the time commitment required and it deters people without sufficient time or commitment from standing. Self-selecting and appointing boards can also have informal meetings with candidates to 'sell' the role and determine whether they have the skills, experience and time to do the job. Some boards will also interview candidates and then choose people who best meet their requirements.

INVOLVING YOUNG PEOPLE IN GOVERNANCE

The Foundation for Young Australians is a national grant-making organisation committed to providing funding, mentoring and capacity building assistance to community projects, which are developed and managed by and for young Australians. In 2007, the Foundation's annual grant and programme budget exceeded AU$10 million from its own capital corpus and co-investment partnerships. At least 20% of the annual funding is allocated to projects that are focused on young Indigenous people. Since its creation in 2000, youth participation has been central to all aspects of the Foundation's governance.

Volunteers make all the Foundation's granting decisions, with at least 50% of the granting committees being made up of young people. Volunteers of 16–25 years of age can join one of its 10 committees, which are responsible either for national programmes or for grant allocations in each state. Each committee runs for a term of two years and the Foundation selects people through individual and group interviews and runs an intensive four-day volunteers' orientation programme to induct the new committees.

These committee members provided a pool of people who can also apply to become members of the board when the opportunity arises. At the time of writing, the board included five members under 25 years old and the founder of a social enterprise for young people, who is also deputy chair (aged 27) and joined the board at 24.

According to the chief executive, the key challenge in integrating young people is 'getting to the point where younger and more experienced members work together effectively, learning how to have challenging and robust conversations with each other and deliver effective governance at the same time'.

The Foundation ensures that the commitment to youth participation permeates everything it does. In addition to the volunteers' orientation weekend, every 18 months the Foundation brings together young people from its projects for 'The GIG' – a four-day event that focuses on leadership development and provides a great opportunity to strengthen relationships with their funded partner organisations.

The great advantage of the principles of the Foundation is that young people determine which projects are funded and they influence the overall direction of the organisation. Youth participation in governance also significantly increases its legitimacy amongst young people in Australia.

Some people may be concerned that formalising recruitment will deter new members from applying. Yet the Charity Commission has records of 900,000 people who act as trustees (*UK Civil Society Almanac*, NCVO, 2008) and there is also the large number of people who sit on boards of organisations that are not registered charities. In other words, the pool of potential board members is large. Furthermore organisations that advertise generally find it easier to attract more diverse membership and often find excellent members from unexpected places.

Some boards develop a structure which allows people to join the board in stages. For example, new members may be expected to become a member of a committee before becoming a board member. This allows them to learn about the organisation and its governance before they put themselves forward for a board position. Some boards co-opt people on to the board for a limited period before inviting them to stand for election.

Most boards have **periods of office** (typically three to four years) and **term limits** (typically two to three terms). This helps the board to avoid becoming stale, and it allows people to leave the organisation with dignity. Some organisations require members to have a break of one year at the end of the term limit before being eligible to rejoin the board. Some have an 'exceptional circumstances' clause enabling boards to keep a member who can continue to make a major contribution to the organisation's development. Others eschew these practices, feeling that everyone should be required to move on to keep the board fresh. The benchmarking study of voluntary sector boards found that the average term limit is six years, with larger organisations tending to have longer term limits than smaller ones. (*BoardsCount*™, John Tierney, Governance Hub, 2007)

Whatever the arrangement, the end of **each period of office** of an individual provides an opportunity to review that member's performance (see sections 4.7, Establishing shared assumptions about governance and 4.8, Managing board development), consider what skills the board is going to need for the next period of time, and decide whether that person should be encouraged to serve another term.

Creating a group of people who can work together as a team is a crucial consideration in recruiting new members. A board can have all the skills required and represent all its constituencies, but be so diverse that members just don't gel as a team. The ability to work effectively as a member of a group is therefore an important criterion for choosing people for both self-selected and appointed boards. Requiring candidates to attend a meeting as an observer and to meet board members informally helps ensure that boards recruit people who can both challenge the status quo and also work as part of a team.

Recruiting people to different types of board

The method of recruiting people needs to be tailored to suit the type of board. Having an **elected board** should not mean that anyone can stand for election regardless of their governance skills. Electoral processes need to be managed to ensure that:

- the membership ultimately has the freedom to choose the board they want;
- candidates for election are advised of the organisation's expectations of board members;
- the board ensures that the organisation is governed by a group of people who have an appropriate balance of skills, experience, values and knowledge.

In this 'managed democracy', action can be taken to ensure that a strong board is elected. Details of the functions that board members are expected to discharge should be widely publicised. Current skill and experience gaps that the board wishes to fill should be announced. Existing members should positively seek out people with the necessary skills and time, and persuade them to stand. Boards that take these actions avoid the danger of leaving its composition to the luck of the electoral draw.

On **self-selecting boards** there is a tendency to appoint friends and contacts rather than to engage in a systematic search and selection process. These boards need to be aware of the risk of becoming stagnant. They need to put extra energy into the search and selection process. They should be particularly aware of the great value of having a diverse board, as these boards tend to recruit people in their own image.

On **appointed boards,** the chair can give details of the skills and commitment required to members of funding bodies and government departments that appoint board members, to ensure that the organisation gets the people it needs and not those who happen to be available.

Involving service users on boards

Service users can make a huge contribution to the effective governance of organisations. Like any initiative to increase diversity, organisations should start by developing a broadly based strategy for involving service users throughout the organisation. This may involve users being recruited to the staff, working as volunteers, assisting with fundraising or being represented on the board. Indeed, the obvious starting place is to include users in the development of the user involvement strategy. User representation on the board and its committees can be part of that strategy.

There are many advantages to involving users in governance:

- they may have skills and experiences that the board requires, in addition to being service users;
- they bring first-hand experience of services to the board;
- they ensure that users' views are heard;
- they are 'empowered' through their commitment to the organisation.

There are also a number of pitfalls to avoid:

- Service users draw on their own experience. Their involvement should not be used as a substitute for more widely based methods of consulting users.
- Members of the board who are not users may feel disempowered by service users. They may feel unable to challenge users, even when challenge is required.
- The term 'users' can become devalued, implying people who have no 'professional' contribution to make because they are 'only' users.
- Users and non-users alike may assume that users' views are somehow more legitimate.

User representation in governance therefore needs to be considered carefully and openly before decisions are taken. It then needs to be managed sensitively, to ensure that the arrangement brings maximum benefit all round.

USER INVOLVEMENT AT ARTHRITIS CARE

Arthritis Care exists to work with people with arthritis and to promote their health, quality of life and independence through services, support, self-help, information and influence. It has branches throughout the country and it aims to put people with the condition in control of their arthritis, their lives and their organisation.

Some time ago, the board agreed that it was desirable for a *majority* of the board to be people with personal experience of having arthritis. At the same time a number of staff posts were also designated specifically for people with arthritis, for example counsellors on the help line, Young Arthritis Care development officers, and trainers. Many of its volunteers are also people with arthritis.

According to the chief executive who led the initiative, 'the changes meant Arthritis Care became a more user-led charity, more vociferous and more visible. New services were developed with more input from people with arthritis and the organisation became more attractive to funders because it was seen as empowering people with arthritis'.

The key challenges in bringing users on to the board are, first, to find people with appropriate experience and knowledge, and then to provide the right kind of induction, training and support to ensure that they are able to contribute to governance. These are of course important for all new board members, but they are particularly so in the case of people unused to having their voices heard, who may lack experience of formal meetings or the confidence to speak in front of others.

Induction and orientation

As boards become more sophisticated and capable of delivering high standards of governance, the learning curve for new members becomes steeper and more demanding. For a board that meets four times per year it can take a year or more to understand the organisation's context, the way it relates to other organisations, the dynamics of board meetings and how to make pertinent and insightful contributions.

As soon as board members have been chosen, a number of things can be done to help them up the learning curve. New members need:

- **induction** – they should receive a briefing on the organisation's work, current strategies and plans, and copies of relevant reports. They should be given written information on their role and responsibilities, the way the board and its sub-committees work, the board's code of conduct and the organisation's expectations of its board members.
- **orientation** – they should be expected to acclimatise themselves by reading past papers and being briefed by the chair and the chief executive or a senior manager on current issues and priorities for governance.
- **a mentor or buddy** – they should be linked to an experienced member who can answer questions, provide guidance and offer reassurance.
- **training** – they should be given opportunities to attend the growing number of training courses available for board members.
- **shadowing** – they should be offered the chance to visit services, shadow meetings at different levels of the organisation and bring their reflections back to the board.

4.3 MANAGING BOARD MEETINGS

Board meetings are the heart of the board's work. Successful meetings can add considerable value to the organisation. To be really effective, they require all the elements of good meeting management to come together at the same time.

Plan an annual meeting cycle

Boards need an annual cycle of meetings that is established at least six months before the start of the cycle. This plan should set out:

- how the work and reports from assemblies, committees, advisory groups and task groups fits into the annual cycle;
- the timetable of board and other meetings throughout the year;

- specific responsibilities that need to be delivered at particular times of the year, such as:
  - a review of achievements;
  - anticipation of key changes in the external environment;
  - a review of the strategic plan;
  - agreement to operating plan and budget-setting guidelines;
  - approval of the operating plan and budget;
  - approval of the annual accounts;
  - a review of the risk register;
  - the appraisal of the chief executive;
  - the performance review of the board.

Ideally the cycle should include at least one or more overnight meetings for the board, away from the office, where board members and the leadership team can review past performance and agree future strategy. These meetings are particularly good for building personal relationships and creating team spirit. When board members and managers participate as equals and the meetings are well prepared and managed, they also strengthen relationships between management and governance.

Establish the right agenda

One of the quickest ways of increasing board effectiveness is to gain control over the agenda. Agenda planning should be done jointly by the chair and chief executive. Together, they are responsible for making good judgements about what needs to be discussed and decided, and what each meeting can achieve in the time available. Their plans should ensure that board members leave every meeting feeling satisfied with what has been achieved rather than frustrated by an incomplete or unsatisfactory meeting arising out of over-ambitious or poorly structured agendas and papers.

Matters which require board members' attention can be categorised into four groups:

- **Items for information.** These include progress reports, background briefings and other information that board members need to receive. These can be sent separately from board meeting papers to avoid overloading board members with reading immediately before meetings.
- **Items for approval.** These include matters which the board needs to formally agree, but are not contentious. They can be grouped together and approved *en bloc* to save precious board time.
- **Items for discussion.** These are the really big matters that require debate. They can include early stage discussion of policy issues, major changes of strategy and new strategic partnerships. They deserve significant time on the agenda

and form the core of the meeting. It is these items that shape the future of the organisation.

- **Items for decision.** These may include items that have been considered before and are now coming forward for final decision. If preparation has been good, they should not require significant discussion.

Achieving control of the agenda means that every item contending for board attention needs to pass through a filtering process in which the chair and chief executive ask:

- Is this a governance issue?
- Does it have policy implications?
- Is it a priority for board time?

Boards should also avoid falling into the trap of repeating committee discussions. This is best managed by ensuring that the board agenda and papers report on the conclusions, recommendations and decisions of committees and only allow issues to be re-opened when members have alerted the chair in advance. This should not be allowed to happen too often, otherwise members of the committee begin to feel disempowered and complain that their efforts were wasted. If the board has to re-open issues frequently, it should consider whether the committee has the necessary skills and experience for the responsibilities it has been given.

Board meetings are highly dependent on the quality of board papers. Carefully crafted papers that present key background information and broad options are needed for early stage discussions. More detailed papers with clear conclusions and recommendations are needed for final decisions. Good papers empower boards to have high-level and strategic discussions. Poor papers inevitably sink boards into fragmented and inconclusive decisions.

Chief executives have particular responsibility for the quality of papers, and need to set high standards. Papers should be submitted in sufficient time to allow improvements to be demanded of their authors if they do not meet the required standard. They should be easily identifiable (e.g. by means of numbers or cross-referencing to agenda items), and the author and purpose of each paper should be flagged on the front page.

Ensure appropriate attendance by management

Directors and managers play an important role in delivering effective governance. For clarity, the term 'director' refers throughout this book to the senior employees of the organisation and not to the legal 'directors' of the organisation, who in many cases are the board members.

Through the chief executive, directors and managers inform, guide and make recommendations to the board. But they need to be careful not to step over the boundary and encroach upon the board's legitimate role. A critical issue is whether members of the leadership team attend board meetings. There are three models which can be followed:

1. Directors can **attend by invitation.** In this model, the chief executive attends board meetings and invites colleagues to join the meeting when their expertise and advice are required. This makes it easier to maintain the boundary between governance and management, but it means that directors and board members are less likely to have a good understanding of one another. It also means the chief executive has to be particularly thorough in reporting back to the leadership team. In this model new directors can be invited to shadow a board meeting, so they understand its role.

2. Directors can **attend as non-voting participants.** Although in law board members have tightly specified responsibilities, the paid directors can attend and participate in all the discussions. It requires the board itself to be comparatively small (otherwise meetings become very cumbersome) and that board members and managers are skilled and experienced at maintaining the distinction between governance and management. If members – and in particular the chair – are not vigilant about keeping the board focused on the governance task, it is very easy for the board to slip into management tasks.

3. Finally directors can **attend as observers.** In this model, members of the leadership team attend, but they are there solely to give advice when required. This emphasises the distinct roles of governance and management and helps to avoid the danger of dominance by management, but there is a risk that important information and insights from management may be overlooked.

Each model has its advantages and disadvantages. The key to ensuring that everyone is clear about their role is to agree which model best suits the organisation at a particular point in time. Problems most commonly arise not from the use of any particular model but when different people are operating on different models in the same meeting. Clarity is essential, and if board members or managers stray over the line into a different role, the matter should be taken up with them.

Private sessions of the board

Whatever attendance regime is agreed, many boards find it valuable to have some time with the chief executive alone. This gives him or her an opportunity to:

- share concerns about individuals' performance;
- brief members on matters relating to individual members of the leadership team;
- ruminate about the overall structure of the leadership team and seek their advice on any changes that he or she may be considering;
- speak more freely about other issues where the board's experience and range of perspective would be valuable.

They can be held at the beginning or end of all or some meetings.

Boards should also have time without the chief executive. This provides an opportunity to receive reports on the chief executive's annual performance review, to confirm recommendations on his or her salary and to agree ways in which the board can be supportive over the coming year. It also provides an opportunity for individual board members to express any concerns.

Private sessions of the board should be built into the annual meeting cycle so they do not come as a surprise to the directors, who might otherwise worry about what the board is discussing. They need to be chaired tightly, to ensure that the board does not drift into discussing topics that should be taken when the chief executive or directors are present. There should also be an agreement that the chair will report back to the chief executive immediately after the meeting, to maintain a high level of trust between the board and management.

A pattern for these private sessions, which should generally be quite brief, is to hold them once or twice a year, at the end of board meetings. Any directors present leave first, so the chief executive can have a session with the board alone. Then the chief executive leaves to allow the board time on its own. Having the session programmed does not mean it always has to be used; it just avoids the awkwardness of having to ask people to leave, and immediately raising their suspicions that there is something they should worry about.

Meeting environment and etiquette

The environment for meetings can be a surprisingly significant determinant of their success:

- Cramped rooms leave people feeling on top of one another.
- Excessively large rooms with people too spread out leave people feeling distant from one another.
- Rooms without daylight are enervating.
- Long tables where people cannot see one another do not allow them to read one another's emotional intelligence.

The space needs to be used appropriately for the type of board meeting. Square tables work well for formal meetings. A cafeteria layout, with tables spread around the room works well for workshops and group work. Settees work well for rumination and informal exploration of issues.

Meeting etiquette is also important. Allowing people to keep mobile phones on or to use laptops to keep up with e-mails, or to send text messages (unless circumstances are exceptional) is distracting and discourteous. People who do this imply that they have more important matters to attend to than the meeting itself, and they are seldom able to give their best contribution.

The chair should take action on inappropriate behaviour and the rest of the board should be strongly supportive.

Communicate extensively after meetings

Managers and staff are interested in, and in many circumstances need to know about the board's deliberations and decisions. They also appreciate having some connection to the board, though this becomes more difficult in larger organisations.

Actions that can be taken to ensure good communications between the board and managers and staff include:

- ensuring that minutes are a succinct high-level summary of decisions and actions, and are circulated within a week of the meeting;
- putting agendas, minutes and papers on the organisation's intranets (excluding any confidential items);
- circulating a summary of board decisions;
- having a regular article about board matters in internal newsletters;
- inviting managers or staff to attend those parts of the board meetings where they have expertise or would benefit from hearing the board's deliberations;
- inviting one manager to shadow each board meeting to learn about the board's role and its work;
- inviting managers and staff to meet the board informally before and after meetings;
- inviting board members to join social gatherings of staff.

4.4 INCREASING COMMITTEE EFFECTIVENESS

The actions needed to increase committee effectiveness (including assemblies, committees, advisory groups and task groups) are similar to those required to increase board effectiveness. All these groups need to be an appropriate size, to have top quality paperwork and to have strong leadership from their chairs.

Committee size

The size of a committee is a significant determinant of its effectiveness. If a committee is too small, it may have insufficient expertise to be effective. If it is too large, meetings become protracted and each member feels less personally responsible for its effectiveness.

The precise size depends on the function of the committee. A committee to advise the board on medical research may need to be large to reflect a wide range of disciplines. An audit committee, in contrast, may need a small number of members to check that proper financial management and audit procedures are in place.

Benchmarking data suggests that the average size of third-sector committees is six people, with 10% of committees having three or fewer members and 10% having more than 11 members (*BoardsCount*™, John Tierney, Governance Hub, 2007).

There are many pressures that lead boards to create committees that are too large:

- No one likes to say 'no' when members volunteer to give their time to a committee.
- Sometimes people are concerned that they will miss out on important decisions if they are not members of committees.
- There are always good reasons for bringing extra people on to the committee and few for keeping them off.

These pressures need to be resisted.

Agendas and papers

The second component of an effective committee is the quality of the paperwork. Effective committees have agendas that are short and prioritised, and that maintain the boundaries of committee and staff responsibilities. Their chairs plan agendas ahead, and prevent the committee from slipping unintentionally into management tasks. Chairs are always aware that the primary role of committees of the board is to undertake governance tasks.

Effective committees also expect high-quality paperwork from staff. Committee chairs can play an important role here by insisting that papers are short, focused, dated, labelled 'for approval', 'for discussion' or 'for information', and include a succinct summary and a clear articulation of options. Anticipation is essential; committees faced with poor papers feel obliged to untangle the issues rather than send them back for improvement. The chair should agree the agenda before it is distributed and, when paperwork is a problem, should **ask to see draft papers as well.**

Leadership from the chair

This is another essential element of committee effectiveness. Members appreciate committee chairs who take the initiative to define the work programme, agree relevant agendas for meetings with the responsible staff member, and ensure that the papers are of a high quality.

Good chairs involve everyone in the discussion but take the initiative when the time comes for decisions. They delegate work to members to free up their own time for the leadership function. They are totally clear about the committee's role and strive to ensure that it makes a significant contribution to governance.

Minutes should be short and succinct, highlighting action points and when they are to be achieved. Minutes should be circulated within a week of the meeting.

4.5 APPOINTING AND APPRAISING THE CHIEF EXECUTIVE

Appointing a new chief executive is one of the most important decisions a board takes. Recruiting the right person can launch an organisation successfully on to the next stage of its development. Making a mistake can lead at best to drift and at worst to a directionless period as the person is moved out and another leader sought. The board therefore needs to be at its very best when seeking and recruiting a chief executive.

Good practices in recruitment are well documented, so points made here will focus on particular issues around appointing a chief executive. The process should begin with a board-level discussion about what the current chief executive has contributed, and what skills and experience are required for the next stage of the organisation's development. This needs to be set clearly into the organisation's current context. It might be that the current chief executive is a great visionary who has built strong external relationships, but has not given internal management sufficient attention. Or the incumbent may have developed great strategies and plans but not established good relationships with the board.

Whatever the circumstances, it is likely that the organisation will benefit from having someone whose skills are different from the current chief executive. This needs be discussed by the board to draw on members' varied experiences in order to begin building a profile of the characteristics of the person required.

The board should also agree the job description, the strategy for seeking applications and the recruitment process, having taken appropriate professional advice.

The strategy for seeking candidates needs to produce a good range of applicants and may include advertising, headhunting and promoting the vacancy by word of mouth. There is a well-established market for chief executives of third-sector organisations and a good understanding of appropriate compensation packages for organisations in different fields and of different sizes. Many potential candidates will know this information, so it is important to pitch the package at a level that will attract candidates with the desired skills and experience.

Chief executives have to deploy an extraordinarily wide range of skills, so the selection process should test those that are most important. Making a presentation, resolving an issue in a group discussion or producing written work under time pressure can all be part of a selection process. Psychometric tests can also provide insights that are valuable in making the choice and second interviews can reveal perspectives that may not have been seen at first-round interviews.

Opportunities for meeting board members and the organisation's leadership team can be created to involve them in the process and therefore own the final decision. It generally makes sense to include the current chief executive in both the selection and the interviews, as he or she will have the best understanding of what the job involves. However there are circumstances when this is not appropriate, such as when a person with very different skills and experience is being sought.

Ideally the process should be led by the chair, who, along with a sub-group of the board, should be empowered to select, negotiate and make the appointment within agreed boundaries.

Recruitment agencies specialising in the third sector are often used in chief executive appointments. They have access to potential candidates and experience in making such appointments which may not be present on the board. The best ones have the capacity to manage the whole process to a high standard, to be an intermediary between the organisation and candidates, the finest of whom it is always worth remembering will be pursuing a number of opportunities.

Recruitment is a two-way process, and candidates will be assessing the organisation and its board as closely as the board is assessing them. Good presentation of the organisation and the board will be important in maintaining the interest of the best candidates.

Appraising the chief executive

A key part of the board's role in supporting and developing the chief executive is to provide an annual appraisal. The actions of chief executives can have wide repercussions for the whole organisation so it is critically important that they are given accurate, insightful and constructive feedback on their performance.

Boards are responsible for ensuring that chief executives are appraised. Research from ACEVO suggests that two-thirds of chief executives are given formal appraisals. The appraisal is carried out by the chair in 70% of organisations, by a group of board members in 18% and by the whole board in 6% of organisations. (*The View From Here*, ACEVO Pay Survey 2007/08). The process for conducting the appraisal should be consistent with that used for other directors and managers (see section 16.3, Getting performance from teams), but there are some special dimensions to this appraisal which need to be considered.

First, board members are potentially a rich source of information on the performance of the chief executive because they see him or her in action. Their views can contribute to an overall assessment of performance.

Second, there will be considerable overlap between the extent to which the chief executive has achieved his or her objectives and the extent to which the organisation as a whole has achieved its annual goals. That said, in an appraisal it is important to separate organisational objectives from personal objectives, focusing more on the latter, because accountability for organisational performance will happen through other processes.

Third, the appraisal process needs to reflect the fact that the chair is not involved in the organisation on a daily basis so it is particularly important to have robust processes for collecting evidence. Ideally evidence should be collected using a 360° review.

Fourth, the outcome should be reported to the board as a whole. This will contribute to strengthening trust between the board and the chief executive.

Fifth, rigorous appraisal of the chief executive is a signal to the rest of the organisation that performance review is taken seriously.

Finally, it allows the board to demonstrate compliance with the relevant Code of Governance.

4.6 ENSURING EFFECTIVE CHAIR–CHIEF EXECUTIVE RELATIONSHIPS

The relationship between the chair and chief executive is the pivotal one in the organisation. Differences of opinion between them or weaknesses in how they work together will quickly become apparent to people across and outside the organisation and risk damaging its reputation.

It can be a particularly demanding relationship to manage when there are weaknesses in the governance and management of organisations. These weaknesses can manifest themselves as pressures on the chair–chief executive partnership. When the chair is striving to resolve governance matters and the chief executive is coping with management challenges, the demands on their time, openness and trust are particularly high.

Some of the functions of chair and chief executive overlap. Issues that these two people need to agree upon include:

- representing the organisation in public;
- responding to media requests;
- visiting the organisation's services and dealing with any issues that are seen or raised;
- dealing with direct approaches to the chair by directors, managers and members of staff;
- dealing with service, HR and other issues raised by board members outside meetings;
- dealing with key stakeholders (including funders and government officials);
- managing the board's work.

Some aspects of governance will be handled by one, and some by the other. The best partnerships build upon the strengths of each individual. Both parties should be willing to have an open discussion about their expectations of each other and agree how the areas of overlap should be divided between them. The division should build on their respective strengths and weaknesses.

The relationship has to achieve a delicate balance between the chair's twin roles of supporting, advising and sharing experience with the chief executive, and holding him or her to account.

Chairs and chief executives therefore need to invest significant time in developing their relationship. They should:

- meet regularly
- talk frequently (perhaps weekly)
- talk openly
- agree expectations of each other
- discuss policy issues together
- plan the board's annual programme together
- prepare for meetings together.

Chairs and chief executives should operate as 'sounding boards' for each other, sharing, shaping and discarding ideas before they are tested more publicly. They should operate on the basis of 'no surprises' for each other. When things go wrong, as they inevitably do, they should quickly admit mistakes to each other and learn from the experience.

Chairs and chief executives have to establish new connections when one or other decides to leave or reaches the end of their term of office. This is a time when extra effort should be invested in the relationship. It requires recognition that no two partnerships are the same and that new expectations and boundaries will have to be negotiated.

A SUCCESSFUL RELATIONSHIP

Watching the chair and chief executive of a national housing association working together, I noticed:

- The chief executive went out of her way to ensure that the chair was always kept informed of major developments, copying papers and talking regularly on the phone
- The chair always defended the chief executive in meetings, and had a private discussion if problems needed to be resolved
- They met before the quarterly board meetings to agree the agenda and the papers needed at the meeting
- They had regular one-to-one meetings to discuss progress and problems
- They had dinner together at least twice a year to review progress and problems in an informal setting
- Once a year they reviewed their relationship and identified potential improvements

4.7 ESTABLISHING SHARED ASSUMPTIONS ABOUT GOVERNANCE

Third-sector boards consist of people from all walks of life. Members have backgrounds in the private, public and third sectors. Although many boards still do not reflect the full diversity of the communities they serve, people do come from different professions, different socio-economic, age and ethnic groups.

This wide range of backgrounds means that when people join boards they bring very different assumptions and mental models about how governance should work. Because boards don't meet very frequently it takes a surprisingly long time for members to understand each other and to develop a common set of assumptions about the way governance should operate in their organisation's circumstances.

People from the private sector are used to unitary boards where full-time directors sit alongside non-executive directors. Such boards are smaller and tend to meet more frequently. People with public-sector backgrounds are used to working with party politics and democratic representation. Each brings different assumptions about effective governance. When they join third-sector boards it is likely that some of their assumptions will have to change.

That does not mean leaving business acumen back in the company offices or becoming disabled by the complexities of third-sector governance. Nor does it mean leaving behind the values of representation and listening to voters at the council chambers. But it does require people to work together to develop and maintain a common 'model' of how governance in third-sector organisations works best.

Another set of distinctions on third-sector boards resides in the involvement of people from different professions, such as accountancy, law, medicine, science, education, health, communications and social services. They too bring their own assumptions and ways of thinking that add further to the complexity.

This all creates great challenges in getting boards and committees to work effectively as teams that appreciate the different perspectives members bring. This means time has to be invested in getting to know each other and the different life experiences that everyone is contributing to the board.

Not everyone will be convinced that this is good use of board time. Some members may feel that all the board's time should be focused on taking decisions. At best this risks missing opportunities to add great creativity and insights to governance and at worst it leads to a vicious circle of deteriorating relationships and unproductive meetings. Boards and committees therefore need to spend time in getting to know each other through awaydays, overnight meetings, gathering informally before and after meetings and undertaking tasks in groups outside meetings.

It also requires having a board whose membership does not change too often, because it takes time to understand new members. Frequent changes or a sudden influx of new members can destabilise boards to the point where they become inefficient because a disproportionate amount of time has to be spent developing shared perspectives on issues and decisions.

Boards should, however, avoid becoming ossified because members know each other too well and are unable to bring new perspectives. So whilst boards may have rules about periods of office, when people come up for renewal, the chair or the nominations committee should be asking whether greater stability or fresh perspectives are needed to get the best from the board as a team. This may require more active management of renewals of board membership than is often the case. Chairs and board members frequently make an assumption that when a member's period of office has been completed it will automatically be renewed (unless a term limit has been reached).

In an ideal world, when members have completed a period they should be able to say to the chair or the nominations committee that they would be delighted to serve another period but they would also fully understand if it was decided that different skills and experiences were now required. This gives chairs or nominating committees greater flexibility in selecting the team that is most needed at that particular point in time.

Getting the board to work as a really effective team is ultimately the responsibility of the chair (see also section 16.3, Getting performance from teams). He or she sets the style and tone of board meetings and other board events that bring people together, encourages members to be open with each other, engenders trust and inspires commitment.

Board and committee chairs often talk about 'herding cats' and that description contains more than a grain of truth in the third sector. It can be challenging to get the board to work as a team. But when the going is tough it is worth reminding members that the very diversity of third-sector boards is a tremendous source of vitality and creativity and a huge asset to the organisation.

4.8 MANAGING BOARD DEVELOPMENT

Effective boards invest in their own development. They strive to improve their performance continuously using a range of different approaches that suit their circumstances. They identify those areas of their performance that most require attention and agree plans and actions that will make them more efficient and more effective. A survey of boards of larger voluntary organisations showed that 32% had a board appraisal system (*Chief Executives on Governance*, ACEVO, 2007).

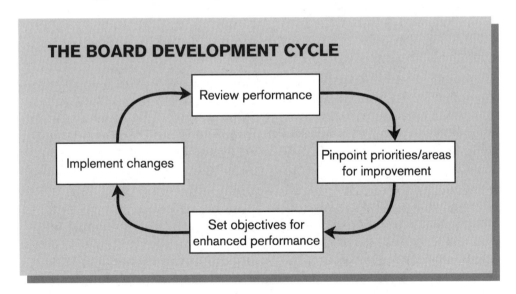

Some boards are reluctant to put time and effort into their own development because board members:

- assume that good intentions and goodwill lead to effective governance;
- find it awkward to talk about things that are not working well;
- fear upsetting other members;
- are anxious that the board might appear to be weak.

Any work on board development therefore needs to start by allowing members to raise their concerns about board development and feel comfortable about discussing the board's performance. Chairs should ensure that they have secured members' commitment to board development before embarking on it.

There are many different ways of developing board performance. Those listed below start with approaches that require little time and commitment and move on to those that require greater commitment.

DEVELOPING BOARD PERFORMANCE

Approach to assessing board performance	Circumstances in which it is appropriate
End-of-meeting review of how the meeting went	When boards wish to begin reflecting on their own performance
Review of legal and regulatory documents and board agendas and minutes	When boards wish to confirm that they are meeting legal and regulatory requirements
Observation of a board meeting by an independent expert	When a board is not operating well as a team and wishes to explore ways of working together more effectively
A short self-assessment questionnaire (say 10–15 questions)	When a board wishes to get a broad overview of members' views on areas of performance requiring attention
A full questionnaire that is compliant with the relevant codes of good practice (say 60–80 questions)	When a board wishes to pinpoint precisely areas of good and poor performance and confirm that it has conducted a code-compliant review
Benchmarking of performance	When a board wishes to compare its performance with other similar boards
A full independent review, including interviews of members and a selection of the above approaches	When a major re-structuring of governance is required

End-of-meeting reviews are a good starting point. They can address questions such as:

- what should we do differently next time?
- what did we most appreciate about the meeting?

These reviews can cover a wide range of topics including the appropriateness of the environment, the structure of the agenda, the quality of papers, the quality of the discussion, the timing of items and so on.

Observations of meetings are valuable when the dynamics of the group are not working well. Although people tend to behave better when they are being watched, a good observer can help a group to explore ways of working more effectively. Observation can be combined with one-to-one interviews and lead to a facilitated discussion on improving governance.

Self-assessment questionnaires can be used to gather views on board performance. Ideally they should be analysed by an independent person, to encourage people to be more open and honest. Short questionnaires can be used to precipitate a discussion about broad areas of governance that might require attention. They can be completed by board members and members of the leadership team. Longer ones can be used to pinpoint more precisely which of the many aspects of good governance most require attention. It is good practice to run one of these longer self-assessments every couple of years.

BOARD PERFORMANCE SELF-ASSESSMENT TOPICS

- Strategic direction
- Roles and compliance
- Skills and experience
- Performance of the board as a team
- Information
- Board meetings
- Decision-making
- The board and the chief executive
- Performance of committees
- Performance of the chair
- The board's overall contribution last year
- Top strategic issues for the organisation next year

Source: Compass Partnership board self-assessment tool

Benchmarking can be used to compare board performance, using a consultant to provide comparative information from other organisations. Allowance needs to be made for the different standards and norms in different organisations, but it can still guide boards on where to focus their development efforts.

Independent reviews are most appropriate when the fundamental structures and processes of governance need significant improvement and when there are vested interests that would be best addressed with the assistance of an independent person or firm. This will be a longer exercise than the other methods described above.

BOARD SELF-ASSESSMENT AT THE WOODLAND TRUST

The chair and chief executive of the Woodland Trust felt that the organisation's governance could add greater value. A preliminary board discussion identified that, whilst some members were keen, others were not convinced it was necessary. A workshop was therefore organised to consider different approaches, and people were surprised to discover that members held a different views about the effectiveness of the board. They agreed to do a self-assessment.

A steering group was established to oversee the work, and held two teleconferences, one to tailor the questionnaire to the organisation's circumstances and one to preview the findings.

The questionnaire was completed by board members and members of the leadership team and the results were summarised into a PowerPoint pack for consideration at a half-day workshop of the board and the senior management team.

The board acknowledged that many aspects of governance were working well but some could be improved. It agreed to:

- implement some improvements immediately
- establish a task group to clarify the key roles of the board, propose detailed changes for the governance of the organisation and improve the planning of meetings

Reviews of individual performance

As well as conducting reviews of board performance, some boards also have regular reviews of individual members' performance. In addition to enhancing the functioning of the board, this presents an opportunity for members to learn more from their experience (indeed some people see it as a benefit of board membership that could not easily be gained in other ways). Individual reviews are often seen as a second stage of developing board performance and are best done when members are comfortable with the concept of board development. A survey of large voluntary organisations showed that 18% had an individual appraisal system (*Chief Executives on Governance,* ACEVO, 2007).

Individual performance reviews can be 'light touch' or more detailed. At the light-touch end of the spectrum, the chair may have a feedback discussion with each member, perhaps covering what each appreciates about the other's contributions to the board, and ways in which they might be helped to develop their input. The discussion might also cover how each person thinks the board as a whole is performing, and the board member's future intentions, for example whether to stand for re-election or to take greater responsibility.

In a more detailed approach, the chair can gather feedback from board members about each other's performance, so that the discussion is less dependent on the chair's own opinions.

The most thorough approach involves all board members completing a short questionnaire on their own and other board members' performance. This enables the chair (or another nominated person) to give feedback based on systematically collected evidence, and to compare members' views of their own performance with those held by other board members. A third party is normally used, to anonymise the findings before the chair sees them. Where appropriate, this information can be collected at the same time as information is gathered for an overall review of board performance.

Whichever approach is chosen, it is usually appropriate that the chair receives feedback first, so that he or she is aware of board members' views on his or her performance before giving feedback to other members. If appropriate, the chair and vice chair can give each other feedback or an independent person can do so. Some organisations share the work of giving feedback between the chair and vice chair, as it is quite an onerous task.

Further significant learning can be gained at the end of the process by having a brief discussion to 'review the review'. Members can say what worked well and not so well, and this learning can be captured and fed into subsequent reviews.

Resource the board support function

Providing proper support for the board takes time and effort from staff. While the chief executive is responsible for ensuring that the board receives proper support, much of the routine work is best delegated to one member of staff. In smaller organisations, management of paperwork, minute-taking and meeting arrangements can all be tightly coordinated by someone who might be called the executive assistant to the board. This person may also be responsible for providing similar support to the leadership team.

Some organisations with more complex governance arrangements appoint a person called a 'governance manager'. This is a more senior position that reports to the chief executive, but works closely with the board and committee chairs. In organisations with complex governance arrangements, the governance manager might be supported by one or more executive assistants.

Document the board's policies and processes

Documenting the board's procedures helps to ensure that members of the organisation, staff, candidates for election, other stakeholders and board members themselves understand the policies and processes of the organisation's governance.

Documentation should include:
- the board's structure, role and responsibilities;
- the processes for electing and inducting members;
- the processes for choosing the chair and the officers;
- terms of reference for all committees;
- the processes for selecting and inducting committee members;
- the processes for arranging and administering meetings;
- the conflict of interest policy;
- the equal opportunities policy;
- the role of the chair;
- job descriptions for board members;
- the skills grid.

In addition, there should always be up-to-date lists of members of the board and its committees, preferably with details of their relevant experience. In an ideal world, all this information is kept on the organisation's intranet.

SUMMARY OF KEY POINTS

Governance requires meticulous management

- Tight management of all the processes is required to get the greatest value from governance
- Team working is the most crucial ingredient for effective governance. It can be challenging to establish high-performing teams because members come from different sectors and professions, each bringing different models of governance

Recruiting and inducting members

- There is a 'market' for board members. Those organisations that put greatest effort into recruitment and present themselves most effectively will attract people with the greatest skills and widest experience
- Job descriptions and person specifications are valuable in thinking through the requirements of board members
- Organisations should have a grid of skills and experience required on the board and recruit to fill gaps
- There are many ways to attract people to join boards and investment in recruitment generally leads to successful appointments
- Different approaches to recruitment are needed for different types of boards
- Diverse boards, including users, have the potential to add greater value to their organisations
- Induction, orientation, buddying, training and shadowing are all elements of introducing new members to boards

Managing board meetings

- Board meetings lie at the heart of good governance. They need to be part of an annual cycle that includes all governance meetings
- Carefully prepared agendas and papers are essential
- Items should be categorised as being for information, approval, discussion or decision
- There are different models for attendance by management. Board and managers need to be clear which model the board is using
- The outcomes of board meetings need to be communicated effectively to stakeholders
- Environment and etiquette are important in having effective meetings

Increasing committee effectiveness

- The size of a committee is a significant determinant of its effectiveness
- Good chairs involve everyone in the discussion but take the initiative when the time comes for decisions

Appointing and appraising the chief executive

- Boards need to specify the profile and type of person they want to take the organisation to the next stage of its development
- The selection process should involve a range of challenges and the chair should be empowered to negotiate a deal within agreed boundaries
- Boards can make a significant contribution to the feedback and learning of chief executives
- The chief executive's appraisal needs to be based on robust evidence, ideally using a 360° review

Ensuring effective chair–chief executive relationships

- This is the pivotal working relationship in the organisation
- It is demanding to manage because weaknesses in governance and management manifest themselves as pressures on this relationship
- There is no clear line between the functions of the chair and the chief executive. It has to be agreed and should reflect their respective skills
- Investing time in nurturing this relationship and having regular and systematic communication are the keys to ensuring success
- When new chairs and chief executives are appointed, different roles and ways of working and communicating will need to be agreed

Establishing shared assumptions about governance

- When people join boards they bring very different assumptions and mental models about how governance should work
- Time has to be invested in getting to know one another and the different life experiences that everyone brings to the board
- Board membership needs to change sufficiently frequently to ensure the board does not become ossified, but not so often that members are unable to operate as an effective team
- The diversity of third-sector boards is a tremendous source of vitality and creativity

Managing board development

- Effective boards invest in their own development using a range of different approaches
- Reviews of individuals' contributions enhance board performance, and give board members opportunities to learn more
- The board support function needs to be resourced to suit the complexity of the governance arrangements
- The board's policies and processes need to be documented and kept up to date

FURTHER READING

Good Governance – A Code for the Voluntary and Community Sector, ACEVO, Charity Trustee Networks, ICSA and NCVO, 2005

The Good Governance Standard for Public Services, Independent Commission for Good Governance in Public Services, OPM and CIPFA, 2004

Competence and Accountability 2004: Code of Governance for Members of the National Housing Federation, 2004

Hallmarks of an Effective Charity, Charity Commission, 2008

More and recent books and reports can be found at www.compasspartnership.co.uk.

5 Strengthening strategic management

5.1 THE RATIONALE FOR MANAGING STRATEGY

The next five chapters are all about creating and managing strategy. Strategy is particularly important in third-sector organisations because they are coalitions of individuals with different aspirations that need to be integrated to enable the organisation to thrive.

Strategic management is a powerful tool for uniting the coalition because it provides an **intellectual connection** between funders and service users. It gives the discipline required to assess needs, orchestrate resources to meet those needs, monitor the outcomes and adjust strategies and plans.

Strategic management is also a **mechanism for building coalitions** around new priorities. The process of analysing needs, setting new objectives and agreeing new strategies can be both motivating and unifying. It provides a structure within which disparate views can be brought together into a shared view of the future of the organisation.

Some organisations have gained greater strategic freedom than they had in the past. Examples include schools being given independence, academies with their own boards and budgets; recreation centres becoming independent social enterprises; government bodies being encouraged to earn income from entrepreneurial activities; and charities expanding into new areas. Such diversification increases the need for boards and managers to **develop new conceptions of their organisations**.

Other organisations are losing strategic freedom as the proportion of their funds coming from contracts and other statutory sources continues to grow. These organisations need to grasp strategic management in order to help find ways to **maintain or increase their independence and their strategic freedom**.

The benefits of improved strategic management are immense:

- Everyone becomes clearer about their objectives and how they fit into the wider goals of the organisation as a whole.
- It leads to more effective use of resources.

- It is an ideal way of building commitment and motivation.
- Diverse constituencies can be brought together around a common purpose.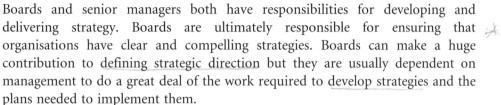

Boards and senior managers both have responsibilities for developing and delivering strategy. Boards are ultimately responsible for ensuring that organisations have clear and compelling strategies. Boards can make a huge contribution to defining strategic direction but they are usually dependent on management to do a great deal of the work required to develop strategies and the plans needed to implement them.

This chapter describes:

- the overall concept of strategic management;
- how to decide which aspects of strategic management require most attention;
- the concepts of vision, mission and values;
- how to create and refresh visions, missions and values;
- how to promote visions, missions and values.

The next four chapters demonstrate:

- how corporate objectives and performance measures are created;
- how corporate strategy is devised;
- how service strategies and operational plans are produced;
- how strategic performance is managed.

The term 'strategy' refers to coordinated sets of actions to achieve specific objectives. Strategies are well-thought-through and integrated groups of activities that give organisations, services and campaigns clarity of direction. They are the result of 'strategic thinking' and they summarise how objectives will be attained.

Strategic plans, on the other hand, document and describe objectives, performance measures, strategies and the resources required to implement them. The distinction is important because the creation of compelling strategies is both more crucial and more difficult than the preparation of a document called a strategic plan.

As well as creating corporate strategies, organisations can have strategies for divisions, regions, services and campaigns. These subsidiary plans need to fit within the overall corporate strategy.

5.2 CONCEPT OF STRATEGIC MANAGEMENT

In recent years a bewildering number of ideas have been developed by management gurus to help people understand organisations and manage them more effectively. Management by objectives, critical success factors, zero-base budgeting, scenario planning, total quality management, corporate culture, business process re-engineering and even catastrophe theory are among almost

200 strategic management concepts recognised by the Strategic Planning Society. All of them have their place. But what matters more than the latest fashion in planning methodology is that every organisation should have a coherent view of its aspirations and how it will manage performance. This view needs to include:

- **a vision** – the organisation's view of the future it wants to see;
- **a mission** – the fundamental purpose of the organisation;
- **strategic objectives** – statements about what the organisation wishes to achieve in a given time-frame;
- **performance measures** – indicators that board members, managers and staff will use to track achievements;
- **strategies** – descriptions of how human and financial resources will be applied to achieve the stated objectives;
- **annual objectives** – specific statements about what will be achieved in the coming year.

Together, these concepts provide an overview of strategic management.

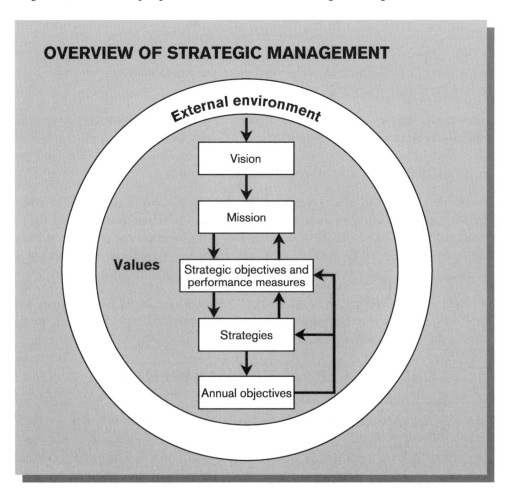

OVERVIEW OF STRATEGIC MANAGEMENT

External environment

Values

Vision

Mission

Strategic objectives and performance measures

Strategies

Annual objectives

Strategic management enables boards and managers to address the key questions that any organisation should be able to answer:

- What specifically does our organisation want to achieve in the next few years?
- What have we learned from past experiences?
- How should we allocate resources among different objectives?
- What quality standards should we aim to achieve?
- How can we make better use of our resources?

The characteristics that distinguish strategic management from other aspects of management are that it:

- is **complex in nature** – it requires all aspects of the organisation to be viewed in the context of the changing external environment;
- usually involves a **high degree of uncertainty** – it requires people to make judgements about the future when information is only partial;
- requires an **integrated** approach – thinking has to cross the functional boundaries (such as fundraising, service delivery and staffing);
- demands **absolute clarity of thought and analysis** – the logic that integrates mission, objectives, strategies and performance measures needs to be impeccable;
- must **move beyond words and rhetoric** – it requires sharp and realistic propositions about the changes the organisation wishes to make to the lives of people, animals or the environment;
- often results in **major change** – that can challenge the values and power of particular groups in the organisation.

5.3 DECIDING WHERE TO START

Most books, including this one, present strategic management as a top-down process, starting with the mission and moving down through objectives to strategy to action, and finally closing the loop with performance monitoring. It is easy to think of it in this way, but the vision and mission may not be the best starting point. Before working on strategic management it is important to identify which aspect of strategic management most requires attention:

- vision, mission and values
- strategic objectives and corporate strategy
- service strategies
- operational plans
- performance measures
- performance management processes.

The choice depends on which will deliver the greatest improvements in management from the investment of time and effort.

Sometimes the overall strategy is well established, but departments do not have clear and compelling strategies for the delivery of services, campaigns, fundraising or back office support. Sometimes the strategy is clear but annual operating plans are weak. Sometimes the plans are well established, but there is no explicit process for reviewing achievements against the original intentions.

The danger of working on more than one at the same time is that the organisation may not have the capacity to manage the change so nothing is done to a high standard.

Just as an 'organisational analysis' (see section 1.5, Deciding where to start making improvements) may have identified that strategic management needs attention before other aspects of the organisation's workings, so a brief analysis of strategic management is required before deciding where to focus people's efforts. Too often, organisations spend disproportionate time reviewing their mission and corporate strategy, when that effort might have produced greater impact if it had been focused on service strategies, operational plans and performance management.

Having made decisions about where to start, it is worth remembering that strategic management is one of the most satisfying aspects of management. People find it motivating to be involved in developing plans and establishing future priorities. They enjoy seeing more clearly how the organisation fits into its environment and how services and campaigns fit into the broader corporate strategy. At the end of a programme of strengthening strategic management, people are likely to be fired up and will endeavour to achieve more ambitious targets and work together in ways that are more effective.

5.4 THE CONCEPTS OF VISION, MISSION AND VALUES

Three ideas sit at the top of the strategic management hierarchy, each of which contributes to building a shared understanding of the fundamental purpose and beliefs of the organisation. All three are needed to establish a deep understanding of the organisation and to promote it to the wider world.

Vision

The best way to understand what is meant by 'vision' in this context is to think of it as an achievable dream. A vision statement describes a world in which the organisation would no longer need to exist. It does not assume that all the work to achieve that desirable future must be done by the organisation on its own. Visions are often articulated in language such as 'We want a world in which. . .' They should be inspirational, specific to the organisation's field of work but not limiting in scope.

VISIONS

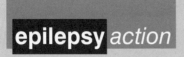

'We want to live in a society where everyone understands epilepsy and where attitudes are based on fact not fiction.'

'Our vision is control over asthma today, freedom from asthma tomorrow.'

St Mungo's
Opening doors for London's homeless

'Our vision is that everyone should have a decent place to live, something meaningful to do, and satisfying relationships with other people – as well as the good health to enjoy them.'

'WaterAid's vision is of a world where everyone has access to safe water and sanitation.'

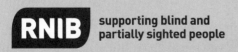

'RNIB's vision is a world in which blind and partially sighted people enjoy the same rights, freedom, responsibilities and quality of life as people who are fully sighted and one in which no one needlessly loses their sight.'

'Our vision is a world where farm animals are treated with compassion and respect.'

'Barnardo's vision is that the lives of all children and young people should be free from poverty, abuse and discrimination.'

'VSO's vision is of a world without poverty in which people work together to fulfil their potential.'

'Our vision. A world in which the poorest and most marginalised people have equitable access to health and improved quality of life.'

'Samaritans' vision is that fewer people die by suicide.'

Third-sector organisations need to have visions of the way they want the world to be. Visions are a powerful motivating influence on people. Founders and leaders often bring the vision, and they need to ensure that it is sustained.

A vision would not normally change until it has been achieved, though organisations do choose to re-word them from time to time.

Mission statement

While an organisation's vision is its view of an ideal world for its beneficiaries, mission is the contribution the organisation thinks it can make to help create that ideal world. So a mission statement should answer the question **'what is the organisation for?'** Some organisations prefer the term 'statement of purpose', but they are the same thing.

The people who lead and drive third-sector organisations are usually highly motivated, with a strong sense of mission. They want to change society in some way, and may assume that everybody else in the organisation has the same view of the world. As a result, the missions of some organisations are implicit. They are part of the accepted beliefs that are not necessarily discussed or written down.

Most third-sector organisations begin with a missionary zeal that is enough to inspire people to join the cause. However, as they grow larger, involve more people and need to communicate with more stakeholders, all of whom may share the overall zeal but have subtly different ideas about what it means in practice, it becomes increasingly important to have explicit statements of vision and mission.

Third-sector organisations often have a much stronger sense of mission than their counterparts in the private and public sectors. Campaigning organisations and membership organisations that are championing a cause have a particularly strong sense of purpose and intention. Service-giving organisations that were set up by people with a disease or disability maintain a strong sense of mission for many years.

Mission statements should identify, succinctly and with clarity, the organisation's users or beneficiaries, what the organisation does for them and the desired outcomes.

Missions have to strike a balance between being so general that they become meaningless and becoming unhelpfully restrictive. Incorporating boundaries in missions helps to make them more specific, for example by stating the geographic territory the organisation aspires to cover or the age range of the people it seeks to support.

Mission statements should clearly differentiate the organisation from others in closely related fields. Many organisations working in the same field might share the same vision, but they should all have unique missions.

The way in which the organisation can best make its contribution may change over time. Mission statements should therefore be reviewed from time to time to ensure that they make sense in prevailing circumstances.

MISSIONS

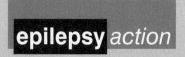

'To take action to meet the identified needs and aspirations of all people with epilepsy and those with an interest in the condition.'

'To improve the health and well-being of people with asthma by building and sharing expertise about asthma.'

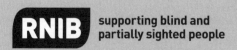

'Our mission is to house, support and care for vulnerable and excluded people who either have been, or are at risk of, sleeping rough and homelessness.'

'Our mission is to challenge blindness by empowering people who are blind or partially sighted, removing the barriers they face and helping to prevent blindness.'

'Our mission is to advance the well-being of farm animals worldwide.'

'Our mission is to alleviate emotional distress and reduce the incidence of suicidal feelings and suicidal behaviour.'

AGE
Concern

'Our mission is to promote the well-being of all older people and to help make later life a fulfilling and enjoyable experience.'

'We are an international organisation working with partners in developing countries to eliminate avoidable blindness and promote equality of opportunity for disabled people.'

Purpose

Some organisations use the term 'purpose' instead of mission.

PURPOSES

'Barnardo's purpose is to help the most vulnerable children and young people transform their lives and fulfil their potential.'

'VSO promotes volunteering to fight global poverty and disadvantage. We bring people together to share skills, creativity and learning to build a fairer world.'

'We work to address unmet health needs of people affected by leprosy, tuberculosis, HIV/AIDS and other health conditions exacerbated by poverty, discrimination and stigma.'

Values

Values are critically important to people who work for and support third-sector organisations. Most people who govern, manage, staff and volunteer for these organisations do so because of deeply held beliefs about social justice, civil society, supporting underprivileged people and building a better world. Often the particular organisation will have been chosen because of great empathy with the cause it champions.

But one person's strongly held beliefs may not be those of the next person, even if they are broadly similar. In a values-driven organisation it is therefore important that the shared beliefs governing policy and decision-making are absolutely clear. The process of articulating these organisation values can also bring the board, staff and supporters closer together as one group.

Sometimes statements of values focus on an organisation's beliefs about its cause, and sometimes they also include values relating to the behaviour that it expects of its board members, staff and volunteers.

Values statements articulate what an organisation stands for, but to be meaningful they have to be 'lived' by people in the organisation, and in particular by its board members and leaders. Carefully crafted values statements only encourage cynicism if people do not behave according to the statements that the organisation has agreed.

VALUES

- 'Epilepsy Action will be representative and inclusive of and accessible to all people with an interest in epilepsy
- Epilepsy Action will encourage and enable the active involvement of its members and other stakeholders
- Epilepsy Action believes that people with epilepsy must have equality of opportunity in their lives to allow them to achieve their full potential'

St Mungo's
Opening doors for London's homeless

'Our core values are:

- **Respect and ambition** – we respect the life histories of homeless people, believe in their potential and will help them realise their ambitions
- **Excellence and creativity** – we aim for excellent and creative solutions to the changing needs of homeless people
- **Diversity and equality** – we are richer as a charity and as a society by valuing diversity and striving for equality of opportunity'

Believe in children
Barnardo's

- 'Respecting the unique worth of every person
- Encouraging people to fulfil their potential
- Working with hope
- Exercising responsible stewardship'

115

- We believe that everyone must be able to exercise their fundamental human rights
- We believe that people working together can achieve positive and lasting change
- We value diversity and cross-cultural understanding
- We value partnerships based on honesty and respect
- We value the innovation and creativity based on shared endeavour
- We value openness to learning

- **'Equity –** We work to improve the health of some of the most disadvantaged people around the world
- **Respect and dignity** – We are a people-focused organisation, working to eliminate stigma and marginalisation caused by disease and poverty
- **Creativity –** We encourage innovation in the solutions we adopt
- **Efficacy and quality –** We ensure that our resources are used in the most efficient and cost-effective manner and that the quality of our services is uniformly high
- **Sustainability –** We believe that the principal responsibility for the provision of health care rests with governments. We work to bring about structural changes which produce long-lasting benefits'

SAMARITANS

We are committed to the following **Values**:

- **Listening**, because exploring feelings alleviates distress and helps people to reach a better understanding of their situation and the options open to them.
- **Confidentiality**, because if people feel safe, they are more likely to be open about their feelings.
- **People making their own decisions** wherever possible, because we believe that people have the right to find their own solution and telling people what to do takes responsibility away from them.
- **Being non-judgemental**, because we want people to be able to talk to us without fear of prejudice or rejection.
- **Human contact**, because giving people time, undivided attention and empathy meets a fundamental emotional need and reduces distress and despair.

The concepts of vision, mission and purpose have been brought together in a model developed at Ashridge Strategic Management Centre. Although it uses the words in a slightly different way, the underlying ideas are very similar. The Centre argues that mission is concerned with both **hearts** and **minds:** the beliefs that come from the heart and the rationale that comes from the mind.

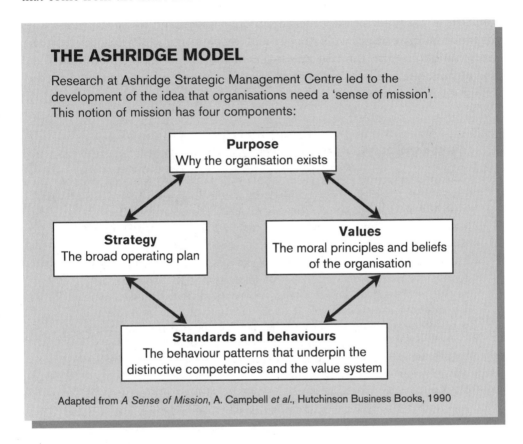

THE ASHRIDGE MODEL

Research at Ashridge Strategic Management Centre led to the development of the idea that organisations need a 'sense of mission'. This notion of mission has four components:

Purpose
Why the organisation exists

Strategy
The broad operating plan

Values
The moral principles and beliefs
of the organisation

Standards and behaviours
The behaviour patterns that underpin the
distinctive competencies and the value system

Adapted from *A Sense of Mission*, A. Campbell *et al.*, Hutchinson Business Books, 1990

5.5 CREATING AND REFRESHING VISIONS, MISSIONS AND VALUES

Vision, mission and values need to be worked on:

- when the organisation's purpose and *raison d'être* have become woolly and unfocused;
- when the organisation has become directionless and people are not totally clear about what the organisation stands for;
- when the motivation of the board, staff and other supporters is low;
- when the gap between the mission and the organisation's capacity to deliver is so large that the mission is just not credible.

An essential pre-requisite for creating a strong sense of vision and mission is having a group of people, on the board and among the staff, who share similar aspirations and are willing to work together to strengthen the organisation. If the top team is not functioning with a high level of trust and openness, work on vision, mission and values will be neither productive nor meaningful. It may be better to address the team and trust issues first.

Timing is another consideration. It often takes longer than people expect to understand the fundamental beliefs of an organisation and to see the varied ways in which beliefs connect with strategy and people's actions. Particularly in larger organisations, it takes time for new board members and managers to understand the organisation's history and context, and it is easy to come to premature views about vision and mission.

THE MISSION OF A MEDICAL CHARITY

This organisation existed to help people with a terminal neuromuscular disorder. It aimed both to raise funds for medical research and to provide care and support for people with the disease. The board included eminent medical researchers, senior social workers and people with the disorder.

One-third of the board believed that the organisation existed primarily to fund medical research, and they grudgingly agreed to fund care for people with the disorder. One-third believed that the organisation should focus on helping social services departments to provide better care, and they felt that medical research was expensive and making little progress. One-third felt that the organisation should provide direct care itself, because it knew best the particular problems people with the disability and their families faced.

Not surprisingly, staff were very confused about the organisation's purpose. Morale was low and a great deal of time and effort were wasted arguing about the allocation of resources to different activities.

To overcome the problem, the board and senior staff held two special workshops, at a neutral venue and with an outside consultant, to clarify the organisation's mission. They began to find common ground when it was agreed that, above everything else, they shared a desire to help people with the disorder. They acknowledged to each other that the medical professionals, the social work professionals and the volunteers all had distinctive contributions to make. They also agreed that close cooperation among these groups would yield more benefit for people with the disorder than working separately for the same cause. Finally, they agreed a formula for allocating resources to different activities.

The mission was clarified, enthusiasm began to grow, arguments declined and the organisation began to thrive again.

The board is ultimately responsible for managing the mission, but it needs to involve staff, members (in membership organisations) and often service users as well, in a joint effort to agree and strengthen the vision and mission.

Management needs to construct a process that informs stakeholders how and when they can make their contribution to the debate. The process could start with a board discussion, or it could start in different parts of the organisation and culminate with a board session that draws together the various strands needed to renew the organisation's understanding of its vision, mission and values.

STRENGTHENING THE MISSION OF A HOUSING TRUST

The senior management team of a housing trust decided that the 'command and control' culture of the organisation was no longer appropriate. They wanted to empower managers and free them up to be more entrepreneurial within a broad mission for the future of the organisation. To achieve this required that some 70 managers be involved in a process of defining a mission that they all felt they owned and believed in.

They embarked on a 12-month programme of activities including:

- Two senior-management team away days to diagnose the problem, establish the precise objectives of the work and define a programme of activities that would eventually involve almost all 700 staff
- Two conferences for the top 70 managers, to allow them to develop their views on the mission and on the obstacles that got in the way of their contributing effectively to that mission. This included training in facilitating group discussions for the next event
- A conference, with half the staff attending on one day, half the next, and all staying overnight, designed to engage everyone in the process of developing the new mission
- Further away days for the senior management team to distil all they had learned from the staff and to create a new mission which reflected the debate over the preceding months
- An action plan which identified how the obstacles of the 'command and control' culture would be removed so that everyone could take the organisation forward with a new mission and a new culture

Debates about the future vision and mission of the organisation should aim to:

1. **Define the purpose of the organisation** at the most fundamental and general level. This can involve asking seemingly simple questions about why the organisation exists, who it exists for and what (at the most basic level) it aims to achieve.

2. **Identify the core values and beliefs** upon which the future of the organisation can be built. Asking questions about what the organisation stands for, what its philosophy is and what position it takes on the central issues of concern can help to clarify values and beliefs.

3. **Clarify its features and competencies**. Identification of those characteristics that distinguish the organisation from others in the same field can help to develop a better understanding of an organisation's distinctiveness. Similarly, looking at its particular competencies can lead to valuable insights.

Developing the vision, mission and values can be undertaken as part of a strategic planning process or it can be a separate management initiative. It often results in sets of words which sound worthy and about which it is easy to be cynical. However, organisations that have ironed out common misunderstandings on the fundamental issues are likely to be more effective and more satisfying to work for than those that leave such issues unresolved.

5.6 PROMOTING VISIONS, MISSIONS AND VALUES

Mission, vision and values statements all document the outcome of an organisation's work in this area. They are also a way of communicating the organisation's purpose to staff, volunteers, funders and the outside world.

It is important to recognise that these statements bring the greatest benefit when people have been involved in their development. Management teams that start by drafting a statement are usually disappointed. The carefully crafted copy sent down with a memorandum from the chief executive usually has the opposite effect to that which was desired. Unless statements have been developed through a process of discussion and debate through the organisation, they are likely to promote cynicism and encourage the view that senior management doesn't know how to make good use of its time.

Vision and mission statements should be cast in terms of the changes the organisation wants to make to people's lives, not what the organisation wants to be. Statements starting with words such as 'We want to be the premier provider of...' or 'We are an organisation that...' focus people on the organisation rather than what it wishes to achieve.

A good mission statement should be:

- **Short** – no more than one or two sentences.
- **Inspiring** – to call people to action.
- **Durable** – designed to last for five or more years.
- **Distinctive** – uniquely describing one organisation's purpose.
- **Specific** – establishing clearly what the organisation does.
- **Credible** – so stakeholders can believe it.
- **Kept alive** – so everyone in the organisation knows it.

A good test of the distinctiveness of a mission statement is to ask whether it could be applied to any other organisation.

Promoting statements

Once the vision, mission and values have been clarified, continuous effort is required to keep them alive and relevant to everyone's work. The larger the organisation, the greater is the effort required. Annual general meetings provide an opportunity to hold workshops that celebrate achievements and plan future developments. Regional meetings can start with a reminder of the mission. Branch chairs and directors can be encouraged to communicate the mission, vision and values amongst their members. Managers can draw the attention of staff to the links between the mission and daily activities and remind people how their work is a part of achieving the mission. Volunteers can be thanked for their contribution to the mission. These are the actions that give an organisation vibrancy, clarity of purpose and a sense of mission.

Every opportunity should also be taken to promote mission, vision and values statements. Annual reports, annual reviews and websites should always include these statements in prominent places. Other ways to promote them include:

- in reception areas and meeting rooms
- at conferences
- on headed paper and business cards
- on directions for visitors
- in strategy documents
- on invoices and compliments slips
- on press releases
- in publications
- on invitations to events
- in catalogues
- on e-mail footers
- in regional and branch offices.

Many people and potential supporters have only limited contact with an organisation, so it is worth taking every opportunity to exploit these under-used channels to communicate the new and carefully crafted statements.

SUMMARY OF KEY POINTS

The rationale for managing strategy

- Strategic management provides the intellectual connection between service users, campaigns and funders
- The process of developing strategy helps to weld together the coalition of interests that is needed for organisations to thrive
- Boards and senior managers both have responsibilities for developing and delivering strategy

Concept of strategic management

- The essential components of strategic management are concerned with clarifying the organisation's vision, mission and values, establishing overall objectives and strategies for achieving them, and setting up systems to manage performance
- Strategy is complex in nature, involves a high degree of uncertainty, requires an integrated approach and absolute clarity of thought and analysis

Deciding where to start

- Careful choices should be made to pinpoint the aspects of strategic management that most need attention
- Sometimes greater benefits accrue from working on service and campaign strategies and performance management than on mission, vision and corporate strategic objectives

The concepts of vision, mission and values

- Vision is a description of a desirable future situation for the organisation's users and for the world at large
- Mission is concerned with what the organisation exists for
- Values describe the underlying beliefs that the organisation holds and that inform its policies and decisions

Creating and refreshing visions, missions and values

- Organisations can increase the strength of feeling about their vision and mission by involving stakeholders in a debate about why the organisation exists and what, overall, it aims to achieve
- The process should define the purpose of the organisation, identify core beliefs and clarify its distinctive features

Promoting visions, missions and values

● Vision and mission statements document the outcomes of a process to refresh the organisation's purpose. The process of preparing them should involve as many people as possible
● Once the vision and mission have been created, continuous effort is required to keep them alive and ensure that they are promoted and referred to in many different types of meetings
● Every opportunity should also be taken to promote mission statements using a wide variety of communication channels

FURTHER READING

Strategic Management for Voluntary Nonprofit Organisations, Roger Courtney, Routledge, 2002

The Wilder Nonprofit Field Guide to Crafting Effective Mission and Vision Statements, Emil Angelica, Amherst H Wilder Foundation, 2001

More and recent books and reports can be found at www.compasspartnership.co.uk.

6 Establishing objectives and performance measures

6.1 LINKING OBJECTIVES TO PERFORMANCE

Many third-sector organisations find it extraordinarily difficult to define precise, measurable and achievable objectives. This is often because they are working in the sphere of the intangible (making the world a better place for particular groups of people or animals, for example) and it is hard to measure intangible change.

It is comparatively easy to produce an inspiring, unifying mission statement and overall goals for the organisation. But the difference between doing this and producing achievable, time-bound statements of the specific differences an organisation, department or individual will make is huge.

The challenge is easier for some types of services and some organisations than for others. Setting measurable objectives for the number of new houses to build or the number of people gaining qualifications is easier than for strengthening couples' relationships or improving the quality of life of profoundly disabled children.

It used to be the case that the identification of performance measures, if it was done at all, came after an organisation had set objectives and agreed its strategies and plans. There is now a growing expectation that measures should be defined as an integral part of planning, because objectives and measures of performance need to be completely aligned if they are to be meaningful.

Leading organisations now plan for impact (what difference the organisation can make in a specified time period) rather than for activities (what the organisation will do). The key difference between this and more traditional planning is the rigour of the thinking. Woolly statements of good intentions are being replaced by tightly specified objectives and performance measures that focus people on results.

Objectives need to be based on people's needs (e.g. for a home, to obtain a qualification or to receive a treatment). Understanding these needs and how services can be constructed to meet them is the fundamental starting point for setting objectives. This needs to be based on good 'market' research that produces evidence of what service users most want, whether and how much they are willing to pay for it, how it should be promoted, and where and how they would like to receive it. These are the 'Ps' of business marketing (product, price, promotion, place) that have been valuably converted into a third-sector context in *Charity Marketing: Meeting Need through Customer Focus* (see Further reading in Chapter 8).

This chapter describes:
- different types of objectives;
- the hierarchy of objectives;
- different types of performance measures;
- how to integrate objectives and performance measures.

It begins the process of pinpointing 'what' organisations set out to achieve. Chapter 7 addresses 'how' organisations achieve their objectives through the development of strategies, and Chapter 8 describes how to establish systems for measuring progress and performance.

Taken together these chapters are further elements of the 'golden thread' that links the mission to specific objectives and to performance reports. With these in place, board members and managers can drive the effectiveness of their organisations.

The term 'output' is used to describe the services or campaigns that the organisation delivers (e.g. training courses or campaign meetings held). The term 'outcome' describes the benefits that derive from the service or campaign (e.g. qualifications gained or government policies changed). The term 'result' is used generically to describe both outputs and outcomes.

6.2 DIFFERENT TYPES OF OBJECTIVES

Objectives are statements of aims which can be created for the organisation as a whole, or for different departments, services or individual managers. They can be both qualitative and quantifiable. They help to focus different parts of the organisation on achieving the mission.

The main types of objectives are:

- strategic objectives
- departmental objectives
- service, campaign and project objectives
- cross-departmental objectives
- individual objectives.

They can all be categorised into externally facing objectives and internally facing objectives.

Strategic objectives

Some organisations call strategic objectives 'goals' or 'aims'. Whatever their name, they have the same effect: focusing the organisation on delivering the things that are most critical to its success. They should be couched in words that concentrate and guide people's actions. They should avoid the common trap of being well-meant statements of good intentions that could be applied to many different organisations.

There is a danger that strategic objectives simply sum up what the organisation is already doing. This type of statement can help to set direction and indicate what the organisation will be doing, but it does not provide the basis for measuring performance.

The trend is towards quantified strategic objectives, because qualitative ones can only establish good intentions. This creates a clear line of sight between the organisation's objectives and the measures of performance that determine how far they are being achieved. Strategic objectives therefore establish the performance that organisations wish to achieve. They are the top-level targets that provide the core content of performance reports which should be directly aligned with each objective.

There is a school of thought that says 'if you can't measure it, you can't manage it'. Measurement can take a number of forms. It can be about numbers, people assisted and the types of assistance delivered. It can also be about 'progress' towards achieving a desired result, for example the steps that are required to catalyse a change in public policy. In some cases it may involve measuring people's opinions about progress or identifying evidence that indicates progress but may not be measurable on a simple scale.

Some large organisations that offer a wide range of services may find it difficult to quantify a limited number of top-level objectives because the outcomes of a wide range of services cannot be 'added together' to create overall performance measures. They find it easier to have qualitative strategic objectives and to quantify the next level in the hierarchy.

WATERAID STRATEGIC OBJECTIVES

WaterAid works with people in 17 countries in Africa, Asia and the Pacific region to improve their quality of life through lasting improvements to water, sanitation and hygiene education using local skills and practical, sustainable technologies. It has an income of £31 million.

WaterAid's eight strategic objectives are to:

1. Work with local partner organisations towards helping one million people gain access to water and one million people gain access to sanitation every year by 2010, ensuring the longevity of these services. This target will be focused in 15 countries in sub-Saharan Africa and South Asia which between them contain 30% of the world's population without safe water and 40% of the world's population without sanitation

2. Enable a further 500,000 people to gain access to water and 500,000 people to gain access to sanitation in these countries every year by 2010, by supporting local partners to raise their own funds and retaining a strong advisory role on how these funds are spent

3. Increase urban work to 30% of programme expenditure

4. Ensure all future water supply and sanitation projects supported by WaterAid address the issues of water depletion and contamination through appropriate integrated water resource management

5. Demonstrate through practical examples that sustainable and equitable water and sanitation services are essential to achieve the overall Millennium Development Goal of poverty reduction and the targets on health, education and the environment. Monitor, support and lobby other organisations to strengthen their own water and sanitation work in this direction

6. Strengthen local governments' ability to provide equitable and pro-poor water and sanitation services on a larger scale

7. Develop innovative approaches and new sources of funding to increase annual income to £35 million by 2010 in order to support WaterAid's country programme activities and advocacy work

8. Expand the number of organisations that work using WaterAid's methods through international partnerships and alliances

CANCER RESEARCH UK GOALS

Cancer Research UK has developed ten goals to measure success over the coming years in beating cancer.

We will work with partners to achieve the following by 2020:

1. **People will know how to reduce their risk of cancer** – Three-quarters of the UK public will be aware of the main lifestyle choices they can make to reduce their risk of getting cancer

2. **The number of smokers will fall dramatically** – Four million fewer adults will be smokers, preventing thousands of new cases of cancer every year

3. **People under 75 will be less likely to get cancer** – The chances of a person developing cancer up to the age of 75 will fall from more than one in four to one in five

4. **Cancer will be diagnosed earlier** – Two-thirds of all cancer cases will be diagnosed at a stage when the cancer can be successfully treated

5. **We will understand how cancer starts and develops** – We will have a detailed understanding of the causes and changes in the body in two-thirds of all cases of cancer

6. **There will be better treatments with fewer side effects** – Treatments that accurately target the cancer and have few serious side effects will be available for at least half of all patients

7. **More people will survive cancer** – Survival rates for all common cancers will increase, with more than two-thirds of newly diagnosed patients living for at least five years

8. **We will especially tackle cancer in low-income communities** – The differences in the risk of dying from cancer between the most affluent and the least affluent will be reduced by half

9. **People with cancer will get the information they need** – At least nine out of ten patients will be able to access the information they need at the time of diagnosis and during treatment

10. **We will continue to fight cancer beyond 2020** – Sufficient scientists, doctors, nurses and infrastructure will be in place to ensure continued rapid progress in the fight against cancer beyond 2020

In some organisations there may be a degree of **conflict between strategic objectives**. The artistic directors of arts organisations often want to present new and challenging works but marketing directors want to achieve high income targets by attracting large audiences. Fundraising directors of aid agencies want to maximise income with dramatic appeals while operations directors want to promote strong and resourceful people in less-developed countries who are struggling to survive in difficult circumstances. The debate about strategic objectives should highlight these tensions and lead to creative ideas that help to establish clarity about strategic direction.

The **time horizon** of strategic objectives depends on the nature of the organisation's work. Organisations with large capital expenditure programmes, such as housing associations, may have specific strategic objectives for five or more years. At the other end of the spectrum, organisations that have to respond quickly to changing circumstances, such as disaster appeals, may have to have shorter-term strategic objectives. Typically strategic objectives have a three to five year time frame, though there is a trend towards shorter time horizons. Some organisations have two to three year rolling objectives that are revised every year.

A **good strategic objective** should:
- specify the intended outcome;
- quantify current and planned performance measures;
- have a specific time-frame;
- be broadly achievable within the resources and influencing powers of the organisation.

A quick test of the quality of objectives is to review whether they are SMART – Specific, Measurable, Actionable, Realistic and Timetabled – a useful mnemonic that can be applied to objectives at all levels of the organisation.

Departmental objectives

Departmental objectives should be more specific. They are easier to quantify and 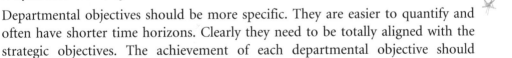 often have shorter time horizons. Clearly they need to be totally aligned with the strategic objectives. The achievement of each departmental objective should contribute directly to the achievement of one or more strategic objectives.

ROYAL BRITISH LEGION WELFARE DIVISION – STRATEGIC OBJECTIVES

'By 2010 we will be providing per year:

- Pensions Compensation and disability advice to 14,500 more people than we deliver at present
- £26 million in immediate need grants for people with urgent needs, of which we expect to be raising 50% from other benevolent charities
- Accommodation and care for 900 people in our homes
- Welfare Breaks for 7,000 veterans, widows, families and young people
- 8,000 students and their teachers with tours to the war cemeteries and battlefields in Europe
- 10,000 adults with guided tours to war graves or battlefield sites across the globe
- 25,000 people with advice from our Civvy Street careers advice web site
- Vocational assessments for 300 early service leavers
- Benefits and debt advice to an additional 10,500 people, increasing their average household income by £600
- 200 local health and well being centres providing monthly activity programmes to 20,000 ex-Service people
- Essential home and garden maintenance and security enhancements to 21,000 people
- £2 m to specialist charities providing assistance to homeless, people with mental health needs and prison leavers'

Cross-departmental objectives

Sometimes objectives will cut across two or more departments. They are entirely legitimate, but it is important to clarify who will take responsibility for leading on the delivery of each one so as to avoid accountability slipping through the net. For example:

- Finance and fundraising will integrate our processes for managing legacy income and reduce annual processing costs by 15% by the end of 2010 – led by the director of finance.
- The director of communications will increase spontaneous awareness of our organisation by five percentage points in three years through coordinated initiatives in all departments and regions focusing particularly on our annual awareness week.

Service delivery, project and campaign objectives

These are even more specific, and will almost always be quantified. Service delivery units are the lowest level of the organisation at which people and money can be managed to produce a desired result; they are defined more fully in section 8.2, Defining services and campaigns.

Service delivery units can have their own long, medium and short-term objectives – their own hierarchy within the overall scheme.

Service delivery objectives should state a very specific desired outcome of the service or campaign. Objectives might include:

- the number of people who will benefit from the service each year;
- the user quality rating targets that will be achieved;
- growth in the number of people supported each year.

Service objectives should be cast in terms of intended outcomes rather than outputs. For example 'increasing the number of people who gain a qualification in food hygiene from 800 in 2008 to 1,000 in 2010' rather than 'providing 30 courses per year'.

EXAMPLE OF A SERVICE OBJECTIVE AND OUTCOME

Strategic objective

To improve security and safety in beneficiaries' homes.

Service output

To provide improved home security measures including key-operated window locks, door locks and other security measures for 5,000 older people per year, starting in 2008 and growing by 15% per year.

Service outcome

By the end of 2012 a total of 33,700 older people will report that they feel more secure and confident to live independently in their own homes (measured by an annual survey).

External and internal objectives

All objectives can be categorised as either externally or internally facing. External objectives relate to the organisation's mission and the tasks it is trying to achieve. These have been the focus of the previous sections of this chapter.

Internal objectives, on the other hand, are primarily concerned with building the capacity of the organisation to achieve the external objectives. They can include:

- **Expanding fundraising** – for example, developing public profile, marketing the cause and raising money from new sources.
- **Strengthening the governing board** – for example, implementing a new induction scheme, improving working relationships with management.
- **Developing HR** – for example, establishing a one-to-one supervision process, creating management development programmes.
- **Investing in management information systems** – for example, improving financial management systems, developing performance measures and investing in information technology.
- **Investing in plant and buildings** – for example, purchasing new equipment and renovating offices.
- **Improving risk management** – for example, taking steps to mitigate risk and making more effective use of the risk register.

CfBT CORPORATE LEARNING STRATEGY

CfBT Education Trust is a leading education consultancy and service organisation. It exists to provide education for public benefit in the UK and internationally. It has over 2,000 staff who provide consultancy, run schools, support education reform, conduct research and deliver training.

It has a cross-cutting, internal objective to promote learning through all its activities. Every operational team in the organisation is expected to report on the impact their work has on beneficiaries. The cross-divisional objectives for this work are:

1. to embed a system for ensuring that teams can provide evidence that their work is having the **desired impact on beneficiaries**
2. to embed **a system for capturing and accessing learning** and for connecting people to new knowledge and opportunities for innovation in practice and professional learning
3. to **design, deliver and disseminate** the elements of good practice to maximise impact for beneficiaries and record progress on our balanced scorecard

It is important to distinguish between external and internal objectives and to ensure that the majority are externally facing. Internal objectives can then be tested to ensure that they are closely aligned with the achievement of external objectives. As the next chapter will demonstrate, objectives for building internal capacity need to be justified by evidence that each will enable the achievement of external objectives.

The value of having clear objectives and of ensuring that everyone has a deep understanding of what they are and what they mean cannot be overstated. The fuzzy and ever-changing environment in which third-sector organisations exist means that managers need to be continuously asking themselves how their activities contribute towards the achievement of strategic objectives and ultimately to the mission.

Together internal and external objectives provide the starting point for an integrated performance management system and the basis for holding people to account for achieving the desired results.

6.3 THE HIERARCHY OF OBJECTIVES AND PERFORMANCE MEASURES

A hierarchy is a useful way of organising objectives and performance measures into a coherent picture for the organisation as a whole. This hierarchy can be linked to the structure of an organisation. The board and the leadership team will concentrate more on the establishment of strategic objectives and managing performance against these. Directors need to focus on divisional objectives and their achievement. Service managers will be most interested in the objectives and performance of their service, and individuals will focus on their personal objectives.

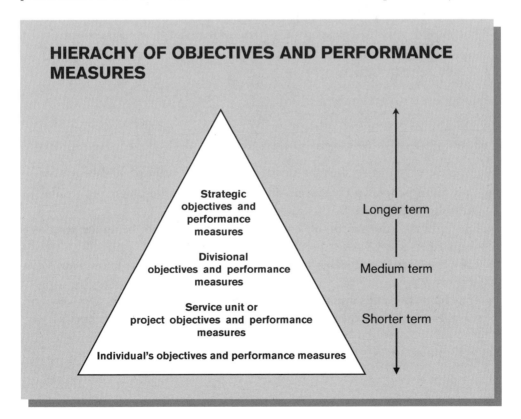

HIERACHY OF OBJECTIVES AND PERFORMANCE MEASURES

- Strategic objectives and performance measures — Longer term
- Divisional objectives and performance measures — Medium term
- Service unit or project objectives and performance measures — Shorter term
- Individual's objectives and performance measures

Many organisations find that having between five and eight objectives and performance measures for each part of the organisation allows for the breadth of their activities but is sufficiently few to maintain a sharp focus on achievable results.

A good test of the robustness of the hierarchy is to plot its elements on a single sheet of paper and ask whether the achievement of the objectives at one level will lead to the accomplishment of one or more higher level objectives.

6.4 CHOOSING PERFORMANCE MEASURES

TERMINOLOGY

Performance measure

The 'scale' that is used to measure performance (e.g. the number of people assisted, or the volume of service provided).

Target or performance indicator

The numerical measure of achievement (e.g. 200 people assisted or 330 sessions delivered).

Key performance indicator

A critically important indicator of 'current' performance (e.g. funds raised last week).

Key results indicator

A critically important indicator of past performance (e.g. number of people provided with a permanent water supply last year).

There are compelling reasons for having performance measures and targets:

- **They focus people and resources on the achievement of objectives** – rather than allowing effort to be dissipated on many activities.
- **They provide information on how efficiently services are being delivered** – so managers know where to focus their attention.
- **They give managers feedback on users' views** – so managers know what to improve.
- **They identify trends and allow comparisons with other similar services** – so managers know how they compare with internal and external benchmarks.

- **They provide evidence of achievements for funders and supporters** – enabling them to see what has been done with their money.
- **They enable organisations to report on achievements to regulators and watchdogs** – and are therefore more accountable for the difference they made.

However, the use of performance measures has attracted much controversy, with advocates arguing that, without measures, no one knows how well the organisation is doing, and those opposed arguing that the complexity of third-sector organisations means that measures are of little practical use. The most common objections are that:

- **It is difficult to measure the quality of services** – and quality is often as important as quantity. A simple measure will seldom reflect the effect on people's complex needs.
- **It is difficult to link cause and effect** – because the relationship between actions and results is often not clear-cut. A campaign that leads to a policy change is usually the consequence of actions taken by many different organisations.
- **Monitoring overemphasises the quantifiable** – because it encourages people to put more emphasis on measurable results, leading staff to focus on achieving specific targets rather than on improvement of the service as a whole.
- **It is hard to obtain reliable data** – for example, information that depends on people reporting on their own behaviour (such as drug misuse). There can also be issues of confidentiality (where service users do not wish to be followed up) and of accuracy (where people who are dependent on a service do not wish to be critical for fear of losing it).
- **It is an unnecessary expense** – particularly when resources are scarce and people believe that funds should be focused on improving or expanding the service rather than setting up systems to measure it.
- **What gets measured gets manipulated** – a well-known adage pointing out that all measurement systems distort their users' behaviour.

Despite these concerns, the overall trend in the sector is towards greater use of measures to track performance. Organisations are discovering ways to measure quality. They are striving to understand better the links between actions and results. They are finding ways to quantify their activities and to obtain reliable data on performance. Many now summarise organisation-wide performance into dashboards of key indicators and are finding ways to minimise the costs of collecting and managing information.

Types of performance measures

Using performance measures does require some knowledge of the terminology around the topic. Basically, they are all about understanding:

- What did the organisation do?
- What did it cost?
- What difference did it make?
- How did it contribute to the achievement of the mission?

In the more technical language of the field, performance measures can be categorised into:

- **input measures,** which track the resources the organisation uses;
- **process measures,** which track the activities the organisation undertakes;
- **output measures,** which track the services and campaigns that the organisation delivers;
- **outcome measures,** which track the benefits delivered to users and public policy changes;
- **impact measures,** which track the wider social consequences of the organisation's work.

Input, process and output indicators are usually measures of current performance. They need to be collected regularly (e.g. weekly or monthly) and can then be used by managers to take action when performance is below target (for example if call waiting times are longer than planned on Monday mornings, more volunteers can be rostered for that time). These are the measures that are used by front-line team managers to track activities and make adjustments.

Outcomes are usually measures of achievements and are sometimes called 'results indicators'. They measure performance over a longer timescale and are the indicators that are particularly pertinent for senior managers and board members. They provide information about the extent to which top-level objectives are being achieved. Actions taken on these indicators have longer time horizons.

Impact measures track the wider social, environmental and economic consequences of an organisation's work. They are the hardest to capture and to attribute solely to one organisation's activities.

The term 'key' is used to distinguish between the indicators that organisations need to track performance and the limited number of critically important indicators that determine the success of a team, department or the organisation as a whole. Many organisations have a great deal of performance information. The best managed ones understand which indicators are most critical to achieve a high level of performance and require closest management attention.

EXAMPLES OF PERFORMANCE MEASURES

Input measures	income, staff time, volunteer numbers and time contributed, gifts in kind
Process measures	response times, backlogs and arrears, clear-up rates, seat and bed occupancy, length of waiting lists
Output measures	housing offers made, enquiries answered, courses delivered, counselling sessions held, number of performances
Outcome measures	people who secured employment, people who stopped using drugs, people successfully housed, qualifications gained
Impact measures	reduced unemployment, reduced street homelessness, increased literacy, reduced re-offending

Performance measures can be combined together to create measures of **efficiency.** Efficiency measures how well the resources were used, and it is usually expressed in terms of the cost of achieving one unit of the desired output, for example cost per enquiry or cost per course participant. Efficiency can also measure the time taken to achieve the desired output, for example time to place volunteers or time to house homeless people.

Measures can also be combined to create measures of **effectiveness.** Effectiveness measures achievements from the available resources and is usually expressed in terms of the cost of achieving one unit of the desired outcome. Examples include the cost per successful placement or the cost per qualification gained. Effectiveness can also measure the time taken to achieve the desired outcome, for example staff hours per person successfully rehabilitated.

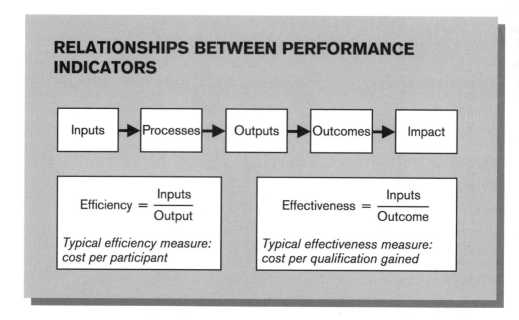

User satisfaction measures

User satisfaction measures can be qualitative and quantitative. Both are important in building an overall picture of user satisfaction. Qualitative information comes from asking users open questions about a service, then looking at the patterns in the responses to determine how users view the service. Quantitative information comes from asking users to rate each aspect of a service on a scale. Quantification is important because it allows managers to aggregate the scores and find out which aspects of the service deserve attention. It also allows organisations to follow trends over time to determine whether users are becoming less or more satisfied.

Milestones

Projects and special initiatives may require different types of measures, since it may be more appropriate to track steps towards achieving objectives, in the short term. Progress is measured using **milestones.** Plans and projects can be divided into stages, and timetables can be attached to the achievement of each stage. This is sometimes called a 'milestone plan'. It sets out what will be achieved and by when, and it can be used by managers as one way of holding people accountable for their work. Milestones are particularly useful for 'one-off' pieces of work, where other performance measures are not appropriate.

6.5 INTEGRATING OBJECTIVES AND PERFORMANCE MEASURES

Objectives establish 'what' an organisation is striving to achieve. They describe outcomes or intended impacts. Performance measures track key elements of the input, process and output chain that need to be managed. They measure 'whether' objectives are being achieved.

Choosing measures

Management has to ensure that objectives and performance measures are all aligned in a way that optimises the performance of the organisation. Nobody should be striving to achieve a target that is not contributing directly to the achievement of a strategic objective.

It is easy to identify a whole range of performance measures and indicators that might be interesting, and there is a real danger that managers become overwhelmed by the quantity of data that could be collected. The trick is to pinpoint those critical measures that can be used to manage performance. This requires careful and thoughtful judgement about which indicators will produce valuable information that will influence decisions. Only indicators that pass this test should be collected and reported on a regular basis. This minimises the risk of information overload.

Each objective should therefore have a very limited number of performance indicators that need to be met for the objective to be achieved.

AN EXAMPLE OF INTEGRATED OBJECTIVES AND PERFORMANCE MEASURES FROM SHELTER

Aim 1

Ensure there are significantly more affordable homes.

Objective

Shelter will campaign at a national, regional, and local level to make affordable housing – especially social rented housing – a key public spending priority.

Performance measures

- A government commitment to fund at least 20,000 social rented homes per annum over and above current plans
- A commitment from the Scottish Executive to fund 24,750 social rented homes (a 50% increase on the current 2005– 2008 target) between 2008 and 2011

High-level objectives and performance measures often need to be divided into sub-objectives and measures that contribute to the achievement of the wider objective – leading to the hierarchy of objectives discussed earlier.

Each manager should be responsible for only a limited number of key performance indicators – usually between five and eight. So chief executives have responsibility for the five to eight critical organisation-wide indicators. Members of the leadership team each take responsibility for five to eight indicators that contribute to the top-level indicators, and may track other aspects of performance as well. In turn, managers reporting to members of the leadership team have their own key indicators.

So at the end of any planning process (described in section 7.5, Developing strategic plans) there will be clarity about the objectives to be achieved, the indicators that measure performance and who is responsible for tracking each measure, praising success or taking action on under-achievements.

SAMPLE OF OBJECTIVES AND PERFORMANCE MEASURES AT RNIB

Blind and partially sighted people can get more out of television and audio-visual culture

- Numbers of people reached directly to raise awareness of audio description
- Percentage of TV programmes required to be broadcast with audio description
- Percentage of the top 100 blockbuster films released on DVD with audio description in the last calendar year

Promoting the teaching and learning of Braille

- Number of active Braille readers, defined as those purchasing or loaning at least one RNIB Braille product a year
- Review of Braille teaching materials completed and agreed revisions made
- Online teaching resource launched

Radically improving the RNIB experience for our key customer groups

- Percentage of units whose customer satisfaction is improving
- Number of books simultaneously published in more than one format
- Call abandonment rate

SUMMARY OF KEY POINTS

Linking objectives to performance

- Organisations need achievable, time-bound statements of the specific differences the organisation as a whole, each department and each service will make
- Planning for activities is being superseded by planning for impact

Different types of objectives

- The main types of objectives are strategic, departmental, service, project and individual. They can be categorised as external or internal
- Strategic objectives focus people on those things that are most critical to the achievement of the mission
- The trend is towards quantification of strategic objectives to establish a clear line of sight between intentions and results
- In some large, complex organisations it is more difficult to quantify top-level objectives so this is done at the next level

The hierarchy of objectives and performance measures

- Objectives and performance measures exist in a hierarchy. A test for completeness is to ask whether the achievement of all the objectives and performance measures at one level will ensure the accomplishment of those at a higher level
- Having between five and eight objectives for each part of the organisation allows for breadth of activity but maintains focus

Choosing performance measures

- Despite the controversy around performance measures, organisations are discovering ways to measure quality, link cause and effect, emphasise qualitative measures, obtain reliable data, summarise organisation-wide performance and minimise the costs of collecting and managing information
- Performance measures track inputs, processes and outputs. Results indicators track outcomes and impacts. Milestones track the delivery of stages of a project
- Use of a limited number of carefully chosen indicators is growing

Integrating objectives and performance measures

- A key management task is to ensure that objectives and performance measures are all aligned
- Each should be allocated to a manager so everyone is clear how their work contributes to the achievement of the mission

FURTHER READING

Key Performance Indicators – Developing, Implementing and Using KPIs, David Parminter, Wiley, 2007

The Nonprofit Strategy Revolution, David La Piana, Fieldstone Alliance, 2008

More and recent books and reports can be found at www.compasspartnership.co.uk.

7 Devising strategies to maximise impact

7.1 STRATEGY FOCUSES ORGANISATIONS

Strategies are broad groups of priorities that describe at a high level how an organisation will achieve its mission and strategic objectives. Organisations can pursue their mission in a wide variety of ways. Strategies should describe how carefully chosen groups of activities will generate and use resources to make the greatest possible progress towards achieving the mission.

Third-sector organisations face countless opportunities to drift away from their primary purpose. They work in an increasingly turbulent environment and, in order to avoid such distraction, they need to be totally clear about the strategies being pursued. Strategies establish direction and priorities. They create a framework within which people can develop detailed plans for individual services and campaigns.

Creating strategies is a process of building coalitions of internal and external stakeholders who are committed to working together to achieve a common mission. Developing strategy should unite the board, the senior management team, staff and volunteers behind a shared conception of future plans and priorities. It should help each person to understand how their part of the organisation fits into the overall picture. It enables senior management to concentrate resources on achieving agreed outcomes, and it should motivate staff to focus their contribution more sharply on key priorities.

In today's demanding environment, managers need to have a clear conception of how their work fits in to the overall strategy of the organisation. They need to anticipate relevant changes in the external environment, so far as is possible, and develop appropriate responses. They have to have a rationale that explains the allocation of resources to different objectives or activities, and they have to demonstrate to funders precisely what will be or has been achieved with their money.

Organisations working in the most rapidly changing environments need more frequent reviews of strategy than those in comparatively stable environments. A major review of strategy used to be on the agenda every five years. Nowadays strategy is kept under constant review and major re-examinations often take place every three years, and sometimes every second year.

Creating strategy should be viewed as a process of learning and discovery. It involves anticipating changes in the external environment, understanding the heart of the organisation's competencies and having an analysis of the organisation's strategic position. Armed with these insights, strategising involves making high-level choices, and devising plans, performance measures and timescales that establish how and when strategic objectives will be achieved. Strategies focus people on a 'narrative' that enables them all to fit the activities of the organisation into a broader context.

This chapter is about the process of developing strategies for the whole organisation. It sets out:

- the different ways strategy evolves in organisations;
- how to analyse an organisation's strategic position;
- ways of making strategic choices;
- how to design a strategic planning process;
- some common strategic dilemmas that third-sector organisations face.

The next chapter focuses on developing strategies for departments, services and campaigns.

7.2 STRATEGY EVOLVES

Strategy changes with time and is influenced by circumstances and people. It is not something that is developed only when a strategic plan is produced. There are three ways in which strategy evolves.

First, strategy develops through **experimentation and learning.** Opportunities are presented or created and initiatives are pursued. These ideas are tested and experience is gained before major new strategies are agreed. Most organisations reduce the risks inherent in any significant new undertaking by establishing pilots, learning from the results and modifying proposals as they are developed. Those that work well may then become an essential part of the organisation's strategy.

Second, the development of strategy is a **political process.** Strategy results from a process of bargaining, negotiation and trade-off between people with competing interests in the organisation. Powerful individuals and groups therefore have a strong influence over an organisation's strategy. How they view an issue may be more relevant than the factual accuracy of their arguments. From this perspective, strategy is not the result of dispassionate analysis – it is a reflection of the power and influence of different stakeholders.

Finally, strategy is the result of an **analytical process.** In this commonly held view, strategy emerges from a systematic and logical analysis of the organisation's environment and its current activities. This leads to the establishment of new objectives and strategies which usually take the form of a strategic plan.

THREE PARADIGMS OF STRATEGY FORMULATION

Paradigm	Characteristics	Assumptions
Experimentation and learning	Strategy requires creative new ideas	Winning strategies can only be articulated in retrospect
Political	Strategy reflects the power and influence of individuals	Strategies are a process of negotiation
Analytical	Strategy is a logical process of setting a mission, objectives and strategies and then taking action	The future can be forecast There is one best solution

In practice all three paradigms are needed and are usually operating simultaneously. Creative new ideas are essential to drive organisations forward, and they don't necessarily happen when the strategic plan is being prepared. But they are not sufficient to give organisations a deep understanding of direction and priorities, and anyhow decisions will eventually depend on the power and influence of people with greater authority. Hence there is the need for a periodic and rigorous planning process that aligns all parts of the organisation behind a shared set of strategic priorities.

POLITICS AND STRATEGY

The National Orchestra faced many competing demands when it began to think about future development:

- the musicians wanted good pay and opportunities to play new and challenging pieces of music
- the education department wanted more musicians to support their community music schemes in schools
- the fundraisers wanted a popular programme of events to attract corporate sponsors
- the board wanted high-profile public events to increase the status of the orchestra
- the conductor wanted more rehearsal time to improve the quality of performances

A strategic plan failed to solve the problem. These competing demands on money and musicians' time had to be resolved through negotiation and agreement.

Strategy is required at every level

Just as objectives are required at every level of an organisation, strategies are also required at every level. In a smaller organisation, strategy may operate at two levels: there will be an overall strategy for the organisation as a whole, and separate strategies for each service or each service user group. Large organisations that are divided into different operational divisions may require:

- an overall strategy
- divisional strategies
- service level strategies.

The overall strategy in both large and small organisations is concerned with the definition of the service user group (i.e. who is included and who is not), the range of services to be offered to these people, and the allocation of resources between different groups of people or different services. The divisional strategy is concerned with the achievement of particular components of the corporate strategy, and service level strategy is concerned with the objectives and performance of individual services.

This does not mean that long and complex strategic planning documents are needed at every level. Indeed there is a danger of 'bureaucratising' strategic planning. What is required is that each level has clearly established objectives, performance measures, priorities and implementation timescales, ideally set out on as few sheets of paper as possible.

7.3 STRATEGIC REVIEWS, POSITIONS AND KEY ISSUES

The management of strategy can be divided into five basic elements These are shown as a diamond to emphasise that strategy making is not a linear process. Although there is a logical sequence to reviewing the organisation, considering alternative ways forward and developing an implementation plan, all the processes are in practice going on simultaneously, each continuously informing the others.

This also emphasises the idea that whilst periodic deep reviews of strategy are necessary, in practice, strategy is continuously evolving, with the current strategic position informing choices that are being made and their implementation, and both informing re-assessments of strategic position and updates to the formal strategic plan.

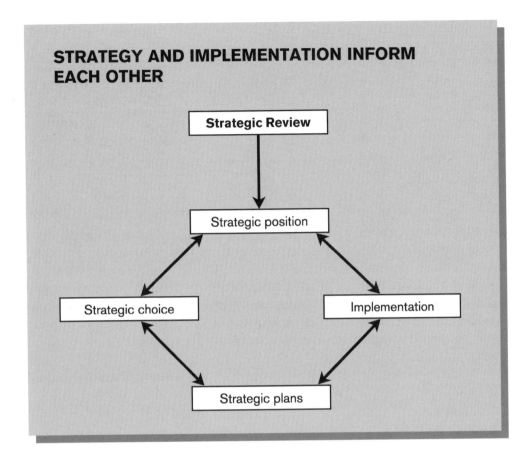

STRATEGY AND IMPLEMENTATION INFORM EACH OTHER

Strategic review

Reviewing strategy is a process of monitoring changes in the external environment and developments within the organisation in order to gain a deeper understanding of the organisation's strategic position. It may involve reviewing the mission, the objectives or the strategies the organisation is pursuing, or any combination of all three.

The process involves collecting data about the way the world around the organisation is likely to change and assessing the impact of these changes. Key strategic information needs to be gathered and assembled in formats that give clear insights into past achievements, current competencies and critically important external trends that will have an impact on the organisation.

The aim of reviewing strategy is to focus people on the most significant trends – those few things that are 'driving change'.

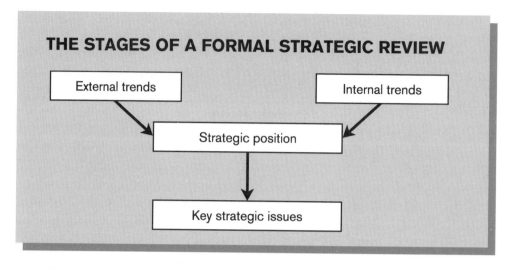

Formal strategic reviews are usually undertaken every few years at the beginning of a strategic planning process. These formal reviews help people to learn about the underlying trends influencing an organisation's strategy. They can also point to important data that the organisation should collect systematically on a regular basis.

Questions which the review may need to answer include:

External review

What are the key social and economic trends directly relevant to the organisation and its objectives (e.g. benefit levels, social exclusion)?

What are the key political trends that will affect the organisation during the plan period (e.g. growth of higher education, European legislation)?

What significant technological developments are likely during the plan period (e.g. for helping people with disabilities to communicate)?

What will the key trends in funding sources and methods be (e.g. contracting and saturation of the direct mail market)?

What will the critical political decisions and actions be (e.g. welfare reform, investment in education)?

Internal review

Who are the organisation's users (e.g. age, gender, minority representation)?

How will their needs change in the plan period (e.g. services may need to change as users grow older)?

What proportion of the total population of potential users is the organisation reaching (e.g. the percentage of each user group that the organisation supports)?

How much subsidy is the organisation allocating to each service and user group (e.g. the amount of unrestricted funds spent on residential homes or on young service users)?

How has the overall allocation of subsidy changed and is it appropriate (e.g. should the proportion spent on older users increase)?

External review

What will the critical changes in the demographics of service users and funders be, and how will their needs change (e.g. demand for different types of services or methods of delivery)?

What cultural trends will the organisation have to respond to (e.g. user-centred service delivery)?

Who will the organisation be competing with during the plan period (e.g. new competitors from the private and third sectors)?

What are the strengths and weaknesses of our competitors (e.g. marketing, bid winning, cost structure, access to capital)?

Internal review

What campaign successes have been achieved and what were the keys to those successes (e.g. parliamentary achievements)?

What are the organisation's critical human, physical and financial resources, and how have they changed (e.g. people's skills, funding sources)?

What are the organisation's key intangible resources (e.g. its key relationships, contacts, reputation)?

The external environment may be analysed in a framework such as PESTEL (Political, Economic, Social, Technological, Environmental and Legal trends) or PESTO (Political, Economic, Social, Technological and Other). Whatever format is chosen, it is important to avoid the trap of simply summarising all relevant external trends. The key to making this kind of analysis really valuable is to pinpoint those **changes that will have greatest impact** on the organisation and, crucially, what those impacts are likely to be.

Internal reviews need to incorporate thorough analysis of costs, a topic often overlooked in third-sector organisations. Reviews should generate new insights into the costs of externally delivered services. In particular they should identify how unrestricted funds are allocated to different services or campaigns, so that people can see how the resources over which the organisation has the greatest control are being used.

Reviews should also identify the full costs of services, per user (e.g. per pupil) and per unit of time (e.g. hour of counselling), taking into account indirect as well as direct costs, to determine whether the organisation is generating and allocating enough money to cover the real costs of what it does. Where this is not the case, organisations need to explicitly determine whether a different distribution would increase the organisation's impact and effectiveness. The same should apply to fundraising costs.

Reviews should also look at the costs of internally delivered services as there may be opportunities to reduce costs by outsourcing services or by purchasing them jointly with other organisations.

Reviews invariably generate a great deal of information. An essential step is to distil the data, focusing on the information that is most pertinent to the future development of the organisation.

KEY CHANGES IN THE EXTERNAL ENVIRONMENT FOR BROOK

Brook is a provider of free and confidential sexual health advice and services for people under 25. Specially trained doctors, nurses, counsellors, and outreach and information workers provide professional advice to over 200,000 young people each year. Brook is a federated network of organisations that work together with one shared vision, mission, values and brand identity.

In 2007, Brook began the process of strategic planning for 2009–19. The process was kick-started with a trustee planning day where a range of stakeholders – including clients, service managers, government officials and voluntary sector leaders – were invited to give 'evidence'.

This process enabled trustees and executive officers to understand the changing external environment to enable the development of a realistic and positive strategic vision. Following this consultation an ongoing process of engagement with staff, trustees and young people across the network began.

Trustees agreed the key drivers in the external environment were:

1. Increasing rates of sexually transmitted infections with continued inequalities in teenage pregnancy, sexual health and the provision of services across the UK

2. Ongoing media interest in issues relating to young people and sex in a culture that is not supportive about young people and sexuality

3. Ongoing challenges and threats to young people's rights to confidentiality, and pressure from some safeguarding boards to follow mandatory reporting protocols

4. Devolution, the changing NHS commissioning environment and an increasing number of services being put out to tender, and a move towards joined-up children's services. Within this, some services are being commissioned across the age range, and some across the range of health issues

5. The increased role of charities in public service delivery and a continued emphasis on partnership working and the provision of integrated services

6. Increasing need to demonstrate service quality and the impact of our education

7. The changing consumer worlds of clients who are increasingly discerning about the services and support they need, and active consumers of new media

8. Rising numbers of younger clients and an increased focus on boys and young men whose needs may not be well met by other services

Developing insights into strategic position

Strategic position sets the organisation in its environmental context. It draws together the information from the internal and external reviews to produce a summary of the situation. There are a number of techniques which can be used to enhance understanding of strategic position. These may sound rather elaborate, but in practice their greatest use is as thinking tools to help people look at the review from different perspectives.

Gap analysis is a method of focusing attention on service users' needs. It involves preparing an assessment of people's needs and comparing these with services currently available. This can be done with a survey of users, by talking with other providers or by seeking views from knowledgeable people inside or outside the organisation.

GREATEST WELFARE NEEDS OF THE EX-SERVICE COMMUNITY

An omnibus survey conducted across the UK led the Royal British Legion strategic review to conclude that there were large unmet welfare needs amongst the ex-service community:

- An estimated 4.4 million ex-service people were living with a long-term illness, disability or infirmity
- An estimated 1.5 million people were experiencing three or more difficulties in their lives
- An estimated 530,000 people reported experiencing difficulties and not receiving the help they need
- More than one in ten veterans aged under 45 were suffering from a mental illness (compared to three in one hundred nationally) and unemployment amongst the 25–49 age group was twice the national average

The research concluded that the greatest unmet welfare needs of the ex-service community were:

- mobility difficulties
- problems maintaining homes and gardens
- exhaustion or pain
- common and long-term mental health issues
- financial or employment problems

The aim is to make judgements that help identify the most pressing unmet needs of service users and thus pinpoint areas where new services are most required or where existing services most need expansion.

Value for money analysis is a method of comparing the benefits of different services with their costs and, more specifically, the subsidy which needs to be found from fundraising or other sources. This involves calculating the subsidy required to provide each service and dividing it by the number of service users to give unit subsidy figures. These can then be compared with people's judgements about the importance of each service. This does not mean that services with higher subsidies are less valuable, but it does help the organisation to understand the costs of expanding each service and the savings gained from reducing them.

COMPARING COSTS AND BENEFITS

An organisation of people with disabilities carried out a review of the cost of services; it yielded the following figures:

	Income £'000	Expenditure £'000	Subsidy £'000	Users	Unit subsidy £
Holiday service	15	55	40	200	200
Help line	–	25	25	2,500	10
Residential care	100	120	20	10	2,000
Employment advice	50	60	10	400	25
Equipment loan	10	25	15	500	30

As a result of the review, the board agreed a strategy of:

- expanding employment advice because it was providing excellent value for money
- reducing the holiday service because similar holidays were available from other charities at a lower cost
- negotiating increased fees from local authorities to reduce the unit subsidy of the residential care home

SWOT is a well-known mnemonic that stands for Strengths, Weaknesses, Opportunities and Threats. These are compared for an organisation or particular services, the aim being to produce a succinct statement of the organisation's strategic position. This is a valuable way of summarising data obtained from a strategic review. It is often used as a group brainstorming technique to encourage people to think about strategic issues. However, when material is generated in this way, it should be tested thoroughly against the evidence of a review, to avoid the danger of producing a series of platitudes.

Identification of key strategic issues

Having gained an understanding of an organisation's strategic position, the final stage of a review is to distil all the learning into a set of key issues that need to be addressed. This is one of the most critical steps in the process; it provides the foundation on which the strategic plan will be built.

Strategic issues are generated by comparing the mission and the objectives with the information generated in the review about the achievements and performance of the organisation. This can be done by individuals and by groups, and it is likely to be an iterative process in which first thoughts are developed and then continuously refined until consensus emerges around the most fundamental questions.

KEY STRATEGIC ISSUES FOR BATTERSEA DOGS AND CATS HOME

Every year the home rescues over 10,000 dogs and cats, re-unites almost 3,000 and re-homes over 5,000. It has an income of over £12 million per annum. The organisation conducted a strategic review which included an analysis of its strengths, weaknesses, opportunities and threats. It also included a review of the impact of changes in the outside world on the Home. The following were identified as the key issues a new, longer-term strategic plan for the Home needed to address:

1. Ways to improve further management of the intake of dogs, in particular in response to the increase in more challenging breeds
2. Ways to improve further the movement of animals through the Home
3. The need to develop a clearer vision of the Home's unique contribution in the animal welfare sector and how to communicate this more effectively through campaigning, through the media, and through education work
4. The need to develop a more comprehensive, longer-term funding strategy for existing fundraising and to establish new funding streams
5. The next steps in enhancing the physical environment of the Home for dogs and cats, for staff and volunteers, and for the public
6. How to promote further responsible dog and cat ownership
7. How to further increase the Home's national profile and presence
8. Clarifying the Home's international remit
9. Further strengthening the leadership and management of the Home, and the way staff are recruited, inducted, rewarded and developed

In some circumstances, a review will raise big issues that will influence the future direction of the whole organisation. In other circumstances, the overall direction will be secure and the issues will be about adjustments to current strategies.

7.4 MAKING STRATEGIC CHOICES

The process of strategic review identifies key issues such as new needs among service users, new or better ways of meeting needs, or new threats such as changing funding arrangements or competition from other suppliers. The priorities may initially seem daunting – too much to do and too few resources to do it. So, governing boards and managers need to make choices about what resources can be raised and what the organisation can realistically achieve with those resources.

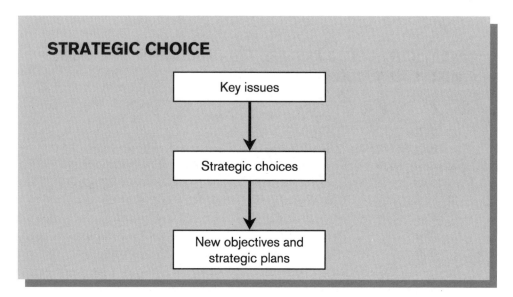

Making choices about priorities will always involve making judgements based on experience and evidence. Every option will have benefits for the people the organisation serves or for the campaign objectives it wishes to achieve. The problem is one of weighing the benefits against the costs and the risks of pursuing different strategies. The process needs to be structured to encourage rigorous debate and clear decisions. A number of techniques can be used to assist organisations to make strategic choices.

Making strategic choice more rigorous

When a range of strategies has been identified, choices have to be made about which to pursue, how much to invest in each and how fast to proceed with implementation. As resources are always constrained, difficult decisions cannot be avoided.

One approach to making this process more systematic is to review and unpack the **theory of change** for each of the organisation's services and campaigns. A theory of change is a series of cause and effect relationships that connect actions to desired results. It is a way of systematically identifying the steps that may be needed to achieve the desired outcome. It encourages rigorous thinking about the content of a strategy and it enables people to make judgements about whether the proposed actions are likely to achieve the desired results.

When this approach is taken to analysing alternative strategies for achieving the same objective, the choice can be based on judgements about which strategy is most likely to achieve the desired outcome.

Considering the resources required to deliver each step also encourages more realistic views on the funding required. Assessing timescales encourages more realistic judgements about the time required to deliver the desired outcomes.

ALTERNATIVE THEORIES OF CHANGE FOR IMPROVING FARM ANIMAL WELFARE

A production-led strategy

IF we fund a few sympathetic farmers to test 'welfare friendly' approaches to farming...

...THEN we can demonstrate that there are alternatives that are less cruel and more economic.

IF we promote these alternative practices to 'semi-sympathetic' farmers...

...THEN farmers will begin to be convinced that different practices are economic.

IF we have farmers who are willing to champion new methods...

...THEN we can persuade less sympathetic farmers to adopt less cruel practices.

IF we persuade large numbers of farmers to change their practices...

...THEN we will begin to reduce cruelty to farm animals on a wider scale.

A regulatory and consumer-led strategy

IF we persuade the EU to require that produce is labelled to identify the welfare of the animal...

...THEN consumers will be empowered to choose high-welfare products.

IF consumers are persuaded to buy high-welfare products...

...THEN retailers will stock more of such products.

IF retailers purchase more high-welfare products...

...THEN more farmers will change their practices and reduce cruelty to animals.

IF some farmers change their practices...

...THEN regulation to end unacceptable practices becomes more achievable.

Another approach is to systematically **review strategic options against the mission.** Going back to the mission provides a rational basis for considering which of various priorities are most important. The mission provides the framework for discussion of the options. However, as we have already seen, strategy is an iterative process, and sometimes the mission has to be changed in order to incorporate new and important objectives. So the method is far from foolproof!

Another approach is to **attach a weighting** to proposals that are competing for limited resources. Managers putting forward a number of proposals are asked to rate them according to criteria such as:

- critical strategic importance
- important but not essential
- pursue when funds available.

This exercise can be carried out twice, once for projects requiring capital funding and once for projects requiring revenue funding.

A similar approach involves identifying the different groups that the organisation is trying to reach and using a 'star rating' system to answer questions such as:

- What is our potential impact on this group?
- What is our current impact on this group?
- To what extent do the proposals increase our impact on the group?

Another frequently used method is **scheduling.** Scheduling is useful both as a way of prioritising (without turning down projects altogether) and because it identifies optimum sequencing of projects where there are inter-dependencies between them.

Organisations can compare themselves with other organisations receiving funds from the same sources. They can ask what their **distinctiveness** will be in future compared with their competitors. They may be better placed to become a low-cost, high-volume supplier of the service, or alternatively to become a niche provider, servicing a carefully targeted service user group. These considerations then influence which projects and initiatives to pursue.

An important source of information for making choices is **the organisation's recent experience** of things that worked and things that did not. Learning from that experience can provide valuable insights which can be used to inform the strategic choices (see Chapter 17, Creating a learning organisation).

Before choices are finally made, organisations can **test strategic choices.** One test is to consult relevant stakeholder groups and seek their reactions to the proposed choices. Another test is to analyse the sensitivity of particular projects to changing assumptions, looking for example at the implications of the loss of funding or the impact of new government regulations. Looking at the financial effects of a growing or declining demand for a service can **test the economic sensitivity** of proposals to different assumptions.

In practice, making strategic choices will always involve a high degree of judgement. Techniques help to structure the problem, but ultimately they cannot replace experience and wisdom.

There are a number of **common pitfalls** to avoid when making strategic choices. Some organisations, quite rightly, thrive on opportunism. The third sector is known for its ability to produce social innovations. New ideas and new funding sources drive the organisation's strategy in a series of unplanned and incremental steps. In these organisations opportunism is a crucial ingredient of a successful strategy. Nevertheless, organisations that are driven exclusively by opportunism risk becoming a hostage to external funders; forced to pursue only those things for which they can raise money, they put their future at the whim of their funders. Organisations that gain control over their strategy begin to determine their own future.

Some organisations compromise when it comes to strategic choice. In part this is necessary – diverse constituencies are often held together by giving a little to each group. But too much compromise is dangerous. An organisation that steps incrementally from focusing on a few key objectives to a brief so wide that it ends up doing a little of everything risks not doing anything particularly well.

Finally, some organisations write the strategy in such general terms that everyone can agree to it. This avoids making difficult choices, but it greatly reduces the value of the strategic management process.

Risks and critical success factors

Once the strategy is clear, the risks of not achieving the objectives can be identified and assessed. This is an effective way of testing the robustness of the strategy. A long list of risks can be developed and then organised to identify the probability of them occurring and the implications for the strategy. It may then be necessary to revise the strategy to minimise the risks or put in place plans that avoid them altogether.

A related test is to identify the **critical success factors**, those things without which the strategy could not be achieved. These will be items over which the organisation has little or no control, but which are essential to achieving the objective (for example agreement of another organisation to work in partnership or approval of the board to borrow funds to finance the plan).

The list of critical success factors can be used to judge how realistic the strategy is and whether it needs to be changed to make it more achievable.

7.5 **DEVELOPING STRATEGIC PLANS**

This section explores the process of planning. It establishes the circumstances that need to exist for an organisation to develop its strategy in a formal way. It explains how to **plan the planning process**, how to improve existing processes, and how to avoid common pitfalls.

Preconditions for strategic planning

There is never an ideal time for strategic planning. Major determinants of when to initiate a strategic planning process will be the time that has elapsed since the last plan was produced, the extent to which it has dated and critical changes in the policy or competitive environment that call for a new strategic plan.

Plans should not necessarily be produced on a regular three, four or five year cycle. These risk creating a bureaucratic process that can consume a great deal of effort, but not add high value. These days new strategies should be created when they are most needed and in response to changing external circumstances.

Having said that, there are a number of circumstances when strategic planning will be less appropriate or will not work effectively as a management tool:

1. **Commitment of the chair and the chief executive.** A high level of commitment, particularly from the chief executive, is an essential ingredient of strategic planning. If the chief executive is not seen to be in command of the strategic planning process and is not dedicated to using the plan as a managerial tool, scepticism will creep in and planning will not be effective. In a similar vein, the chair needs to be involved and committed to demonstrate to the board that planning is for real and not just a paper exercise.
2. **The senior management team needs to be stable.** If a number of senior managers are in the process of leaving or if a major re-organisation of the senior management team is imminent, there is a danger that strategic planning will become dominated by internal politics. This is not a moment for sitting back and dispassionately reviewing the organisation and its prospects.
3. **Lack of major crises.** If the organisation is in crisis or if one is imminent, short-term pressures will predominate. The loss of a major source of funding, deep divisions between key individuals or the resignation of a number of board members are all circumstances that militate against a participative approach to planning. For planning to be effective, there needs to be adequate stability in the organisation and a willingness on the part of senior staff and the board to be dispassionate.

In strategic planning, both the planning process and the substance of the plan are ultimately matters for the board and senior management, in consultation with staff and volunteers and sometimes with service users and other stakeholders.

Whilst much work is done jointly, management is usually responsible for proposing strategy and the board is always responsible for approving it.

Planning in different circumstances

Organisations' external circumstances influence the freedom they have in determining their future. Some organisations have a great deal of **strategic freedom**. They have broad objectives, most of their income is not tied to specific activities and they can choose not only what they do but how they do it.

Other organisations have very little strategic freedom. Most of their income is restricted to tightly prescribed projects, and there are few options for raising unrestricted income.

Organisations with a lot of freedom can be expansive in their strategic thinking. They can carry out wide-ranging environmental reviews, establish significantly different strategic objectives and reallocate resources to different or new activities. The advantage is that they can be creative in their planning, but the disadvantage is that their plans risk becoming too broad and general and not focused on the specific objectives that the organisation wishes to achieve.

Organisations with little freedom, such as those that are highly dependent on winning contracts, have to focus more sharply on strategic developments that are within their control. They may plan to increase their strategic freedom, but the core of their strategy is likely to be concentrated on developments arising from their existing services, knowledge and expertise.

Some organisations have a comparatively **predictable environment**. They know broadly how many users there are in their area of work and how their needs will change as they grow older. These organisations can plan for the longer term and they need to revise their plans less frequently.

Others have a much less predictable environment which may change significantly in a short space of time. Campaigning organisations are a common example. These organisations need to plan to have the capacity to respond to different circumstances. Their plans will have shorter time horizons. They will need powerful campaign strategies, but they will also need to concentrate on building the organisation's capacity so that it can respond decisively when the next opportunity arises.

Planning the planning process

The objective of strategic planning is to build a widely shared conception of the future of the organisation and its managerial priorities. The glossy document is a by-product. Getting the planning process right is therefore just as important as getting the right plan. Issues that managers should consider as they embark on a planning process include:

1. **Legitimising the process throughout the organisation.** People in significant positions in the organisation need to be committed to planning. Their involvement in the decision to embark upon strategic planning and in the design of the strategic planning process is an essential ingredient for success. Some people may have genuine concerns about the process and its implications for the organisation. If so, they too need to be involved in the design of the process.

2. **Clarifying who will be involved at different stages.** Ideally, strategic planning should involve as many people as possible from the organisation's different constituencies. However, there is a trade-off to be made. Consultation takes time and not everyone can be involved in every stage. Decisions must be made about whom to involve at different stages of the process and how to involve them, in order to maximise their commitment to the plan. Once these decisions have been taken, everyone should be told how and when they will be expected to make their contributions.

3. **Integrating with other management procedures.** The strategic plan needs to fit with budget preparation and other important procedures such as submitting grant applications and preparing for performance reviews commissioned by funding bodies. Managers should anticipate having to make trade-offs because the timetable can never meet everyone's requirements. In practice, strategic planning, even in a small organisation, is likely to take at least three or four months. In larger organisations and those where more extensive consultation is required, between six and nine months is more likely to be appropriate for a major review of strategy. Successful integration requires that the timetables for planning, budget-setting and performance management all fit together.

4. **Challenging conventional wisdom.** Strategic planning is a process of challenging existing beliefs, checking whether assumptions still hold and developing new perspectives. This may require the involvement of outsiders and of people who are close to the organisation but not an integral part of it. Designing them into the process will help to ensure that there is independent challenge to conventional wisdom.

5. **Communicating strategy.** Communication is an essential ingredient for effective implementation. Sometimes there are external stakeholder groups who can contribute more to the organisation if they understand its strategic priorities. These can include funding bodies, members, major donors, service users, branches, local centres, local committees and any other group that has a relationship with the organisation.

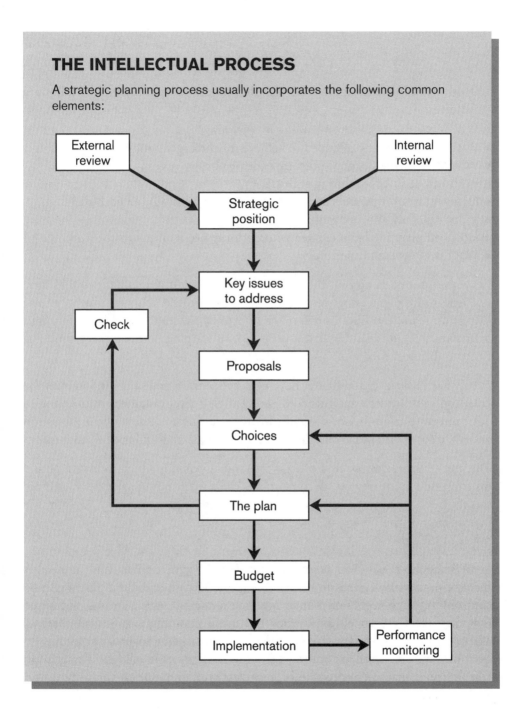

THE INTELLECTUAL PROCESS

A strategic planning process usually incorporates the following common elements:

Preparing strategic plans

Preparing strategic plans needs to be thought about in terms of a 'social process' that involves different people at different stages. It usually starts with management designing a process and consulting on their initial ideas with staff and board members. This should result in a short document that describes the proposed process and is formally approved by the board as the basis for planning.

The document about planning the planning process should answer the following questions:

- Why is the organisation embarking on planning?
- What is the planning intended to achieve for the organisation?
- What are the key stages of preparing the plan?
- Who will be involved during each stage?
- How will board members and staff be consulted at the end of each stage?
- When will decisions be taken?
- How will planning be integrated with performance management?
- What is the overall timetable?

Once the process is agreed, the review stage can begin. Organisations that have not engaged in planning for some time, and those with a relatively new leadership team, can find the internal and external reviews time-consuming. This is unavoidable, not least because a great deal of learning is taking place while the review is being carried out.

Even when basic facts and figures have been collected, it takes time to interpret the data and develop new insights into the changing circumstances. Allow time to draw out conclusions before summarising the strategic position of the organisation and identifying the critical questions that the strategic plan will need to address.

The end of the review stage is often a convenient point at which to have a period of consultation. A review document can be circulated to a wide variety of stakeholders, and workshops can be held with key groups to explain the conclusions of the review in order to seek their input and to explain the next stages in the process.

Sometimes the review will point to a small number of critical strategic choices that the organisation needs to make. One of the keys to successful planning is to confront these choices, rather than agreeing strategies which are so generalised that they meet everyone's aspirations but avoid choosing between alternatives. These choices may need to be the subject of a consultation process, leading to decisions by the board on future directions and priorities. When consultation takes place, management needs to be very clear with everyone about:

- who is being consulted
- when consultation ends
- who is taking decisions
- when they will be taken
- how they will be announced.

Sometimes the review will require that a series of task groups be established to address specific issues that the plan needs to resolve. Such groups can involve staff and board members working together, since this will increase ownership of the final plan.

Eventually the time comes to put the plan together. It may include contributions from task groups and from senior managers, and it may be put together by a senior manager. In the end, though, the content of the draft plan needs to have a significant input from the chief executive. He or she has the overview, understands the politics of the organisation and needs, more than anyone, to own the plan.

A temptation at this stage is to be excessively ambitious and to adopt priorities that far exceed the organisation's resources and, more usually, its management capacity. This should be avoided by ruthless prioritisation.

Draft plans benefit from widespread consultation with staff and the board and, sometimes, other stakeholders. Following a number of re-drafts (usually necessary to get the thinking really straight), a final plan can be put to the board for approval.

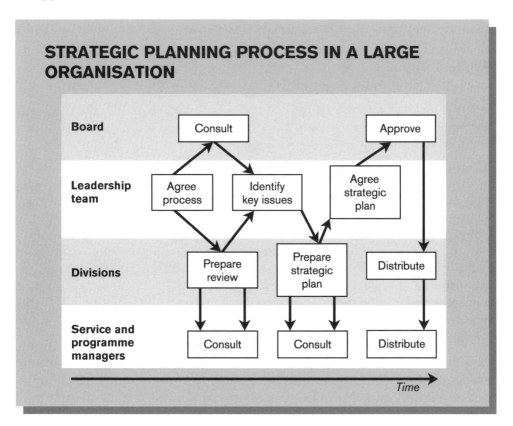

STRATEGIC PLANNING PROCESS IN A LARGE ORGANISATION

SCENARIO PLANNING

Scenario planning is a technique used to encourage managers to think the unthinkable. It is particularly valuable when significant changes in the external environment are anticipated and when managers have become set in their ways and need to be encouraged to be more imaginative.

One way to prepare scenarios is to put together a group of managers and ask them to prepare a number of scenarios for the future based on fundamentally different assumptions. The assumptions could be significant increases or declines in unrestricted income, the possibility of a major technological breakthrough or the consequences of a new government policy.

Managers should work in an iterative way, brainstorming the possibilities, working out the consequences and then writing them up in a series of different scenarios. Generally three scenarios are developed: an optimistic one, a pessimistic one and a middle-of-the-road one.

These can then be used by other managers to test the consequences of the scenario on their area of work. The results can be fed into the strategic plan in the form of a sensitivity analysis that shows where the plan is most sensitive to changes in assumptions.

Content of plans

The content of the plan needs to:

- reflect the organisation's values
- communicate the key messages
- provide the basis for reviewing progress.

In smaller organisations the document is usually called the 'strategic plan'. In larger organisations, which have separate strategic or operational plans for each of their services, the document is sometimes called the 'strategic framework'. This sets the overall context for the detailed service and campaign strategies that will be prepared subsequently.

When it comes to preparing the document itself, the most useful plans:

- are **short** and to the point – say 10-20 pages;
- **mix communication methods** – such as text, diagrams, bullet-point lists and charts;
- are **inspirational** – demonstrating what will be done;
- **avoid detail** – that can be documented separately.

Each time a planning process is undertaken, the organisation will learn how to create more effective plans. The first time is usually the most difficult. Subsequent processes should become more sophisticated, use a wider range of techniques and drive the organisation up the planning learning curve.

Requirements for top-quality plans

The best plans have the following characteristics:

- They establish a compelling mission.
- The contain a limited number of achievable SMART strategic objectives, which can be used to track progress and measure performance.
- They articulate the key strategies for achieving each of the objectives.
- They embody realistic judgements about what can be achieved within the resources and timescale of the plan.
- They are specific but adaptable, not set in concrete but not so generalised that they can mean anything to anyone.
- Strategies for raising money from donors are tightly integrated with service and campaign strategies.
- They set a clear financial framework.
- The allocation of resources to particular objectives is clear.
- They assess risks and establish mitigating actions.
- They contain a summary implementation timetable.
- The allocation of responsibilities is clear and ideally aligned with the organisation structure.

Ultimately, the key to successful planning is the synthesis of external and internal information that enables people to concentrate an overview of the organisation. This allows people to engage in clear strategic thinking. Penetrating thought and good judgement can then be used to create powerful strategies.

One trap is making an assumption that a top-quality plan will solve all the organisation's problems. Postponing actions until the plan is completed can be tempting but it is usually an excuse for avoiding a decision. Plans are not a panacea; they are a structured means for conducting a rational debate and coming to an agreement about future priorities.

STAGES IN THE DEVELOPMENT OF STRATEGIC PLANNING CAPABILITY

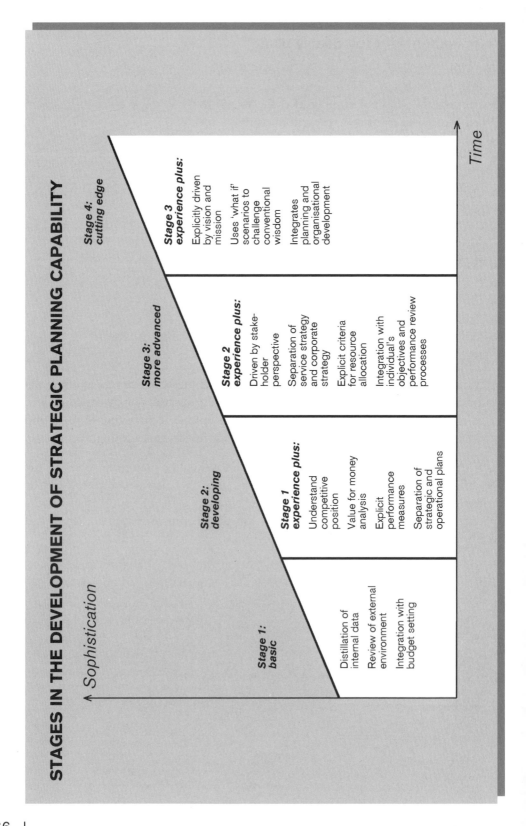

← *Sophistication*

Time →

Stage 1:
basic

Distillation of internal data

Review of external environment

Integration with budget setting

Stage 2:
developing

Stage 1
experience plus:

Understand competitive position

Value for money analysis

Explicit performance measures

Separation of strategic and operational plans

Stage 3:
more advanced

Stage 2
experience plus:

Driven by stake-holder perspective

Separation of service strategy and corporate strategy

Explicit criteria for resource allocation

Integration with individual's objectives and performance review processes

Stage 4:
cutting edge

Stage 3
experience plus:

Explicitly driven by vision and mission

Uses 'what if' scenarios to challenge conventional wisdom

Integrates planning and organisational development

7.6 **RESOLVING COMMON STRATEGIC DILEMMAS**

Organisations often discover that there are some fundamental dilemmas to be considered. These usually emerge at the strategic choice stage.

The strategic dilemmas which appear most frequently are set out here to illustrate some of the common issues that organisations have to address. When the strategy-making process has reached one of these dilemmas, managers know the time has come to make judgements.

1. **A little help for many or a great deal of help for a few**
   Many organisations have to choose between making a substantial difference to a limited number of people or applying their resources more widely to give a little help to a lot of people:
   - Development agencies may have to decide whether to make a substantial difference to a few communities or spread their resources more thinly across many countries.
   - Disability organisations may face a choice between offering substantial support to a few service users (perhaps people with the most profound disability) and giving a little help to many people with a mild disability.

2. **Treat the symptoms or the cause**
   Most organisations want to strike at the fundamental causes of the problem they seek to address, but are also acutely conscious of the day-to-day impact of the problem itself:
   - Health and disability organisations may have to decide how much money to spend on support and services for people with the illness or disability and how much to put into research towards a cure.
   - Social service organisations may have to make choices between meeting people's immediate needs, doing preventative work or undertaking research into the more fundamental causes of a problem.

3. **Provide services or campaign for change**
   Many service-giving organisations start to campaign for changes in government policy or funding when they realise that their contribution will always be small compared to the size of the problem. Similarly, some campaigning organisations start to provide services to demonstrate what needs to be done:
   - Disability organisations may have to find a balance between providing services and campaigning. They may decide that they can potentially achieve much more by changing people's attitudes towards disability than through direct service provision.
   - Development agencies may have to balance lobbying activities with practical projects. They recognise that, for example, successfully campaigning for debt write-offs might achieve much more than the practical projects they fund – but complete write-off may take many years to achieve, and people need help now.

- Medical charities may have to balance lobbying government to put more money into their field of research with using that money to fund their own research programme.

4. **Focus or diversify services**

   Organisations can choose between concentrating on relatively few services and building their expertise in those tightly specified fields, or diversifying their expertise and delivering a wide range of services.

   Many pressures encourage diversification. Funds may be offered for a new service; members or service users may call for new services to meet changing needs as people grow older; and staff may push for new services because they offer new challenges and career-development opportunities.

   Despite these pressures there are powerful arguments for concentrating on particular services. Economies of scale mean that services can be provided to more people at lower cost. Focusing leads to increased expertise in all aspects of the service.

   - Campaigning organisations may have to choose between spreading their efforts over a number of campaign fronts and focusing on the achievement of a few tightly specified objectives.
   - Research organisations may have to decide whether to put new investment money into a limited number of specialities, thus gaining a reputation in these fields, or spread the money over a wider range of specialities.

5. **Hold virtuously to beliefs or be tempted by new resources**

   Many organisations face the dilemma of whether to hold righteously to their core beliefs or to compromise in order to gain new resources:

   - Choices have to be made between accepting funds from government initiatives or turning the money down because the organisation is being seduced away from its core cause.
   - Organisations have to decide whether to seek sponsorship from industries they may not approve of or to hold tightly to their values and accept that fundraising costs may rise.
   - Fundraising organisations know that pushing the emotive side of the cause (the starving baby, the child with profound disabilities) will sometimes raise more money. But it also distorts the public's perception of the beneficiary group, whose ultimate wish is likely to be a fair chance in life rather than charity.

All these dilemmas are best resolved by allocating time to discuss and debate alternative ways forward to maximise support for final decisions.

SUMMARY OF KEY POINTS

Strategy focuses organisations

- Strategies are broad groups of priorities that describe how an organisation will achieve its mission
- Creating strategies builds coalitions of people committed to achieving the mission
- Creating strategy is a process of learning and discovery

Strategy evolves

- Strategy evolves in three ways: as a process of experimentation and learning, as a political process and as a rational analytical process
- Strategy is required at the corporate, divisional and service levels of an organisation

Strategic reviews, positions and key issues

- Strategic reviews gather data on internal and external trends, summarise the organisation's strategic position and identify the key issues which the strategic plan needs to address
- Insights into strategic position can be gained through gap analysis, value for money reviews and reviewing strengths, weaknesses, opportunities and threats

Making strategic choices

- Analysing the 'theory of change' implied by proposed strategies can help to draw out the underlying assumptions on which the strategy is based
- Techniques to help make strategic choices include:
  - reviewing options against the mission
  - weighting proposals
  - scheduling proposals
  - reviewing against distinctive competencies
  - reviewing against recent experience
- Organisations can also test strategic choices with stakeholders and analyse the sensitivity of proposals to changing assumptions or economic circumstances
- Common pitfalls to avoid include excessive optimism, failing to make tough choices and making the strategy so general that it has no real value

Developing strategic plans

- These days new strategies should be created when they are most needed and in response to changing external circumstances rather than on a regular three, four or five-year cycle
- Preconditions for strategic planning include: commitment of the chair and chief executive, a stable leadership team and lack of major short-term crises
- Planning the planning process is critical. Key considerations are:
  - legitimising the process
  - clarifying who will be involved at different stages
  - integrating planning with other management procedures
  - challenging conventional wisdom
  - communicating the new strategy
  - developing systems to monitor strategic performance
- Top-quality plans embody clear thinking, are specific but adaptable, show how funds will be raised and have a clear allocation of responsibilities, an implementation timetable and measures of performance
- Planning is a 'social process' that typically happens in stages:
  - agreeing the planning process
  - carrying out a strategic review
  - consulting on key issues from the review
  - making strategic choices
  - drafting the plan
  - consulting on the plan
  - approving the plan

Resolving common strategic dilemmas

- Many organisations face fundamental dilemmas about strategy:
  - provide a little help to many people or more help to a few
  - treat the symptoms or the cause
  - provide services or campaign for change
  - focus or diversify services
  - hold virtuously to beliefs or be tempted by new resources

These are best resolved by allocating time to discuss and debate alternative ways forward.

FURTHER READING

Breakthrough Thinking for Nonprofit Organizations, Bernard Ross and Claire Segal, Jossey-Bass, 2002

Creating Change: Chief Executives on Strategic Planning, Margaret Bolton, ACEVO, 2008

Strategic Planning for Public and Nonprofit Organisations, John M. Bryson, Jossey-Bass, 2004

More and recent books and reports can be found at www.compasspartnership.co.uk.

8 Creating competitive service strategies

8.1 CREATING STRATEGIES AND PLANS FOR SERVICES

When previous editions of this book were written, voluntary income was the single largest source of resources for the charity sector, though not the wider third sector. Now income from government is the largest source of income, much of it from contracts that are subject to competitive tender. This requires a very different set of skills from seeking grants or raising voluntary funds.

Increasingly, the third sector finds itself competing for contracts with private sector organisations and public sector suppliers, as well as with other third-sector organisations, and competition is expected to grow in future.

The previous chapters described how overall strategies are needed to give organisations direction and to build stakeholder commitment to the achievement of strategic objectives. Within the umbrella of the overall strategy, organisations need strategies for each of the services and campaigns that they deliver. Many of these will need to demonstrate how the organisation will compete with other suppliers. Organisations also need operational plans that demonstrate how each service or campaign strategy will be pursued in the coming year.

These strategies and operational plans do not need to be lengthy documents. They need to capture the essential thinking that will ensure the success of the service or campaign. Their value comes from the discipline they impose on thinking about the future in a rigorous and strategic way.

Some organisations have 'business plans' for the organisation as a whole or for individual services, and some funders require a document with this title. A business plan is usually a combination of strategic and operational plans, articulating both longer-term strategy and a more detailed plan and budget. The concepts of strategic and operational plans are dealt with separately in this chapter to establish the clearest possible distinction between strategic and operational thinking.

This distinction also recognises the different psychology of the two processes. Strategic planning is a cooperative and consultative venture in which everyone is striving to discover ways to maximise the impact of the service and so deliver the organisation's mission. Operational planning is about negotiating resources, timescales and responsibilities to ensure that the current year's objectives will be achieved.

This chapter:

- explains how to define services and campaigns as separate 'units' for planning and management;
- describes competitive strategy and explains how to build the capacity to compete successfully;
- shows how to develop service and campaign strategies;
- demonstrates how operational plans are created.

The term **purchaser** refers to the organisation that is purchasing and therefore funding the service. Purchasers are sometimes known as commissioners. The term **provider** refers to the organisation that is delivering the service and the term **service user** refers to the person who is receiving the service.

8.2 DEFINING SERVICES AND CAMPAIGNS

Most organisations deliver a range of interconnected services, often to the same user group. A pre-requisite for developing strategies for these services is to define **service delivery units**. This enables management to put boundaries around activities and to identify clearly who is responsible for them.

Defining services requires careful thought. The very nature of services with social objectives is that the problems they attempt to address are multi-faceted, so service users often need a variety of services to be delivered in an integrated way. Furthermore many services, and particularly innovative ones, tend to be evolutionary in nature, making boundaries harder to establish. When a housing association uses existing staff to offer residents benefit advice or employment training and other 'foyer' services, they are initially inseparable from the housing service. But when they become a significant activity, with their own staff and separate funding, they may need to be considered as a separate service.

Similarly, when an orchestra's musicians do a few school workshops to drum up interest in a particular locality, these are inseparable from its main purpose. When the orchestra is selling its education service to local authorities, using significant amounts of players' time, it eventually becomes a separate service.

Being clear about the definition of the services and campaigns that organisations run is an essential pre-requisite for effective planning. It pinpoints responsibility at a particular point in time for activities that are inevitably evolutionary. The definition should draw boundaries so people preparing plans can specify objectives and prepare strategies for achieving them. This is not to say that, once clearly distinguished, service and campaign managers do not cooperate and coordinate with each other. Indeed, in today's competitive environment, units that work closely together can offer significant advantages to funders looking for integrated solutions to people's problems. But it is essential to start by being clear about the definition of each service and who is responsible for it.

Criteria for establishing service delivery units

Defining services should be based on:

- the needs of service users;
- the different professional skills required to deliver the service;
- the need to relate to different funders and their requirements;
- whether service delivery units should be local, regional or national;
- the need to limit the number of services that are given to each manager (so they focus on doing a few things really well);
- the need to position service delivery units within the organisation's line management structure.

Once a service delivery unit has been defined it requires:

- a clear description of its service user group;
- specified objectives to be achieved with its users;
- a strategy for deploying the resources needed to achieve the objectives;
- a distinct competitive position in relation to other providers;
- systems to monitor achievements against plans;
- timely financial information that sets out income and expenditure of the unit;
- a manager who is responsible (whether part time or full time) for planning, delivering and monitoring the service.

8.3 CONSTRUCTING COMPETITIVE STRATEGY

Competitive strategy has been elaborated extensively in business textbooks, so will not be explored in detail here. The essence of competitive strategy for third-sector organisations bidding for public service contracts involves:

- ensuring that the services fit with the organisation's mission;
- building the skills, abilities and organisation capacity needed to win contracts;
- having a financially viable service proposition that will meet service users' needs and purchasers' requirements better than those of other potential providers;
- knowing how to bring together the necessary skills, processes and management capacity to manage and deliver the services;
- producing a financial surplus to cover all overhead costs, and ideally to contribute to future investments as well.

The first question organisations must ask is whether to compete at all. Some organisations take the view that they do not wish to be in the business of delivering public services for government. They believe that it would reduce their independence and that it could constrain their freedom to campaign vigorously, because of a perceived risk of 'biting the hand that feeds you'.

The Compact between the government and the voluntary sector clearly states that public authorities must 'recognise and support the independence of the sector, including its right... to campaign, to comment on Government policy, and to challenge that policy, irrespective of any funding relationship that might exist'. Nevertheless some organisations do not wish to feel compromised.

Organisations also need to give proper thought to whether or not the proposed service fits with their mission. Some organisations have been seduced into bidding for contracts that have taken them away from their mission and have subsequently withdrawn from that activity. Others have found that considering potential contracts helps them to realise that their mission needs to be reviewed, and that much more could be achieved by delivering contracts. Working in partnership with public bodies may be the best way of achieving their mission.

Organisations also need to consider whether they have the capacity needed to diversify into the business of public service delivery. In the past some organisations have been tempted by attractive financial packages, but found, to their regret, that they have not got the planning, management, HR and financial skills needed to deliver the service successfully.

Building capacity to compete strategically

Building the capacity to compete should start long before opportunities to bid become available. The first step is to build a thorough understanding of the 'competitive advantage' that the organisation wishes to establish over its rivals. Examples of competitive advantage include:

- knowledge and expertise;
- brand and reputation;
- a focus on quality and quality accreditation;
- a research base that informs service delivery;
- economies of scale;
- local knowledge and networks;
- ability to work in partnership;
- the ability to report on outcomes and impacts.

Different combinations of competitive advantage enable organisations to offer purchasers better value for money than their rivals.

Whatever the sources of competitive advantage, being really clear about it also helps organisations to take the all-important decision about whether to bid for a particular contract.

The concepts of marketing, including market segmentation, competitor analysis and market positioning are particularly pertinent here and are described in detail in *Charity Marketing: Meeting Need Through Customer Focus* (see Further reading at the end of this chapter).

Building capacity to win bids

Organisations wanting to deliver or to expand their public services work have to build bid-winning capacity that includes:

- learning precisely what purchasers want by quizzing them and listening very closely to what they say. In a well-designed procurement exercise the purchaser will encourage bidders to be imaginative about how best to deliver, but it is essential also to understand exactly what the purchaser requires;
- structuring, writing and presenting proposals that are clear and succinct and address the requirements of the specification;
- preparing and making presentations that give purchasers confidence in the organisation;
- establishing robust and realistic pricing;
- learning the art of contract negotiation;
- having access to appropriate legal skills;
- reporting on performance and maintaining purchasers' confidence;
- establishing effective and ongoing relationships with purchasers;
- building the organisation's reputation as a reliable provider that adds high value and is easy to work with.

Within all of this they need to ensure that the proposed service will meet the real needs of service users. It is easy to slip into thinking only about the purchasers' conception of needs and forget that providers often have a much clearer understanding of users' needs and how they can best be met.

Bidding is sometimes seen as a distraction from the 'real' work of delivery, but it can often be a highly creative process which requires providers to question how they do their work and how they could do it better or more cost effectively. Opportunities to bid for the first time allow organisations to be imaginative and propose new approaches to solving a problem. Re-tendering for an existing contract is harder because organisations need to challenge their current practices. Bringing in someone who has not been involved previously can help to open people's minds, generate new approaches and create bid-winning proposals.

Putting bids together takes time and effort so organisations should assess their chances of winning before making this commitment. Considerations include:

- the number of bidders there are likely to be;
- the fit between the organisation's aspirations, values and skills and the purchaser's requirements;
- the organisation's ability to add value, to benefit service users, over and above the purchaser's requirements;
- the purchaser's willingness to allow the provider to add value, e.g. the extent to which the specification defines outcomes rather than inputs;
- the provider's capacity to prepare the bid.

Service managers are usually hired for their ability to manage a service, care for people and develop their staff. They may lack the skills required to compete for contracts, so need support from senior managers, board members or consultants. In particular the ability to write well is quite an unusual skill. For large or particularly important contracts, a bid team should be put together including functional, financial and bid-writing expertise.

Competitor analysis

Competing to deliver public services places new demands on the strategy-making process and requires a different mindset. For these organisations, service strategies have to incorporate a sharp understanding of:

- current and potential competitors
- their strengths and weaknesses
- their service offers
- their distinctive competencies
- their competitive advantages
- their pricing strategies.

Some of the information needed on competitors can be gleaned from:

- their publicity materials
- the internet
- previous employees
- purchasers (particularly after successful and unsuccessful bids)
- networking at conferences.

Many organisations are now operating both as charities, with unrestricted income raised in a variety of ways, and as competitors vying for resources in social markets. Each requires a particular mindset, but when it comes to strategic planning these need to be brought together into a coherent whole. The next section looks at this.

COMPETITIVE STRATEGY AT THE CHILDREN'S CHARITY

The long-standing Children's Charity had grown very rapidly for five years as local authorities contracted out the provision of children's centres, residential services, family support and other services. It delivered over 100 different projects that were categorised into 10 different services. The projects were spread across the country, with concentrations in particular areas.

Although the organisation did some terrific work, providing services that were highly tailored to individual needs, it became clear that it had not invested sufficiently in its infrastructure including systems for managing quality, developing people and measuring outcomes.

Rising requirements in the children's services sector, growing competition and reductions in available funding necessitated significant change. The board approved substantial investment to address the key issues, but changes were also required in the fundamental business model in order to return to a sustainable position. It became clear that delivering a wide range of services across a large geographic area was not a tenable competitive strategy.

The charity had won lots of contracts but it had not built its own competitive advantage and reputation. It was in danger of losing further contracts to other organisations that offered greater value to purchasers, including specialist knowledge, economies of scale and stronger reputations.

The organisation had to sharpen its strategy and undergo a major re-organisation to focus on fewer services where it had high expertise to give it the competitive advantage that was missing.

8.4 DEVELOPING SERVICE STRATEGIES

Before working on service strategies, organisations need to establish or further develop a planning architecture that defines how the overall strategy, the service plans and the operational plans all fit together.

Theoretically, large organisations could have strategic and operational plans at the corporate, divisional, departmental, regional and local levels. In practice, choices have to be made and the planning architecture needs to define:

- the types of plan required at each level;
- the purpose of each type of plan;
- the frequency of preparing them;
- their time horizons;
- the time of year when they should be prepared.

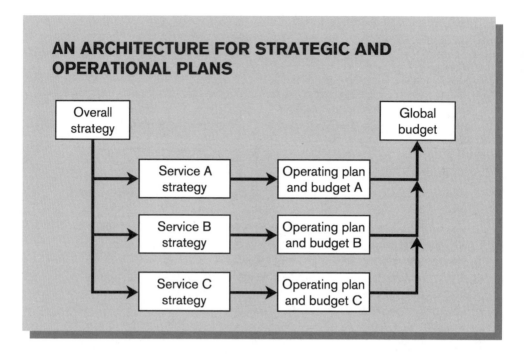

In larger organisations offering a number of services, senior management needs to develop and coordinate an organisation-wide process for service strategic planning. Tidy logic suggests that service managers should prepare their strategies when the corporate plan has been completed. In practice this is not always possible, because the total timetable for preparing corporate and service strategies and then creating operational plans and budgets becomes too extended.

Sometimes there is a need to review all service strategies at the same time, for example to ensure that they are well integrated. Sometimes a rolling programme may be more appropriate as this will allow each to be given closer and more rigorous scrutiny. In other situations, changing competitive circumstances or the appointment of a new manager may require the development of service strategy at a time that does not fit neatly with the corporate planning timetable.

An overall architecture of plans is therefore needed so managers understand how their planning activity fits into wider organisational processes.

In organisations where service managers report directly to the chief executive, the architecture will have two levels (see box). In longer, divisionalised organisations and those with separate geographic regions a third tier may be required. Planning in this tier is likely to be 'light touch' setting out summary objectives, timescales and finances, but not requiring extensive documentation.

When the planning architecture is clear, each service delivery unit needs to prepare its own strategy, usually covering a period of two to three years, which sets out objectives and how they will be achieved.

THE VALUE OF SERVICE STRATEGIES AND PLANS

They help service managers:

- to focus on delivering the organisation's objectives
- to manage their workload better
- to cope with change
- to have confidence
- to recognise achievements

They help senior managers:

- to coordinate between functions
- to allocate resources
- to ensure priorities are achieved
- to hold people accountable for progress

They help the organisation:

- to develop a shared understanding of priorities
- to promote the organisation to its funders and stakeholders
- to learn in a more systematic way about what works

Process for preparing service strategies

Managers need to involve staff (and, depending on circumstances, board members and volunteers) in the preparation of service strategies:

- to exploit their knowledge and creativity;
- to ensure that the strategy is owned by people who will be involved in delivering it.

The preparation of the plan can be divided into a series of steps, none of which should be too onerous, but each of which may be needed.

EIGHT-STEP APPROACH TO DEVELOPING A SERVICE STRATEGY

Developing a service strategy can be divided into easily manageable steps:

Step 1   Review current service provision and the changing external environment

To get a deeper understanding of the longer-term trends in what has been provided in the past and what will be needed in the future.

Step 2   Establish new objectives and performance measures for the service

To create new aspirations and high-level targets to track achievements.

Step 3   Develop strategies for achieving the objectives

To get to the heart of the 'big things' that need to be done to achieve the objectives.

Step 4   Identify key interdependencies with other departments

To ensure that time and resources required from others are in their plans.

Step 5   Determine how the service will be financed

To identify sources of income and how they will be secured.

Step 6   Set out broad timescales and responsibilities

To establish milestones, dates for meeting targets and who will be held accountable.

Step 7   Forecast income and expenditure

To ensure that the service delivers a financial margin capable of sustaining the organisation.

Step 8   Identify risks and mitigating factors

To see where things could go wrong and put in place actions that minimise the chances of this happening.

A good approach involves staff and board members in a discussion of how the review and planning are to be carried out, and a number of meetings to consider the review data, define the key issues that need to be addressed and prepare the plan.

Service managers sometimes need help with their strategic thinking. Some may have been promoted from a service delivery role to their first management post. Well trained in their own specialism, they may be unfamiliar with the task of bringing together service delivery, HR, financial and other concepts to create a strategy. Some may feel that senior management ought to take responsibility for service strategy.

Others are driven by seemingly never-ending demands for their service and feel that they do not have time to stand back from the daily pressures of crises in the hostels, refugees queuing for advice or the deadline of the opening of the night shelter. In all these circumstances, senior management is responsible for providing service managers with the necessary support, training and coaching to produce a top-quality plan. In some situations they may need to procure additional resources to ensure staff have the extra time needed to help prepare the plan.

Preparing the first review of a service is particularly challenging because it requires definition of the service and the nature of the service user population, and the collection and analysis of data which may not have been drawn together before.

Senior managers should expect to make a significant contribution to the content of service strategy. They are usually more experienced strategists; their job is to provide the insight and judgement that can help turn an adequate service strategy into an excellent one. This means helping service managers to define the key issues and shape the emerging strategy.

SCRUTINISING SERVICE STRATEGIES

Service strategies should be carefully scrutinised before being approved. This stage is often overlooked and needs to be built into the planning timetable. Rigorous scrutiny can lead to significant improvements in the quality of service and campaign plans.

The Royal British Legion Welfare Division asked all its service managers to prepare service strategies that demonstrated how the service would contribute to the achievement of the Division's objectives. They were all required to set out objectives, strategies and performance targets in a common template.

Each service manager presented his or her plan to a panel consisting of the division director, an external person who knew the sector, and representatives of other divisions that needed to integrate their work with the service, such as finance, HR and fundraising.

Each plan was scrutinised for an hour. The tone was that of a 'critical friend' wanting to help the manager produce the best possible quality plan. Managers were then able to make significant improvements to their plans and support departments were able to meet the needs of the service managers.

Reviews of current services

Service reviews should consider a range of questions, and the following checklist can help to identify which are most pertinent:

External issues

How are current and potential users' needs changing?
Looking at changing expectations, and different ways of meeting them

What are the trends in the numbers of people requiring the service?
Reviewing demographics of the user group and the numbers who need the service but are not getting it

Who are the competing providers and what distinguishes them?
Identifying other organisations (whether private, public or third-sector bodies) that provide similar services, and understanding what is distinctive about your or their services

What are the relevant changes in public policy that will affect the service?
Considering new social policy trends, regulatory requirements and different approaches to procurement

What are the key changes in the ways the service is provided?
Looking at different ways of delivering the service and the effectiveness of different approaches

What are the trends in funding for the service?
Looking at who future funders could be and what combinations of finance might be required

What will the future requirements of purchasers be?
Looking at what purchasers may require in future such as economies of scale, better outcomes measurement, more localised delivery

Internal issues

Who are the current service users?
Segmented by need, age, socio-economic group and geography. In some cases the service users may be other organisations

How many people benefit from the service?
Trends in the number of each type of user receiving the service

What are the benefits to service users?
Assessing quantitative and qualitative outcomes of services, using satisfaction surveys where appropriate

What skills are being used?
Identifying the critical competencies the organisation requires in order to deliver the service

What have we learned?
Focusing on what has been learned, from users and others, about the services provided. Identifying what needs to change in order to improve services

What staff skills and staff training are required to improve the service?
Looking at different ways to develop people's skills

How much does it cost?
Identifying the full costs of providing the service, including direct and indirect costs, and pinpointing the income, expenditure and (where relevant) subsidy per user

Campaigning organisations can consider a similar set of issues for each campaign. External considerations include:

- public policy developments that present new campaigning opportunities;
- reviews of political party policy that might change their positions;
- opportunities for new sector-wide coalitions to make an impact on the issue.

Internal considerations include:

- the current relevance of campaign objectives;
- the need for new research;
- the need to build campaigning capacity (e.g. on the web, with members or supporters, with politicians, with civil servants, with local partners);
- effectiveness of past use of people and money;
- understanding why some campaign objectives have been advanced whilst others have not progressed.

Service and campaign strategies

Services and campaign strategies should be succinct, establishing objectives, articulating a strategy and setting out groups of actions needed to achieve the objectives. Typical contents might include:

- summary of the review;
- description of the service or campaign;
- summary of existing and potential service users or current campaign strategy;
- objectives and key results indicators for the next three years;
- the overall strategy;
- timetable for implementation;
- HR requirements;
- financial requirements;
- potential purchasers and other sources of funding ;
- value for money analysis;
- risks and mitigating actions.

TESTS FOR THE QUALITY OF SERVICE AND CAMPAIGN STRATEGIES

- Are plans short, succinct and compelling?
- Do they use clear and consistent language for objectives, performance measures and strategies?
- Do they challenge conventional wisdom?
- Are they too modest or too ambitious?
- Are they owned by the people responsible for delivery?
- Are they live documents that can be used by managers to hold people to account?

A SERVICE STRATEGY FROM THE ROYAL BRITISH LEGION WELFARE DIVISION

Service description

Individual grants are used to help members of the ex-Service community overcome a short-term crisis or problem. The scheme gives immediate assistance for financial, household or mobility needs and can provide white goods and payments against priority debt within criteria designed to satisfy need and not want.

The scheme contributes to three of our strategic objectives:

To increase the household income of people living in poverty.

To help an increasing number of people to live independently.

To improve the quality of life for isolated or excluded people and families.

Principal aim

To meet the immediate needs of our service users through a series of structured grants and loans programmes.

Implementation strategy

Through our network of trained caseworkers, we will carry out detailed and holistic assessments of our service users' needs. Once the criteria have been satisfied, we will provide goods, payments or services, as required, to meet immediate needs.

The service will be delivered through our extensive team of field staff and volunteer caseworkers. We will undertake a caseworker recruitment programme and revise our caseworker training. Goods and services will be delivered through national preferred provider programmes, to ensure a common standard is achieved across the UK; these programmes will also generate rebates for the Legion. The service will also link in to our longer-term preventative programmes to minimise future disadvantage.

Targets

1. We aim to be reaching 35,200 people per year with an immediate need grant in 2010 – this will make 7,900 people independently mobile, enable 14,120 people to continue to live independently, provide immediate financial support to 7,300 people and assist 5,100 people with personal items and expenses.
2. We will recruit and train 500 new volunteer caseworkers.

8.5 **FORMULATING OPERATIONAL PLANS**

Operational plans should link proposed activities with budgets and key results indicators **for the coming year.** A trap that some organisations fall into is putting more effort into establishing the budget than into planning the underlying activities or specifying performance measures. The operational plan should be a single short document that **integrates activity, money and indicators.**

Operational plans flow from strategic plans. Strategic plans give broad directions for three to five years ahead and the operational plans set out a programme of work for the next twelve months, or in some cases two years. Operational plans should concentrate on what will be done, when, and how much it will cost. They:

- provide the basis on which managers and their bosses can negotiate and agree future priorities;
- create a structure for delegating work and responsibilities;
- describe desired outcomes and specific targets to be achieved;
- establish the activities upon which the budget will be based;
- create a tool for measuring progress.

Most organisations benefit from requiring managers of all services to prepare short, succinct operational plans. Whether they are called campaign plans, operational plans or work programmes, they provide a structure to the teams' work and are an important tool for communication within the organisation. They should be developed by both the service delivery units and by support services (e.g. finance, HR, ICT). Support service plans should aim to provide the best possible service to front-line teams and senior management.

Operational planning process

Operational planning processes generally start with the board and senior management agreeing planning guidelines. These set the parameters for the process, such as broad targets and budget boundaries. In a small organisation, the guidance may cover a single sheet of paper on which the board sets out its aspirations for the next 12 months. In a large organisation, it will inevitably be more detailed because of the need for a consistent approach to corporate budget-setting.

Managers then work with their staff to prepare operational plans, which should be short, encapsulating critical thinking, proposed actions, costs and any associated income.

Draft operational plans and budgets **need to be reviewed and challenged** before being agreed by line managers. This stage of rigorous scrutiny is often overlooked. It can be an activity where managers add real value to the plans from people who work for them.

Once approved, the documents need to be brought together into an overall operating plan and budget for the organisation. This should contain key proposals for the year, the timetable of major events, and income and expenditure budgets. It should be approved by the board a few weeks before the start of the organisation's financial year.

Content of operational plans

Operational plans should set out:

- what will be done;
- who will do it;
- what the benefits will be to service users;
- how many people or organisations will use the service;
- what quality standards will be applied;
- the implementation timetable;
- mechanisms for reviewing performance and outcomes.

They should include a budget which specifies:

- the cost of providing the service;
- income to be raised from supplying the service (if appropriate);
- the surplus generated or subsidy required.

A common mistake is to allow the process to become too bureaucratic. A year or two after initial enthusiasm for the process, it is easy to fall into this trap. The process becomes so routine that once a year everyone automatically cranks out a plan. People give it little thought and quickly come to regard the plan as work that has to be done to satisfy the system, rather than as an essential managerial tool.

There is a degree of inevitability about this. All new processes have greatest leverage when they are first introduced, which decays with time. So senior management needs to revitalise the process periodically. The guidance can be adjusted to meet new circumstances. Managers can be encouraged to identify more precisely the benefits to service users, to seek ways of streamlining their services, to improve quality and reach out to more people.

Timescales are a particular problem in large organisations, where individual service plans may need to be integrated with other delivery or internal service plans, before being submitted to the board as part of a global financial and operational plan. Plans can end up having to be prepared many months or more before their start date. The process needs to be streamlined so that it does not become an end in itself. The scope required of plans should be agreed (e.g. one page each describing benefits to users, actions, a timetable and a budget) so that the minimum number of steps needed to involve people in preparing and agreeing it can be established.

In both the private and public sectors, there is an assumption that every year organisations will achieve 'efficiency savings'. Managers are expected to find new ways of working that reduce costs and enable more money to be spent on the organisation's primary purpose. This assumption is far less prevalent in the third sector, and organisations may consequently miss an opportunity to do their work more efficiently. Requiring managers to identify such efficiency savings should be an integral part of operational planning.

OPERATIONAL PLANNING IN SENSE

Sense is a large organisation providing a wide range of services and campaigning on behalf of people who are deafblind. Most services are delivered regionally, and their budget is £75 million per annum. The organisation reviews its overall strategy every four to six years.

An example of their operational planning process is as follows:

21 October	Finance committee agrees inflation and cost-of-living assumptions.
26 October	Senior management team agrees guidelines and timetable for operating plan and budget preparation, together with assumptions on fee increases.
3 December	Current year budget and expenditure to date and blank pro formas mailed to senior management team members. Directors review plans with service managers and consolidate them into departmental and regional plans and budget bids.
9 December	Progress report to governing council.
17 January	Deadline for submission of all completed operating plans and budgets to director of finance.
18 February	Summarised national operating plan and budget mailed to senior management team.
27–28 February	Residential meeting. All directors present plans for scrutiny by colleagues. Revisions agreed for submission to governing council.
22 March	Council agrees operating plan and budget.
1 April	New financial year begins

SUMMARY OF KEY POINTS

Creating strategies and plans for services

- Organisations need strategies for each of the services and campaigns that they deliver
- None of these need to be lengthy documents that consume large amounts of management time

Defining services and campaigns

- The notion of service delivery units helps to distinguish separate services
- Service delivery units require:
  - a defined user group or campaign purpose
  - their own objectives and strategies
  - a distinct competitive position
  - systems to monitor achievements against plans
  - information on income and expenditure
  - a manager to plan, deliver and monitor the service or campaign

Constructing competitive strategy

- Third-sector organisations are now competing with the private and public sectors as well as each other
- Organisations have to decide whether they have the capacity to get into the business of public service delivery
- Competitive advantages can include:
  - knowledge and expertise
  - brand and reputation
  - ability to report on outcomes and impacts
  - focus on quality and quality accreditation
  - a research base that informs service delivery
  - economies of scale
  - local knowledge and networks
  - ability to work in partnership
- Organisations have to build bid-winning capacity and to understand the characteristics of their competitors

Developing service strategies

- Organisations need a planning architecture that defines how strategy, service and operational plans fit together
- Service plans describe the objectives, strategies and plans for each service the organisation delivers
- The process for preparing service plans needs to be coordinated at the corporate level
- Preparing a service strategy can be divided into eight stages
- Service strategies should be short, with clear targets and neither too modest nor too ambitious

Formulating operational plans

- Operational plans link proposed activities to budgets
- The process starts with approval of guidelines by the board and ends with agreement of a budget for the year ahead
- Operational plans should be subjected to rigorous scrutiny

FURTHER READING

Charity Marketing: Meeting Need Through Customer Focus, Ian Bruce, ICSA, 2005

The Complete Guide to Business and Strategic Planning, Alan Lawrie, DSC, 2001

Exploring Corporate Strategy, 8th Edition, G. Johnson, K. Scholes and R. Whittington, Financial Times Press, 2008

More and recent books and reports can be found at www.compasspartnership.co.uk.

9 Managing strategic performance

9.1 FOCUSING ORGANISATIONS ON RESULTS

Managing performance is the next essential component of strategic management. People who have put great effort into strategic planning are sometimes disappointed when their organisation keeps moving in the old direction. The 'push' behind the plan existed, but there was nothing to 'pull' people on to the new priorities.

Organisations need mechanisms to focus people at all levels on the new objectives and strategies and to let them know how well they are performing against the plan targets. Establishing or strengthening systems for managing performance is one way of moving attention from planning to implementation.

Managing performance is particularly important in third-sector organisations because, unlike businesses, most do not have the benefit of strong, direct market forces or the discipline of accountability to shareholders to provide external checks on performance. This problem is particularly acute in pure charities that raise funds for re-distribution to their beneficiaries. It occurs to a lesser extent in organisations where the funder of the service requires performance measures but is not the ultimate beneficiary of the service. In all these circumstances, self-imposed measures of performance are needed to ensure that the best intentions lead to actions and results.

It is rather surprising that most third-sector organisations have well-developed systems for measuring their financial performance, but remarkably under-developed systems for tracking the achievement of their mission. Clearly it is much more difficult to monitor achievements; unlike financial management, there is no common currency for monitoring strategic performance. However, those organisations that have risen to the challenge have discovered that four great benefits flow from strengthening processes for managing performance.

1. It **focuses people on results.** The existence of clear performance measures encourages people to think more clearly about the relationship between the work they do and the results they achieve.
2. It drives people to be more **realistic about the objectives** they set. People who work in third-sector organisations are notorious for setting enormously ambitious objectives – an understandable characteristic, given their commitment to their cause. Systems for managing organisation performance force people to think much more rigorously about what can be achieved with available resources in a given timescale, and consequently to set plans that are more achievable.
3. The existence of systems for managing performance helps **people to concentrate their attention on the agreed priorities** when the very nature of these organisations is that they are surrounded by other needs that may all fit with the mission and are therefore difficult to resist.
4. Organisations that have strengthened their systems for managing organisation performance report that great benefits flow from **the process of establishing the system,** as well as the resulting performance reports. Time spent thinking about performance at each level in the organisation helps to clarify priorities and deepen understanding of how resources should be deployed to achieve the desired outcomes.

This chapter describes how to establish and develop the central processes needed to manage organisation performance. It demonstrates:

- how tight management of performance encourages learning and improves accountability;
- how 'scorecards' or 'dashboards' can be used to maintain an overview of performance;
- how to go about strengthening systems for managing performance.

The chapter then describes further ways in which organisations can enhance their performance, including:

- how quality-management systems can improve performance;
- how to use benchmarking to compare performance within and between organisations.

Tightly controlled ways of managing the progress that the organisation or individual services and campaigns make has become increasingly important as organisations have striven to understand and promote the difference they have made to people's lives. Organisations are expected to articulate their achievements and to do that they need systems that produce evidence for what they have done.

The term 'performance management' can refer both to managing organisation-wide performance and to managing individual performance. This chapter concentrates on organisation performance, recognising that one aspect of managing organisation-wide performance is concerned with ensuring that individuals meet their objectives. Managing individual performance is described more fully in sections 17.2, Developing individuals, to 17.4, Encouraging coaching, mentoring and shadowing.

The term 'performance monitoring' is more limited in scope and refers to the process of gathering and assembling information on performance.

Before starting this chapter it should be noted that some systems for managing performance have been the subject of some criticism, particularly in academic literature. Researchers point out that the 'balanced scorecard' was developed for the private sector and is better suited to tracking the performance of profit-seeking organisations. Even with the adjustments made by its creators for use in the third sector, some argue that it requires further tailoring to suit individual organisations' circumstances.

9.2 ENCOURAGING LEARNING AND IMPROVING ACCOUNTABILITY

Effective management of performance provides the foundations for:
- learning from experience and modifying plans;
- holding boards, managers and staff to account.

It completes the loop that begins with planning, leads on to the measurement and assessment of performance, encourages people to learn from experience and ends with a better understanding of how effectiveness can be improved.

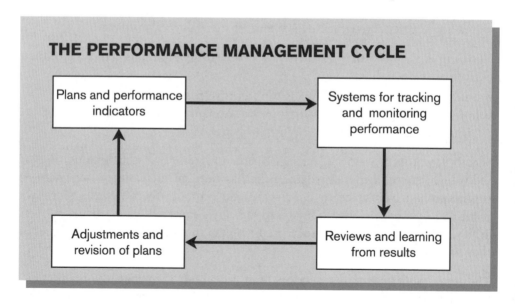

THE PERFORMANCE MANAGEMENT CYCLE

Plans and performance indicators → Systems for tracking and monitoring performance

Adjustments and revision of plans ← Reviews and learning from results

Effective arrangements for managing performance also provide a basis for holding people accountable for their work in a structured and systematic way. Accountability needs to exist at each level in an organisation. Board members should be holding the chief executive accountable for the overall performance of the organisation, senior management should be holding their department managers accountable, and they in turn should be holding individual staff accountable for performance. All this needs to be happening in a constructive two-way dialogue. Good management of performance information allows this accountability to focus on results and priorities for future action.

Different types of performance management

There are four different types of performance that need to be managed:

- strategic performance
- operational performance
- individual performance
- outcomes or results of the organisation's work.

Managing strategic performance is concerned with the overall and longer-term performance of the organisation and its main services. It addresses questions about:

- what progress the organisation has made in achieving its longer-term goals;
- trends in numbers of people assisted and types of assistance given;
- financial trends;
- major campaign achievements;
- whether major developments have been introduced on schedule;
- whether unrestricted funds have been allocated appropriately;
- whether services have provided value for money and whether campaigns have been cost effective.

Strategic performance is tracked by measuring key results indicators and it focuses on long-term outcomes. It might be reviewed six-monthly or annually.

Managing operational performance compares shorter-term achievements against targets. It enables managers to make regular adjustments to activities. It is concerned with such things as:

- volumes of services provided
- campaigning activity
- funds raised by different methods and the costs of raising them
- income and expenditure.

Operational performance focuses on process and outputs. The frequency of measuring operational performance depends on circumstances. Some indicators are tracked weekly, so action can be taken quickly when performance is below the target. Others may be tracked monthly or quarterly. Operational performance is tracked using key performance indicators.

Managing individual performance is concerned with individuals' objectives, monthly one-to-ones and annual appraisals (described in more detail in Chapter 17).

Outcomes or results are measured to track the effect that the organisation is having on the issues that it exists to address, such as medical research, support for people with long-term physical or mental health conditions, homelessness, lack of skills, disability or animal welfare.

Measuring outcomes has become increasingly important as funders and boards have wanted to get a much tighter grip on the difference organisations are making. This has led to the creation of a wide range of tools that are used to measure outcomes. Each examines a range of 'outcomes' to measure the effect the organisation is having in its sphere of work. This can be difficult to pin down because what organisations are trying to achieve is often hard to measure.

One area which has attracted growing interest is **outcomes for service users.** These measure the progress that each user of a service is making in overcoming the problem that brought them into contact with the organisation, such as substance misuse, mental health problems, preparing for employment and homelessness. Sometimes these are called 'soft' outcomes.

EXAMPLES OF SERVICE-USER OUTCOMES

- Managing money
- Living skills
- Personal motivation
- Relationships
- Leisure activity
- Family support

- Eating and sleeping
- Readiness for work
- Reading, writing and arithmetic
- Skills for finding work
- Risk to self and others
- Alcohol and drug misuse

Each outcome is given a scale which can be used to track the progress that the individual is making. Judgements can be made about how well service users are progressing towards achieving the desired outcomes by the service user or their support worker, or both of them working together. Some of these tools are designed to help the service user understand the progress they are making, some help the agency measure progress and some do both. Details of the many outcomes tools (18 at the time of writing) and how to choose the most appropriate one can be found at www.homelessoutcomes.org.uk.

Service-user outcomes provide an excellent way for organisations to demonstrate the differences they have made to service users' lives, The outcomes can be added together to measure the difference that the organisation as a whole has made to all its service users. This information can be fed into the organisation's performance measurement system, so organisations can report on the total difference that they have made to people's lives over a specified period of time.

THE OUTCOMES STAR

The Outcomes Star is one method of tracking individual outcomes. It consists of ten ladders, each of which helps service users and their key workers to track progress in changing their behaviour or way of life. Each ladder has a series of defined steps that the individual needs to take. These are used to 'score' the progress that the person is making.

10 No emotional or mental health issues or can manage with outside support

9 Enjoying life and mostly feel fine. Just need support now and then

8 More content and getting on with life. Need help with 'blips'

7 More on an even keel. Understand how to help myself

6 Can see options and will try out ways to help me feel better

5 See why I feel like this. Need to pick myself up and get on with things

4 Going along with treatment and feel OK some of the time

3 Want change – want to get out of this hole and feel better

2 Don't like feeling like this but there is nothing anyone can do about it

1 There is nothing wrong with me (though I often feel pretty bad)

The ten ladders are then represented in a summary 'star' that gives an overview of how they are doing on each of the criteria.

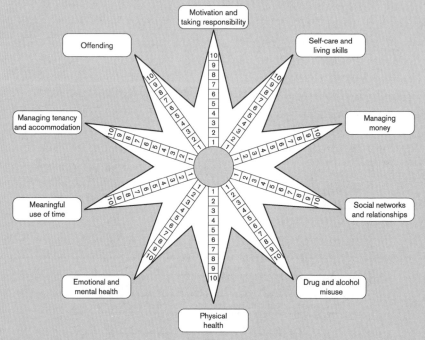

Source: © The London Housing Foundation and Triangle Consulting

ST MUNGO'S ANNUAL REVIEW

The work of homelessness agencies is often measured by 'hard outcomes': how many clients have been successfully re-housed or how many clients have successfully given up drugs or alcohol. Many of the vulnerable men and women St Mungo's works with are at a stage where 'hard outcomes' are unrealistic.

St Mungo's has an income of £44m pa, helps over 1,300 people off the streets and provides employment training for over 2,000 people. It recognised the need to develop more attainable goals for their clients to enable them to feel they are moving onwards and upwards, whether or not they are ready to take the big steps into training, work or resettlement. They pioneered the measurement of 'soft outcomes' for homeless clients.

By using the outcomes star they were able to state in their annual review that nearly 75% of their clients made positive progress with their 'soft' outcomes during the year. Most progress was shown by clients who were resident in one of their projects for between six and twelve months.

9.3 **CREATING SCORECARDS**

Organisations need a structured way to assemble and manage performance information. Whilst most maintain financial information in highly prescribed and systematic ways, many report information on the achievement of their objectives in surprisingly unstructured and fragmented ways.

Information on performance is often collected in different parts of the organisation, on different timescales and in different formats. It is therefore hardly surprising that some organisations find it difficult to report an overview of performance on a regular basis.

To give board members, managers and staff an overview of performance it is necessary to tell them, amongst other things:

- what the organisation has achieved in a prescribed period of time compared to agreed targets;
- how 'healthy' it is in terms of people, money and reputation;
- how these measurements compare to previous years (i.e. trends).

Organisations need to have information on the critical dimensions of performance and present it in a coherent format. One way of doing this is to use a 'scorecard' or 'dashboard'. The idea of a scorecard was originally developed by two Harvard Business School professors for profit-seeking organisations and is known as the balanced scorecard. It tracks performance on four dimensions known as perspectives. These are the:

- financial perspective
- customer perspective
- internal perspective
- learning and growth perspective.

They have modified this for public-sector and nonprofit organisations and include the mission as a fifth perspective. Other organisations have taken the notion but defined dimensions of performance that suit their circumstances. These are sometimes called 'dashboards' and sometimes 'scorecards'.

The simplest form of scorecard captures a range of key results indicators and corrals them into a standard format that provides an overview at a glance. The more sophisticated forms attempt to track the underlying drivers of strategic performance and the growth of the organisation's capacity to deliver its mission.

The idea of scorecards fits well with the values of the third sector because people want performance information that goes beyond financial reports. They need to systematically track progress in achieving a wide range of objectives to give a rounded overview of performance.

EXTRACT FROM MACMILLAN CANCER SUPPORT DASHBOARD

☐ Performance is consistent with the plan/budget.

▨ Remedial action is needed to keep the activity on track and it needs careful watching.

IMPROVE ACCESS TO, AND THE QUALITY OF, CANCER SUPPORT ACROSS THE UK

	Q1 Status	Comments
Calls to Cancerline	6,364	In line with target
Benefits helpline, people helped	2,013	On target
Macmillan grants, people helped	5,385	On target
Mobile information services (EM, NE and LASER) people helped	Only just started tours	On target so far
Visitors to website	495,000	87% increase on the same time last year
Number of posts in partner organisations committed to	On track	Lower than targeted, but confident we will hit year-end target

RAISE AWARENESS OF MACMILLAN'S SERVICES AND CANCER ISSUES AND ACT AS A THOUGHT-LEADER AND FORCE FOR CHANGE

	Q1 Status
Spontaneous awareness	Awaiting May nfp synergy survey results
Total awareness	
Brand awareness campaign	Wave 1 in Feb/March completed successfully
Better deal campaign	Slow progress due to vacancies in the CPPA team
Working through cancer campaign	Parts of project on hold, no project manager at present
Involvement in development of cancer strategies	Good progress made
Coalitions led and influenced	Not yet available, work in hand to monitor
Events and conferences held	Not yet available, work in hand to monitor

RAISE AND SPEND OUR MONEY WISELY AND WELL

	Q1 Status	Comments
Legacy income	£xx m	Slightly ahead of budget
Fundraised income (excluding legacies)	£xx m	On budget
Existing supporters	xx	Up x% on the same time last year
Total number of active committed givers	xx	Up x% on the same time last year
Charitable expenditure	£xx m	£xx m under budget, but £x m more than the same time last year and we are confident we will hit budget by year end
Cost/income ratio for the whole charity (SORP)	x%	Better than budgeted and our latest estimate shows that at year end we will be on budget
Charitable spend/total spend ratio	x%	Less than budgeted, but we will hit budget by year end
Fundraising strategy review	Draft discussed at March EMT, principles were agreed and a more detailed implementation plan has been prepared in April	

BUILD OUR ORGANISATIONAL CAPABILITIES

	Q1 Status	Comments
Staff turnover	x%	Higher than last year, figures being investigated
Number of established posts	xx	As planned
Number of vacancies	xx	Vacancy rate of x%, figures being investigated
Appraisal and reward review	On track	
Fusion project	Analysis phase completed successfully, next stage is to create an implementation plan	
Organisation review project	Workstreams are reporting their recommendations to EMT as planned	
Cancerbackup merger	Progressed well, but having knock-on effects in other parts of the organisation	

EXTRACT FROM SHELTER'S SCORECARD

Shelter helps more than 170,000 people a year 'fight for their rights, get back on their feet, and find and keep a home'. It provides housing advice, campaigns for housing, undertakes research and delivers training.

Indicator	Target	Q1 result	Performance
Clients			
Clients assisted: all services	32,700	33,020	GREEN
Clients assisted: Helpline	15,000	16,500	GREEN
% clients satisfied with services	95%	94%	GREEN
% statutory funding contracts achieved	100%	94%	AMBER
Number of clients taking part in user involvement events	125	222	GREEN
% clients from BME groups	14%	15%	GREEN
Organisation			
Number of staff (full-time equivalent)	842 (baseline)	819	GREEN
Staff turnover	5%	4%	GREEN
Staff sickness	5%	3.8%	GREEN
% appraisals completed by deadline	95%	90%	AMBER
Average training spend per employee	£75	£68	GREEN
IT expenditure per employee	£750	£900	RED
Communications			
Number of media items	875	1,010	GREEN
Opportunities to view	220m	310m	GREEN
Awareness of Shelter	80%	81%	GREEN
Page views of website	3m	2.87m	AMBER
Finance			
Income to budget variance	<5%	4%	GREEN
Expenditure to budget variance	<5%	3%	GREEN
Net fundraising income	£4.8m	£4.7m	GREEN
Net profit from trading activities	£300k	£306k	GREEN
Free reserves	£6.4m	£6m	AMBER
% services funded by statutory sources	75%	72%	GREEN

(Data is indicative)

Common dimensions of performance in the third sector include:

- achievements for service users
- fundraising
- staff and volunteers (numbers, turnover, diversity etc)
- finance
- internal processes
- learning and development.

Some organisations attempt to summarise performance on one or two sheets of paper (or computer screens), usually on a quarterly basis.

Some have taken the idea further and elaborated their scorecards by highlighting achievements and problems with a 'traffic light' system. This marks each performance indicator in green, amber or red to identify whether performance is on target, giving cause for concern, or in need of management attention.

Scorecards are generally used to measure past performance. Some organisations also use them to predict future performance. As well as reporting results to date they ask managers to predict the out-turn for the next quarter or the year end. The scorecard can then reflect seasonal differences and changes in performance that are not linear. For example a new service may not expect many users in the first quarter, but may be achieving more than the annual average by the end of the year.

Yet another elaboration is to combine predictions with traffic lights. In this way it is possible to see at a glance which services are predicted to achieve their targets by the end of the year. There may, for example, be services that are on target now but are not anticipated to achieve their year-end targets.

As well as reporting performance, some organisations also include a commentary column on their scorecard. This allows a few words to explain over and under-performance. Others also add an actions column to inform readers about the actions managers plan to take on areas of under-performance.

Clearly it is not possible to include all categories of data past, present and future plus narrative columns on a side or two of paper. So choices have to be made about what it is most important to communicate.

Some organisations produce a summary sheet with supporting pages that provide greater detail. Others work electronically and provide a 'drill down' facility so that readers can investigate results that are particularly important to them (such as performance by region or performance of different services or by different fundraising methods).

9.4 **STRENGTHENING SYSTEMS FOR MANAGING PERFORMANCE**

Strengthening the management of performance is dependent on other stages of strategic management having been successfully introduced. Directors and managers need to be clear about the overall strategy of the organisation and the objectives and performance measures of individual services before putting too much energy into developing processes for managing performance.

Symptoms suggesting that improvements are needed include:
- required information being located in various parts of the organisation;
- information being held on a variety of manual and electronic systems ;
- information being stored at different geographical locations;
- information which is not summarised or moderated for quality;
- information presented in ways that do not help people to see the big picture and make judgements about performance;
- information that does not compare performance with targets;
- underdeveloped processes for the board and senior management to review overall performance regularly.

Deciding what information best captures performance

Performance measures should have been agreed when objectives were set. A basket of measures will be required, so managers have to decide which indicators most accurately capture the overall performance of the organisation. This is likely to be a process that has a number of iterations as a deeper understanding of the drivers of performance develops.

Although a permanent set of indicators is a tempting proposition, the truth is that, although some indicators may remain comparatively stable, quite a few will change over time. This may happen when new services are introduced, but it is just as likely when it becomes clear that new information should be gathered to get an even better fit between the impact of the organisation and the performance measures that track it.

Deciding where to start

A first step in improving the management of performance is to carry out a brief review of current arrangements and pinpoint aspects that most require attention. This should be done by those who will be most involved in making improvements, as it is an early opportunity to gain ownership of the process.

The review should identify where to start making improvements and how ambitious to be. Experience suggests that it is better to concentrate improvements on a few areas and to be modest in aspirations.

MANAGING PERFORMANCE AT NSPCC

The NSPCC's purpose is to end cruelty to children and its vision is of a society where all children are loved, valued and able to fulfil their potential. It has 180 projects and services for children and young people ranging from helplines like ChildLine, to teams that work directly with those who are at risk.

NSPCC has been striving to improve the way that it measures and demonstrates both its efficiency and its effectiveness. It has a performance framework which divides reporting into:

- reporting progress in achieving the organisation's strategy
- reporting progress in achieving the strategy to end cruelty to children

NSPCC makes the distinction between steps to achieving an outcome and an outcome itself, and ensures that it is measuring the contribution of each outcome to achieving the charity's four strategic objectives.

Each 'function' (called 'division' in this book) produces a quarterly balanced scorecard which is used to manage the function. These are reviewed at quarterly challenge meetings. They are also scrutinised by a trustee sub-committee. The corporate scorecard is reported quarterly to the board of trustees using colour coding and exception reporting. Where any indicators are highlighted red or amber, the causes of the under and over-performance are identified and the actions to be taken are made explicit.

NSPCC recognises that challenges remain in improving the quality of the indicators and in ensuring that there is a focus on measuring outcomes in all the work that they do.

Examples of their performance indicators include:

- **Serving the customer**
  % of children and young people who know what to do to stay safe
  % of NSPCC service users who demonstrate improvement
  Number of volunteer hours at ChildLine
- **Running the business**
  % of calls from children and young people to ChildLine that get through to a counsellor
  Staff turnover
- **Learning and growth**
  % of planned consultations with children and young people that have been undertaken
  % of staff reporting managers communicate effectively
- **Managing resources**
  Total income as a % of budget
  FULL STOP appeal total

The following diagnostic tool can be used to help make choices.

PERFORMANCE MANAGEMENT DIAGNOSTIC TOOL

⟨ℕ⟩ Compass Partnership **Aspects most requiring attention**	Very	Quite	Not very	Not at all
Section A Clarity of objectives and performance measures				
1. How clear are corporate objectives and performance measures for the next three to five years?	☐	☐	☐	☐
2. How measurable are they?	☐	☐	☐	☐
3. How clear are the objectives and performance measures of services?	☐	☐	☐	☐
4. How measurable are they?	☐	☐	☐	☐
5. How clear are the intended outcomes of campaigns?	☐	☐	☐	☐
Section B Readiness of people and culture				
6. How well do managers understand and work for the achievement of corporate and service objectives (ie are they integral to 'the way we do things here')?	☐	☐	☐	☐
7. How comfortable are managers about collecting performance information?	☐	☐	☐	☐
8. How comfortable are managers about the dissemination of performance information?	☐	☐	☐	☐
Section C Quality of data management				
9. How good is the quality of the data collected about the outputs of services?	☐	☐	☐	☐
10. How good is the quality of the data collected about the outcomes of services?	☐	☐	☐	☐
11. How integrated is the flow of output and outcome information to senior management and board members?	☐	☐	☐	☐
12. How well is performance information summarised?	☐	☐	☐	☐

Compass Partnership — Aspects most requiring attention	Very	Quite	Not very	Not at all
Section D Alignment of reporting process				
13. How well developed are the processes for reporting corporate performance against objectives?	☐	☐	☐	☐
14. How well developed are the processes for reporting service and campaign performance against objectives?	☐	☐	☐	☐
15. How integrated are the processes for planning and performance reporting?	☐	☐	☐	☐
Section E Reporting performance				
16. How well does the organisation communicate the scale of the problems it sets out to resolve?	☐	☐	☐	☐
17. How well does the organisation communicate why it has chosen its priorities?	☐	☐	☐	☐
18. How well are the differences the organisation has made to people's lives reported on its website?	☐	☐	☐	☐
19. How well aligned are statements of objectives and reports of performance in annual reports and reviews?	☐	☐	☐	☐
20. How transparently does the annual report link achievements to income and expenditure?	☐	☐	☐	☐
21. How systematically does the organisation report on achievements to major donors?	☐	☐	☐	☐
22. How systematically does the organisation report on achievements to contractors?	☐	☐	☐	☐
23. How systematically does the organisation report on achievements to the general public?	☐	☐	☐	☐
24. How well does the organisation report on planned compared to actual performance to staff and trustees?	☐	☐	☐	☐
25. How well does the organisation shout about its overall successes in all its fundraising and publicity materials, publications and in other places?	☐	☐	☐	☐

Practicalities of strengthening performance management processes

Establishing or strengthening processes for managing performance should be treated as a project. It needs to have clear objectives, a timetable, a team of people from each department affected by the proposals and a project champion who has clear responsibility for seeing it through to completion. The champion and the project team need the authority of the chief executive and the leadership team to ensure that the actions required in each division will be carried through.

When establishing processes for managing performance for the first time the team will need to agree:

- the data that needs to be captured to inform people of progress;
- the format in which data will be reported;
- how often to review performance;
- who will be responsible for preparation of performance information;
- how the results and any associated commentary will be communicated to the board, the staff and other stakeholders;
- how feedback from the board and senior management will be reported back down the line.

The stages of a project to establish a system for managing performance could be as follows:

1. Check the pre-requisites are in place:
   - that people understand the need and that concerns they may have (for example, about confidentiality or the consequences of reporting poor performance) will be considered;
   - that there are clear objectives and strategies for the areas of work to be monitored and well-established planning processes;
   - that people are clear what level of performance requires better management (e.g. corporate or service).
2. Establish a project team:
   - involve a cross-section of people at different levels and people from parts of the organisation that will be affected by the proposals.
3. Build commitment to the value of managing performance:
   - discuss the purpose and need with staff and allow people an opportunity to raise their concerns;
   - plan how the process of strengthening the management of performance will be undertaken with staff and trustees;
   - set boundaries on the scope of the project to ensure that it is not too ambitious;
   - agree that proposals will be piloted.

4. Decide on a simple set of data:
   - brainstorm a long list of potential performance indicators for the areas of work being considered;
   - distil these down to a first approximation of a scorecard of indicators;
   - review the measures that are 'ideal' with the information that is realistic to collect;
   - ask for a mixture of quantitative and qualitative measures;
   - keep them simple.
5. Set up a reporting process:
   - draft and agree a format for reporting performance;
   - keep reports to the minimum necessary to avoid over-bureaucratising the process. Ideally, the first report should be a 'scorecard' that can be distributed in the same way as budget performance is reported to managers, directors and board members;
   - agree frequency of reporting to different groups.

PERFORMANCE MONITORING AT BSS

bss provides information and advice services to citizens on behalf of the public sector, other charities and broadcasters, to advance education, promote health and relieve poverty. It identified the lack of a performance-monitoring system as a key reason for difficulty in implementing a strategic plan. Consequently, when a new plan was established, management went to great lengths to involve as many people as possible to ensure ownership of the corporate priorities.

The plan has five strategic objectives which guide all activities in the organisation. These objectives are hung on the wall of every office to ensure that people do not lose sight of them!

The main performance report to regular board meetings is partly organised under five headings, corresponding to the objectives. Each section of the organisation reports quarterly on its achievements, broadly following the five objectives. The senior management team reviews progress against the plan objectives monthly.

According to bss,

'the key to the success of our system is that we have kept it short and simple. Our first attempt was too complicated. Now it's simplified it keeps staff and the board acutely aware of the corporate priorities. It has been a major contributor to our successful development over the last few years'.

9.5 **CONTINUING IMPROVEMENT THROUGH QUALITY MANAGEMENT**

A different approach to improving performance is to use one of the established systems of quality management to catalyse change. Although people generally strive for quality in their work, some organisations have taken a more formal and rigorous approach to improving quality. Some have acquired formal accreditation for their quality management regime and some seek external assessment to compare their achievements against wider standards.

Quality management is concerned with improving all aspects of an organisation's work, not just with the quality of its services. It should lead to improvements on three levels: people, processes and performance.

QUALITY PRINCIPLES

The National Council for Voluntary Organisations Quality Standards Task Group established six principles that define a quality voluntary organisation. An organisation committed to quality:

- strives for continuous improvements in all it does
- uses recognised standards as a means to continuous improvement and not as an end
- agrees requirements with stakeholders and endeavours to meet or exceed these first (and every) time
- promotes equality of opportunity through its internal and external conduct
- is accountable to stakeholders
- adds value to its end users and beneficiaries

This section introduces three quality systems that are most appropriate to third-sector organisations, and identifies where further information can be found.

Quality management systems have been the subject of some criticism in academic literature because they are seen to satisfy the needs of funders, but may not deliver benefits to service users. Research suggests that sometimes the benefit of the systems may come from the discussions that they trigger, rather than from the systems themselves. All of this suggests that they should be used with some caution and in ways that are appropriate to each organisation's context.

The Excellence Model

The Excellence Model is a self-assessment framework which recognises that there are many approaches to improving quality. The model has nine elements, each of which can be assessed to determine the organisation's progress towards achieving excellence. The nine elements are divided into two categories: **enablers,** that are concerned with how the organisation is managed, and **results,** that are concerned with what the organisation achieves.

Each element is measured using a set of criteria. The elements are weighted to determine the overall performance of the organisation (e.g. leadership accounts for 10%, processes 14%, results 15%). In total, the enablers account for 50% of performance and results account for 50%.

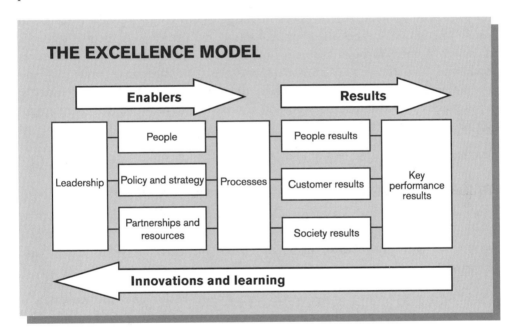

Further information can be found at www.quality-foundation.co.uk.

Investors in People

Investors in People aims to improve organisations' performance by linking objectives to investments in people's skills and abilities. The system focuses on performance in:

- business strategy
- learning and development strategy
- people management strategy
- leadership and management strategy
- management effectiveness
- recognition and reward

209

- involvement and empowerment
- learning and development
- performance measurement
- continuous improvement.

Investors in People is based on four principles:

1. **commitment:** to invest in people to achieve organisation goals;
2. **planning:** how skills of individuals and teams are to be developed to achieve these goals;
3. **action:** to develop and use necessary skills in a well-defined and continuing programme directly linked with organisation objectives;
4. **evaluation:** measuring progress towards goals, added value and future needs.

Organisations applying for Investors in People status have to collect evidence to show whether they meet the required standards. Investors in People status is achieved in stages through a process that can take one or more years. It involves reviewing how the organisation compares with the standards, preparing and implementing an action plan to bring the organisation up to the standards, assessment by an external assessor, and continuous improvement in preparation for re-assessment three years later.

Further information can be found at www.investorsinpeople.co.uk.

Practical quality assurance system for small organisations

Known as PQASSO, this system provides a flexible, step-by-step approach to working out what an organisation is doing well and what could be improved. It uses a self-assessment work pack, to enable managers to set priorities and improve performance.

PQASSO is a systematic 'health check' that is designed for small organisations. It helps to identify where to focus improvement efforts from 12 quality areas.

1. planning for quality
2. governance
3. management
4. user-centred service
5. staff and volunteers
6. training and development
7. managing money
8. managing resources
9. managing activities
10. networking and partnership
11. monitoring and evaluation
12. results.

Each area has three 'levels of achievement', and 'suggested evidence' to help identify what needs to be improved. The self-assessment helps users to decide what action needs to be taken, by specific people and within specific timeframes. A quality mark is awarded to organisations that undergo a peer assessment process.

Further information can be found at www.ces-vol.org.uk.

Selecting a system

These quality systems help organisations take a structured approach to developing the quality of their work. Up-to-date details of all of them can be found on the web. They provide an intellectual framework which managers can use to launch a quality initiative. They also allow organisations to demonstrate to their stakeholders that they take quality seriously.

Managers need to decide which system best suits their organisation's circumstances. Investors in People has the advantage of independent external validation and the award of a widely recognised badge. The advantage of the Excellence Model is that a version of it has been tailored to the third sector, and training in its application is available from Charities Evaluation Services. The advantage of PQASSO is that it is particularly suitable for smaller organisations and for projects in larger organisations.

9.6 BENCHMARKING CATALYSES PERFORMANCE IMPROVEMENTS

Another approach to improving strategic performance is to make comparisons with other organisations.

Benchmarking is a systematic process for making comparisons between organisations and identifying best practices. Crucially, it is about using comparative information to catalyse people into making improvements.

It is widely used in the private and public sectors and is growing in popularity in the third sector. It is a valuable tool for developing an understanding of why performance is different in similar organisations.

Benchmarking works well in the third sector because:

- The sector has a culture that values cooperation as a way of achieving the best results for service users.
- There is a strong tradition of developing best practices – an important outcome of benchmarking exercises.
- It can be a highly participative process.

Benchmarking is not just about **comparing statistical data** on performance. Indeed there is much evidence that excessive effort applied to gathering ever-more detailed numbers can be counter-productive. It is about **identifying good practices** that are qualitative in nature. Most important of all, it aims to understand *why* performance differs and *what* needs to change for an organisation or service to achieve or exceed the benchmark.

There are three types of benchmarking:

- **service benchmarking** – which is used to compare the performance of services that organisations offer;
- **process benchmarking** – which is used to compare the processes, work practices and management procedures organisations use;
- **strategic benchmarking** – which is used to compare organisations' structures and strategies.

Benchmarking can be done in a number of different ways. **External benchmarking** requires organisations to join a scheme that has been established to compare particular functions such as HR, finance and governance. These enable organisations or services to assess themselves against a previously defined set of benchmarks. In the third sector there are well-established schemes for comparing the performance of fundraising, finance and HR.

In larger organisations comparisons can be made between different parts of the organisation. **Internal benchmarking** can compare the performance of different services, regions or branches. This type of benchmarking encourages people to explore why there are variations in performance. Sometimes differences result from diverse circumstances that cannot be changed, such as the geography of a region or the types of people using a service. In other cases it identifies different ways of working that can help an under-performing part of the organisation improve its efficiency. Internal benchmarking has to be sensitively managed because it raises the spectre of league tables and humiliation for poor performance. It needs to be set clearly in a context of learning from differences and identifying best practices.

Informal benchmarking involves one organisation taking the initiative to gather data from a number of organisations and sharing the results with all of them. Each can then compare its performance with the others.

Benchmarking clubs are more formal arrangements that require organisations to work together with other members to compare performance with each other. Club members can both share the information and work together to identify the underlying reasons for the differences in performance. They can then support each other in developing ways to improve their performance in areas that fall below the benchmark.

Before embarking on a benchmarking exercise, it is important to make a realistic judgement about the time and effort that will be required. A survey of benchmarking in over a hundred businesses found that the average project lasted twenty-three weeks and involved thirty person-weeks of time (*From knowledge to action*, Stephen Drew, Long Range Planning, 1997).

A benchmarking exercise typically has six stages:

1. **Determine what to benchmark.** This should identify where performance is thought to be poor and identify whether the service, the process or the strategy should be benchmarked.
2. **Form a benchmarking team.** Using a team ensures that many people feel ownership of the project. Decisions need to be taken about leadership of the team and whether to involve service users, board members and other stakeholders.
3. **Identify benchmarking partners.** Decisions are required about which approach to take. In external benchmarking, decisions need to be taken about which organisations to compare performance against. The options include:
   - organisations in the same sector and field of work (e.g. another housing organisation providing a similar service);
   - organisations in the same sector but in a different field (e.g. charities in different fields of work);
   - organisations in different sectors that provide similar services (e.g. comparing third-sector suppliers with organisations in the public and private sectors).

   It is worth putting considerable effort into this stage, as the experience of the other organisations will be a major determinant of the overall success of the exercise.
4. **Collect and analyse benchmarking information.** Decisions need to be taken about what information to collect, how to collect it and how it will be drawn together. Issues of confidentiality may arise at this point. Where people have concerns, a third party can be used to collect and analyse the data. It can then be reported back in a format that allows each organisation to compare their performance with the other contributors, without identifying them individually.

   It is tempting to collect a wide range of information to ensure that all participants are confident that nothing important will be missed. However, experience suggests that there is a grave danger of being over-ambitious and unrealistic about the time it takes to analyse and report on findings.

   There is also a trade-off to be made between collecting a lot of poor-quality information and a little really good information. Since the credibility of the benchmarking process is entirely dependent on the data gathered, it is usually better to err on the side of caution and, if necessary, collect further information when the value of the initial information has been proven.

5. **Identify the underlying reasons for differences in performance.** This stage is critical to the ability to move beyond interesting information and gather insights into why performance differs. A process of discussion and investigation within and between the participating organisations is needed to explore how things are done differently and to identify what might be changed to improve performance.

6. **Take action on the findings.** This final stage requires organisations to take decisions on changes and to establish groups to implement agreed actions. This will ensure that the results of all the effort are turned into improved performance.

BENCHMARKING COMMUNITY DRUGS AGENCIES

A project was undertaken to compare the performance of 18 community drugs agencies, funded by the Department of Health. Information on what to benchmark was gathered through a series of interviews and workshops with leaders of the agencies. A questionnaire was prepared and tested on a sample of agencies.

Topics covered included overall management of the agencies, governance, service delivery methods and performance of each of the services offered, such as needle exchange, counselling, drop-in and therapy. The project identified good practices in governance and management and developed a set of performance benchmarks which agencies could compare against their own performance. The report made a series of recommendations on ways in which community drugs agencies could increase their effectiveness.

The range of topics that third-sector organisations can benchmark includes:

- service delivery and quality
- user involvement and satisfaction
- membership services
- trading operations
- volunteer management
- HR practices and training
- contracting practices
- financial management.

Benchmarking does require investment of significant time and effort. It requires strong support from senior management and it works best if there is a project champion. When these conditions exist, it is particularly good at convincing people of the need for change and identifying creative ways to make improvements.

Benchmarking is always the start of a process. It is an unthreatening way of introducing people to change, enabling people to share best-in-the-class performance, and encouraging them to go on to establish ambitious aims and action plans to achieve or exceed current best practice.

SUMMARY OF KEY POINTS

Focusing organisations on results

- Establishing or strengthening a system for managing performance moves attention from planning to implementation
- Organisations have well-developed systems for measuring their financial performance, but many have remarkably underdeveloped systems for tracking the achievement of their mission
- Managing strategic performance:
  - focuses people on results
  - makes people more realistic about objectives
  - helps to concentrate people's attention on agreed priorities

Encouraging learning and improving accountability

- Management of performance helps people at every level understand how well they are doing and what they are learning
- Good management of performance information allows this accountability to focus on results and priorities for future action
- The four types of performance are strategic, operational, individual and service user
- Outcomes for service users track the progress that each user of a service is making in overcoming his or her problems

Creating scorecards

- Board members, managers and staff need an overview of performance covering:
  - what has been achieved in a prescribed period of time compared to targets
  - how 'healthy' the organisation is in terms of people, money and reputation
- Scorecards track performance on a series of dimensions
- Some scorecards highlight performance using 'traffic lights', some predict future performance and some combine both to highlight predicted out-turns. The more sophisticated systems have a 'drill-down' capacity to provide access to more detailed information

Strengthening systems for managing performance

- The first step in improving the management of performance is to review current arrangements and pinpoint aspects that most require attention.
- Improvements should be treated as a change management project, with objectives, a timescale, a project team and a champion

Continuing improvement through quality management

- Quality management is concerned with managing all aspects of an organisation's work that should lead to improvements in people, processes and performance
- Quality systems appropriate to the sector include:
  - The Excellence Model
  - Investors in People
  - Practical Quality Assurance System for Small Organisations
- Managers need to decide which quality system best suits their circumstances

Benchmarking catalyses performance improvements

- Benchmarking aims to show why performance differs between organisations and what needs to change to exceed the benchmark
- A benchmarking exercise typically has six stages:
  - determine what to benchmark
  - form a benchmarking team
  - identify benchmarking partners
  - collect and analyse benchmarking information
  - identify the reasons for underlying differences in performance
  - take action on the findings

FURTHER READING

Balanced Scorecard Step-by Step for Government and Nonprofit Agencies, Paul R. Niven, John Wiley & Sons, Inc., 2003

The Balanced Scorecard: Translating Strategy into Action, Robert S. Kaplan and David P. Norton, Harvard Business School Press, 1996

Managing and Measuring Social Enterprises, Rob Paton, Sage, 2003

Your Project and its Outcomes, Sally Cupitt and Jean Ellis, Charities Evaluation Services, 2007

Practical Monitoring and Evaluation: A Guide for Voluntary Organisations, 2nd Edition, Jean Ellis, Charities Evaluation Services, 2005

More and recent books and reports can be found at www.compasspartnership.co.uk.

10 Managing knowledge and reporting on performance

10.1 PEOPLE WANT TO KNOW ABOUT ACHIEVEMENTS

Most third-sector organisations are given tax or other advantages because they strive to make social, environmental and other improvements. In return they are expected to be open, transparent and accountable for their actions. This 'public settlement' is designed to ensure that people can trust organisations to meet their obligations. The settlement is particularly important for fundraising charities because people have to have confidence that these organisations will use donations effectively. It is also important for charities, housing associations, regeneration organisations and other bodies that receive government funds.

Public interest in what these organisations do and how they spend their funds has risen dramatically over recent years. People now want to see evidence of achievements and clear accounts about how funding has been allocated and spent. Most third-sector organisations are required to report to a regulator (for example the Charity Commission, or the Regulator of Community Interest Companies). Charities are also subject to much greater scrutiny than they were in the past, with numerous websites offering information and comment on their performance. GuideStar presents information on all charities in a standard format; Intelligent Giving assesses annual reports against a wide range of criteria and comments on their quality. Charities also face the challenge of reporting 'public benefit' as required by the Charities Act 2006.

Funders are also looking more acutely at performance and expecting reports not just on activities but on the differences that organisations have made to people's lives. Many of the new generation of large donors made their fortunes from running tightly managed businesses that focused on performance. They bring the same focus on performance to the charities they support. Some seek the advice of organisations such as New Philanthropy Capital, which identifies and directs funds towards organisations that deliver high social impact.

Users are also taking a growing interest in how organisations perform. Parents want to know how schools are performing, tenants want to know how quickly housing repairs are done, members expect organisations to report on what has been achieved with their subscriptions.

These trends are part of a broader movement towards greater transparency and accountability, with companies now expected to include a 'business review' in their annual report, and central and local government being required to report annually on their performance.

So a significant new challenge for all organisations is to capture and report information that gets to the heart of performance and present it in ways that are appropriate for many different internal and external audiences.

This chapter sets out:
- the principles of knowledge management;
- how to report on performance to internal stakeholders;
- how to communicate achievements externally;
- how to set about improving performance reporting.

10.2 MANAGING KNOWLEDGE

Performance reporting requires good management of information and knowledge. As organisations become larger and more complex, so the challenge of managing the information and knowledge needed by different groups increases.

Third-sector organisations have four types of assets: physical, human, financial and knowledge assets. They have to invest in developing systems to manage knowledge effectively, just as they have staff and processes to manage people, buildings and money. Properly managed, knowledge assets can help organisations to:
- drive improvements to services by gathering and using knowledge about what works best in service delivery and what could be done differently;
- demonstrate, with evidence, the differences that services have made to people's lives;
- present the organisation's achievements more confidently;
- attract more funding from donors, particularly the new philanthropists who want to see hard evidence of progress;
- offer a competitive edge in contract bids;
- motivate staff by making them feel proud of their organisation's achievements.

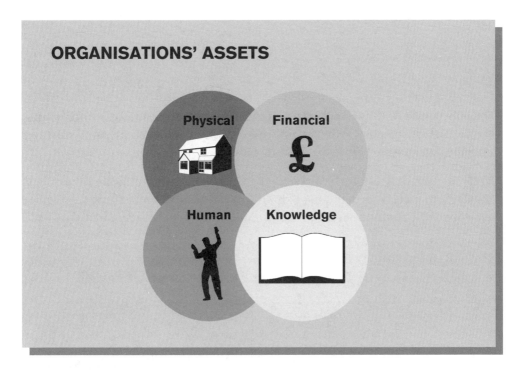

The terminology of knowledge management is as follows:

Data consists of raw facts and figures (e.g. the number of calls to the help line)

Information is data that is set in a meaningful context (e.g. the trend in the number of help line calls compared to last year)

Knowledge is information that has been condensed and distilled (e.g. comparisons of five-year trends in requests for different types of information).

Knowledge is the end result of collecting data, organising it into information and presenting it in ways that offer new insights. Knowledge management is the process of capturing, creating, distilling, sharing and using data, information and knowledge to drive improvements in organisations' effectiveness.

Managing knowledge begins with the **collection** of raw data such as the number of people assisted, the types of assistance given, the qualifications achieved or grants given. This requires judgements to be made about the most meaningful information to collect, how to gather it and how to store it. It may also require the preparation of tight definitions of 'what counts', as many services have fuzzy boundaries. For example, when does an enquirer become a service user? How is one person using a service multiple times counted? How can a person who leaves part way through a service be counted? Data collection will also require decisions about how frequently data should be collected (daily, weekly, monthly) and how it should be captured and stored.

Data from services then needs to be **amalgamated** and validated. Information may come from different services or different parts of the country or the world and someone has to take responsibility for assembling it, checking that it has been collected on a consistent basis and 'cleaning', for example to exclude anomalies.

For information to be valuable it needs to be **contextualised** to set it into context by comparing results with targets, by presenting trends or by explaining significant variances. This helps users to gain meaning from the information.

Lastly information has to be **presented** in ways that communicate quickly and efficiently to users. Raw data can be almost meaningless, whereas a graph, presented in colour with a summary headline can communicate everything required at a glance.

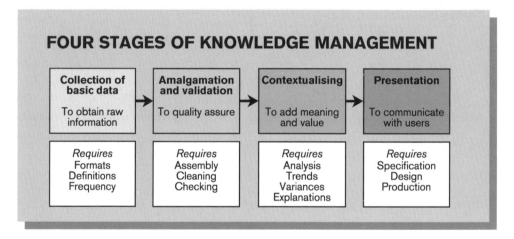

As well as working through the 'substance' of knowledge, managers need to build people's commitment to the 'purpose' of making improvements. People need to believe that the work will make a difference to stakeholders such as service users, donors, managers, board members or the wider public. They need to be convinced that the benefits will justify the time, effort and investment required. This is challenging because people can be sceptical and view knowledge management as unnecessary bureaucracy. Being clear both about why knowledge is needed and about what benefits it will bring is therefore crucial.

Questions that can encourage people to consider whether knowledge management needs improving include:

- Could we collect better evidence of the difference we make to people's lives?
- Could we use this evidence to make more informed decisions about what we do and how we do it?
- Could we communicate the difference we make to people's lives more effectively and therefore attract more funding?
- Do other organisations communicate the difference they make more effectively than we do?

IMPROVING PERFORMANCE REPORTING AT MACMILLAN CANCER SUPPORT

Macmillan joined a group of four organisations that decided to work together to improve performance reporting. Early work with service managers included tightening up the definitions of objectives that services set out to achieve and agreeing key performance indicators and measurable targets/project milestones.

The overall aim was that 'by 2008 we can report to internal and external stakeholders relevant information about the difference we are making to the lives of people affected by cancer, and we are continuously improving what we do based on this information'.

The specific objectives were that:

- 'We have an integrated system for collecting, storing, analysing and disseminating information about the difference we make
- The information gathered is used for management decisions and also filters back to the people who collect it in a valuable form
- We develop meaningful measures of costs and benefits to help us prioritise our activities
- We create tools and a shift in culture so that performance management and impact reporting are seen as useful
- The information we collect can also be used to shout about successes to the outside world'

A senior champion led the work, supported by an information manager.

Initially, work was done to reformat the chief executive's quarterly reports to the board so that they were shorter, more visual, and drew out key themes, numbers and reasons for variances. Later a draft balanced scorecard was presented to the board using traffic lights to indicate performance. The board requested quarterly performance reports even though the data for some performance measures would not be available for many months. This gave the initiative added momentum.

Every year an 'Achievements' report was prepared, comparing objectives with results and setting these alongside past trends and the objectives for the following year. This was used primarily to communicate with staff and key external stakeholders.

Work to improve performance reporting was always founded on a desire to improve service delivery and increase the impact of the organisation.

The quarterly dashboard reports have stimulated directors to manage performance more robustly and take collective responsibility for action needed. End-of-year reports (such as the annual report) describe Macmillan's achievements in terms of the benefits to people affected by cancer. This, in turn, sharpens up how Macmillan describes objectives and KPIs.

Advances in information technology, and particularly in the establishment of **intranets** in many organisations, have made knowledge management considerably easier. Intranets enable data to be gathered, managed and presented on one system, saving large quantities of time. They allow more knowledge to be managed at lower cost and so they open up new possibilities for better and more extensive knowledge management.

Making significant improvements to knowledge management, and maintaining them over time, requires a **community of people** committed to the task. This community may include people who are responsible for the collection of primary data, people who assemble data and people who use it to manage services or report on performance. Heroic efforts by one or two people striving on their own to make improvements are unlikely to be successful.

Improving the analysis and management of knowledge needs to be **appropriately resourced**. Organisations are likely to make significant strides forward when someone becomes responsible for knowledge management and has time to dedicate to the task. Another key step can be to make someone responsible for the administrative work involved. When these functions are part of people's jobs, knowledge management is more likely to become fully embedded in the way the organisation works.

Knowledge management architecture

Organisations need to create an 'architecture' that defines how data, information and knowledge will flow from source to end users and back to the original supplier. This needs to map:

- who will provide the raw data
- who it will be sent to
- who will manage it
- how it will be distributed.

Knowledge management begins with managers collecting and possibly contextualising information on key dimensions of performance. These may relate to inputs (money and time), processes (what work was done) or outputs (what we delivered) or outcomes (what was achieved). This information needs to be brought together into a central information bank. This could be as simple as a spreadsheet, it could use 'off-the-shelf' performance software or it could be a bespoke system.

When the information has been checked and cleaned, it can be fed into a knowledge bank that can be made available to a wide range of users who will need it for different purposes.

An overarching model for knowledge management could be based on the following model:

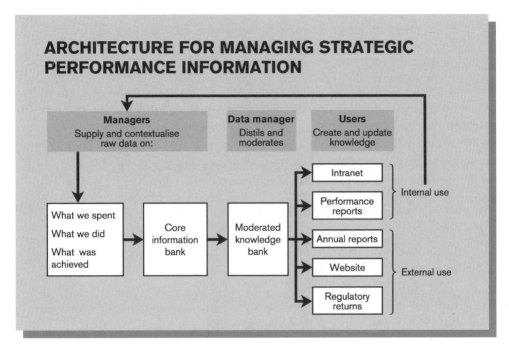

ARCHITECTURE FOR MANAGING STRATEGIC PERFORMANCE INFORMATION

The aim should be to streamline the flow of data from managers through to information and knowledge that can be used to inform decisions. Ideally information should only be 'keyed in' once, checked once and then fed into a knowledge bank that is accessible to managers and possibly board members as well.

In the private sector there are many suppliers of 'Executive Information Systems' that provide the software to support this type of knowledge management and, at the time of writing, systems were just starting to be developed for third-sector organisations. They are also called 'Decision Support Systems'.

Experience in the business world is that:
- The 'people' aspects of knowledge management require as much attention as the 'technological' design of the system
- Solutions need to be flexible to respond to changing circumstances
- Implementation takes longer and requires more effort than most people anticipate.

KNOWLEDGE MANAGEMENT AT SENSE

Sense is a large organisation providing a wide range of services and campaigning on behalf of people who are deafblind (both deaf and blind). It operates throughout the UK and is dependent on a wide range of income sources. It has demanding knowledge management requirements. Its managers worked hard to identify and track the differences it makes to people's lives. This involved pilot exercises with a number of services to test different approaches to gathering information about performance.

The senior management team agreed that the primary objectives of improving knowledge management were:

- to provide high-level data on the difference the charity makes to individuals in order to facilitate strategic decisions on service priorities
- to improve operational planning for frontline services through a greater focus on impact data and targets for enhancing impacts
- to produce external reports containing meaningful achievements

Sense developed an architecture for its information management processes to give managers an overview of the way key management activities and information flows relate to each other.

Data and information management model

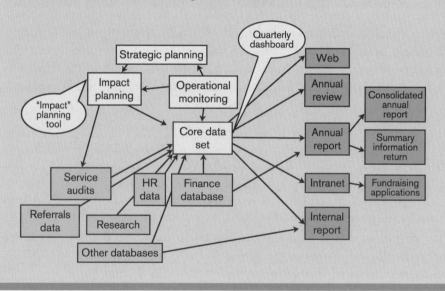

10.3 REPORTING EFFECTIVELY TO INTERNAL STAKEHOLDERS

Some performance information, such as overall achievements and funds raised last month, needs to be easily available to everyone in the organisation. They need to feel proud of what the organisation has done. More detailed information on performance is needed by the board and senior managers. Heads of departments require information about the performance of their services.

In most organisations, information sources grow in fragmented ways as new services are developed, new methods of fundraising are established and new managers are appointed. This information resides in different formats, in different databases and sometimes in different locations. It is often almost inaccessible to other potential users. Managers consequently spend a great deal of time preparing and manipulating it for different users. And different departments often hold different versions of what is essentially the same information; for example, fundraisers write up a project in a way they think will appeal to donors; meanwhile the publications team writes it up for the annual review. Quite apart from the waste of time, the organisation runs the risk of embarrassment if the two accounts differ and left hand appears not to know what right hand is doing.

Taking a more strategic approach to making performance information accessible helps to overcome such frustrations. Getting on top of this issue requires that managers:

- define the most important requirements of people who want performance information;
- make it easily available, ideally on an intranet so users can access it when they want it;
- make clear commitments in contract bids about what performance information will be available, to avoid the problem of different funders requiring similar information in different formats or at different times;
- spend more time on developing systems that meet the majority of requests than on responding to 'one-off' requests.

Once good quality information is easily available, there are many ways of promoting it across the organisation:

- It can be fed regularly into the organisation's intranet.
- Performance can be highlighted in the chief executive's newsletter.
- Posters can promote 'achievements last month'.
- E-mails can alert people when summary information has been updated.
- Meetings can begin with updates on performance.

The key is to continually refresh both the information and the means by which it is communicated.

TRACKING PERFORMANCE AT GUIDE DOGS

Guide Dogs established a corporate measurement system linked to the five aims contained in their strategy 'Moving forward together':

1. Improving and expanding the guide dog service.
2. Extending services to children and young people.
3. Defining and campaigning for better rehabilitation services for all blind and partially sighted people.
4. Campaigning for equal access for guide dog owners and other blind and partially sighted people.
5. Helping to reduce the onset of blindness and promoting eye care.

Their system tracks the performance of 26 teams around the country and makes this information available to managers so they can see how their performance compares with other teams.

The performance system was developed by one of the team leaders in conjunction with his colleagues, reducing the potential for resistance to an idea that could have been seen as being imposed on teams.

Key performance indicators were identified and agreed. Each was given a weighting so that achievements could be summed up to give an overall performance rating for each team.

The information was managed on an intranet, so managers could view current performance and, through drill-down graphs, compare this with past performance.

District team service level

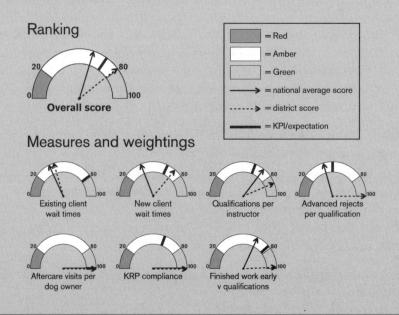

Ranking

Overall score

= Red
= Amber
= Green
→ = national average score
----> = district score
━━ = KPI/expectation

Measures and weightings

Existing client wait times

New client wait times

Qualifications per instructor

Advanced rejects per qualification

Aftercare visits per dog owner

KRP compliance

Finished work early v qualifications

LEARNING FROM SENSE

Sense, the organisation for deafblind people, put considerable effort into improving its knowledge management and performance reporting because senior management wanted to encourage managers to learn from their work and to enable the organisation to promote its work more effectively.

The learning reported by the chief executive after two years' work was that:

- Impact measures need to be a combination of hard data, feedback and stories
- Sense's strategic goals aren't exciting to everyone
- Information needs to be tailored to suit different audiences
- Proposals for new information management processes need to be integrated with existing activities and not presented as 'additional'
- Improving knowledge management needs champions at senior and other levels
- Continuous improvement is better than 'big bang' change
- Staff have developed a new appetite for knowing how well they are doing, as part of the culture shift that this initiative engendered

10.4 INCREASING THE IMPACT OF EXTERNAL REPORTS

The achievements of many third-sector organisations are often quite extraordinary. But some organisations do little to shout about their successes, and consequently receive less credit for their achievements than is deserved.

The terms 'transparency' and 'accountability' often trip off the tongue together when considering external reporting. Each has a different meaning. **Transparency** is about being easy to understand, and being open, frank and honest in all communications, transactions and operations. It is not just about making information available, it is about taking all the necessary steps to ensure that when people look into an organisation they can see clearly what it has done, how it did its work, what policies it adopted, what risks it took and how it raised and spent its money.

Accountability is the acknowledgment and assumption of responsibility for actions, decisions and policies. It encompasses the obligation to report, explain and be answerable for the consequences of the organisation's work.

In order to be accountable, organisations need to be transparent. Without transparency it is possible to hide or 'spin' reality. Whilst it is entirely appropriate that organisations create a narrative that presents their work in the best light, today people expect the highest standards of honesty. Indeed, organisations that report under-achievements honestly are often trusted more highly than those that report only good news.

Performance can be reported externally in many places including:
- the annual report;
- an annual review;
- on the organisation's website;
- on websites that present comparative information (such as GuideStar)
- in the Summary Information Return (for charities)
- in newsletters, appeal documents and promotional materials;
- on posters, exhibition stands, e-mail footers and so on.

One person needs to be given responsibility to ensure that the organisation promotes its achievements as effectively as possible in all these media. As there are now so many different places for promoting achievements, it is important to ensure that the same objectives and performance are being reported in different media. It is easy for different parts of an organisation to report on overall performance in different ways, and inadvertently dilute the messages that the organisation wishes to communicate. Some organisations establish a central record of key performance messages for staff to use, and regularly check that these messages are appearing consistently in the many different places where performance can be reported.

While consistency is important, **performance reports also need to be tailored** to meet the needs of different audiences. An annual review aimed primarily for supporters will probably place more emphasis on individual stories, whereas a review aimed at purchasers of services will need to highlight quantitative achievements of different contracts or schemes compared to objectives. A review aimed at members might focus on benefits achieved from members' subscriptions.

Websites present particular challenges, because they are accessible to all audiences. However, they offer great flexibility to allow users with different interests to 'drill down' into those areas of performance that most interest them. Structuring the website to present top-level reports on performance, supported by more detail in drill-down pages, provides great scope for being open about performance without overloading readers with detail.

Whilst the aim of reporting externally is to communicate achievements, it can have the added benefit of **protecting organisations** from inevitable pieces of bad publicity. It is harder for criticisms to stick to an organisation that is highly transparent about its achievements than it is for one that is more opaque.

TESTING EACH ACHIEVEMENT STATEMENT

The best statements of achievements for external stakeholders are fully transparent, and do not present partial information that may look good superficially but falls short of the complete picture that discerning readers now expect. Here are some quick tests for each statement:

✓ Does it pinpoint the difference made to users, the environment or public policy?

✓ Does it compare that difference with the desired objective?

✓ Does it state the period over which the change was achieved?

✓ Does it set the achievement in the context of trends?

✓ If a percentage is given does the statement give the starting figure on which the percentage is based?

Examples:

✗ We are pleased to report that we are continuing to grow our services, with a 20% increase in the number of courses offered.

✓ In 2008, over 750 people achieved our externally validated care qualification, representing a 7% increase on the previous year and keeping us on target to reach our aim of achieving 1,000 qualifications per year by 2010.

10.5 SETTING ABOUT IMPROVING PERFORMANCE REPORTING

Expectations about the quality of performance reporting, particularly in annual reports, have risen dramatically in the private, public and third sectors. Tomorrow's Company, a think tank on corporate reporting, has set out a series of proposals for improving company reporting. They recommend companies move beyond reporting historic financial information and describe their 'success model', their relationships with their stakeholders and the value they add to the community. Public sector bodies are expected to report on performance as well as finances, and the Audit Commission has set out new standards for them to meet.

Research commissioned by the Charity Commission (*Reporting Aims and Performance*, 2008) and others has demonstrated that there is also considerable room for improvement in the quality of annual reports and websites in the charity sector. Topics requiring attention include stating objectives, comparing performance against objectives, focusing on external achievements (i.e. outputs and outcomes) and reporting under-achievements.

Making improvements requires strong **support from the chief executive.** He or she needs to believe improvements are needed and demonstrate personal commitment to seeing through the changes. This support is crucial because it is so easy for initiatives to improve knowledge management to lose momentum or get bogged down in detail.

Improvements also require strong **support from the board.** If board members are demanding better information, management has the incentive to ensure that it is collected and presented in meaningful ways.

There are always many improvements that can be made, so management needs to **prioritise** those changes that will bring greatest benefits. It might, for example, be better to have a dashboard with some data missing than trying to complete it all first time. Alternatively it might be better to get good information on some services and leave those that have less accessible information until later.

This type of work needs **proper resourcing.** In particular it requires a **champion** who can drive the initiative relentlessly forward. It also requires that the managers who are expected to gather additional information are supported and that the task is made as easy as possible for them. Investments may need to be made in computer hardware or software to make the overall process as streamlined as possible.

Opportunities should also be taken to **scrap processes** and data that are no longer required. This can bring great relief to hard-pressed managers who are wondering where they will find the time to undertake new tasks.

Finally, **small but significant improvements** should be given priority over grandiose schemes. An overall plan for longer-term improvements is necessary, but the best way to gain momentum is for managers to see big gains for little effort.

SHOUT ABOUT SUCCESS

Four national charities worked as a group over a two-year period to improve significantly the ways they promoted their achievements. I brought the group together and facilitated quarterly meetings at which we reviewed progress and agreed next steps.

From this programme I learned that:

- Working as a group provided a strong incentive for each organisation to work hard between meetings, so they could report significant progress at quarterly meetings
- The organisations that had a project champion and strong support from their chief executive made the greatest progress
- It takes much more time and effort than anyone anticipated to get all parts of an organisation aligned behind a corporate performance management system
- Once a system has been established and is used it quickly becomes part of the culture and the way people work

Testing for transparency of reporting

It is surprisingly easy to report on performance but not get to the heart of the real difference that the organisation has made. The following tests can be used to check rigorously whether performance reports are truly transparent.

Content: reports should give an overview of performance presented in an honest way. Questions to test the quality of the content include:
- Do reports summarise the organisation's biggest or most important external achievements?
- Have reports said how many people used the organisation's services?
- Have they set out the difference the services made to people's lives?
- Do reports demonstrate the linkage between objectives, achievements and the next year's plans?
- Have under-achievements been reported honestly?
- Have achievements (and under-achievements) been linked directly to the relevant objectives?

Starting from the readers' perspective: reports should start from the perspective of what the reader wants or needs to know, rather that what the author wants to describe. Questions to test whether reports meet readers' requirements include:
- Are the needs of the external reader at the top of the author's mind?
- Is the purpose and work of the organisation contextualised for lay readers?
- Is the language used accessible to lay readers?
- Do reports make assumptions about previous knowledge of the organisation and its activities?
- Is hard evidence of achievements combined with stories and testimonies?

Style: people are inundated with information these days. Tests to check ease of access include:
- Are reports short and succinct, written to ensure every word counts?
- Do they avoid the use of acronyms and jargon?
- Do they use design devices (e.g. text boxes, tables, diagrams) to liven up communication?
- Do they put financial and numerical information in a graphical format?

Wider availability: once information has been prepared, it should be put to greatest use:
- Are all performance reports easily available on websites, intranets and in printed formats?
- Are they accessible to different audiences (e.g. the visually impaired) and in different languages?
- Is information presented consistently in different media (e.g. annual reports, websites)?

SUMMARY OF KEY POINTS

People want to know about achievements

- Public policy gives concessions and advantages to third-sector organisations and in return they are expected to be open, transparent and accountable to the public
- Expectations of the public, funders and the media for clear, complete, honest and meaningful reports of performance have risen dramatically

Managing knowledge

- Knowledge is an asset that needs to be effectively managed to drive improvements to services, improve competitive position, attract donors and motivate staff
- Data consists of raw facts and figures. Information is data that is set in a meaningful context and knowledge is information that has been condensed and distilled
- The four stages of improving knowledge management are collecting basic data, amalgamating and validating it, contextualising it and presenting it. Each stage requires different skills
- Winning people's commitment to improving knowledge management is critical to achieving enduring improvements
- Improvements need to fit into an overall 'architecture' for information management

Reporting effectively to internal stakeholders

- Information develops in very fragmented ways
- Diverse requests for information are frustrating for managers, so establishing systems to make it easily available can bring great benefits
- A wide variety of communication channels should be used to communicate achievements internally

Increasing the impact of external reports

- Transparency is about being easy to understand, and being open, frank and honest in all communications, transactions and operations. Accountability is the acknowledgment and assumption of responsibility for actions, decisions and policies
- Performance needs to be reported externally through many different channels, highlighting information appropriate to the audience

Setting about improving performance reporting

- Organisations make most progress when:
  - the board requires that improvements are made
  - there is strong support from the chief executive
  - priority areas for improvement are carefully selected
  - the work is given the resources required
  - one person takes responsibility for leading the work
  - processes and data no longer required are quickly scrapped
  - small but significant improvements are given priority over grandiose schemes

FURTHER READING

Learning to Fly – Practical Knowledge Management from Leading and Learning Organizations, Chris Collinson and Geoff Parcell, Capstone, 2004

The Complete Idiot's Guide to Knowledge Management, Melissie Rumizen, Alpha, 2002

11 Creating flexible management structures

11.1 ANTICIPATING FUTURE REQUIREMENTS

Structures are central to our understanding of organisations. When people describe how their organisations work, they talk about them being structured into five departments, or about having monthly meetings of the leadership team or working on cross-functional task groups. Structures define the way the parts of the organisation should fit together.

In the past, structures were seen as relatively fixed and were altered infrequently. The environment around organisations is now changing much more rapidly. New sources of funding, new methods of delivering services and the need for greater efficiency all mean that organisations need to be highly flexible. And flexible organisations are better able to adjust to the more uncertain and more demanding environment than those with more rigid arrangements.

Managers need to anticipate future needs and organise around them. Growth, changing priorities and new funding methods may all require new structures. Management's task is to adjust the structure to meet the future demands on the organisation.

It is well known, though, that structure itself is seldom a fundamental determinant of an organisation's performance. It is all too easy to blame the structure for all sorts of management problems, to invest great effort in designing and implementing a new structure, and to cause much personal angst during the transition. Months later, the original difficulties reappear because underlying problems have not been resolved.

Nevertheless, organisations do grow. New ventures are established, new posts are added and spans of control become elongated. Within a relatively short period, what looked like a rational structure can become confusing to people inside and outside the organisation. In these circumstances, structural change is required.

Although this chapter is about structuring organisations into departments and divisions, it should be recognised from the outset that management structures create barriers which can become obstacles to effective working. Departments find themselves competing against each other for resources, people become protective of their departmental interests and managers' egos become attached to the success of their department.

Managers can take actions to break down these barriers. People can be promoted across, rather than within, departments. Staff can shadow colleagues in other departments as part of their professional development. In some circumstances, people can swap jobs for a limited period of time to broaden their experience.

This chapter explains:

● how cultures and structures evolve;
● the criteria for choosing a line management structure;
● how to work across the line management structure;
● the appointment and role of deputy chief executive;
● how to integrate management and meeting structures;
● how to implement changes to the structure.

For clarity, the term 'back office' is used as a generic term to describe finance, HR, ICT and facilities management. The term 'support functions' is used to describe back office functions and all other activities that support the delivery of the organisations' services and campaigns including fundraising, communications, public relations, strategic planning and governance support.

11.2 CULTURES AND STRUCTURES EVOLVE

The term 'management structure' refers to the way in which paid management and staff are organised into units that are held accountable to senior management and ultimately to the chief executive. The term is often used to describe reporting lines on an organisation chart or an organogram. These define how the different roles in an organisation relate to each other. In practice, organisations are much more complex creatures. The way people are formally accountable to each other is determined by the lines on the organogram. But this is only one influence on the way organisations work. That is determined by tradition, behavioural norms, informal relationships and power structures.

So, before thinking about the lines on the chart, consideration needs to be given to the type of culture that will enable the organisation to deliver its strategy most efficiently.

Developing a management culture to fit circumstances

Management guru Charles Handy has described four types of management culture. Elements of each culture may exist in all organisations, but one is likely to be predominant.

- **The role culture** is the conventional hierarchy with the chief executive at the top and all staff having roles that fit into the hierarchy. This culture works for larger organisations and when the future is reasonably predictable. Role cultures use cross-functional groups to coordinate different departments. This culture is often predominant in large service delivery organisations.

- **The task culture** is built around groups of people that are established to work on problems or projects and are then disbanded. Groups bring together the expertise needed to solve the problem. Staff may report formally to a functional manager, but their daily work will be done through a series of different teams. This culture works well for organisations that deliver time-limited projects or programmes. Think tanks and organisations offering consultancy-type services often have this culture.

- **The club culture** is built around an individual, sometimes the founder, and is more informal. Relationships between members of the club are more important than the lines on the chart. This culture is good at responding quickly to opportunities and changing circumstances because people tend to be conscious of what others will be thinking. This culture is likely to be predominant in young campaigning organisations and new organisations.

- **The existential culture** exists when individuals are more important than the organisation. The talent of the individuals is the organisation's critical asset, and coordination between them may be less than in other cultures. This culture is likely to predominate in research institutes and arts organisations.

The **fit** between the culture needed to deliver an organisation's strategy and the structures and processes that exist at present will be a significant determinant of its effectiveness. For example, in organisations where the majority of the work is organised around delivering projects, developing team relationships, project management and systems for sharing knowledge will be more important than the lines on the organisation chart. An example of poor fit might be a new organisation that has outgrown the club culture and needs to develop the arrangements that create a culture where roles are more clearly defined and reporting lines more important.

Culture, and in particular levels of culture, are discussed further in section 13.2, Understanding organisation culture. The central point here is that structures and processes need to be developed to suit the work that the organisation does. When organisations grow significantly or when the type of work they do changes, they will need different types of structures and processes.

Stages in the evolution of management structures

A further dimension of management structure relates to organisations' size. The growth and development of management structures follows a common pattern in many organisations:

- **Stage 1   The start-up structure.** In this stage all staff report to one manager. The club culture may predominate. But when organisations grow beyond about 10 people some structure is needed, and reporting lines need to be established, though all staff may continue to meet as one group. As growth continues this arrangement eventually becomes untenable and gradual re-organisation into the next stage begins.
- **Stage 2   The departmental structure.** In this stage management is structured into a series of departments (for example service delivery, finance and fundraising). Each department will have a 'head' who is a member of the leadership team. Growth in the number of departments (e.g. different services, different fundraising methods, different internal support departments) eventually leads to too many people reporting to the chief executive, and so the management structure has to move on to the next stage.
- **Stage 3   The divisional stage.** In this stage departments are grouped into divisions. Departmental managers report to directors who in turn report to the chief executive. In this stage, there needs to be a clearer distinction between the functions of the 'centre' and of the 'service delivery units' (see section 8.2, Defining services and campaigns).

Developing clear and consistent management structures can be difficult when organisations are on the cusp of moving from one stage to another. They may be too large to continue effectively in the previous stage but not big enough to justify moving fully to the next stage. Half measures may be required with a mix of departmental and divisional heads on the leadership team.

The role of the centre

As organisations move through each stage the role of the 'centre' of the organisation needs to evolve. In the start-up stage the centre is just the chief executive. He or she will be responsible for coordinating many of the activities of the organisation, where possible encouraging people to work in small teams on particular issues.

In the departmental stage the 'centre' will be the leadership team. The team will share responsibility with the chief executive for both coordinating and providing leadership.

In the divisional stage there are more options for the role and size of the centre. In some circumstances it will be more appropriate to delegate a great deal to service managers and expect them to coordinate across organisation boundaries.

This is appropriate when an organisation is delivering a wide range of loosely related services. In other circumstances, tighter control by the centre is more appropriate, for example when an organisation is delivering a comparatively standardised service.

A key question the corporate centre has to consider is whether it is maximising the value it is adding to the organisation. Is it delegating sufficient functions and setting high expectations of its departmental managers, or is it expecting too much to be referred to the centre?

Considerations include:

- Whether there are economies of scale in delivering a particular function (e.g. finance, ICT and employment advice) from the centre or whether local delivery would better meet local needs (for example HR or property services)?
- Whether managers are being fully empowered and whether they have capacity to take on greater responsibilities and deliver more for the organisation.

Management will need to determine which critical matters need to be centrally managed and which can be delegated. A few areas may need to be tightly controlled by the corporate centre (e.g. resource allocation and overall strategy), and many others might be better handled if they were delegated to front-line managers and subject only to loose control.

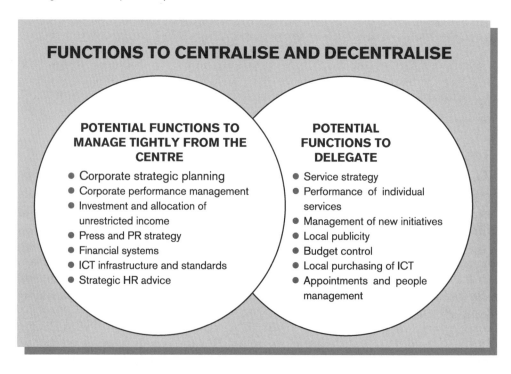

FUNCTIONS TO CENTRALISE AND DECENTRALISE

POTENTIAL FUNCTIONS TO MANAGE TIGHTLY FROM THE CENTRE

- Corporate strategic planning
- Corporate performance management
- Investment and allocation of unrestricted income
- Press and PR strategy
- Financial systems
- ICT infrastructure and standards
- Strategic HR advice

POTENTIAL FUNCTIONS TO DELEGATE

- Service strategy
- Performance of individual services
- Management of new initiatives
- Local publicity
- Budget control
- Local purchasing of ICT
- Appointments and people management

Some organisations fall into the trap of not decentralising activities as they grow so the centre becomes a bottleneck. Despite increasing efforts of senior managers, their workload grows inexorably. So, someone needs to determine which tasks can be decentralised. It is seldom whole areas of work; more often it comes down to decentralising certain aspects of each area of work.

Another trap that organisations fall into is failure to control those issues that are the critical determinants of success. The centre should have a tight grip on the overall allocation of resources to different objectives or services; it should be very clear about what specifically is being achieved for each group of service users, and it should know what it costs to achieve the benefit. Sometimes the centre may need to gather additional information to enable it to manage these critical success factors.

A further problem occurs when organisations have capable middle and front-line managers who are not given clearly specified boundaries to their work. In these circumstances it is tempting for senior managers to involve themselves in the detail of the services to the detriment of their primary task of setting objectives and boundaries and delegating practical responsibilities to their unit managers.

Overcoming conservatism

It is an ironic truth that many organisations committed to social and environmental change and development can be conservative when it comes to changing themselves. Examples of arrangements that have passed their 'use-by' date include:

- Small organisations committed to consensus-style management, with everyone having a say in everything, growing beyond the point where this is possible.
- Medium-sized organisations continuing to operate with one person attempting to coordinate everything, when a leadership team is required to manage across functional boundaries.
- The hierarchical structures of some long-established organisations making decision-taking tortuously slow, even when urgent action is required.

So managers, and sometimes boards, must be alert to the need for change and be prepared to invest the time needed to precipitate change in conservative organisations.

Some organisations are easier to change than others. The pressures for change are strongest in organisations funded by the sale of their services. Here, market forces work to demonstrate a clear linkage between the need to change and the organisation's survival. In donor-funded organisations, where money may continue to flow in long after the organisation has lost its cutting edge, particular vigilance about the appropriateness of structures is called for.

11.3 **CRITERIA FOR CHOOSING A MANAGEMENT STRUCTURE**

At the simplest level, management can be divided into the services (or campaigns) that the organisation delivers and the support functions (such as finance, fundraising and HR) that enable the organisation to deliver them.

Services can be structured in four fundamentally different ways:

DIFFERENT WAYS TO STRUCTURE SERVICES

Structure	Examples	Advantages	Disadvantages
By service user	• Young people • Adults • Elderly	Focuses the organisation on the particular needs of each client group	Less suitable when service delivery is dependent on specialist skills
By content	• Education service • Housing service • Benefit rights service	Focuses on professional skills needed to deliver the service Recognises different nature of services	Cumbersome for service users who need to access different services
By funder	• Contract services • Charitable services • Sales-funded services • Membership services	Separates out different 'business' logic that applies to different services	Risks fragmentation of service delivery
By geography	• Countries • Regions • Counties • Districts	Puts decision-making close to clients Allows for regional differences	Danger of over-stretching professional skills

Support functions tend to be grouped by specialist skills. Combinations include:

- finance, ICT, facilities, planning and performance;
- fundraising and communications;
- communications, public relations, press.

Some organisations create a chief executive's department which can include planning and performance, governance support, new initiatives and legal advice.

The criteria that determine the choice of a preferred structure include:
- the size of the leadership team;
- current managers' skills and experience;
- the span of control of leadership team members;
- the strategic importance of different functions;
- the size of divisions or departments.

Size of the leadership team

A starting point for determining the management structure of an organisation is the number of people who report directly to the chief executive. Although the size of the leadership team depends on circumstances, many chief executives find that having between four and six people reporting to them is optimal. This allows for a diversity of views on the top team, whilst maintaining a size that allows free and easy discussions at team meetings and gives the chief executive a workable span of line management responsibility. Providing managers with high-quality support including regular one-to-ones, an annual appraisal as well as meeting to discuss their services or campaigns takes considerable time, and many chief executives find that doing this for more than six people becomes too demanding. Teams as small as two can be appropriate, however, as can teams larger than six.

The main issues that influence decisions on the size of the leadership team are:
- **The rate of change in the external environment:** more rapid change requires faster responses by management and calls for a smaller leadership team that can meet at short notice and take quick decisions.
- **The complexity of the organisation:** more complex organisations require smaller leadership teams so that members can spend more time together coordinating activities and coping with the complexity. Working in a complex environment with a large leadership team is a particularly difficult combination to manage.
- **The need to have specialist knowledge on the team:** having people with critical specialist knowledge that is needed at most meetings may be important.
- **The stability of the leadership team:** when a group of managers have been in a post for a few years and they understand each other's assumptions, styles and skills, then the team can be larger.
- **Past experience of the leadership team:** when the experiences of members of the team are very divergent (for example, from private, public and the third sectors), large leadership teams are difficult because members are making judgements based on different assumptions.

- **The extent of delegation:** a larger management team means that more decisions will be taken in sub-groups rather than by the team as a whole. A smaller team, however, can necessitate more levels of management, with the attendant increase in bureaucracy and communication problems.

EVERYONE WANTS A SEAT AT THE TOP TABLE

Every department can make a compelling case for having a seat on the leadership team:

- Regional managers argue, 'We deliver the services – without us the leadership team moves into an ivory tower, utterly removed from practical service management issues'.
- The fundraising department makes the case that 'We need to be in a position to give donors a strategic view of the organisation and to represent their views to the leadership team'.
- The communication division reasons, 'Unless we are on the team, we will not have an overview, so we won't get our public image right and consequently won't be able to raise the money or win the campaigns'.
- The research department suggests, 'We hold the keys to long-term success. If we're not on the team, investment may be wasted'.
- The HR department pleads, 'People are our main asset; HR management must have an overview and be represented'.
- The new initiatives team believes, 'We represent the future services that will be critical in the long term – we cannot be demoted to a second-tier position'.

And so on. The only department that seldom has to argue its corner is finance, though even they may find themselves subsumed within a resources division in some organisations.

Tough choices have to be made to create a workable team.

Current managers' skills and experience

A crucial determinant of management structure will always be the current managers. Their skills and their development needs cannot be separated from the structural issues. Holding on to talented people, giving them growth opportunities and widening people's experience will always be vitally important. People are the organisation, and the primary purpose of the structure is to create arrangements that enable them to work together effectively. Structures that are perfect in theory are of no use if they do not capitalise on the available people.

Judgements by the chief executive and board members about individuals and their potential are therefore often the most crucial determinant of a management structure.

Span of control of directors

Another major determinant of the composition of the top team is the span of control of each member of that team. They can have more direct reports than the chief executive because they have less responsibility for managing relationships with external stakeholders and the board. Furthermore, people with more homogeneous departments reporting to them, for example all the area managers, can have more direct reports than those with heterogeneous group of services. Typically directors might have between five and eight people reporting to them. When one of them has too many people reporting to them decisions will be needed either to divide their role into two (and have an extra person on the top team) or to combine posts in their division.

Spans of control can become stretched when organisations deliver services in all the nations and regions of the UK. Decisions have to be taken on whether some or all of their managers should be represented on the top team. None will want to be left out, but having all represented can make a top team too large. One way around this is to have a wider group of directors who meet less frequently with the leadership team (see section 11.6, Integrating management and meeting structures.)

Fit with the organisation's strategy

Ideally there should be close alignment between the organisation's strategic objectives and its management structure. This means that responsibilities and job titles should map as directly as possible on to the objectives in the strategic plan. This makes it much easier to hold individuals to account for the achievement of each objective.

Since organisations should have more externally oriented strategic objectives than internal ones, it follows that the majority of posts on the top team should ideally be externally oriented.

Size of divisions or departments

The size of departments is sometimes a further consideration. A department that accounts for a large percentage of the organisation's staff and activity usually has better claim to be represented at the top than a small department. Conversely, a small department whose work impacts significantly on the future (e.g. new ventures) may have a strong claim. In practice, many organisations end up with some large and some small departments represented on the top team.

RE-STRUCTURING MANAGEMENT AT CITIZENS ADVICE

The Citizens Advice service helps people resolve their legal, money and other problems by providing free information and advice from over 3,200 locations, and by influencing policymakers. The service helps around 2 million people to resolve nearly 5.5 million problems every year. All Citizens Advice Bureaux are members of Citizens Advice, the national charity which provides leadership and support and sets standards for advice and governance.

The senior management team of Citizens Advice consisted of directors of advice, the network, policy, communications, finance, HR and ICT. A review concluded that a smaller team, better able to focus on leading the delivery of a new strategy and driving new business development, was needed.

It also concluded that some heads of department could take on greater responsibilities and that relations between directors and department heads could be strengthened.

Options for the structure of the top team were considered by the chief executive and the chair's committee, and when a preferred option was agreed the chief executive carefully re-organised departments into the four new divisions.

The resulting structure was as follows:

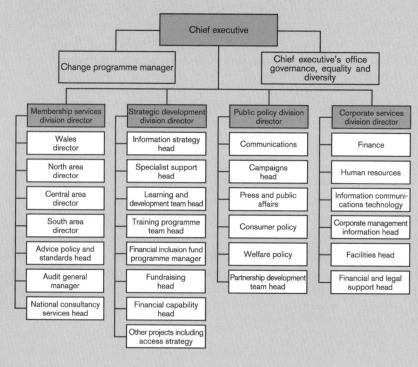

11.4 WORKING ACROSS LINE MANAGEMENT STRUCTURES

In most organisations the line management structure is the predominant model of the organisation in people's heads. However, many organisations also require extensive cross-functional working in order to be effective. A few organisations have tried to recognise this by having a 'matrix' structure where managers report to two bosses (for example a regional director and a functional director). Formalising this across the whole of an organisation has been found to be complex and bureaucratic. A more accurate model of reality may be one in which cross-organisation groups are treated as being as important as the line management structure, but everyone has only one boss.

Cross-functional groups can be temporary or permanent. Temporary groups may be called task groups or project teams. They have a specific task to carry out in an agreed timescale and are dissolved when it is completed. Permanent groups are valuable when integration across the organisation is required on a continuous basis. The membership of the group may change from time to time, but its purpose remains comparatively constant. Examples include groups that integrate service delivery with fundraising and groups that integrate fundraising and communications.

Cross-functional groups provide an excellent opportunity for involving people from different levels of the organisation in management. These people can bring new and different perspectives to issues and, by forging personal links across functional boundaries, will strengthen the ability of management to resolve issues. Involving people from different levels allows people to demonstrate their potential for future promotion. Making adjustments to cross-organisational groups is much less demanding than changing the line management structure. This makes them an important source of flexibility in the management structure.

Establishing cross-functional groups

Establishing cross-functional groups with the potential to succeed requires that:

- **Each group has a very clear brief.** It should specify the desired outcome and also the scope of the task. It is easy for a group to drift into many issues that are not central to the task, so specifying the boundaries helps to keep the group focused.
- **Each cross-functional group needs to have a plan.** It should establish objectives, performance indicators and milestones to monitor progress.
- **The group has a leader with the authority and internal credibility to carry out the task.** The leader must command the authority needed to complete the task, either through his or her position in the organisation or through personal persuasiveness and the support of senior management. The leader's brief should clarify to whom he or she is accountable (which may or may not be his or her line manager).

- **The skills of the group are appropriate.** The group needs members with the skills and experience required to achieve its tasks. Every member should be able to make a significant contribution (to justify their involvement in the group). Standardised membership guidelines (e.g. all groups should have a representative from communications) should be avoided.
- **The group has the resources to carry out the task.** This may include giving the group a budget so that it does not have to prise resources from line departments. A budget also signifies that the group is valued and that its task deserves resources.
- **Team members have the time required for the task.** The most common reason for groups not working is that members have not estimated the time the task will require or taken this into account when planning the rest of their work. A good discipline is to require members to make the estimate and agree the time allocation with both the team leader and their line manager.

For permanent groups, planning needs to be integrated into the organisation's planning cycle. In some cases, groups may need to circulate outlines of their plans to line-management departments to ensure that their requirements are incorporated into departmental and service delivery unit plans. In other cases, cross-functional group leaders may wish to review line-management plans before they finalise the cross-functional plan. In both cases, time may have to be included in the organisation's planning cycle to mesh together the line and the cross-organisation group plans.

The resulting plans should be subject to the same rigorous scrutiny that line-management plans receive and be approved in a similar manner. Their approval will help to give the group the authority to command the time and resources required to carry on with or complete the task.

Managing cross-functional groups

The essential requirements for a well-managed cross-functional group are that:

- **Leaders report in to the management structure.** The line of accountability of the leader should be known in all the departments contributing to the group.
- **Groups should ideally be of between three and eight people.** With more than eight, coordination becomes increasingly complex and time consuming.
- **Members work to the leader on cross-functional tasks.** Members of the group should be accountable to the group leader for their cross-functional tasks. They can delegate work to other members of their line department, but they remain accountable to the group leader for delivery.
- **Group leaders are responsible for managing communications with line management departments.** This work can be delegated to group members, each of whom should take responsibility for reporting progress and problems back into their own departments, and sometimes to other cross-departmental groups as well.

CROSS-DIVISIONAL PROJECT TEAMS AT CHRISTIAN AID

Christian Aid is the agency of the British and Irish churches that provides more than £90 million to support relief and development work in 60 countries. It had a matrix structure based on regions of the world (Africa, Asia, Latin America and UK/Ireland) with cross-cutting functions for education, communication, fundraising and finance. Although this worked for 10 years, it was eventually replaced by a conventional structure, supported by a series of cross-divisional project teams. A high level of cross-departmental working is essential to the success of Christian Aid, so, to ensure that project teams were successful, the leadership team (known as the Directorate) agreed the following guidelines for project teams:

Definition

A cross-divisional project is a major piece of work that can be implemented only by two or more departments, divisions or teams working together. These project teams, task forces or strategy groups have clear terms of reference, an agreed membership and adequate support for achieving their results. Cross-organisational projects and the teams have to be approved by directorate. The current cross-divisional projects are:

- Christian Aid Week
- Campaigns strategy group
- Specific change management project teams
- Major emergencies
- Supporter care and fundraising

Project planning

- **All projects must have a plan** that establishes the goals, specific objectives, actions and performance indicators of the project. The timespan for achieving each of these must be clearly stated. Project plans must also have responsibilities allocated to teams or individuals, a financial budget and a time budget. The time budget should include unallocated time to take account of the unexpected.
- **Project plans should be prepared as part of the annual planning cycle,** except in the case of emergencies. Projects may have timescales of more than one year but they will still have a new plan each year.
- **Planning formats for projects should be the same as those for teams.**
- **Project managers must be responsible for agreeing time estimates** with each team leader and staff member who is responsible for implementing part of the plan.

- **Project plans must be approved by Directorate** before implementation can begin.

Integration into the annual planning process

- **The objectives of cross-organisational projects should be sent** to all teams at the same time as the paper on 'really important priorities'.
- **Embryonic cross-organisational project plans should be circulated** to all teams before they start to prepare their annual plans.
- **Directorate should take responsibility for providing robust challenge** to project plans and for ensuring that each is realistic and achievable.
- **The planning process must allow time for team leaders to mesh team plans** with project plans before Directorate approves the annual plan.

Project management

- **All projects must have a project manager** who has overall responsibility for achieving the goals and objectives. Project managers should be responsible specifically for planning, managing and evaluating their project. They should take decisions, consulting where necessary, chase progress and directly manage the work of people who contribute to the project. Project managers will usually be Associate Directors.
- **Line accountability of project managers** to the director or an Associate Director should be clear to all staff. Team leaders and staff should have an up-to-date list of project managers and their accountability.
- **Project managers should be responsible for holding group members accountable** for carrying out agreed tasks within agreed timescales and budgets.

When groups have completed their tasks or are no longer required they should celebrate their achievements and be swiftly disbanded.

Cross-functional groups are an essential part of an organisation's management structure. However, if too many are established, they can become an obstacle to effective working. People find themselves in a never-ending round of meetings and have no time to meet the commitments they have made to all the groups to which they belong.

Responsibility for making good judgements about the numbers and tasks of groups lies with senior management. If management is overloaded with groups, action may be required in order to:

- abolish groups that are not critical at this time;
- reduce the scope of their work so their tasks are achievable;
- reduce the size of groups so they take less staff time in total;
- set tighter timescales so tasks are completed and groups disbanded;
- improve working practices so groups are more effective;
- establish time budgets to ensure that more realistic judgements are made about the tasks that can be achieved within the available time.

11.5 APPOINTING A DEPUTY CHIEF EXECUTIVE

The chief executive's role in many third-sector organisations is extraordinarily demanding. They are often expected to be the public face of the organisation, to manage relationships with external funders and stakeholders, to drive the strategic management process, to ensure that governance is well managed, to ensure that the organisation is well managed internally and to have a personal presence across the whole organisation.

Sometimes, overstretched chief executives consider appointing someone to take responsibility for some of their 'leadership' functions. Sometimes boards recommend this course of action because they can see that the overload on the chief executive is constraining the organisation's development.

Before considering this type of appointment it is worth recognising that an overloaded chief executive may be a symptom of other problems, and it might be better to address those issues directly rather than attempting the tricky task of appointing a deputy:

- The chief executive may not be delegating effectively and might need coaching to learn how to delegate and hold people accountable.
- The tasks the organisation is attempting to deliver may have grown beyond the abilities of some members of the leadership team and they may be too dependent on the chief executive's support. The organisation might need to appoint more skilled and experienced directors.
- Members of the leadership team might deliver their own functions effectively but fail to share responsibility for supporting the chief executive in leading the organisation as a whole. Leadership team development might therefore be required.
- The interest of the chief executive may be waning when he or she has been in post for a long time, or is approaching retirement. This might be a performance issue that needs to be addressed by the chair.
- Some chief executives are just unwilling to do parts of the job they do not enjoy. This might need to be addressed through a performance review.

In any of these circumstances, tackling the root cause of the problem can be more productive than appointing someone to a deputy chief executive role.

However, there are circumstances when a deputy chief executive is just what is required:

- To create management capacity to enable the organisation to grow and develop.
- To release the chief executive to focus on external relationships.
- To give someone specific responsibility for driving the 'internal leadership' to the organisation.
- To retain a key person who is ready to take additional responsibilities and might otherwise leave the organisation.

This position might be called deputy chief executive, managing director, chief operating officer or deputy director. There is no standard name for the post, so the term 'deputy chief executive' has been used here as the generic description and the other terms have been used to distinguish between the different types of deputy chief executive.

None of the terms should be confused with the notion of asking someone to 'deputise' for the chief executive when he or she is away, on leave or ill. Deputising can be done by one of the current directors, or it can be a role that is rotated amongst members of the leadership team.

Making an external appointment to any deputy chief executive role is difficult, particularly if the post has been newly created. The person appointed has to both establish the role and personal relationships with everyone involved, some of whom may feel they have been demoted even though they may have agreed the need for the appointment.

There are **four types** of deputy chief executive. All four require particularly clear definitions of the respective roles and high levels of trust between the chief executive, the deputy chief executive and members of the leadership team. They also require a great deal of flexibility between these people, as role definitions will never cover all circumstances that the team will encounter.

The managing director

The managing director is a role where one person takes overall responsibility for managing all the organisation's services and support functions. The chief executive may take direct responsibility for managing external relationships, new initiatives and for managing governance and relationships with the board.

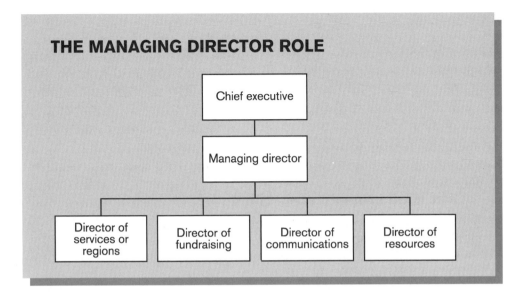

THE MANAGING DIRECTOR ROLE

The advantages of this role are that:

- It recognises the difference between the skills required to create and manage external relationships and those needed to manage delivery of the organisation's services.
- It makes recruitment of the organisation's chief executive easier because the person appointed will not need such a high level of internal management skills.

The big risk in this arrangement is that the chief executive and the managing director do not work well together. This structure requires the highest levels of trust and personal chemistry, and a willingness by both to compromise when necessary.

Another danger of this arrangement is that the chief executive becomes semi-detached from the organisation, developing initiatives and relationships that the organisation is unable or unwilling to support.

Appointing a managing director for the first time can be difficult because all the other directors may feel that they are being demoted. Their involvement in the decision to create the post and the appointment itself will therefore be crucial to managing the change and to minimising any legal risks (see box on legal issues on p. 255).

This arrangement requires that senior managers do not attempt to bypass the managing director to get decisions from the chief executive and that the chief executive turns down such requests.

The chief operating officer

The chief operating officer is a role involving responsibility for a number of departments. In one model the chief operating officer takes responsibility for all internally facing departments. This can include finance, fundraising, communications, HR, facilities, information systems, branches and planning and performance. The primary aim of this arrangement is to reduce the workload and span of control of the chief executive.

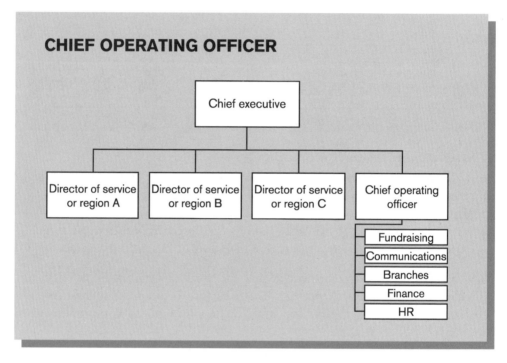

It works well when the chief executive is a great visionary, campaigner or entrepreneur but needs someone who can ensure that the systems, procedures and processes needed to manage a successful organisation are established and managed to a high standard.

When this role is introduced for the first time, managers of support functions may feel that they have been demoted and that their contributions are less valued that those of the service or regional directors. Again, this needs careful management both to gain people's support and to minimise legal risk. The perceived 'demotion' is placed into sharp relief as the regional and operational directors have maintained their reporting line to the chief executive.

SENSE – THE STRUCTURE GOES FULL CIRCLE

When Sense was growing very rapidly and the entrepreneurial chief executive was overloaded with management responsibilities, consultants recommended the appointment of an executive director to manage all the business affairs of the organisation. Regional managers reported to the chief executive, and all the other departmental managers reported to the executive director.

The arrangement worked well because the chief executive and executive director built on each other's strengths, worked closely together and trusted each other. As confidence grew, the executive director was promoted to become managing director with full responsibility for managing the leadership team.

When, eight years later, he left to become chief executive of another charity, Sense promoted one of its regional managers who was ready for promotion to take on the additional responsibility of coordinating all the regions. Many improvements had been made by the executive director and there was no longer a pressing need for that role, so the other directors reverted to reporting to the chief executive.

Another arrangement for a chief operating officer is to combine all the main service and campaigning functions under this role and leave the support functions reporting to the chief executive. Some organisations might just call this a director of services.

CHIEF OPERATING OFFICER FOR SERVICE DELIVERY

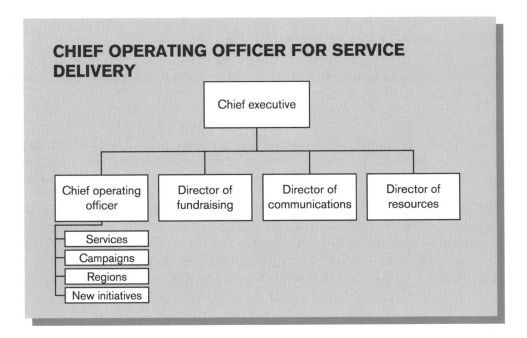

This works well when the chief executive is a good strategic manager but does not have extensive experience of the type of services that the organisation delivers or the professional skills required to deliver them. It can also provide a good promotion opportunity for a service director who is ready to take greater responsibility and might otherwise leave for employment elsewhere.

Its main disadvantage is that the leadership team is dominated by support functions rather than service delivery.

The associate director

Another option is to have a 'floating' associate director who has no line responsibilities but is used as a fixer and is given specific time-limited tasks to reduce the burden on the chief executive.

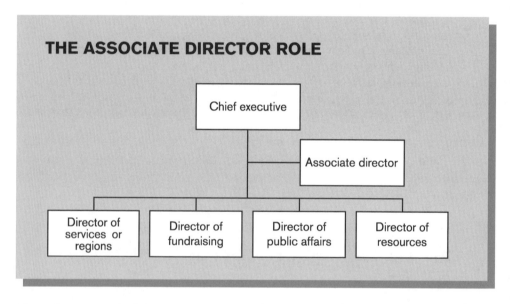

The advantage of this arrangement is that it provides significant additional management capacity for the leadership team that can be used flexibly in response to changing circumstances. It can also provide an honourable promotion for a director who has skills to offer the organisation but is not the person to take his or her current division on to the next stage in its development.

Successful operation of this arrangement depends on close working relationships between the associate director and all the other members of the team, to avoid their feeling that she or he is interfering in their responsibilities. It is also important to assess whether in practice the associate director is taking on any aspects of the other directors' roles. This may require careful management to address the risk of complaints or legal claims by the directors to the effect that their status or the express terms of their contract have been breached.

SOME LEGAL ISSUES TO CONSIDER WHEN APPOINTING DEPUTY CHIEF EXECUTIVES

Whether making an internal or external appointment it is important to consider and manage the potential legal risks that may arise from grievances and claims being brought by members of the leadership team who have previously reported directly to the chief executive.

A detailed analysis of the scope and substance of the contractual and statutory claims that may be brought by a disappointed member of the senior team is beyond the scope of this book. Points to bear in mind are that:

- Even if all other terms and conditions of the individual members of the senior management team will be unaffected by the appointment of a deputy, their actual or perceived status and their reporting line may change.
- There may be express flexibility in the employment contracts of the senior managers for the organisation lawfully to interpose a new post holder as the chief executive's deputy to whom the senior managers will report. But, if the contract does not anticipate potential changes to reporting lines the imposition of such a change may amount to a breach of both an express term of the contract and the mutual trust and confidence which is implied in all employment relationships.
- If so, this could result in an employee raising a grievance concerning the impact of the change (and possibly its manner of implementation) and, ultimately, a complaint of constructive dismissal. Constructive dismissal arises where an employer's conduct towards an employee is such that the employee is able to regard that conduct as breaching terms which go to the root of the employment relationship, enabling the employee to say, in essence, 'treating me in this way is tantamount to you dismissing me'.
- Constructive dismissal or raising a grievance centred on discrimination is not likely to be a step taken lightly by employees, and if the employee secures a new job at a similar remuneration package with a new employer comparatively quickly, there may be little practical incentive for a claim to be brought. However, it might be used by an employee who has had a series of complaints, and is therefore motivated to bring a claim.
- Some employers will have an equal opportunities policy that will deal with the process of making appointments and is likely to involve internal and external advertisements. It may be necessary to allow members of the leadership team to apply for the new role. Preventing internal applications may amount to both direct and indirect discrimination and therefore be both tactically and legally unwise.
- Even if a chief executive has received the support or agreement of his or her senior team for the need or appropriateness for a new structure to be adopted, the implementation of the appointment, including internal and external communications, needs to be handled carefully, and with appropriate legal and HR advice, in order to manage the exposure to claims or complaints from members of the senior team.

11.6 INTEGRATING MANAGEMENT AND MEETING STRUCTURES

The management structure and the structure of key meetings need to be considered together as they both contribute to the overall management arrangements, and because proposals for the structure of management influence the types and frequency of meetings required. Consideration needs to be given to:

- which groups of people need to meet regularly;
- who attends these meetings;
- how often they happen;
- who chairs them;
- how they are managed.

Most people can recount stories of meetings that are held too frequently or too infrequently, are attended by people who didn't really need to be present, are poorly prepared and managed, achieve little and consume a great deal of time. Systematic development of the meetings structure can help to overcome these problems.

Management has to decide which types of meeting are needed for which purposes, who should attend and how frequently they should be held. Clearly, choices have to be made so as to avoid people spending all their time in meetings.

The choice should ensure that the meetings structure and the management structure are aligned. So, for example:

- the creation of a smaller leadership team could be combined with the introduction of meetings of a wider management team;
- the establishment of service teams could point to reduced frequency of all staff meetings;
- the delegation of greater authority to divisions could lead to their teams meeting more frequently.

Chief executives need to be aware of and sensitive towards the perceptions of managers who have traditionally attended a particular category of meeting, who are then told that they will no longer be expected to do so. A decision to exclude employees from participating in certain meetings or a decision to dispense with certain meetings altogether may still have legal implications. Managers may feel that they have been demoted in practical terms and their status within the organisation diminished, and that colleagues will view the situation in the same light. Careful handling of these situations, allowing time for concerns to be raised, should minimise the risk of someone taking legal action.

TYPES OF MEETINGS

Group	Common purposes	Typical frequency
Leadership team	To provide leadership and strategic direction to the organisation as a whole To coordinate across divisions and departments To prepare policy advice for the board	Monthly or quarterly
Wider management team	To coordinate planning and review performance across the whole organisation To address issues that benefit from a wide range of perspectives	Quarterly or half yearly
Divisional team	To provide leadership to the division To plan and manage the division's work	Weekly, monthly or quarterly
Service and campaign teams	To manage delivery of services and campaigns and support functions To develop plans for the future To help one another solve tricky issues	Weekly, monthly or quarterly
All managers	To brief managers on important issues To consult them on future plans To report on performance	Bi-annually or annually
All staff (In departmental and divisional stage organisations)	To allow everyone to feel part of one enterprise To hear about progress To consult on future plans	Annually or biennially
All staff (In start-up organisations)	To coordinate between individuals To develop future plans To review achievements	Weekly, fortnightly or monthly

Regular meetings develop a life of their own, so their purposes need to be reviewed regularly to confirm that the value they add to the organisation justifies the time invested in them.

MANAGEMENT STRUCTURE AND MEETINGS IN A CAMPAIGNING ORGANISATION

This campaigning organisation exists to protect and improve the environment. It is a large and complex outfit with operations at local, national, country-wide and international levels.

It had directors for each of the four nations of the UK, for campaigns, activism, supporter development, communications, organisation development, information systems and finance. The top management team was therefore large.

This team worked well as a strategy group, meeting quarterly to review progress and establish future priorities.

Monthly meetings of the team to manage operations were less effective, so a consultancy review recommended that:

● Monthly meetings should be replaced by meetings of task groups of directors attended only by people responsible for delivering those tasks
● Each meeting should be well prepared by the leader of the task
● Meetings should be time limited, with agendas identifying decisions required and the time allocated to each item

These groups would also prepare cross-organisation items that required decisions from the full team, so that each item was well thought through before the quarterly meeting.

This arrangement was designed to reflect the need for a large top team, but to ensure that operational decisions could be taken by smaller groups of directors.

11.7 CHANGING MANAGEMENT AND MEETING STRUCTURES

Making significant changes to the management structure is a sensitive and time-consuming task. Getting agreement to the process, developing alternatives, consulting the board and staff and dealing with the human implications all consume effort and energy. It is a major decision which should not be taken lightly.

Before embarking on making changes to organisation structure, the highest level of **organisation analysis needs to be revisited** (see section 1.5, Deciding where to start making improvements). The sequencing of major change initiatives (such as a new strategic planning process, re-structuring governance or merging with another organisation) will influence whether and when to begin a significant re-structuring of management.

Choosing between strategy and structure is a common conflict, particularly for a newly appointed chief executive. In some cases, a new strategy may be needed before decisions can be taken about the structure. In others, the structural problems may be so pressing that the chief executive has to accept an imperfect strategy and wait until the new leadership team is established before developing a new strategy. Although logic suggests that structure should follow strategy, sometimes it is necessary to get the right people in place in order to develop a top-quality framework for action.

The next consideration is **which aspects of management structure need to change** to deliver the required improvements. Options include:

- changing team membership and reporting lines (a conventional 're-structuring');
- changing the meetings structure;
- changing cross-functional working groups;
- appointing one or more 'interim managers';
- improving or making better use of existing management processes.

The third consideration is the **scale of the re-structuring**. It may be possible to change the structure of the leadership team and make only essential changes to the departments which report to that team. The structure of departments could be changed later when a new leadership team is in place. Alternatively, the scale of change to the leadership team may necessitate that changes are made to the next level at the same time.

The fourth consideration is whether change is best achieved by **incremental adjustment or in one 'big bang'**. Major structural change is very disruptive, and it is sometimes possible to achieve the same end in a sequence of smaller changes. If the chief executive and the board have a view of the broad structure that needs to be developed over the coming years, they can sometimes use opportunities created by growth, departures, retirements and promotions to make a series of alterations that eventually create the desired structure.

A final consideration is the option of **appointing 'interim managers'** for a limited period of time to carry out agreed roles or specific tasks. They could be appointed to work full time or part time and they may or may not become members of existing management teams.

This option can be used when a position needs to be filled at relatively short notice. It can also buy time when a chief executive wants to avoid making a permanent appointment. It also allows very specific and sometimes short-term skill gaps to be filled. A longer-term arrangement, which may require different skills, can be made at a later date.

Tricky issues around consultation

Before embarking on a re-structuring, it is essential to consider the pros and cons of consulting with staff who may be affected. In some organisations, particularly those with a highly consultative management style, there may be an expectation that staff will be consulted in the usual way.

However, this may not be appropriate, because the interests of the individuals involved in the change (for example, promotion, a new role or more status) will not automatically coincide with what the chief executive determines are the interests of the organisation as a whole (for example, a more streamlined structure or a smaller leadership team). In these circumstances it is difficult for individuals to give impartial opinions on the different options for the re-structuring.

Although some employees may well have, or be expected to have, personal or vested interests in seeking to resist potential change, it may still be better, from a legal perspective, for the chief executive to canvass the thoughts of such employees about the proposed changes before they are presented more widely to an organisation, even if they are not going to have direct input into the formulation of the options that are under consideration.

This may not be the level of input or legal consultation that the manager may want, but it helps the chief executive to manage the risk of an employee asserting that the manner of the implementation of the change was contrary to mutual trust and confidence.

Re-structuring and redundancy

Re-organisations are often needed because organisations are growing. As they grow, the skills needed to manage them change and become more demanding. Unless people are developing their skills at the same pace as the organisation is growing, they may well not meet the organisation's future needs.

Whilst re-structuring should never be undertaken purely to deal with an issue of under-performance, it is often impossible entirely to separate the need to re-structure management and this issue.

In these circumstances, chief executives and senior managers need to anticipate that re-structuring and redundancy will become inter-connected. This can arise where the need to change a number of roles is triggered by a failure of a specific post-holder to meet their targets. Clearly a direct replacement may be one option but the circumstances may also necessitate a broader change which simply does not allow time for managing the performance of an individual.

Ideally, issues of under-performance should be dealt with promptly and through annual performance appraisals and formal capability programmes rather than at the time of a re-organisation. But, managerial and organisational *realpolitik* often dictate that formal warnings and final written warnings are not used for senior managers.

When a re-organisation might involve one or more redundancies, advice on the process should be sought from a lawyer specialising in employment at the earliest opportunity. Employment law requires that a prescribed consultation is held with people whose jobs are directly affected by the changes. This should be factored into thinking about the costs, risks and the time needed to implement the change.

Stages of a major re-organisation

The work of making major changes to the management structure should be divided into stages. The number and content of the stages depends on:

- the extent of re-organisation envisaged;
- the culture of the organisation ('the way things are done');
- expectations about the way individuals will be consulted;
- constraints on timing;
- whether there are likely to be redundancies.

Some of the stages described below can be combined in organisations that are smaller or have a less consultative tradition, or when the re-organisation involves few people. The stages are set out separately here, to clarify the logic underlying the process of implementing change.

The process set out below describes re-organisation of a leadership team and posts that might be affected by that re-organisation. The same process can be applied to re-organisations within divisions and departments, though in these cases there will be less, if any, involvement of the board.

Stage one: agree the process – The chief executive should seek agreement with the board that a re-organisation is necessary. Since re-organisations are a sensitive issue, this may require preliminary discussion with the leadership team and, sometimes, an announcement to other staff that the management structure is going to be reviewed. This preparatory stage is vitally important. The aim is to ensure that everyone involved is clear from the start why changes are necessary and how they will be consulted. It will also help to clarify that, while there will be consultation, the final decision will be taken by the chief executive and the board. In many circumstances, a chief executive will want to retain the right to propose a preferred structure to the board. But the board may also want an input into this sensitive decision because it affects the overall balance of power in the organisation and the importance attached to different activities.

The chief executive should agree with the board:
- the main reasons for considering a re-structuring;
- the scope of the exercise (involving all departments or just a few; involving senior management or other levels as well);
- the way the review will be carried out and when staff and board members will be consulted (i.e. the process);
- how final decisions will be taken (for example, by chief executive with the support of the board);
- the timetable for consultation and implementation of decisions.

Stage two: instigate a review – A review needs to be carried out to pinpoint specific problems with the current structure. This is sometimes carried out by an independent person. It may involve looking at the meetings structure as well, since the two issues need to be considered together. This review may conclude with a shortlist of key issues that the re-organisation needs to resolve and which may require wider discussion. The review can be a vehicle for gaining agreement among staff and board on the exact nature of the structural problems. It can also be used to establish clear objectives for changing the structure.

Once the need for change has been settled, attention can focus on the changes that will best achieve the agreed objectives. In straightforward circumstances, stages one and two can be combined.

Stage three: develop and evaluate options – Options need to be created, and the advantages and disadvantages of each identified. At this point, options may be either about principles (for example, to structure around services, regions or functions) or about more specific organisation structures.

Criteria for evaluating options can help to guide the choices that need to be made. Potential criteria might include:
- enhancing the capacity of the organisation to meet its strategic objectives;
- creating teams of people who will work together effectively;
- establishing teams of appropriate sizes;
- integrating teams that need to work closely together;
- keeping the costs of transition with agreed limits.

Privately, the chief executive and the board may also need to bear in mind:

- keeping the managers the organisation wishes to retain;
- managing out people who are not seen as being part of the future.

The latter inevitably need to be factored into risk analysis and planning. It is important to bear in mind that the paper trail – including memos and e-mails – may be subject to disclosure if employment claims are brought. So great care is needed when preparing documentation. The involvement of external legal advice may be advantageous to rehearse and explore options because communications between lawyers and their clients for the purposes of providing legal advice are privileged and so not disclosable.

Even with the criteria listed above, there is no way round the reality that management structures are a matter of judgement, and that ultimately the board and the chief executive are responsible for taking decisions about which management structure will best deliver the strategy. Chief executives can listen to advice from many people, but in the end a key part of their job is to create a structure and a team that will enable them to do their jobs.

Stage four: prepare a detailed structure – One or more of the options needs to be worked up into a detailed structure, fitting individuals into the emerging organogram, so that the chief executive can identify:

- posts that will remain unchanged
- posts that disappear
- posts that change partially
- entirely new posts.

Stage five: take decisions – The chief executive needs to take decisions, in consultation with the board. Once a preferred structure has been developed, individuals who may be affected need to be informed of the implications for them individually, assuming that the re-organisation proceeds as planned. A timetable for individual consultations will be required at this stage.

Appropriate consultation is an important element of a successful re-organisation – and a legal requirement in some circumstances. There will always be people who gain and those who feel they have lost out in the changes; if the chief executive has been demonstrably fair in the process, however, there will be less cause for complaint.

Consultation with staff and trade unions can be undertaken between any of the five stages.

In some circumstances it may be anticipated that that the need for changes could result in an unfair dismissal case. One way around this is to agree a way forward with the person concerned through a 'compromise agreement'. It is important to be aware that certain statutory employment claims can only be validly waived or compromised via a statutory compromise agreement – where an independent legal advisor provides advice to the employee. In these circumstances a separate strand of 'without prejudice' negotiations can be conducted to resolve and document dismissals on mutually agreeable terms.

Avoiding mistakes

Mistakes made during re-organisations include:

- springing surprises on people;
- re-organising too many levels of management at the same time;
- using re-structuring primarily to solve other problems;
- being heavily influenced by lobbying from powerful individuals or groups.

So, when preparing for a re-organisation:

- ensure people understand that there are no ideal solutions – compromise is always necessary;
- recognise that the skills of people currently in the organisation will be a significant determinant of the appropriate structure;
- ensure that the board supports the proposals;
- at the right time, consult openly with the staff and their trade union or staff association (where appropriate);
- set a clear timescale, let everyone know when decisions will be made, and stick to the timetable;
- be willing to see changes through – this is not a time for vacillation;
- manage paperwork and e-mail correspondence with care and explain why this is necessary;
- obtain HR and legal advice on the process when appropriate.

SOME LEGAL POINTS ON RE-ORGANISATIONS THAT LEAD TO REDUNDANCY AND DISMISSALS

Re-structuring raises the potential for the dismissal of employees on the ground of redundancy. The following points will need to be considered:

- Redundancies may arise if posts are amalgamated or if a new, much broader role is felt to be necessary
- Even if a re-organisation results in a new potential role which is felt to fall short of a redundancy there is still a separate question of whether the changes can be implemented merely by instructing the post-holder to undertake the revised role. Much will depend on the terms of employment and the actual circumstances
- If an employee refuses to accept the revisions to his or her role and they are not felt to be changes that are sufficient to amount to a redundancy situation then it may be necessary to dismiss the employee and offer re-employment on the revised terms of the new role.
- This may involve considering whether the affected employee can be appointed to a new, expanded role – which must involve assessments of their performance and capability
- Employees with at least two years' continuous service qualify for a statutory redundancy payment calculated according to a statutory formula. However, they will not be eligible to receive the payment if they unreasonably refuse an offer of 'suitable alternative employment'
- Whether a new role is suitable alternative employment will depend on both an objective comparison of the two roles and a subjective assessment by the employee. An employee who is offered a revised, albeit significantly different, role will need to give careful consideration as to whether to accept it (and not reject it out of hand)
- Consultation with people affected does not mean that they have a veto over the imposition of a new structure. Consultation requires that their views are considered and, if they are to be rejected, it is always better for there to be a clear and, as far as possible, objective basis for doing so. Ultimately, there may be an 'agreement to disagree' on the decision, but provided the process is conducted with appropriate vigour the risk of claims for unfair selection or discrimination can be managed sensitively
- Unfair dismissal claims can result in awards of compensation for actual loss subject to the obligation to take reasonable steps to mitigate losses and a statutory limit of just over £70,000

Management consultants often work closely with legal advisors on re-structuring of managment. The consultants focus on developing the most appropriate structure and the lawyers work on legal implementation.

SUMMARY OF KEY POINTS

Anticipating future requirements

- Management is responsible for adjusting structure and processes to meet the future demands on the organisation

Cultures and structures evolve

- One of the four cultures (role, task, club and existential) will be predominant in most organisations
- The fit between the culture needed to deliver the strategy and the culture that exists at present will be a significant determinant of an organisation's effectiveness
- Structures evolve in three stages; start up, departmental and divisional
- Managers need to agree roles for the 'centre' of the organisation, to manage them tightly and to delegate other roles
- Organisations committed to social and environmental change can be conservative when it comes to changing themselves

Criteria for choosing a management structure

- Criteria include:
  - the size of the leadership team
  - current managers' skills and experience
  - the span of control of members of the leadership team
  - the strategic importance of different functions
  - the size of divisions or departments

Working across line management structures

- Cross-functional groups bind organisations together
- They can be temporary or permanent
- They require clear briefs, a strong leader with the authority to carry out the task, resources and members with the time required to deliver the task
- Cross-functional plans need to be fully integrated with line-management plans
- Cross-functional leaders should be responsible for communicating progress and problems to the rest of the organisation
- Senior management must make judgements about the number and scope of groups and take care not to overload the organisation with too many of them

Appointing a deputy chief executive

- An overloaded chief executive may be a symptom of other problems. It might be better to address those issues directly rather than appoint a deputy
- There are circumstances when a deputy chief executive is just what is required to take an organisation to a new level of development
- The four types of deputy chief executive are:
  - the managing director
  - the chief operating officer (for support services)
  - the chief operating officer (for primary services)
  - the deputy director
- Specialist HR and legal advice should be taken to ensure that changes are implemented in line with legal requirements

Integrating management and meeting structures

- The management structure and the structure of key meetings need to be reviewed together
- Organisations have to choose which types of meeting are needed for which purposes, who should attend and how frequently they should be held

Changing management and meeting structures

- Before embarking on making changes to organisation structure, chief executives need to:
  - identify which aspects of management structure need to change
  - consider the scale of the re-structuring
  - decide whether it would be best achieved by incremental adjustment or in one 'big bang' and whether appointment of interim managers is appropriate
- Tricky issues around consulting with staff who may be affected need careful and thorough consideration before starting
- The process for major structure generally has five stages: agreement to the process of review, development and evaluation of options, preparation of a detailed structure, decision-taking and implementation
- Establishing criteria that the structure should meet helps to evaluate proposed changes in a systematic way

FURTHER READING

Understanding Organisations, Charles Handy, Penguin Books, 1997

More and recent books and reports can be found at www.compasspartnership.co.uk.

12 Managing strategic partnerships

12.1 PARTNERSHIPS DRIVE GROWTH AND DEVELOPMENT

The last few chapters described how organisations establish, manage and report on strategy, and how they structure their management to deliver it. These are essential elements of effective management, but they are not sufficient. Organisations grow when they are bubbling with creative ideas, when they inspire people to support their cause and when they both compete and collaborate with other organisations. This chapter is about the wide range of strategic partnerships that third-sector organisations can form with other organisations and in particular about the management and governance of such partnerships.

The extent of collaborative working is greater than might be expected. Charity Commission research showed that 22% of all charities work collaboratively with other charities, and of these 45% had between two and five collaborations at the time of the survey (*Collaborative Working and Mergers*, 2003). The extent and total volume of collaborative working is much larger than these figures suggest because collaboration grows with organisation size. The 5,000 charities with an income of more than £1 million per year account for three-quarters of the income of the sector. Almost 40% of these report that they work collaboratively with other charities. Conversely collaborative working is much less common among smaller organisations.

Organisations also form different types of strategic partnerships with the private sector that can involve activities such as joint marketing and staff development as well as the more traditional fundraising and sponsorship. They also form relationships with the public sector on issues such as policy development and the delivery of services.

Merger activity is also more prevalent than might be expected. The same Charity Commission survey reported that 5% of all charities (i.e. some 9,000 charities) are the result of a merger; this too is more prevalent amongst larger ones, with 13% of big charities having either merged or actively considered a merger in the last 10 years. A further 6% considered merging but decided not to proceed (*Collaborative Working and Mergers,* Charity Commission, 2003).

Organisations form partnerships and merge because they see opportunities to:
- improve services – by reaching more people and enhancing quality and consistency;
- share knowledge – by bringing different skills and experiences together;
- increase efficiency – by finding more effective methods of delivery and by reducing overhead costs;
- deal with difficulties that one or more of the partners is facing.

Establishing strategic partnerships presents many challenges. They require high levels of trust, effective leadership, the capacity to manage the partnership and extraordinarily high levels of communication between partners and with other stakeholders. Mergers present additional challenges because they have a much greater effect on board members' and managers' roles, so people leading the initiative can not always be as open with everyone as they might wish.

This chapter sets out:
- different types of strategic partnerships that are established between third-sector organisations;
- the types of partnerships that are formed with private and public-sector organisations;
- issues to consider when creating strategic partnerships;
- the characteristics of successfully managed partnerships;
- different types of mergers and how to manage the process of merging.

12.2 SELECTING PARTNERSHIP TYPE TO SUIT CIRCUMSTANCES

There are many ways in which organisations can work together. Whilst defying easy generalisation, they can be organised into four broad groups: collaborations, strategic alliances, intermediary organisations and integrations. Each category can be divided into a series of distinct types of strategic partnerships. These in turn can be seen on a spectrum, with less intensive relationships and greater autonomy at one end and closer relationships and greater integration at the other.

THE CONTINUUM OF STRATEGIC PARTNERSHIPS

Collaborations	Strategic alliances	Intermediary organisations	Integrations
Affiliations	Joint ventures	Specialist intermediary organisations	Group structures
Buying groups	Management service organisations	Generalist intermediary organisations	Takeovers
Mutual help	Franchises	International federations	Mergers
Delivery partners Collaborative services	Federal structures		
Collaborative campaigns			

◄───►

More operational   **More strategic**
Greater autonomy   **Greater integration**
Less intensive relationships   **Closer relationships**

Collaborations

Affiliations offer organisations the opportunity to demonstrate support for each other, share knowledge and work together without making any long-term or strategic commitments (for example independent local environmental organisations that affiliate with Friends of the Earth).

Buying groups enable organisations to exploit economies of scale in purchasing (for example the Charities Buying Group operated by Leonard Cheshire Disability).

Mutual help partnerships are established when organisations with similar aims recognise that more can be achieved by supporting each other in a long-term strategic relationship (for example the Strategic Network for Mental Health enables Advance Housing and Support to extend its reach by providing strategic assistance to four smaller organisations, and at the same time gain easy access to their specialist expertise).

Delivery partnerships enable one organisation to provide services by paying others to deliver some of them. This is essentially a 'sub-contracting' relationship, though it may involve a cooperative relationship rather than competitive tendering (for example Christian Aid has long-term relationships with church-based partner organisations in less developed countries who deliver projects that it finances).

Collaborative services are created where two or more organisations work together to provide a service within the institutional structure of one of them (for example the Royal British Legion works with Citizens Advice to provide welfare rights information to members of the ex-Service community).

Collaborative campaigns are collaborations where organisations come together to generate public interest in a particular issue and lobby for policy change (examples being End World Poverty and Stop Climate Change).

Strategic alliances

Joint ventures are created when two or more organisations create an additional organisation to deliver a service which none could provide on their own, or which would be more effectively provided by an independent organisation (Universities UK and Guild HE set up the Leadership Foundation for Higher Education, so that one body provides leadership development across the whole of the higher education sector).

Management service organisations are established to provide shared back-office support (such as finance, HR, ICT and facilities management) to a number of organisations (for example CAN provides offices and support services to over 40 third-sector organisations at its Mezzanine 2 offices by London Bridge).

Franchises are established when one organisation has developed a 'model' service and wishes to roll it out across the country using other organisations to both raise the funds and deliver the service (for example the Food Bank was established by the Trussell Trust in Salisbury, and it now encourages, trains and supports other organisations to provide a similar service in their own localities).

Federal structures are established when local organisations providing similar services 'federate' together to establish national standards, a national brand and to represent their common interests whilst maintaining their local autonomy (well-known examples include Citizens Advice, Samaritans and Relate).

Intermediary organisations

Specialist intermediary organisations are established to represent the interests of organisations working in the same field (for example the Social Enterprise Coalition, the Long-term Conditions Alliance and Alcohol Concern).

Generalist intermediary organisations are established to provide advice and support on issues such as governance, management, fundraising and partnerships to all types of organisations and to represent their interests to local and national government (examples include Councils for Voluntary Service and NCVO).

International federations are established to enable organisations to support each other across national boundaries and to represent their interest at an international level (Greenpeace International and the Red Cross are two examples).

Integrations

Group structures are established when a number of organisations come together under one 'parent' body but each retains legal and operational independence (the most common example being housing associations that have a number of subsidiaries operating in different areas or with different specialisms).

Takeovers happen when one organisation approaches others to ensure the future of their service but does not wish to, or is unable to, retain its independence (for example ChildLine was taken over by NSPCC).

Mergers happen when two organisations decide that they can have greater impact as one organisation rather than separately (for example the two largest cancer organisations merged to form Cancer Research UK).

Separations

It is also possible for organisations to make moves in the opposite direction and separate parts of their organisation to improve services:

De-mergers happen when organisations spin off some of their activities because they have the potential to achieve more as independent organisations (for example NCVO established and incubated organisations that were spun off many years ago and have now become Age Concern, the Charities Aid Foundation and Citizens Advice).

Service moves happen when a whole service is moved from one organisation to another because it can grow, develop and be better supported by a new 'owner' (for example United Response took some children's services from Barnardo's).

Outsourcing happens when organisations decide to purchase services from agencies that can offer economies of scale or greater flexibility (for example the Charity Technology Trust provides a credit and debit card processing system for online transactions for other charities).

These separations can increase organisations' effectiveness because they can focus on activities that make best use of their specialist skills.

Purpose of different types of partnerships

Partnerships ultimately exist to improve mission impact. They also achieve other purposes including sharing knowledge and building the capacity of the third sector. However, each also has a primary purpose that should be used to determine the type of partnership that is most suitable for each circumstance.

SUMMARY OF THE MAIN PURPOSE OF DIFFERENT PARTNERSHIP TYPES

Type of strategic partnership	Main purposes
Collaborations	
Affiliation	To share knowledge and demonstrate support for a cause
Buying group	To save costs through joint purchasing
Mutual help	To share skills and experience
Delivery through partners	To deliver through better-positioned organisations
Collaborative service	To provide a service more effectively
Collaborative campaigns	To raise the profile of an issue and achieve greater impact
Strategic alliances	
Joint venture	To deliver a service that is best provided by a third organisation
Management service organisation	To create efficiency improvements and cost savings
Franchise	To grow a service whilst giving local providers some independence
Federal structures	To apply national standards whilst maintaining local independence
Intermediary organisations	
Specialist intermediary organisations	To share knowledge and to represent views of a sub-sector
Generalist intermediary organisations	To offer organisation development and represent the interests of groups of organisations
International federations	To share knowledge and coordinate internationally
Integrations	
Group structure	To provide independence with the managerial support of a larger organisation
Takeover	To rescue struggling organisations
Mergers	To increase delivery capacity, reduce competition and generate cost savings
Strategic separations	
De-mergers	To give a service greater freedom to grow independently
Moving services to other organisations	To gain better strategic fit with other services
Outsourcing	To exploit economies of scale, and reduce costs

benefits

Partnership structures

Each type of strategic partnership can take a number of legal and structural forms. These do not map precisely on to the different types of partnerships. Choices have to be made about which structure best suits each set of circumstances.

Collaborations can be delivered by agreements between participating organisations on 'who does what'. They do not necessarily require the creation of a separate organisation. More straightforward arrangements may be set out in a legal agreement. More complex arrangements may require a separate organisation.

Strategic partnerships can draw on the resources of two or more organisations while one of them takes legal and line management responsibility on behalf of the others. In this arrangement, management of the partnership can be overseen by representatives of each participating organisation, while, if necessary, governance oversight can be provided by board members from one of the participating organisations. Legal responsibility lies with the organisation that employs staff and delivers the service. In complex or risky partnerships a legal agreement may be appropriate to specify each partner's responsibilities. In simpler arrangements an exchange of letters may be all that is necessary.

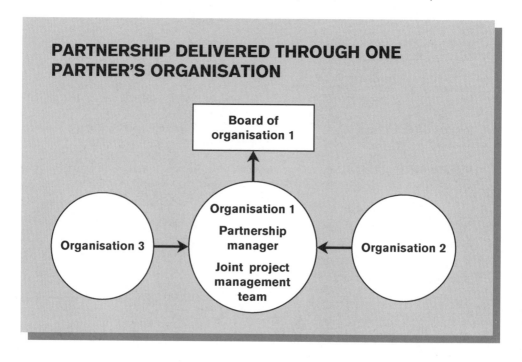

PARTNERSHIP DELIVERED THROUGH ONE PARTNER'S ORGANISATION

Board of organisation 1

Organisation 3 → Organisation 1 / Partnership manager / Joint project management team ← Organisation 2

THIRD SECTOR LEADERSHIP CENTRE

The Third Sector Leadership Centre was established by a number of voluntary organisations that recognised the need for better information about the wide range of leadership development activities to be made available to third-sector organisations.

The NCVO agreed to 'host' and manage the Centre, which was based at Henley Management College. No new legal entity was established. The staff were employed by NCVO and an advisory board was established to provide oversight of the initiative.

Alternatively, collaborations and strategic partnerships can deliver their services through a separate organisation with its own legal structure. Members of the partnership board can be managers or board members from the participating organisations. This arrangement can include an independent chair and/or independent directors, since both can bring a broader perspective to decision-taking. This can help when members have conflicts of loyalty (see section 3.7, Standards board members should meet) between their responsibilities to the partnership and their roles in their own organisations. In some cases it may be appropriate for independent directors to be in a majority.

PARTNERSHIP DELIVERED THROUGH A SEPARATE ORGANISATION

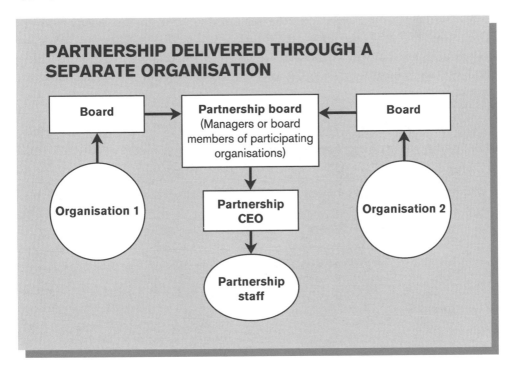

275

THE DISASTERS EMERGENCY COMMITTEE

Formed in 1963, the Disasters Emergency Committee is an umbrella organisation for humanitarian aid agencies. Member agencies include British Red Cross, Christian Aid, Oxfam, Save the Children and World Vision.

At times of overseas emergency, the DEC brings together a unique alliance of the UK's aid, corporate, public and broadcasting sectors to rally the nation's compassion, and ensure that funds raised go to DEC agencies best placed to deliver effective and timely relief to people most in need.

DEC is governed by a board of trustees that comprises the chief executive of each member agency plus up to four independent trustees, a treasurer and a chair.

DEC has its own chief executive and staff who manage the organisation and report to the DEC board.

Franchises, federal structures, intermediary organisations and confederations nearly always require a separate organisation which franchisees or members join. Franchises and federations also require a separate legal agreement setting out the rights and responsibilities of all parties. This document provides the basis for regulating the relationship between the federal body or franchisor and the members of the federation or franchisees. Subsidiary documents set out the standards which each expects the other to achieve and the mechanisms for holding each other to account when standards are not met.

A FRANCHISE STRUCTURE

The North East Social Enterprise Partnership launched a scheme to create a franchise for renewable energy social enterprises across the UK. The Community Renewable Energy (CoRE) project advises fledgling renewable energy organisations on how to generate sustainable, low-cost energy supplies.

In return, CoRE, itself a social enterprise, holds a stake in the enterprises it sets up and uses the income to create more sustainable energy organisations. Responsibilities are regulated through a franchise agreement.

Choosing the most appropriate type of partnership and legal structure depends on the circumstances. Criteria for selecting the most appropriate type include:

- **permanence** – how long is the partnership expected to last?
- **mission impact** – which will offer the opportunity to best achieve the mission?
- **freedom** – which will maximise partners' ability to do what they do best?
- **control** – which provides appropriate control over the partnership?
- **sustainability** – which offers the greatest chance of long-term viability?
- **staff motivation** – which will motivate staff and give them the greatest security?
- **management time** – which will make best use of limited management time?
- **governance** – which will be easiest to govern?
- **costs** – which will be most cost effective?
- **risks** – which best balances the risks and rewards for the partners?

Possible benefits

12.3 PARTNERSHIPS WITH THE PRIVATE AND PUBLIC SECTORS

In addition to the growth of partnerships within the third sector, organisations are increasingly establishing partnerships with the public and private sectors. Almost 40% of respondents to a Charity Finance survey (*Mergers and Collaborations*, 2004) reported that they had partnerships with public and private-sector organisations.

Managing these partnerships presents additional challenges over and above those of partnerships within the third sector, because the cultures of the private and public sectors can be very different. They often work in different ways and there will often be different implicit expectations of each other that have to be surfaced and understood. The need to invest time in clarifying assumptions, expectations, roles, plans and ways of working together is paramount.

Private-sector partnerships

Relationships with the private sector have traditionally been about fundraising and sponsorship. They have now become much more sophisticated. Research in the USA (*The Collaboration Challenge* by James Austin) established the notion of a continuum of types of relationships between companies and third-sector organisations. They begin with a **philanthropic stage**, in which the company is a charitable donor. The resources may be significant to the nonprofit organisation, but are not strategically significant to the company.

When the philanthropic stage is successful, the relationship can move to the **transactional stage**. This is a more active relationship in which both parties expect more significant benefits. Activities can include cause-related marketing, event sponsorship, product certification, licensing agreements to use logos and employee volunteering.

When a transactional stage is successful the partners can move onto the **integrative stage**. In these cases missions, people and activities are increasingly joined together. Each partner might have a member on the other's board, marketing strategies for new products might be developed together and staff might move between the two organisations. The relationship becomes more deeply embedded in both organisations' corporate strategies and the resources involved are progressively more significant.

THE COLLABORATION CONTINUUM

Relationship stage	Philanthropic → Transactional → Integrative
Level of engagement:	Low → → → → → → → → → → High
Importance to mission:	Peripheral → → → → → → → → Strategic
Magnitude of resources:	Small → → → → → → → → → → Big
Scope of activities:	Narrow → → → → → → → → → Broad
Interaction level:	Infrequent → → → → → → → Intensive
Managerial complexity:	Simple → → → → → → → → → Complex
Strategic value:	Modest → → → → → → → → → Major

Source: *The Collaboration Challenge*, James Austin, Jossey-Bass, 2000

Corporate-sector relationships present great opportunities for learning from each other and discovering different ways of working. The American research concluded that 'Cross-sector partnering was distinctive because the participants in such partnerships were likely to have noticeably different performance measures, competitive dynamics, organisation cultures, decision-making styles and personnel competencies'.

Corporate-sector partnerships are becoming more sophisticated and can include:

- charity of the year
- employee involvement
- secondments (in either direction)
- corporate events
- sponsorship
- cause-related marketing
- payroll giving
- team-building days
- gifts in kind
- public relations opportunities.

Partners need to be selected with great care, both to ensure strategic fit, and to avoid establishing a relationship that could damage either organisation's brand or reputation or create conflicts of interest or loyalty. Companies need to find partners that have a good strategic link with their business objectives (for example Carphone Warehouse and the Get Connected help line for young people). Third-sector organisations need to find partners that will bring a range of benefits without devaluing their brand and reputation.

Partners also need to have compatible values and to be able to work together in relationships of mutual trust. Compatibility is required both amongst the people who 'strike the deal' and amongst the staff in both organisations who will make the partnership work in practice.

Public-sector partnerships

The third sector is involved in a wide range of strategic partnerships with the public sector. National government, local government, the health service and a wide range of non-departmental public bodies have strategic partnerships with organisations concerned with education, health, crime, children and young people, sport, housing, culture and many other aspects of life.

Some of these partnerships go beyond straightforward funding relationships. They can involve a number of public bodies and a number of third-sector organisations working together over an extended period of time on issues such as the needs of service users, policy and strategy and appropriate methods of commissioning. They can lead to new visions for the future of services, improved delivery of services and better representation of users' views. They can attract additional sources of funding which might not have been available to organisations working separately.

Partnerships are not always necessary

Partnerships are not necessarily the best way to deliver solutions to social problems. They are extraordinarily time-consuming, and the investment of time and effort has got to justify the desired results. Greater impact can sometimes be achieved by one organisation working on its own to deliver the service and consulting with others as work progresses, or by organisations taking on contracts to deliver commissioned services.

Sometimes funders encourage partnership working, and this can be entirely appropriate. But sometimes the lure of the funding can lead to false partnerships that are only established to secure the funding and are not based on genuinely shared interests. Organisations considering such partnerships should ask themselves whether they would enter into this partnership even if there were no funding involved. If not, a commissioning relationship might be more appropriate.

Partnerships are not an end in themselves; they are a means to an end that can be more effectively achieved by working together than working independently.

12.4 CREATING STRATEGIC PARTNERSHIPS

The most appropriate approach to establishing a partnership depends on the type of partnership and the extent of its ambitions. Partnerships which require little integration and a small loss of autonomy will need less time and resource to establish. Those at the other end of the spectrum will require careful planning and extensive investment of time, effort and leadership.

A number of questions need to be addressed before serious consideration is given to establishing or joining a partnership:

- Do all the partners have spare organisation capacity to meet the demands of the partnership or the resources to create new capacity?
- Are any of the potential partners in a crisis of any form? (Those pressures will inevitably spill over into the partnership.)
- Is there any history of poor relations between any of the partners? (These too can resurface in the partnership.)
- Do potential partners have a track record of working in partnership or strategic plans that establish their commitment to work in partnership?

The single most important action in the creation of successful partnerships is to establish **good relations** between the partners. Time spent getting to know potential partners, their organisations and their contexts will be time well invested. Understanding people's values, their priorities and how their organisations work will pay dividends when the partnership has to resolve difficult issues. Seeing where missions overlap and where there may be differences of objectives or approach will also help to provide a solid foundation for the establishment of a partnership.

Investment of time in the early stages of a partnership will lead to increased **trust**, the second ingredient needed to establish a successful partnership. Ideally, relationships and trust should be built at both the governance and management levels, particularly in partnerships which have higher levels of integration or involve greater loss of autonomy for the partners.

Clarity of **objectives** is crucial, and whilst it may be straightforward to agree a few crisp sentences, it is important that new partnerships explore precisely what their objectives mean to each partner, how their achievement might be measured and whether they are achievable. Some words and phrases may have particular meaning to one partner and other partners may be unaware of them. It is easy to agree loose wording to gain agreement from the partners, but this may be regretted when partnerships have to address difficult issues and different interpretations of the original objectives emerge.

Robust **business plans** should be used to agree strategies, plans, timetables and resource requirements. Plans for partnerships also need to set out clearly the responsibilities of each partner and the commitments each is expected to deliver. They should establish governance arrangements for the partnership, and line management accountabilities. They should also provide the basis for measuring progress and, when necessary, adjusting aspirations.

It is important to estimate the **costs and time** required to establish a successful partnership. One of the more common features of partnerships is that managers and board members greatly underestimate the time required. Without sufficient time, misunderstandings occur, relationships become frayed and trust starts to ebb away. A rule of thumb is to estimate the time required from each person in each organisation, and then double it! Clearly more time is required when there are more organisations in the partnership, when partners come from different sectors or cultures and when the aspirations are more ambitious.

Risks also need to be identified and managed. In a partnership it is important to distinguish between partners who have a stake in the objectives of the partnership but are not carrying any of the risk, and those who are carrying the risks. Partners not carrying risk need to respect the roles and actions of those that are carrying risks. The types of risks partnerships have to consider include:

- short-term funding not being renewed;
- dependence on key members of staff;
- delayed decisions (particularly those requiring agreement from all organisations in the partnership);
- reputational damage resulting from disagreement amongst partners;
- keeping partners focused on the common objectives and not allowing 'mission drift' by the partnership.

When the partnership is being established, there needs to be an explicit commitment to **good faith negotiations**. Three ground rules can be useful in the set-up phase. Without the prior agreement of all partners:

- there must be no material changes in the partnership proposition;
- negotiators must be named, and should not be changed during negotiations;
- there must be no private or parallel negotiations with other external parties.

Planning, chairing and management of meetings turns out to be a crucial ingredient in the early stages of creating a partnership, so it is important to be clear who is responsible for these functions and to ensure that they are all given sufficient attention. Sometimes an independent chair can be valuable at this stage. Preparation of agendas and papers, identifying potential issues before meetings, ensuring that difficult issues are not avoided and following up actions after meetings all contribute to establishing good relationships and ensuring momentum is maintained.

One of the most difficult issues to deal with can be agreeing the right **management structure** and developing the **partnership agreement.** These come towards the end of the process of establishing a partnership, and it is important to anticipate the time and attention they will require from the negotiating team.

A strategy for managing **communications** will also be required, to ensure people are informed and consulted at appropriate times. The importance of engaging fully with front-line staff who will be directly affected by a partnership also needs to be recognised and given careful attention.

THE GOVERNANCE HUB – A VOLUNTARY SECTOR PARTNERSHIP

In response to the need to improve the governance of voluntary organisations, 10 national infrastructure organisations came together to plan and deliver a £1.5 million investment in improving information, support and advice on good governance.

A series of six 'long half-day' meetings were held with a 'core group' of members to assess the most pressing needs, to establish an overall aim and agree three specific objectives for the hub. It also agreed a management structure for the delivery of the programme and governance arrangements. A wider advisory group was established to encourage ongoing communication with stakeholders.

Preparation of a business plan was the main vehicle for getting agreement, a deep understanding of the proposal and the assumptions underlying it. The long half-day meetings helped to establish good relationships and a high level of trust between the partners.

12.5 LEADING STRATEGIC PARTNERSHIPS

Once a partnership has been established, attention has to turn to its ongoing leadership. Much of the guidance that applies to the leadership, management and governance of organisations is equally applicable to partnerships, but each element has a distinctive feature in the context of a partnership.

Leadership is a crucial ingredient. Partnerships succeed because someone champions the partnership and gives it the requisite attention, drive and commitment. Partnerships also require 'leaders' in each of the member organisations to manage relationships between the partnership and their organisation. They can also ensure that their organisation delivers on its commitments and make sure that there are excellent communications between the partnership and the member organisation.

Continuing to develop and nurture **relationships** is also a high priority. This requires that most critical of resources: time. All key participants need to give the partnership sufficient time. If they genuinely cannot, then they should appoint someone else with appropriate authority and status to be their representative. There is a danger that senior people establish a partnership and then delegate its management without conferring the appropriate power and authority. It is particularly debilitating for a partnership to have members who want to take the kudos of the initiative but do not make a fair contribution to its management and development.

Board commitment is important in closer and more strategic partnerships. The boards of all participating organisations need to be strongly committed to the partnership and willing to support it through the good times and the difficult times. Actions to help maintain commitment can include:

- establishing a board committee, serviced by one organisation, consisting of members of the boards of all the participating organisations;
- requiring that each partner has a seat on the other's board;
- expecting counterparts, including chairs and board members, to meet each other frequently to encourage good personal relationships.

A key requirement is continued access to **resources** commensurate with the size of the partnership's ambitions. Success depends on honesty and realism about the continuing time and financial commitments each organisation will have to make to the partnership. If there are insufficient resources, it may be better to cut the ambitions and achieve realistic targets rather than always chasing after unattainable ones.

There will always be the challenge of creating **open and honest communications** between partners. Managers need to recognise that many different stakeholders, such as funders, board and committee members, staff, local groups and volunteers, may be affected by a strategic partnership. Each requires regular and thorough communication. Formal communications should be supported by plenty of informal communication, ideally at board, senior management and staff levels. Sharing information across two or more organisations to keep staff, managers and board members of all organisations in touch with progress and problems requires even more effort and attention than communication within organisations.

Finally it is easy in partnerships to overlook the need to **admit failures** when things go wrong and to **celebrate success** when milestones and objectives are achieved. Maintaining the shared morale of the partnership is as important as maintaining morale in the individual organisations.

Conflicts of loyalty

Conflicts of loyalty can occur when establishing and managing partnerships. They are never far from the surface because the interests of individual members are seldom exactly the same as those of the partnership. For example, the partnership might attract funding and publicity that could have gone to one or more member organisations. Or the partnership might gain knowledge and experience that cannot be easily transferred to member organisations. It is important to acknowledge and manage these conflicts rather than pretend that they do not exist (see section 3.7 for a description of the distinction between conflicts of interest and conflicts of loyalty).

Partnerships can benefit from having a conflict of interest and loyalty policy and associated procedures, for use when members become aware that:

- there is a clear conflict between loyalty to their organisation and to the partnership;
- one or more members have a financial interest in a matter under discussion;
- there is a real danger of bias (for example because a decision will be affected by a professional or close family relationship).

For trust to be maintained amongst members, conflicts of loyalty and interest need to be raised when they are perceived, before they arise in practice. When conflicts are perceived, simple rules about absenting conflicted members from discussions and decisions about those items can be applied.

CHALLENGES FOR PARTNERSHIPS

Each type of partnership presents its own challenges:

Type of partnership	Particular governance and management challenges
Affiliations	• Continuing to give affiliates value and not taking their support for granted
Mutual help collaborations	• Maintaining commitment when the pressures of members' own organisations are likely to predominate
Delivery through partners	• Ensuring the quality of the service delivered • Managing relations with partners
Collaborative services	• Maintaining trust between partners
Campaigning coalitions	• Securing agreement on policy without threatening members' independence
Joint ventures	• Managing relationships with 'owners'
Management service organisations	• Maintaining motivation of staff and quality of service when the mission is to provide business services
Franchises	• Securing and supporting franchisees • Franchisees raising the required funding
Federal structures	• Maintaining appropriate central control and local autonomy • Systems to develop and maintain standards across the federation • Managing breaches of standards
Specialist intermediary organisations	• Commitment of members • Managing relationships with members • Financial sustainability
Generalist intermediary organisations	• Range of services and funders to manage • Financial sustainability
International federations	• Long-distance communications • Managing across different cultures • Sustainability of funding

There are also particular management challenges when parts of the organisation have been separated off into other organisations:

Type of separation	Governance and management challenges
De-merging or spin off	• Establishing new and effective governance arrangements • Securing long-term sustainability of the spun off organisation
Moving services to other organisations	• Keeping good people • Managing integration into a new culture where norms and expectations will be different
Outsourcing	• Managing quality and prices • Managing relationships with people responsible for delivering services

12.6 MANAGING MERGERS

Merger activity has grown dramatically in recent years, driven by public policy that encourages third-sector organisations to merge and a widely held public view that there are too many with similar purposes.

The term 'merger' is something of a euphemism that is often used to encourage good feelings between the organisations involved. In the majority of charity mergers, 75% according to the Charity Commission (*Collaborative Working and Mergers*, 2003), a large organisation merges with a small one, which is perhaps struggling or in distress, so in practice they are 'takeovers' or 'acquisitions' of one organisation by another.

Merger is one of the most challenging change management projects that organisations attempt, because it involves people, power and politics and there are a large number of inter-dependencies. There will be winners, losers, uncertainties and resistances. It requires extraordinary effort from the organisations' leaders. There are likely to be structural, legal and practical challenges to overcome. In the long term, cultural differences are often the hardest nut to crack.

Mergers are also expensive. Reported costs vary from £25,000 for a straightforward merger to £250,000 and more for large and more complex ones. More than 50% of them fail to be successfully completed, according to Charity Commission research. They are also virtually irreversible. Careful consideration is essential before embarking on an initiative that, by any standards, is risky.

Despite all this, there have been many successful mergers. They can lead to stronger organisations with greater 'critical mass', capable of delivering a wider range of services and having greater impact. Done well, they can re-energise the boards, management and staff of organisations.

ORGANISATIONS THAT RESULTED FROM MERGERS

Asthma UK	Norwood
Cancer Research UK	Parentline Plus
Carers UK	Rainer
CLIC Sargent	Terrence Higgins Trust
Eating Disorders Association	Thames Reach Bondway
Homeless Link	Volunteering England
Jewish Care	Working Families

Mergers have been particularly prevalent in the housing sector, where economies of scale can be significant. Here, organisations have often merged into group structures to allow the subsidiaries to maintain their own identity and governance whilst simultaneously integrating their 'back office' services.

Reasons for merging

The main reasons for merging include:

- improving services for users
- exploiting economies of scale
- raising profile and attracting more funding
- sharing knowledge and expertise
- reducing overhead costs
- avoiding duplication.

However, there may also be reasons that may not be so explicit including:

- rescuing an ailing charity;
- loss of direction and leadership;
- loss of the will to remain independent;
- using it as a way of overcoming seemingly insuperable difficulties;
- averting a major crisis.

Types of mergers

Mergers can be broadly categorised into four types.

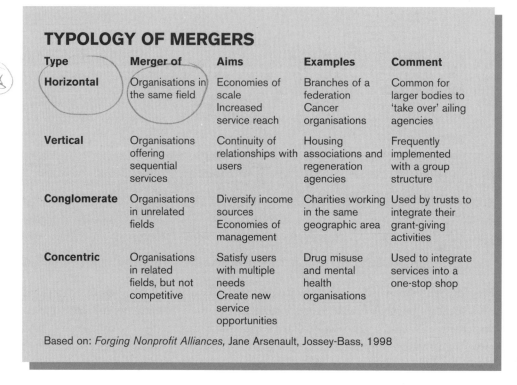

TYPOLOGY OF MERGERS

Type	Merger of	Aims	Examples	Comment
Horizontal	Organisations in the same field	Economies of scale Increased service reach	Branches of a federation Cancer organisations	Common for larger bodies to 'take over' ailing agencies
Vertical	Organisations offering sequential services	Continuity of relationships with users	Housing associations and regeneration agencies	Frequently implemented with a group structure
Conglomerate	Organisations in unrelated fields	Diversify income sources Economies of management	Charities working in the same geographic area	Used by trusts to integrate their grant-giving activities
Concentric	Organisations in related fields, but not competitive	Satisfy users with multiple needs Create new service opportunities	Drug misuse and mental health organisations	Used to integrate services into a one-stop shop

Based on: *Forging Nonprofit Alliances*, Jane Arsenault, Jossey-Bass, 1998

For each of these types there are four options for the legal structure of a merger:

- one or more organisations merge into one of the existing organisations (the most common);
- one or more organisations create a new organisation that all merge into (less common);
- the board members of one become the board members of the other (the least common);
- establishment of a group structure (most common amongst housing associations and described more fully in section 2.5, Group structures).

In some situations, the organisations can merge but retain their name, brand and reputation. This offers all the advantages of back-office integration and reduced overheads without losing public appeal or fundraising potential. ChildLine, for example, became part of NSPCC, but retained the organisation's brand and reputation. It is managed and governed by NSPCC, but has kept its well-known name and continues to present its own image and logo, that are so closely associated with the services it provides.

In other situations, merging into a group structure allows organisations to retain operational and some strategic independence but have the security, financial strength and support that this arrangement provides.

Stages of a merger

There is no template or magic formula for success; all mergers have to address different issues in a different order, so the following guidance should be treated as a starting point for considering how to approach the management of a merger.

Although all mergers are different, the process can be loosely defined into a series of overlapping stages. It is seldom a 'linear' process and there will usually be surprises.

An early decision in any merger is who to involve at each stage. Here confidentiality must be balanced with the need to bring people along with the process.

1. **Exploration** – Mergers begin in a number of different ways:

- Some begin when senior people in an organisation (usually the chair or chief executive) have an idea about merging with a specific organisation.
- Others begin when an organisation decides it wants to merge and goes out to seek partners.
- Some begin when an organisation in distress approaches another for assistance.

However the proposition emerges, it is important at this early stage to establish a clear rationale for the merger and make a very preliminary assessment of the specific benefits of the merger for the organisation's mission. These can be set against the time, effort and costs that merger implies to determine whether it is worthwhile proceeding to the next stage.

Organisations that wish to find a number of potential partners and choose the most appropriate will need to take a proposal to their board at this stage, setting out the rationale and the proposed approach. This can happen when an ailing organisation wants to choose who it is acquired by, or when a successful organisation is looking to acquire others. In either case, the board needs to agree on the investment of time and money.

2. **Preliminary assessment** – Irrespective of how the merger process has begun, a preliminary assessment of any proposition will be required. This may be more open when an organisation has had to legitimise the process and seek partners through open tender. In more sensitive situations, perhaps only a few people will know about the proposition at this stage.

A preliminary assessment should be designed to identify the 'big issues' that the merger process will need to address. This is somewhat iterative, as the process for addressing these questions will depend on the big issues, and the nature of the big issues will determine the most appropriate process for addressing them.

It may be appropriate to consider 'deal breakers' at this stage. Alternatively, it may be judicious to identify them but postpone consideration until later in the process when good personal relationships have been established. Potential deal breakers include:

- disagreement over who should chair the merged organisation;
- neither chief executive being willing to work for the other;
- neither organisation being willing to relinquish its name or combine it with the other organisation's name;
- lack of strong support from one board.

A merger proposition might end at this point, avoiding unnecessary work and the disappointment that results from failing at a later stage in the process.

If a merger proposition still looks attractive, it is important at an early stage to **'define the prize'**: the vision of a merged organisation assisting more people, mounting stronger campaigns, providing better quality and more integrated services, or whatever it is. The prize can then become the touchstone which everyone can hold on to when negotiations become difficult.

3. **Legitimising, planning and agreeing the process** – At this stage more people will need to be involved. It may be appropriate to establish a merger task group, comprising representatives from potential partners. Its role, brief and timescale will need to be defined and agreed by the organisations involved. The task group should attempt to identify all the issues that might arise and then agree which ones need to be solved before the merger can proceed.

Timescale is important, but it depends on circumstances and complexity. Mergers create uncertainty, so it is important not to allow discussions to take any longer than absolutely necessary, but it is equally important that the work is thorough and that important issues are not overlooked or pushed under the carpet. According to Charity Commission research, charity mergers can take between one and two years, but some mergers can be done faster when circumstances require quick action.

A communications strategy may be required at this stage to identify who should be told what and when.

The proposed process should assume that difficulties will arise, and should therefore include a mechanism for resolving serious obstacles. One way of dealing with this is through a meeting of the organisations' chairs with an independent facilitator; such a person can be very helpful more generally as negotiations proceed.

4. **Planning and negotiating** – This is when the detailed work of jointly agreeing a merger proposition is done.

Whilst negotiations are at an early stage the focus will be on the key issues that need to be addressed for the merger to succeed. If potential 'deal breakers' have not been resolved earlier, they will need to be addressed now.

Decisions will also be needed on what to change before the merger and what to leave until later. Some issues can be resolved temporarily, allowing for a thorough review after the merger has taken place. For example, it may be appropriate to establish a temporary governance structure and commit to a full review in the first year following the merger. It may be appropriate to use both organisations' names initially to allow a complete re-branding to happen later.

It may not be possible to solve all the issues at this stage, but it is not good to postpone too many decisions. So, decisions will be needed on what to decide upon! With a list prepared, the task group should address the biggest obstacles early on in the process rather than leaving them to the end.

At this stage it can be valuable for management and governance to be working in parallel, being kept abreast of discussions and having opportunities to contribute to the process. Having boards that are united in their determination to make the merger work will be important, but this can be difficult because they themselves are likely to be re-organised as a consequence of the merger. It might be appropriate to consider establishing an interim or 'shadow' board at this stage, so that they can start the process of 'forming, norming, storming and performing' and hit the ground running when the decision to merge is announced.

Ideally, at this stage organisations should be moving from negotiation to collaboration. It should be becoming increasingly clear whether or not a deal is going to be possible, in which case the focus of attention can move to making it work in practice. If discussions are going well, a business plan for the merged organisation might start to be developed. This can be very motivating, as it keeps 'the prize' in sight.

People bring their own organisation cultures to the negotiating table and expect others to share their point of view, not realising that their organisation has different beliefs and norms. Trust between the negotiators will therefore be important, as will trust within each organisation, since it is not possible to tell everyone everything at delicate stages of the discussions. True and deep commitment from chairs and chief executives is crucial to maintaining momentum, anticipating problems and finding creative solutions.

5. **Implementation planning** – Before decisions are taken, detailed implementation planning is required, as different types of actions will be needed with different stakeholders when an announcement is made.

When it becomes clear that a merger is likely to proceed, some trustees may see it as a natural time to leave. So this could be a good time to refresh the board and ensure it is a manageable size, reflects its diverse stakeholder groups and includes a mix of skills. If a new board is required, a selection process and criteria will be needed (see section 4.2, Recruiting and inducting board members).

6. **Decision-taking** – If all the planning has been thorough and there has been appropriate consultation with the boards, and if necessary the legally responsible members of the organisations, the decision itself should be a formality, and discussion can focus on making a success of the merger.

7. **Implementation** – An implementation team will be needed, as there will be much to do. People issues should take priority as they are the ones that leave bad feelings after the merger has been completed.

8. **Post-merger integration** – It is likely that cultural integration will be the greatest challenge. All organisations have subtly different approaches to matters such as:

- Delegation – giving managers extensive freedom or expecting lots of consultation.
- The board – being strategic or more 'hands on'.
- Accountability – having tight or loose systems for reporting.
- Meeting management – holding short and sharp meetings or long and thorough ones.
- Risk – being entrepreneurial or being more cautious.

So it will be important to manage expectations and encourage differences to be viewed as opportunities for learning rather than obstacles to progress.

Failing to deal with difficult and sensitive issues, particularly those concerned with redundancies, relocation and redefined jobs, can often re-emerge as problems years after the formal completion of the merger.

Sometimes mergers remain 'un-consummated' for years: the organisations may have been legally merged but the people and processes have not joined together. So post-merger actions need to include activities that ensure people are brought together in formal and informal ways and that key business processes are integrated across the new organisation.

Merged organisations have a remarkable ability to re-create within themselves the very problems that they were established to solve. Unless managed carefully, the grand aspirations for a more strategic, decisive, action-oriented organisation with greater delegation and tight accountability can be lost in a series of processes and procedures that emulate the very behaviours that led to the need to merge in the first place. So it is important to be acutely aware of approaches and behaviours that need to be managed out of the merged organisation.

CHECKLIST OF ISSUES TO CONSIDER WHEN MANAGING A MERGER

- The rationale for the merger
- The benefits to each organisation's mission and service users
- Whether the power to merge exists in the governing documents of all the merging organisations
- Filling the key roles of chair and chief executive
- Name of the organisation and branding of services
- Informing and negotiating with funders – particularly where one organisation funds two or more of the merger partners
- Checking donor lists to discover the extent of duplication
- Governance structure and processes
- Management structure and processes
- Location issues
- Finance (particularly special trusts, restricted funds and permanent endowments which are being transferred to the new organisation)
- Balancing the need for confidentiality with the need to bring everyone along with the merger
- Communication strategy, both internally and externally
- Involving the 'legal' members (where the governing documents make it necessary)
- Employment issues (such as any TUPE requirements*, pension liabilities and compliance with employment law)
- Assessing the risks associated with both a successful merger and one that does not proceed
- The extent of due diligence required
- Costs of the merger process and of an unsuccessful merger
- Ensuring continuity of services during the process
- Planning and managing the integration of organisation cultures
- Allowing for a year or so of reduced output while the merger settles down

(* TUPE protects employees if the organisation in which they are employed changes hands. Its effect is to move employees and any liabilities associated with them from the old employer to the new employer by operation of law.)

SUMMARY OF KEY POINTS

Partnerships drive growth and development

- Organisations grow when they are bubbling with creative ideas, when they inspire people to support their cause and when they both compete and collaborate with other organisations
- Third-sector organisations form partnerships with each other and with the private and public sectors
- Organisations form partnerships and merge because they see opportunities to improve services, share knowledge and increase efficiency

Selecting partnership type to suit circumstances

- Partnerships can be organised into four groups: collaborations, strategic alliances, intermediary organisations and integrations
- Organisations also make moves in the opposite direction and re-locate some of their work in other organisations
- Partnerships are created to improve mission impact, to share knowledge and to build the capacity of the sector
- Each type of strategic partnership can take a number of legal and structural forms
- Criteria for selecting the most appropriate type include permanence, mission impact, freedom, control, sustainability, staff motivation, management time, governance, costs and risks

Partnerships with the private and public sectors

- Organisations are increasingly establishing partnerships with the public and private sectors
- There is a continuum of types of relationships between companies and third-sector organisations which has a philanthropic stage, a transactional stage and an integrative stage
- Corporate-sector partnerships can include charity of the year, employee involvement, secondments, corporate events, sponsorship, cause-related marketing, payroll giving, team building days, gifts in kind, and public relations opportunities
- The third sector is involved in a wide range of strategic partnerships with the public sector that go beyond funding relationships

Creating strategic partnerships

- Pre-requisites need to be established before even considering whether to establish or join a partnership
- Creating partnerships requires the establishment of good relationships, trust, clear objectives, robust business plans, estimates of time and costs, assessment of risks, good faith negotiations, effective management of meetings, partnership agreements and communications strategies

Leading strategic partnerships

- Guidance that applies to the leadership, management and governance of organisations is equally applicable to partnerships, but each has a distinctive feature in the context of a partnership
- Successful partnerships require strong leadership, board commitment, appropriate resources, open and honest communications and a willingness to celebrate success and admit failures
- Each type of partnership presents its own distinct challenges
- Conflicts of loyalty and interest need to be acknowledged and managed

Managing mergers

Merger is one of the most challenging change management projects that organisations attempt.

- There are four types of merger and they can each take four different legal forms
- All mergers have to address different issues in a different order
- The stages of a merger include:
  - exploration
  - preliminary assessment
  - legitimising, planning and agreeing process
  - planning and negotiating
  - implementation planning
  - decision-taking
  - implementation
  - post-merger integration.

FURTHER READING

Collaborative Working and Mergers, Charity Commission, 2003

Forging Nonprofit Alliances, Jane Arsenault, Jossey-Bass, 1998

Managing Mergers – a Guide, ACEVO, 2003

The Collaboration Challenge, James Austin, Jossey-Bass, 2000

More and recent books and reports can be found at www.compasspartnership.co.uk.

13 Managing change

13.1 MANAGING CHANGE IS AN ESSENTIAL SKILL

Third-sector organisations have had to respond to the increasingly turbulent and demanding external environment. New opportunities and rising expectations on the part of users, funders, staff and the public have all contributed to the need for more frequent, more rapid and better managed change:

- Organisations have to be more creative and innovative to grow and develop in the face of increasing competition.
- Funders expect to give fewer grants for loosely defined purposes and more contracts with tightly specified performance requirements.
- Users expect to be more closely involved in service providing organisations than they were in the past.
- Staff and volunteers expect to get learning opportunities as an integral part of their compensation package.
- The public expects good governance, low overhead costs and high standards of probity.
- Developments in technology are changing what organisations can do and the ways they can do it.
- Partnerships and coalitions with other organisations are presenting new opportunities to increase impact.

Taken together, these mean that organisations face a significant 'change management' agenda, and all the evidence suggests that such pressures are likely to grow in the coming years.

Change management draws together a group of ideas that helps managers to understand what type of change they are embarking on and how to make appropriate changes happen. Change management is a rigorous approach that underpins many of the activities described in other parts of this book such as re-organisations of governance, implementing strategic plans, establishing new partnerships and changing management structures. These principles can also be applied to quality standards initiatives, cost reduction programmes and the redesign of management processes.

This chapter sets out the principles and practices of effective change management. It starts by describing the theory of organisation culture, because culture is a major determinant of the ways organisations should set about making change happen. Insights into culture help managers to identify which levers of change will have the greatest impact, to understand which communication methods will be most effective and to ensure that changes can be fully embedded into the ways organisations work.

The chapter describes:
- how organisation culture influences change;
- the fundamental concepts of change management;
- the characteristics of change processes;
- the eight critical stages of a major change initiative;
- the essential skills of successful change leaders.

The term 'change leader' refers to the senior person responsible for managing a programme of change. The term 'sponsor' refers to individual or group (e.g. a board) that has commissioned or approved a change programme.

13.2 UNDERSTANDING ORGANISATION CULTURE

Organisation culture has been defined in many ways, including:
- the way we do things around here;
- the way we think about things around here;
- the commonly held and relatively stable beliefs, attitudes and values that exist within an organisation.

Three levels of organisation culture

Different types of organisation culture were introduced in section 11.2, Cultures and structures evolve. Culture can be more deeply understood by considering the three different levels at which it is expressed. At the most superficial level, there are the **visible representations** of an organisation's culture – its buildings, the routine procedures of meetings, the management structure and the language that people use. Visit a well-established housing association with its offices in the business park, and one cannot help but notice the smart photographs of its properties on the wall, the tidy reception area and the calm sense of order. Contrast this with an under-funded campaigning organisation with its offices in a dilapidated property in a rundown area of town, newspapers piled high waiting to be recycled, desks crammed close together, walls with T-shirts, pamphlets and posters piled to the ceiling, and the sense of pressure and urgency. Two extreme cases, perhaps, but they illustrate the different physical manifestations of culture.

At the second level of culture, there are common patterns of **group behaviour**. This level is about how people act and react in various circumstances. Organisations work in subtly different ways: they vary in their decision-making processes, in the level of respect accorded to particular groups of people, in the processes they consider important and those they disregard. Examples of group behaviour include:

- how the organisation treats users;
- how board members behave towards staff;
- how the leadership team behaves towards staff;
- how staff treat each other.

Once behaviour patterns have been established, they strongly influence people who join the organisation. New employees, volunteers, managers and board members watch how people conduct themselves and adjust their own behaviour accordingly. As a result, the way the organisation works becomes embedded in their unconscious behaviour patterns.

At the third and most fundamental level, there are the **underlying beliefs** held by the staff, board members and members of the organisation. These are assumptions that are taken for granted. They are the unconscious values that inform people's behaviour. For example:

- Social welfare providers may have underlying beliefs about respecting
  service users.
- Managers may have underlying beliefs about the importance of costs and the
  effectiveness of services provided.
- Campaigners generally have strong underlying beliefs about the impact of
  social and environmental policy on people's lives and the need to change policy
  to make the world a better place.

The power of culture in determining how an organisation works should not be underestimated. It is comparatively easy to change the visible representations of culture; the intangibility of values makes them much more difficult to change.

Characteristics of culture

The concept of culture can be understood more thoroughly by considering some of its characteristics:

- **It is learned**. It results both from people's experiences before they joined the
  organisation and from the influences of the organisation itself.
- **It is determined by the organisation's history**. It is defined by decisions
  people have taken in the past, particularly those taken by significant individuals
  such as the founder.
- **It is influenced by the organisation's environment**. The context of a third-sector
  organisation's work (ranging from international development to social welfare to
  justice and human rights) is a major determinant of organisation culture.

- **It is partly subconscious**. Over time, assumptions develop and become implicit influences on people's behaviour. These beliefs and assumptions affect the way people think about things.
- **It is heterogeneous**. Different parts of an organisation have different cultures. A commonly observed difference is that between staff in the headquarters of an organisation, who may be concerned with public profile, fundraising, lobbying and the inevitable politics of large organisations, and people in the local branches, who may be more concerned with service delivery and valuing volunteers. Offices on split sites, or even two floors of the same office, can exhibit surprising differences in culture.

Culture and change are inter-dependent

The culture of an organisation significantly affects change. It influences:

- how ambitious change should be
- how change should be introduced
- how much consultation will be needed
- how fast change can be implemented.

Changes that break too many of the 'rules' about the way the organisation works may be destined to fail. People in the organisation will push back or deploy delaying tactics against change and the power of change makers will diminish.

Nevertheless, change makers do have to challenge the culture. They propose new objectives, new initiatives and better ways of working that will alter 'the way we do things'. It is a question of balance. Lack of ambition in changing the organisation can lead to lost opportunities and reduced mission impact. But pressing for change that is too ambitious, not introduced in ways that respect the culture or implemented too fast will lead to tension, unnecessary argument and eventually to loss of morale and motivation amongst those affected.

Managers who understand their organisation's culture are therefore in the best position to manage change effectively. This understanding gives them insights into how to maximise the impact of their efforts. It points to the 'levers' to pull at different points in the process in order to have the greatest effect. They know that when new initiatives are carefully introduced they will lead to changes in the organisation's culture and 'new ways of doing things'.

Understanding culture comes from conscious observation of the patterns of behaviour in an organisation. Reflecting on changes that were successful, and identifying what it was that enabled them, leads to insights into how to implement future changes more effectively.

Influencing culture

Culture guru Edgar Schein, who first unpacked the analysis of culture described above, believes that five types of action are the most significant determinants of culture.

First, culture is influenced by **what leaders pay attention to**. The issues leaders systematically work on send signals to the rest of the organisation about what is considered to be important. The leader who consistently pays attention to financial management encourages a culture in which tight financial control rises up the agenda. The entrepreneurial leader who welcomes new ventures encourages a culture that values innovation and development.

Second, the explicit and implicit **criteria used to allocate resources** to different activities influences people's view of the culture. They send out signals about the types of activities that are perceived to be valued. For example, if the board consistently approves projects for people from ethnic minorities, the importance of minority groups will rise up everyone's agenda.

Third, the explicit and implicit **criteria used in the recruitment and promotion** of people are an indicator of beliefs. The organisation that champions the rights of people with disabilities, and takes positive action to recruit people with disabilities to its own staff, gives important signals about its underlying beliefs.

Fourth, the **way people react in a crisis** is an influence on culture. Crises are important in this respect because people are watching each other's actions more closely than at other times, and because they often lead to learning that sticks in the mind. For example, an organisation that handles redundancies badly leads people to perceive that it doesn't put high value on caring for its staff.

Finally, deliberate **role modeling and coaching** influences the culture. Managers are implicitly teaching their staff through their actions. Reviewing people's plans, commenting on achievements and guiding people on how to improve their work are all ways of exemplifying beliefs and values that managers want staff to adopt.

Embedding change into organisation culture

Embedding changes in an organisation's culture requires action at all three levels: visible representation, group behaviour and underlying beliefs. The easiest level is through visible representation – but this also has the least long-term effect. A particularly symbolic change is to move offices, for example from an old building in a rundown area of town to smarter, open-plan offices in a new development. This can be a powerful element of a programme for modernising an organisation and the way it works.

Changes to group behaviour happen most easily through new appointments. New people can bring new assumptions and ways of working that challenge old behaviours. The appointment of a new chief executive is a particularly significant determinant of behaviour. The experience and characteristics of the person appointed to this post will be a significant influence on group behaviour and therefore of the culture of the organisation.

The most difficult level at which to effect change is that of people's underlying beliefs. Changing these requires time and the coordination of many different influences, but once achieved this kind of change will last. The new ways of working will become part of the unconsciously accepted culture of the organisation.

13.3 CHANGE MANAGEMENT CONCEPTS

This section builds on the concepts of organisation culture and:

- defines what change management means in third-sector organisations;
- describes different types of change;
- explains the art of combining leading and listening;
- illustrates how the 'coalition of interests' has to be maintained;
- explains how changing one element of an organisation has impacts on all the other elements.

The nature of change management

The ideas that underpin change management are valuable for managers who wish to introduce significant change into their organisation. Organisations are littered with examples of changes that did not produce the desired results. Indeed, much of the cynicism about change that managers encounter results from the failure of previous initiatives to have a significant impact. Introducing change is a subtle and sensitive process, and a misjudgement in any of the stages of change can easily result in good proposals being consigned to the pile of failed management initiatives.

Change management is **the skill of catalysing significant improvements in the performance of organisations**. It is a set of skills that managers need to apply in order to achieve the greatest results for their efforts.

Change management **involves people from many parts** of the organisation. The actions usually cut across departments and may involve users, branches and board members.

Change management is a **combination of substance and process**. It is about developing a clear view of the improvements that are needed and integrating this with a sequence of activities for achieving the change. It combines the head (the vision and the analysis) with the heart (the people and their emotions).

At a more fundamental level, change management is about **'re-framing' a situation** so that people see their circumstances in a different way. It is about creating a new mental model or paradigm that enables people to think and act in ways that will help the organisation achieve its objectives more effectively.

There is **no one approach** that can be applied to all change situations. While this chapter aims to help managers to plan and implement major changes by setting down some principles and a general approach, there is no avoiding the harsh reality that good judgements at each stage of a change process are critical to success. It is impossible to predict how the process will evolve and it is almost certain that something will go awry in a complex set of changes.

Flexibility is therefore critical. Plans have to be prepared, communication methods agreed and timetables established. But, particularly in large-scale change, effective managers are always ready to make adjustments and sometimes to take a different approach in order to achieve the desired objective.

Types of organisational change

Three types of organisational change have been defined (by L. Ackerman):

- **developmental change** – concerned with improving current activities or ways of working (for example, by doing more or doing it better);
- **transitional change** – concerned with replacing current activities or ways of working with new ones (for example, introducing new services or systems);
- **transformational change** – concerned with changing beliefs and awareness about what is possible, requiring a leap of faith (for example, adopting an entirely new strategy or completely re-structuring the organisation's service delivery system).

Transitional change may also involve an element of developmental change, and transformational change may involve both the other types.

The key point for aspiring change leaders is to determine the type of change they are embarking upon, since the complexity and resource requirements grow exponentially from developmental to transformational change. This chapter focuses on transitional and transformational change.

TRANSITIONAL CHANGE AT VSO: REDESIGNING THE RECRUITMENT PROCESS

VSO aims to send over 900 people per annum on two-year overseas assignments. They are selected from around 75,000 enquirers in a complex process that has to:

- recruit people with a wide range of skills and abilities
- prepare applicants for selection boards
- select people as potential volunteers
- post people to appropriate overseas assignments
- train people for the post
- prepare them for departure

In the 1990s the recruitment division wanted to increase the number of volunteers working overseas, reduce the time from initial inquiry to departure, and reduce the unit costs of the division. It used the principles of change management to diagnose the problem and develop new ways of working.

A steering group, led by the division director and representing all parts of the division, was established to oversee the whole process. It established 11 task groups to investigate every aspect of the problem. Their reports were drawn together by the consultants assisting the director in an overall diagnosis of the situation. There was widespread consultation on this to ensure that it was owned by key people in VSO and the recruitment division.

The steering group established specific objectives and targets which the new process needed to achieve. A new process was designed and piloted for 18 months and evaluated against agreed success criteria. After detailed consensus-building work between the steering group and the other staff, more radical changes were made. The new structures and systems were then implemented throughout the division. Although some issues remained (particularly around workloads in the new structure), most staff believed that the new process provided a better way of working.

Combining leading and listening

Organisations often pursue one of two routes into change management. The first is a 'top-down' approach, inspired by a vision, pushed by management and driven energetically through the organisation with plans, briefings and an element of razzmatazz. This approach tends to be strong on analysis, and aims to achieve a pre-determined objective.

The second route is a 'bottom up' approach in which leaders facilitate change, managers help their staff to use skills and experience that are already embedded in the organisation, and the development of people is seen as the key to successful change. In this approach, sometimes called 'organisation development', change happens incrementally.

A third view of change management (first elaborated by George Binney and Colin Williams) stresses the need to adopt both approaches simultaneously. From this perspective, the most effective change happens when there is a combination of:

Leading	Listening
• a clear view of the future	• a desire to build on the best of the past
• strong leadership	• strong commitment to hear the concerns of people at all levels of the organisation
• a focus on action	• time for reflection
• investment in training	• commitment to learning
• a timetabled plan with targets	• freedom to act within broad guidelines

This combination is particularly important because trustees, managers and volunteers place a very high value on the meaning of their work to them personally. People are often closely attached to their work because they are motivated by the organisation's mission. Since change management is about altering an aspect of people's work, it can threaten to take away some of the meaning of that work for those people. It may also be perceived as the organisation placing less value on a role, department, region or branch, or on particular individuals.

These concerns are articulated in many different ways. Sometimes they are expressed in terms of the implications for service users of the proposed changes. Sometimes the objections are practical and sometimes they are philosophical. They are seldom expressed in terms of people's anxieties about the value that is being placed on their work. In these circumstances it is difficult to untangle people's concerns about how their work is valued from objective views about the proposed changes.

If these concerns are not listened to, or if their underlying meaning is not understood, there is a danger that change will be opposed. Opposition of this kind may be voiced through the organisation's formal decision-making processes, but it may also arise through the powerful networks of informal communications that determine how any change initiative is viewed in the organisation. Successful change managers go out of their way to meet such concerns head-on and to understand what people have to gain and to lose from the proposals.

People's concerns have to be treated as genuine. Managers have to try to bring to the surface the underlying meaning of the proposed changes for the people affected and find accommodating ways forward before the opposition becomes an insurmountable obstacle to the overall change process. Railroading proposals through may be possible, but there is often a large price to pay in terms of reduced motivation and willingness to cooperate with the new arrangements.

Broadly speaking, people affected by a change initiative can be divided into those who are committed to change, those who are uncommitted and see it neither as an opportunity nor as a threat, and those who are likely to oppose change. The key group to win over is the uncommitted; the people who are willing to change but need to be convinced that it is necessary. In many situations these people may well be the silent majority, who are not ready to stand out and champion change. They need to be motivated by the planned improvements, and any concerns they express about the consequences need to be given particularly close attention.

Maintaining coalitions

One of the distinguishing features of third-sector organisations is that they are a coalition of different interests, held together by shared objectives and interests.

Major change can put the coalition at risk. Any significant part of the coalition (volunteers, branch members, board members in particular) that does not support the change or feels that their views have not been listened to may take their voluntary effort elsewhere. This could have damaging consequences for the organisation's ability to deliver its services and campaigns, as well as for its reputation.

A key requirement of a change process is that it should keep all the stakeholders on board. Not only does massive effort have to be put into communication at every stage, but critics have to be listened to. Sometimes, decisions may have to wait until it is quite clear that the change will receive the support of the majority.

In circumstances where there are fundamental disagreements, the consequences of taking actions that alienate a group need to be carefully weighed before taking decisions. This is particularly important in organisations with a high public profile, as any stakeholder group can threaten to go to the press with their views and cause significant damage to the organisation's reputation.

Managing the impact of change

Changing one aspect of an organisation inevitably has an impact on many other elements of the organisation. The McKinsey 7S model of organisations offers a valuable tool for thinking about these inter-dependencies. The model identifies the seven factors that contribute to a successful organisation and proposes that they are all dependent on each other.

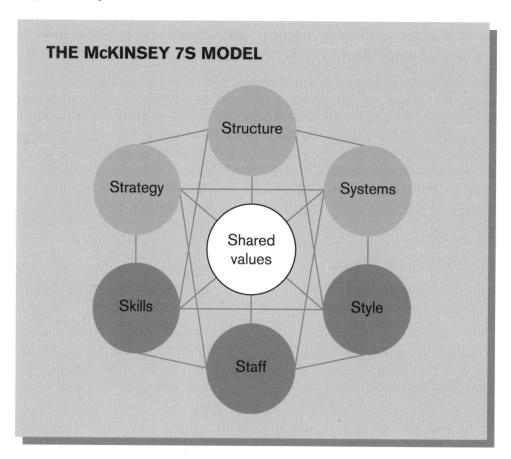

THE McKINSEY 7S MODEL

Strategy, structure and systems are known as the 'hard' elements of the 7Ss, and skills, style, staff and shared values are known as the 'soft' elements. The hard elements are easier to define and easier for managers to influence. The soft elements are more difficult to manage and are more strongly influenced by culture.

The model is based on the theory that, for an organisation to perform well, all seven elements need to be aligned and mutually reinforcing. So, the model can be used to help identify what needs to be realigned to achieve fully the objectives of a planned change. The key point is that any changes to any one of the elements has a larger or smaller influence on all the others. These need to be anticipated as part of planning a change process.

13.4 CHARACTERISTICS OF CHANGE MANAGEMENT PROCESSES

Large-scale change processes have four common characteristics:

- complexity and clarity vary with time;
- confidence and support vary during the process;
- they require massive communication;
- change is demanding of leaders.

Complexity and clarity vary with time

Change leaders and their teams should anticipate that the complexity of a change initiative will vary with time. At the start of the assignment the issues can look remarkably straightforward. However, gathering data and building the case for change produces masses of detail, and soon the problem can look overwhelmingly complicated. Then, as the information is analysed, perhaps assisted by the preparation of a summary review, the big picture starts to become clear again. The key issues that have to be addressed become more obvious, and consensus about the next steps emerges.

When planning starts in earnest, matters may once again look more complex, leading to a renewed sense of being overwhelmed with detail. But preparing the plan should in itself clarify and simplify the actions that are required to make a success of the initiative.

Finally, when implementation begins, the team may yet again feel swamped in detail, but, as issues are resolved and new mindsets are established, clarity should once again return.

Confidence and support vary during change process

People's feelings and attitudes towards change will also vary during the process. Their support for it, and their confidence about coping with change, will fluctuate as the project proceeds.

Typically, at the start of a change process some people will enthusiastically support the need for change; some will feel the way things worked in the past has always been successful, so changes are not required; others will feel anxious about the implications of the initiative and concerned for their jobs. Once the initiative is underway, more people will come to understand the need for the change, and support will begin to grow.

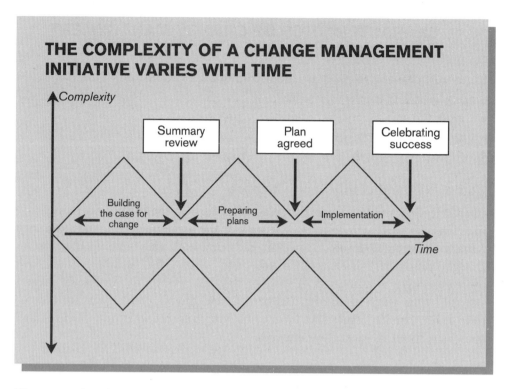

THE COMPLEXITY OF A CHANGE MANAGEMENT INITIATIVE VARIES WITH TIME

There are often one or more false dawns. People see glimpses of a new future but feel overwhelmed by the scale of change required to achieve the new vision. Frustration levels rise, and with them a level of scepticism about whether the desired changes will ever be achieved. Some may feel that they lack the skills or the energy to make the necessary changes.

Some people may find change impossible to accept, and it is not unusual in major change for them to decide to move on, sometimes graciously and, unfortunately, sometimes bitterly. The hard reality for change leaders is that this is inevitable, and should not distract them from the bigger picture of the organisation's longer-term future.

As time passes, the need for the change becomes clearer and people start to see its potential to have a positive impact on their work or offer them new opportunities. They start to let go of the history of the situation and acknowledge that new approaches are needed. Small steps forward increase their confidence in implementing change. People start to internalise the progress, and they incorporate changes in the way they think and behave. A new frame of reference becomes increasingly accepted as the way things work in the organisation.

This pattern of progress and setbacks should be anticipated as an inevitable part of a change management process.

Change requires massive communication

The need for extensive and repeated communication around a change programme cannot be underestimated. It is extraordinary how often messages have to be repeated to different audiences and through different media for everyone involved to understand the purpose of the change, the benefits that will arise, who will be involved, what needs to be done, when it needs to be done and how it fits with other initiatives.

The key test is not whether change leaders and managers think they have communicated sufficiently but whether everyone involved has heard, internalised and acted on the communications.

ENSURING GOOD COMMUNICATION

Watching the chief executive of a large nationwide service delivery organisation undergoing transformational change in its service delivery model I noticed that she:

- Wrote a personal progress letter to all managers once a month
- Made a DVD every few months to be shown at each of the organisation's centres
- Visited every centre to explain the rationale for the changes, listen to people's concerns and respond to them personally
- Always linked the changes to the organisation's mission and the need to improve the services delivered to users
- Ensured that there was good documentation on the need for change, the principles that underpinned change and the stages of implementation

Change is demanding on leaders

Leading change, particularly transformational change, is personally very demanding. It requires commitment to stay with the change for the duration. It also requires the stamina to work incredibly hard during key stages of the process (and a willingness to take holidays during quiet periods to recharge personal batteries). And it calls for the strength of personality to stand up to criticism and cope with being pulled in different directions by different stakeholder groups.

Change leaders recognise that their own energy and personal strength are a critical resource in a major change process. They take care to look after themselves, both physically and psychologically.

TRANSFORMATIONAL CHANGE AT VICTIM SUPPORT

Victim Support provides free and confidential support to help people affected by crime deal with their experience. It contacts over 1.5 million victims and supports 250,000 witnesses every year.

It was a federal organisation with 90 member charities supported by a National Office. The need to deliver more consistent quality, to be more accountable to its main funder and to be more cost effective, combined with the opportunity of significant additional funding to establish a new network of 'victim care units', led the organisation to agree to merge all the charities into one.

This transformational change began with the creation of a 'Future Group' to establish the case for change and the options. Thirteen project groups were set up to review the implications for volunteers, performance management, IT, governance and other topics.

The vision of a stronger organisation better able to reduce the effects of crime was strongly promoted. Two rounds of consultation meetings, led by the chair and chief executive, were held with groups of branches in all parts of the country. In order to build commitment to the proposal, which required the support of 75% of member votes at an Extraordinary General Meeting, a case for change was prepared. E-mail updates, a regular bulletin, a prospectus and videos were all used to communicate the proposal.

The member charities were the electorate for choosing the members of the board, so merger meant that new systems had to be established to choose the board. New arrangements for board succession, and for representation of volunteers' views, had to be agreed in parallel.

In addition, a new management structure had to be developed for the National Office (re-positioned as the National Centre) so that it could move from managing standards to line management of the delivery of the service.

All the planning and consultation paid off when 90% of members voted in favour of the changes at the EGM in June 2007. Change management moved into implementation from that point. In the following year the National Centre moved to new offices, an action that powerfully symbolised the change in culture from federal to a line-managed organisation.

13.5 STAGING CHANGE MANAGEMENT INITIATIVES

The success of transitional and transformational change is highly dependent on following a series of sequential stages, and not falling into the trap of beginning any of them prematurely. This section sets out eight essential stages that should be followed in order to implement change successfully. It draws on the experience of third-sector organisations and the thinking of a number of people who have written about change, including Professor John Kotter of Harvard Business School.

In summary, these stages are:

1. to **clarify the scope and scale** of the proposed change initiative;
2. to **establish a change team** with the power and expertise needed to ensure the change will succeed;
3. to **prepare a diagnosis of the problem** so people can understand why change is needed;
4. to **build strong commitment** to the need for the change and listen to people's concerns;
5. to **develop a motivating vision** for what the change will achieve;
6. to **plan and communicate** extensively about the proposed change;
7. to **implement by empowering** people to take the required actions;
8. to **incorporate change** into the culture of the organisation.

These stages should proceed sequentially. The change leader and members of the change team need to be thinking ahead about subsequent stages, and indeed these thoughts may influence their approach to a current stage. But ensuing stages should not be rolled out more widely into the organisation until people have understood and internalised the previous stages.

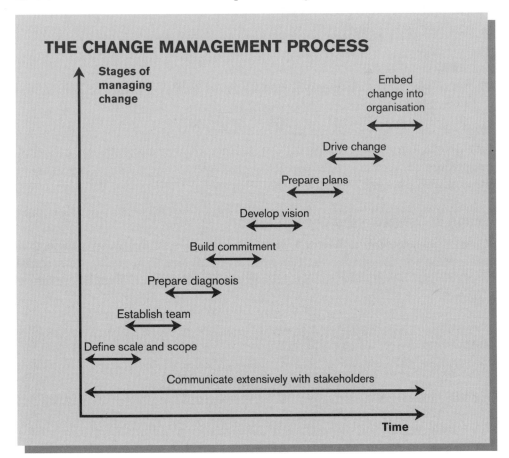

Stage 1: Clarify the scope and scale of the proposed initiative

Before deciding to proceed with a change initiative, critical judgements need to be made about its scope (what its boundaries will be) and its scale (how significant it will be).

Scope – It is all too easy for a change initiative to stray into many different areas that seem to be connected to the issue, leading to loss of the sharp focus required for success. Clear boundaries need to be established around levels of the organisation to which the initiative applies, the departments or divisions covered and the issues that should and should not be considered. Connections with other change initiatives should also be identified at this point, to allow dovetailing and integration by management before they are presented to the organisation. A common mistake is to present a number of change initiatives to the organisation in ways that appear to other people to be unconnected.

Scale – Change initiatives need two resources: staff time and money. The former is usually the hardest to obtain in the required quantities. Although it is difficult to make accurate estimates before plans for the initiative have been agreed in detail, the scale can be clarified by considering:

- Who will be involved?
- How much of each person's time is required to ensure that the initiative will be a great success?
- What will the key individuals be relieved of, in order to free up the required time?

In the third sector, one of the most common problems is that workloads of the key people can spiral out of control so that change initiatives lose all their momentum. For change to succeed, it is critical to keep significant amounts of time free to cope with the unexpected.

Stage 2: Establish the change team

Change management initiatives require a team to ensure that many perspectives can be considered, to give the initiative to champions in different parts of the organisation, to improve the quality of decision-making and to take effective action.

The team needs a leader who cares about the issue and has the skills and authority to deliver a successful result.

Four types of team can be considered:

- a **line management team** – consisting of the managers responsible for the areas where the change is happening;
- a **cross-cutting team** – consisting of managers from the different parts of the organisation that will be affected by the initiative;

- a **representative team** – consisting of carefully selected representatives from those levels and parts of the organisation that have a stake in the initiative (including trustees, front-line staff, regions, branches and volunteers). This is sometimes called a 'diagonal' or 'slice' team;
- a **mixed team** – consisting of a combination of the above.

The critical tests are whether the team has sufficient:

- **Expertise to do the job.** The specialist and managerial skills required to review the problems and implement solutions should all be represented.
- **Power to drive through the changes.** People with the power to make the change happen and those with the power to block it should all be represented. This may include board members, staff association or union officials, branch members, user representatives and individuals who are significant opinion-formers who may not hold any formal positions of power.
- **Connections to listen to the views of everyone affected.** The tentacles of the team should reach out to all parts of the organisation that will be affected by the changes.

When change is transitional, the chief executive should create the team. This confers immediate authority on the initiative – though, as time passes, the team will have to earn their authority from their work and their actions. When it is transformational, the chief executive will almost certainly be the team leader.

The team leader should estimate the time that will be required from each team member from the start so that everyone realises the level of commitment that is likely to be required. The team leader will then need to agree people's availability with their managers. Being explicit about the time required and reducing team members' other commitments will ensure that they can allocate sufficient time to make a success of the initiative.

Loyalty to the whole of the organisation is a critical ingredient of a successful change team. If team members are more committed to their department or their region or to a section of the organisation than they are to the organisation as a whole, the change process will be more difficult. Team members should be willing to put the team's work ahead of these allegiances in order to ensure the success of the initiative. Applying other good practices in team working, as described in section 16.3, will help to ensure that the change team works effectively.

The team is the core of people who champion the initiative. Their influence will need to spread out across the organisation as the initiative gains momentum. In particular, they will need to listen to, involve and influence the key stakeholders as the change process gets underway. These key stakeholders will in turn have to do the same with an ever-widening group of people.

Stage 3: Prepare a diagnosis of the problem

The first task of the change team is to develop a diagnosis of the situation. This may involve an analysis of the issues that led to the creation of the team and the development of a shared understanding of the underlying causes of the problem.

Start by thinking through how the diagnosis should be prepared. Topics to consider include:

- the issues to be investigated;
- the division of the issues into manageable chunks of work;
- responsibilities of individuals and teams preparing parts of the diagnosis;
- ways of bringing elements of the diagnosis into an overview;
- the timescale for the work;
- the process for agreeing the diagnosis.

For a comparatively small-scale change initiative, members of the change team may do all the work. In larger initiatives, sub-groups may be needed to do specific jobs and feed their work into the change team. Involving people across the organisation in gathering data helps to build commitment to the change process. Setting up task groups to gather information on specific issues, each of which could be led by a member of the change team, is one way of gaining support. External and internal sources of information may be needed to review the current situation, identify the key issues and summarise the reasons why change is required.

External information – This ensures that the case for change takes advantage of perceptions of people who see the organisation from outside. These external views and comparisons are valuable, even when the change initiative is mainly about internal matters, because they bring new perspectives which can catalyse change.

User information is particularly valuable because it helps to challenge any complacency that may have developed about the quality of the services provided. With appropriate support, and guarantees about not attributing information, it can be gathered from virtually everyone who receives services from third-sector organisations. People with learning difficulties have contributed to Mencap's strategic review; people attending counselling with Relate have provided feedback at specified times after the counselling was completed; and drug mis-users have given feedback on the use of illegal substances.

Other sources of information include funders, members, visitors, other organisations in the same field, suppliers, prominent people who know the organisation, past employees, trustees, patrons and people from the media, and others (such as elected representatives who know the organisation).

Internal information – This is equally important in building the case for change. Gathering people's views – as well as facts and figures – has the added advantage of involving people in the initiative and listening to their opinions. People need to be given time to raise their concerns about the issue and to explain previous decisions that led to the current situation. This ensures that people feel fully involved in the change process.

Remember to **ask what works well**, and do not allow the change initiative to become an opportunity for people to do nothing more than air their grievances. People forget that, for much of the time, many things are working well, and a natural desire to highlight problems may lead them to give undue emphasis to the difficulties.

When pulling new information together, task groups and the change leader should go to great lengths to **be respectful of the past.** Acknowledging the commitment people have given to improving the organisation in the past ensures that their previous work is appreciated and is not unintentionally devalued.

Change leaders also **build on achievements,** rather than criticising what people did in the past. Each person who feels that his or her previous hard work is not being appreciated is potentially someone who will not give wholehearted support to the change process. A good test is to check that all reports and presentations give as great a weight to strengths, capabilities and achievements as they do to weaknesses, problems and criticisms.

This is the first point in the change process when widespread understanding is crucial. People need to comprehend why change is needed and how the process will proceed, and the diagnosis stage usually results in a summary document that makes all this clear. It might confirm the original thoughts on the nature and extent of the problem, or it might redefine the problem. Alternatively, it might conclude that no change is necessary or that the costs and upheaval of change outweigh the anticipated benefits.

Whatever conclusions are reached, decisions will be required from the sponsor of the change about whether and how to proceed.

Stage 4: Build commitment to change

Change initiatives are most successful when a critical mass of the people involved has a deep understanding of the need for the changes and the benefits that will be gained. The best way to achieve this understanding is to build a **robust case for change**.

Change is easiest when there really is external pressure for change: a financial crisis, loss of public confidence, demonstrably poor performance or a succession of missed opportunities. However, well-managed organisations anticipate change.

They see new opportunities or issues on the horizon and introduce change in advance of their arrival. Changes of this kind require stronger and even more robust cases to be made.

The case for change needs to **take account of both the facts and the emotions** of the situation. Change therefore requires hard information on the situation which can be analysed and summarised for presentation to key stakeholders. It should diagnose the problem and pinpoint what needs to change, without making proposals for the actual changes required. The case for change also requires a deep understanding of people's concerns about the current state of affairs and their future aspirations, both for the organisation and for themselves. By taking these on board, the change team will earn the support and respect of the people who may be most affected by the change process.

STAKEHOLDER ANALYSIS

An organisation that provides lifelong services for over 2,000 people in the UK set out to modernise and reconfigure the way it delivered its services. At the start of this transformational change process, it prepared an analysis of internal stakeholder views to identify contributions people could make and obstacles that they might present:

Group	Major concerns	Key contribution	Obstacles they might present	Actions to win their support
Trustees	Financial viability	Setting new direction and targets	Divided views on the future	Staged approach to key decisions
Senior managers	Personal futures	Communication with stakeholders	Opposition to proposed changes	Focus on benefits to clients
Staff	Jobs and professional integrity	Champions for change	Lack of response to required changes	Massive consultation and communication at every stage
Branches	PR image of the organisation	Continuing support for the organisation	Declining support for the organisation	Keep branch chairs well informed
Service users	Security of service facing the organisation	Understand situation	Public opposition to proposals	Keep them well informed
Other related organisations	Effect on them of new strategy	Form new partnerships	Lack of cooperation	Consult at each stage of change

The analysis identified where the change team needed to concentrate its effort and pinpointed the need to increase the effort put into communication with stakeholders.

One way of ensuring that all the appropriate groups are considered is to list key stakeholder groups and, for each, to identify:

- their major concerns
- the key contribution they need to make
- the obstacles they might present
- the actions required to win their support.

The summary case for change should be limited to the arguments for change. Although proposals may be beginning to emerge, do not be tempted to put them forward at this stage; that would be premature and would risk generating opposition about proposals before the reasons for change have been accepted.

Stage 5: Develop and communicate the change vision

Change initiatives need a vision that describes the desired improvements. This should not be confused with the organisation's overall vision as described in Chapter 5. The change vision should state as succinctly as possible the ultimate objectives of the initiative. It should describe **desired objectives and outcomes** and, where possible, these should be quantified.

The vision should be **motivating**. It should inspire people to support the project by connecting its aim with the overall mission of the organisation. People should be able to see how the initiative will help the organisation to achieve its overall objectives more effectively.

VISION FOR THE FUTURE OF VSO'S RECRUITMENT DIVISION

The change process in VSO's recruitment division (described in an earlier box, section 13.3) was driven by a series of visionary objectives to:

- increase the number of volunteers working overseas
- increase the satisfaction of overseas organisations that employ volunteers
- increase the average length of stay of volunteers
- fill a higher percentage of vacancies
- fill vacancies more quickly
- become more responsive to volunteers' requirements
- give staff more responsibility and hold them more accountable

Each of these objectives was accompanied by a quantitative target for the division to achieve from its redesigned recruitment process – for example, reducing the early return rate to less than 15%, filling 80% of placement opportunities within three months of the agreed start date, and ensuring that 80% of volunteers depart within three months of their availability.

The case for change and the vision should be communicated to stakeholders in the change initiative and more widely through the organisation. A wide variety of means should be used to ensure that people get the messages by different methods and at different times. Workshops and briefing sessions are likely to be more powerful than written communications, which tend to get swamped in the morass of internal communications circulating in any organisation. Meetings also have the advantage of allowing two-way communication, so people can raise their concerns and alert the change team to potential obstacles.

When planning communications, remember that the change team will have spent many hours building the case for change and developing the vision, so other people must be given the time to consider, discuss and understand the purpose of the initiative, its scope and the problems that it is designed to overcome. This may involve holding a number of workshops with different groups of people and tailoring presentations to meet the needs of different stakeholder groups. The effort required here should not be underestimated. It is a critical investment in the long-term success of the initiative.

Effective change leaders do not expect to get things right first time, so both the case for change and the vision should go out as drafts to enable people to improve and buy into them before they are finalised.

Stage 6: Plan and communicate the changes

It is tempting to start a change initiative by thinking about solutions and preparing detailed proposals for change. This is a mistake. Unless the preceding stages have been completed, there is a danger that proposals are likely to land on infertile ground. Once the preparatory steps have been concluded, however, a plan becomes essential.

The plan needs to address both the substance of the change and the process for implementing it. The substance may include:

- **principles** that will underpin the change;
- **models** of different ways of working in the future;
- **options**, setting out alternative solutions to the issues;
- **proposals** describing what the changes will be.

The process part of the plan needs to address:

- **practical issues**: what will happen, in what order;
- **people and group issues**: who will do things, who needs to be consulted, and how activities will be coordinated;
- **timetable issues**: deadlines, milestones and fitting in with existing decision-making processes.

A critical judgement at this point is the **division of the work into manageable pieces** that can be completed within available resources and the available time. This provides another opportunity to involve people through task groups. The change team should identify each of the tasks that need to be undertaken and estimate the number of days required to complete the task and the time it will take to complete the change. When this has been done, tough decisions may have to be made either to cut out some activities or to increase the resources available to the team. It is extraordinarily easy to underestimate time and resources, and a misjudgement at this stage can lead to unduly ambitious commitments that cannot be met at later stages.

This is the stage when **pilots** of possible ways forward may be appropriate. This allows managers to discover whether proposals will really work. Practical experience helps to improve the proposed solutions and, most critically, helps to build commitment to the proposals. Pilots may delay organisation-wide implementation, but they ensure that when change is rolled out it is rooted in practical experience and has champions who have real credibility.

There is nothing more disillusioning for managers than being asked to support initiatives that appear to conflict with other programmes in the organisation. The plan therefore needs to **consider other initiatives** and activities running concurrently in the organisation. It should identify them and their timetables, to ensure there are no conflicts. This avoids inconsistency later in the process and demonstrates to everyone that the initiative has taken account of other activities and will integrate its work with them.

This stage often ends with the documentation of a plan and formal decisions to proceed on the proposals set out in the plan. It is the second point in the process when it is essential to explain clearly to everyone what is going to happen, why it will happen, and when it will happen.

TRANSFORMATIONAL CHANGE – A STEP-BY-STEP APPROACH

The board of a major UK charity began a process of transformational change by appointing a new chief executive, who was briefed to address some fundamental issues faced by the organisation. It also reviewed its own ways of working and decided that, for the period of major change, all board committees would be suspended and that the board would meet monthly instead.

With the help of consultants, the chief executive embarked on a change process that had the following steps:

1. A plan for the first few stages was prepared, consulted upon and agreed

2. A steering group of representatives of all stakeholder groups was established

3. A review of the strategic position of the organisation, the key issues it faced and broad options for the future, involving contributions from task groups, was prepared

4. A major consultation exercise, involving the chief executive attending workshops in all regions of the country, was carried out

5. The review was published and stakeholders were asked to respond

6. The board took two major decisions on the overall direction of the organisation and agreed six principles as the basis for preparing an implementation plan

7. The plan was prepared, and was the subject of further workshops throughout the country

8. The plan and the implementation document were published

9. Ten task groups, involving staff and board members, were established to drive implementation. Some were due to last a matter of weeks – to ensure some 'quick wins'. Others had tasks that were likely to take one to two years

10. The board agreed a programme of decision-taking, timed to coincide with completion of the work of each task group, and to re-launch the organisation after eight months' work had been completed

Communications strategy was central to the whole process. The chief executive wrote a letter to all staff every few weeks to report on progress. After key board meetings there was a cascade briefing, to inform staff of decisions. Regional meetings were held for service users and branch representatives. Video reports by the chief executive were sent to each region, because people preferred to hear news in this way, and 'hot news' from the steering group was circulated 24 hours after each meeting.

Stage7: Implementing change

When all the previous stages have been meticulously followed, implementation can begin. A key role for the change leader, supported by the team, is to keep track of progress. This means anticipating deadlines and chasing people before it is too late to take remedial action.

The leader and the team also need to keep their ears close to the ground as work progresses, to enable them to identify issues as they arise and deal with them before they become an impediment to the change programme. The change team should meet regularly to review progress and take remedial action when problems begin to emerge.

Prioritise quick wins – Change initiatives need to demonstrate results in order to maintain enthusiasm and momentum. If people work for months without seeing significant results, the whole project begins to lose credibility. People become available for meetings less often, will put in less effort and will focus on other matters.

So 'quick wins' are a critical element in a change initiative. Unfortunately, they do not necessarily come easily; they have to be vigorously sought after and pushed up the change team's agenda.

Examples of quick wins include:
- a successful pilot for a new way of working;
- a new service up and running;
- a marked improvement in quality in one area;
- a new performance report that captures information of the type required to work in new ways;
- an old or disliked process or set of forms being scrapped.

Any initiative should aim to achieve a quick win within months of the start; a smaller initiative should expect a quick win sooner than that. Once achieved, a quick win provides an ideal opportunity to communicate the success to all stakeholders and give the initiative new momentum.

Supporting implementation – Change leaders can take a number of actions to support implementation:
- **Offer training**. People may need training, the opportunity to shadow someone who has done something similar before, or additional support to implement the change proposals. A mini skills audit to determine whether individuals or groups of people have training needs may shed light on the requirement for training.

- **Adjust people's personal objectives and performance review targets**. Increasingly individuals have annual objectives. Problems may arise if these omit points related to the change initiative or, worse still, contain expectations that conflict with the new priorities. A review of personal objectives will help to assimilate change at all levels of the organisation.
- **Appoint new staff**. Appointing new staff who bring new assumptions and ways of working is one of the quickest and most effective ways of making change happen. Making one or two key appointments can significantly increase the speed of change and implant new beliefs into the organisation culture.
- **Encourage consistency**. Changes inevitably lead to inconsistencies with existing activities and processes. Change leaders need to ask people to identify inconsistencies at the earliest opportunity and then attend to them before they become irritations.
- **Hold celebrations**. Change is always hard, so every opportunity should be taken to record progress with activities and events that mark progress.
- **Promote people who implement the change**. In the long term, promotions for people who embody the new behaviour and methods of working will do more than many other measures to ensure lasting success for the change initiative.

When implementation runs into problems, it is often because either a misjudgement was made at an earlier stage about the scale or scope of the initiative, or a stage was omitted or carried out only superficially. In these circumstances, it may be necessary to go back a stage rather than pressing on against the odds.

Stage 8: Incorporate changes into the organisation's culture

Change leaders want their initiatives to be long-lasting. Changes are irreversible only when they become fully embedded in the organisation's culture.

Changing culture is undoubtedly the hardest part of change management; it takes the greatest time and requires the most consistent effort. Experience suggests that culture change happens as a consequence of actions and the results of change programmes, rather than as a consequence of attempts to change the culture directly.

Change leaders should recognise that the timescales over which culture change happens are long – usually measured in years rather than months. However, effective change leaders do speed up the process of change by judicious application of the most appropriate actions at the most appropriate times.

Ways of embedding changes into the different levels of an organisation's culture include:

- Changing visible representations of culture:
  - develop a new performance report;
  - introduce a new corporate image;
  - rename the organisation;
  - re-organise office space;
  - move to new offices.
- Changing behavioural norms:
  - create new management processes;
  - re-organise the meetings structure;
  - develop new meeting agendas;
  - improve or create new internal communication mechanisms;
  - establish user groups to strengthen 'customer' orientation;
  - hold joint board/management meetings to create a new strategy;
  - celebrate specific achievements with a memorable event.
- Changing underlying beliefs:
  - recruit people who hold the new beliefs;
  - promote people who show commitment to the new ways of working;
  - demonstrate how new practices are improving results.

Change management and changing people

The staged approach to change can become significantly more complicated when the need to change key posts or people is itself part of the change programme. Frequently the arrival of a new chief executive in an underperforming organisation presages the beginning of transformational change. In some circumstances, the board will have appointed someone with a mandate to bring about substantial change. In other situations, ambitious chief executives will see their appointment as an opportunity to make a significant difference by bringing new ideas and methods to organisations that are looking for strong leadership. Similarly, the arrival of new senior managers with a brief to transform a department can be the trigger for a major change process.

Large increases in income and significant changes in legislation can imply the need for new services, new appointments, new structures, new roles and new ways of working, all of which are likely to add up to transitional or transformational change.

In any of these circumstances major change often implies changes in people's jobs. Some people may be required to take on additional responsibilities, some may have to make significant changes to their roles (and apply for newly created posts), and some may no longer be required by the organisation. This greatly complicates change, because the team that a change leader has at the start of the process may not be the same group that will be implementing the agreed changes.

It means that change leaders sometimes have to make decisions about people, often when they do not have much evidence as to their performance or their potential. Change leaders have three options. They can **change the team before initiating the change process**. This is appropriate when leaders judge that the organisation does not have the management capacity to bring about major change and that there is time to establish a new team before change becomes unavoidable. This may be appropriate when funding is secure and the board is comfortable that change can await the establishment of a new team. It minimises the potential for people changes and a change programme interfering with each other.

When the pressure for immediate change is stronger, change leaders may have to **change the team during the change process**. This significantly complicates change, because success requires openness, transparency and extensive communication. However, the process of moving people within or out of the organisation requires discreet discussions, private negotiations and confidentiality. It may therefore not be possible for the change leader to be completely open with colleagues about the future of some members of the team. It is a particularly demanding time for change leaders as there are many aspects of major change and of moving people that just cannot be delegated.

While the process of moving people is underway, those who will be part of the new team will have to trust the change leader. Once changes have been agreed, remaining members should be given reassurance concerning their own future at the earliest opportunity. People who are not directly affected but who may be worried when the people changes are announced should also be told that their position is not at risk.

The third alternative is to **adjust the team after the change process**. This is appropriate when it would have been difficult to predict the required changes at the start and when the change process itself has shed light on people's capacity to contribute in the new circumstances. However, if this route is chosen, the change-management process may have to be revisited once the new appointments have been made, so as to help new people understand the rationale behind the changes and the actions required to implement the agreed changes fully.

Ups and downs of change

Presenting major change as a sequence of eight stages makes the process appear as a sequence of events that always move forward. In practice, organisations going through significant change tend to take two steps forward, followed by one step back.

The critical point for the change leader is to anticipate that there will be ups and downs in the process and that it is difficult to predict when a down will come and what will cause it. Experienced change leaders are not disheartened. They know there will be setbacks, but they also have the confidence and commitment to adjust the process and ensure that they do not lose sight of the overall objective.

Project management is a form of change management

Project management is an approach to managing change that helps managers to plan and implement particular pieces of work. There is a body of knowledge about project management that is similar to change management. Many of the principles set out in this chapter also apply to projects. Both require clear commissioning, strong leadership, unambiguous objectives, staged implementation, appropriate resources, clear reporting processes and agreed timetables.

The term 'project management' often applies to the management of specific pieces of work, whereas change management is more often concerned with the implementation of wider change across and organisation.

Both project and change management use techniques to assist managers to develop and implement their plans, the most useful of which are **Gantt charts** (named after Henry Gantt). These set out the activities that need to be delivered to complete a project on a timeline, showing those that have to be completed before subsequent ones can be started.

SUMMARY GANTT CHART FOR THE TRANSFORMATION OF VICTIM SUPPORT

	Month																		
	1	2	3	4	5	6	7	8	9	10	11	12	13	14	15	16	17	18	19
Develop vision, goals and outcomes	■	■	■	■	■	■	■												
Establish projects, leaders and plans	■																		
Publish plans				■															
Initial local consultation meetings			■																
Revised plans published						■													
Chair/CEO tour of areas								■	■	■	■								
Chair/CEO live webchat											■								
Final plans published as prospectus											■								
Extraordinary general meeting													■						
Recruit interim service director						■													
Appoint divisional directors																			
Appoint regional service managers											■	■	■	■	■				
New governance structure developed							■	■											
Due diligence begins																	■		
First charities merge into new organisation																			■

13.6 **SKILLS OF THE CHANGE MANAGEMENT LEADER**

Managing change is an art. In addition to the skills described so far, change leaders need to:

- **Be very clear about the key issues and flexible about the detail**. Leaders need to keep sharply focused on the critical changes that are required and to ensure that timely decisions are taken on the big issues. They also need to give the change team and other stakeholders plenty of freedom to make their own contributions in imaginative ways.

- **Understand people's frustrations**. When people feel that their concerns are being listened to, they are more likely to support change initiatives. Successful change leaders listen particularly to people who are resisting change and understand what fears underlie their opposition. Addressing such fears allows people to contribute constructively to a change programme.

- **Manage the sponsor**. Change leaders are ultimately accountable to another manager, the chief executive or the board. Their continued support for the change will help to give the initiative priority and send important signals to the other stakeholders about how it is regarded. Take steps to build the sponsor's support, to involve them as work proceeds, and ensure that they champion the initiative.

- **Expect to be criticised**. It is not possible to keep everyone happy all the time, so anticipate criticism. The key skill is to distinguish between the vocal minority, who do not actually endanger the overall process, and a quiet majority who may not be fully supportive and who could at a late stage endanger the initiative.

- **Allow time for reflection**. In the maelstrom of activity in busy organisations, it is easy to forget that learning comes in part from reflecting on progress and problems. This helps change leaders to keep their eye on the big picture and ensure that their efforts are directed towards the critical issues and not the minutiae.

The task of the change leader 'involves bringing together apparently contradictory qualities. Successful leaders shape the future *and* they adapt to the world as it is. They are clear about what they want to change *and* they are responsive to others' views and concerns. They are passionate about the direction in which they want the organisation to go *and* they understand and value the current reality of the organisation, why it has been successful and what its people are good at. They lead *and* they learn' (*Leaning into the Future*, Binney and Williams, 1997).

Common obstacles to overcome

Unfortunately, change management is best learned by practice and not by reading books on the subject!

The following guide is designed to help change leaders to overcome common problems that they may encounter:

The problem	Possible solutions
No one has sufficient time to commit to the initiative	• Review resources and time budgets. They may need to be increased and agreed with the appropriate managers • Go back a stage and build more commitment to the initiative
There is lots of action, but nothing fundamental changes	• Ensure the diagnosis is correct. Effort may be focused on the wrong issues or on the symptoms, rather than on the fundamental causes
Inability to make real and significant progress	• Ensure key stakeholders are behind the initiative • Ensure the leader has a strong team with the authority to drive the process • Check the scope has not been defined too widely
Change appears to be blocked by key people	• Review whether these people are fully committed to the change. If not, it may be necessary to arrange for them to leave to secure the best interests of the organisation as a whole
Insecurity among staff and managers	• Identify the root causes of the insecurity. Some concerns may be assuaged, others should be acknowledged as real
People are not changing their habits	• Identify what needs to change and then go back a stage in the process
Too many initiatives are crowding each other out	• Establish priorities. One success is better than two failures
A gap between the people driving the change and people who feel they are being driven	• Create opportunities to listen harder and to respond to people's concerns • Increase two-way communication

SUMMARY OF KEY POINTS

Managing change is an essential skill

- As stakeholders' expectations of organisations rise, change management becomes an essential skill for managers
- The principles of change management apply to many of the changes described in other parts of this book

Understanding organisation culture

- Culture is the way we do things and the way we think about things
- Culture has three levels: visible representations, group behaviour and underlying beliefs
- Culture is learned, historically determined, influenced by the organisation's environment, partly subconscious and heterogeneous
- Culture influences
  - how ambitious change should be
  - how change should be introduced
  - how much consultation will be needed
  - how fast change can be implemented
- People who understand their organisation's culture are in a strong position to manage change more effectively

Change management concepts

- Change management is the skill of catalysing significant improvements; it is a combination of substance and process that enables people to understand why change is necessary and consequently begin acting in different ways
- The three types of change are developmental, transitional and transformational
- Change leaders need to listen closely to people who oppose change to understand the underlying meaning of their concerns and to meet objections head on

Characteristics of change management processes

- Well-managed change processes have periods of confusion and complexity, followed by periods of clarity and simplicity
- Change leaders expect setbacks but maintain the momentum of the initiative
- Change is demanding on leaders

Staging change management initiatives

- The eight essential stages of change management are to:
  - clarify the scope and scale of the proposed initiative
  - establish the change team
  - prepare a diagnosis of the problem
  - build commitment to change
  - develop a motivating vision
  - plan and communicate extensively about the changes
  - implement change by empowering people
  - incorporate change into the organisation culture
- Implementing change can involve training, adjusting personal objectives, encouraging consistency, holding celebrations and promoting change implementers
- 'Quick wins' are an essential element of a change process

Skills of the change management leader

- Change leaders need to be clear about the key issues and flexible about the detail, understand people's frustrations, manage the sponsor, expect to be criticised and allow time for reflection
- Change processes inevitably encounter obstacles, often because the leader has missed one or more of the essential stages of a change process

FURTHER READING

Leading Change, John Kotter, Harvard Business School Press, 1996

Organisational Culture and Leadership, 3rd Edition, Edgar Schein, Wiley, 2004

More and recent books and reports can be found at www.compasspartnership.co.uk.

14 Leading an organisation

14.1 THE DEMANDING ROLE OF CHIEF EXECUTIVE

Over the last thirty years, the role of senior paid employee of third-sector organisations has changed dramatically. The post used to be called 'general secretary' or 'clerk to the council', and the role was seen as being the administrative servant of the board. The post-holder was given comparatively little strategic authority and governing bodies took a hands-on role because most organisations were small.

During the 1970s, the title 'director' started to creep on to organisations' letterheads, reflecting a change in the duties that the board expected the office-holder to discharge. In the 1980s the language and the role changed again. Organisations began to seek 'chief executives'. They wanted people with substantial management experience who could take charge of these increasingly large and complex organisations.

It is now widely accepted that having a talented chief executive is a critical ingredient of a successful organisation. Chief executives are expected to be figurehead, politician and manager all rolled up in one person. They have to deploy a combination of managerial, entrepreneurial and political skills. They need management skills to get everyone to work together towards achieving common goals. They need entrepreneurial skills to take risks and seize opportunities, attributes that are usually associated with the private sector. They also need the ability to unite diverse political constituencies behind activities that everyone is willing to support – a skill that is more often associated with public-sector management.

The job is demanding, both mentally and physically, but it is also immensely satisfying. Effective chief executives are rewarded with the knowledge that their work has a huge effect on the lives of the organisation's users, its staff and its volunteers.

However, the burden of leadership should not fall on the chief executive alone. A clear distinction has to be made between the 'leader' of an organisation, the person who holds the most senior position, and 'leadership', a function which should be shared by all levels of the organisation. The leader is the person who has most responsibility for providing leadership of the organisation as a whole, but managers and staff at all levels can contribute by providing strong leadership of their divisions and departments. Indeed, the board also contributes by giving strong leadership to the governance of the organisation. In this notion of 'distributed leadership' everyone has responsibility for the leadership of their areas of responsibility and for contributing, in large or small ways, to the leadership of the organisation as a whole.

The modern view of leadership is that leaders are expected to possess high levels of emotional intelligence. This is not to suggest that leadership is all about relationships, but to stress that investing time and energy in developing and maintaining open and trustworthy relationships with the board, the leadership team and other stakeholders is an essential part of the chief executive's job.

This chapter:

- draws a distinction between management and leadership;
- describes the special characteristics of the chief executive's role;
- establishes the importance of honesty and trustworthiness;
- sets out ways of structuring chief executives' work;
- explains actions chief executives take to maintain authority;
- shows how chief executives set about enhancing their skills.

There is a huge literature on leadership, and indeed a number of books exclusively on the leadership of third-sector organisations. This section does not attempt to summarise this vast literature. It does set out to give busy leaders some simple tips. Details of some of the most relevant books are given in the further reading section.

14.2 DISTINGUISHING MANAGEMENT FROM LEADERSHIP

The concepts of management and leadership are closely related and they overlap. However, in unpacking and describing the special contribution made by chief executives, it is helpful to make a distinction between the two functions.

Management is concerned with the efficient administration of the organisation. It is about the establishment of processes that make the organisation work, the creation of structures that link people together in an organised way, the development of plans, the control of budgets and the costing of services. Chief executives have to master all these and more.

Effective chief executives have to rise beyond management and provide leadership. **Leadership** is what clarifies the mission, motivates people, seeks new opportunities, gives organisations a sense of purpose and focuses people on the task.

This is not to suggest that management is all boring administration and leadership is the enjoyable activity. Organisations need an appropriate combination of management and leadership for their circumstances. Those that are over-led and under-managed can be exciting places to work, but they may not have the practical capacity to deliver the work. Those that are under-led but over-managed may be capable of doing the work, but they are eventually overtaken by imaginative organisations with the flair and creativity to take entirely new approaches to achieving their missions and inspiring their people.

Effective chief executives understand the difference between being a manager and being a leader. They strive to delegate managerial tasks so as to create the time they need to be the leader. They manage their time in such a way that they can turn their attention away from the daily deluge of seemingly urgent activities and on to the important task of providing leadership.

14.3 SPECIAL CHARACTERISTICS OF THE CHIEF EXECUTIVE'S JOB

The role of the chief executive is very different from all other posts.

It is less structured. Being responsible for everything the organisation does means the chief executive can become involved in anything. This lack of boundaries differentiates the job from all other posts. The range, scope and wide responsibility of the job mean that there is an almost limitless opportunity to be ineffective unless chief executives are totally clear about how they are going to set about the job.

It is highly exposed. Chief executives have nowhere to hide. They are expected to speak in public, to make press statements, to report to the board, to make presentations at gatherings of staff, and to approve publicly available documents. Chief executives are on stage every day of their working lives.

It requires the widest range of abilities. Chief executives need to master an extraordinary range of skills. They need to understand the fundamentals of finance, marketing, service and human-resource management; they are expected to deploy strong inter-personal skills and at the same time master the policy issues of their field; they need consummate political skills to make things happen; they need to be tough when hard decisions have to be made and tender when compassion and sensitivity are required.

It involves the widest range of constituencies. Chief executives have to operate with many different groups, including funders, service users and umbrella organisations, as well as staff and board members. They have to adjust their style and approach to suit groups that often have different interests and different motives for contributing to the organisation.

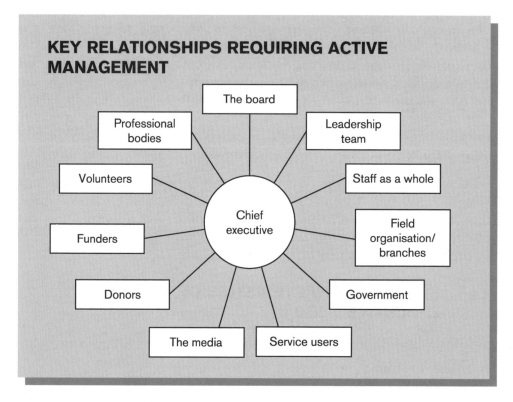

KEY RELATIONSHIPS REQUIRING ACTIVE MANAGEMENT

- The board
- Professional bodies
- Leadership team
- Volunteers
- Staff as a whole
- Chief executive
- Funders
- Field organisation/branches
- Donors
- Government
- The media
- Service users

It is a lonely position. The chief executive often has no one inside the organisation to seek advice from on sensitive issues, because the very act of raising them can cause unnecessary anxiety, particularly if the ideas are not subsequently pursued.

It depends on maintaining a reservoir of goodwill. Chief executives need the trust and active support of their board and their staff. They have to maintain the confidence of both groups in order to do the job.

It is the critical link between the board and the staff. Chief executives have to operate effectively both as head of the leadership team and as the servant of the board. These two groups frequently have different working styles and priorities. Chief executives have to work with both and manage the information flows between the two.

It requires a long-term perspective and short-term actions. Chief executives have to think years ahead, and simultaneously solve current problems that have not been resolved elsewhere in the organisation.

Three further aspects of the role are common in managing third-sector organisations.

The position is not well understood. The special characteristics of the chief executive's job are sometimes not well understood by the board, the staff or other people outside the organisation. This results in conflicting expectations that can pull chief executives in different directions.

Chief executives have to **bridge many fundamentally different value systems**. Third-sector organisations tend to have a skill-base such as medicine, education and social welfare. Each skill-base is associated with a set of values that are predominant in that field. These values are seldom consistent with a managerial mindset. The chief executive has to bridge the different values and help each group see the organisation and its issues from the other's perspective.

Sometimes chief executives have to **challenge inappropriate values**. Modern management textbooks (including this one) stress the importance of the organisation's culture and values. But values can also be a source of difficulty for the chief executive, when they permeate all aspects of an organisation's work in ways that are inappropriate. Take, for example, the training organisation whose commitment to training its own staff grows out of proportion to their need to perform their jobs; the trade union that is frightened to challenge the union that its own staff belong to; or the social-services agency that cannot bring itself to sack members of staff who are consistently not performing to the required standard. In these circumstances, it falls to the chief executive to challenge the inappropriate application of values and beliefs.

Most leadership textbooks contain lists of the characteristics and competencies of chief executives. Those described above have been selected because they are particularly pertinent to chief executives of third-sector organisations.

However, chief executives do not need to have or to use them all the time. Leadership has to be highly sensitive to the context in which it is being applied, so the key to being a really effective chief executive is the ability to apply the right characteristics and the right competencies for the circumstances. This ability to judge the context is a crucial skill. If an organisation has lost momentum, then visionary, inspiring leadership is required to set new directions and aspirations. If, on the other hand, an organisation is facing a crisis, then decisiveness, minimal consultation and speedy decision-making are the right characteristics to display.

The need to provide leadership that is highly sensitive to context also applies when dealing with different circumstances in the daily pattern of a chief executive's work. One meeting may require a thoughtful and sensitive approach to a situation where people's roles may need to change; the next may require a tough conversation to hold an under-performing manager properly to account. Chief executives therefore have to have an ability to 'switch their mental software' extremely quickly so they can adopt different attitudes to deal with different circumstances in different ways.

14.4 CHIEF EXECUTIVES NEED TO BE GENUINE AND TRUSTWORTHY

Despite the many demands for perfection, chief executives have to remember that they are not super-human; they have strengths and weaknesses. The best ones understand what they are particularly good at doing and where they most need support from other members of their team.

Chief executives need to set high expectations of their colleagues, but they also need genuinely and deeply to appreciate the efforts made by other people. They must praise more often than they criticise, and when work does not meet their expectations they must strive to give clear and honest feedback. They express gratitude for what people have done and they don't duck the difficult task of telling people when their work is not up to standard. They have to recognise that no one is perfect, and therefore have to make important judgements as to when work is 'good enough'.

Chief executives also need to be patient, because change will always take longer than they would like, and it will appear to be simpler in prospect than in practice. They have to establish high expectations and at the same time be tolerant about the time and effort required to bring about change.

Chief executives' humility and their deeply held commitment to support others to deliver their best are important elements of being the 'servant leader': the person who has the capacity to bring the best out of other people, to support them when they need assistance and to allow them to take credit for achievements even when the chief executive may have been a major determinant of their success.

Ultimately it is these 'human' characteristics that are the mark of a great chief executive, and not their ability to have the most ambitious vision, the perfect strategic plan, the most creative partnerships or the greatest fundraising skills. Frances Hesselbein, the American guru of nonprofit leadership, says that leaders need to understand 'how to be'. She describes this as having 'quality, character, mind-set, values, principles and courage'. Leaders who appreciate 'how to be' 'build dispersed and diverse leadership and hold forth the vision of the organisation's future in compelling ways that ignite the spark needed to build the inclusive enterprise'.

Her view is echoed by Parker Palmer, author of *Let Your Life Speak*. Interviewed in the *Leader to Leader* journal, he said 'The best leaders work from a place of integrity in themselves, from their hearts. If they don't they can't inspire trustful relationships. In the absence of trust, organisations fall apart. It takes courage to lead from the heart because you're putting your own identity and integrity into the public arena. You're standing for things you believe in. You're professing values that are important to you – and in the public arena you will always draw slings and arrows for doing that. But you will have the best chance of creating something of true and lasting value'.

WHAT FOLLOWERS EXPECT FROM THEIR LEADERS

The authors of the best-selling book, *The Leadership Challenge*, have asked survey respondents over twenty years to select from a list the seven qualities that they 'most look for and admire in a leader, someone whose direction they would willingly follow'. The results have been striking in their consistency, and they do not vary significantly by demographics, organisation or culture.

Characteristic	% of managers selecting it			
	1987	1995	2002	2007
Honesty	83	88	88	89
Forward-looking	62	75	71	71
Inspiring	58	68	65	69
Competent	67	63	66	68

Other characteristics in descending order in 2007 were intelligent, fair-minded, straightforward, broad-minded, supportive, dependable, cooperative, courageous, determined, caring and imaginative. This suggests that followers are not looking for someone with godlike characteristics. Rather they want their leaders to be:

- **Honest:** truthful, ethical and principled. People who know right from wrong, who will not mislead and who disclose clear values and lead by them
- **Forward-looking:** having a sense of direction, the ability to imagine or discover a desirable destination for the organisation and to connect it to the hopes and dreams of the organisation's constituents
- **Competent:** having a good track record, being able to challenge, enable and encourage (but not necessarily having expertise in the core skill areas of the organisation)
- **Inspiring:** enthusiastic, passionate about the cause and communicating a vision and giving people a greater sense of worth

Source: *The Leadership Challenge,* Kouzes and Posner, Jossey-Bass, 2007

14.5 STRUCTURING THE CHIEF EXECUTIVE'S WORK

Because chief executives' jobs entail endless variety, it is all the more important that they structure their work. Without structure there is always the risk that they will become the servants of their in-trays – dealing with what appears to be most urgent rather than with those things that are most important (and which usually do not appear in the in-tray).

One way to structure the chief executive's work is to think in terms of his or her responsibilities for the five Ps:

- the **purpose** of the organisation;
- the **plans** and **performance** of the organisation;
- the **processes** for managing the organisation;
- the **people** who work closely with the chief executive.

This structure builds on the insightful and enduring description of all managerial work first expounded by John Adair. He established the notion that managers always have to think about the **task**, the **team** and the **individuals**.

The purpose

Chief executives have a wide range of responsibilities relating to the purpose. Their first responsibility is to ensure that all parts of the organisation are **focusing on achieving the purpose**. This is easier said than done. Sometimes it is hard to stop the process of getting things done becoming more important than the task itself. A delicate balance has to be struck between gaining sufficient consensus on the way forward and spending too much time and effort on seeking everyone's agreement. Chief executives who take too many initiatives to further the purpose without seeking consensus will ultimately encounter opposition. On the other hand, chief executives who miss opportunities, or who slow the pace of change because they are always striving to gain consensus, risk losing momentum and being branded weak and indecisive.

As well as setting direction, in conjunction with the board, chief executives have a particular responsibility for setting the scale of an organisation's ambition and activities. Lack of ambition and unwillingness to take new initiatives can be demotivating for everyone involved. But attempting to expand too quickly can put many strains on the organisation and eventually lead to reductions in the quality of work and stressed-out staff. It can be a fine judgement. The board and directors are able to give their views, but ultimately the chief executive's opinion will determine the scale of the organisation's ambitions and activities.

Chief executives need to concentrate on the **quality of the organisation's services**. As their core activity, organisations have to provide services to an agreed user group and or deliver campaigns on agreed issues, to a specified standard and within agreed cost and time parameters. The chief executive needs to know whether this is happening, what the organisation is doing to improve the quality of its services and what has been learned about the most effective ways of improving them.

Chief executives also need to ensure that all **'back office' services are delivering high added value** to the rest of the organisation. These include finance, marketing, HR, IT, property maintenance and so on. It is remarkably easy for the people working in these areas to become engrossed in their own concerns and gradually lose sight of the fact that they exist solely to support the externally facing departments. The absence of market mechanisms to keep managers of these services on their toes means that chief executives have to make sure the managers are always focused on meeting internal users' needs to the highest standards, and don't become too engrossed in the intricacies of their own professional function.

Chief executives are also responsible for ensuring that the organisation generates an adequate financial margin. In the past, some chief executives believed their financial role was to ensure that the finance director produced a balanced budget. Today chief executives have to be involved in the formulation of financial strategy and to ensure that, over time, it will deliver a financial surplus to pay for future investments, innovation, experiments, and finance for working capital. This gives the organisations strategic flexibility to achieve their mission in ways that they believe will be most effective.

In many third-sector organisations, fundraising plays a role in balancing the organisation's financial equation. Although most have professional staff running fundraising, chief executives need to play **three critical roles in fundraising.** They have to:

1. Ensure that the organisation has an ambitious, realistic and achievable fundraising strategy. This is a challenging task. Fundraising is among the most difficult and subtle activities in third-sector management. It is surrounded by opportunities to make errors of judgement. Chief executives have to challenge fundraising plans, ensure that they are robust, provide imagination when they are dreary, and give special support to the person who is responsible for their delivery.
2. Give personal attention to key fundraising initiatives. Ultimately, large donors and grant-makers expect chief executives to be personally involved in fundraising. They need to be assured that their grant or donation is being given special attention, and the best way to signify that is by the presence of the chief executive.
3. Ensure that each type of fundraising investment is producing an appropriate return on investment for that source of funds.

Chief executives also play a crucial role in **establishing new partnerships**. Most chief executives spend more time 'outside' the organisation than any other employee, putting them in a strong position to spot new partnership opportunities and to know people from other organisations who might be potential partners. The helicopter view that chief executives must have enables them to see their organisation in the context of others in the field, who may be both competitors and potential partners.

Finally, chief executives have to **encourage innovation**. They have to ensure that the organisation is continually moving forward and finding ways to campaign and deliver services that meet new circumstances. This means searching for new ideas, sometimes from other countries, sometimes from local branches and sometimes from organisations in other fields. It means putting staff time and money into new ideas and acknowledging that, while many will fail, some will become the engine for the organisation's future development.

The plans and performance

Plans and performance have been discussed extensively in Chapters 5 to 9, and they are both the direct responsibility of chief executives. In summary, chief executives have to ensure that the organisation creates **clear and consistent strategic and operational plans** for itself as a whole and for each of its services and campaigns. More than anyone else chief executives have to ensure that every person concentrates on achieving planned objectives and that **performance is managed against plans** at all levels of the organisation. They need to be certain that plans and performance reports are well communicated, that actions are taken when plans are not being realised and that achievements are widely celebrated.

The processes

Above anyone else, chief executives are responsible for ensuring that processes are established and developed to make things happen in a purposeful and widely understood way. They have to make sure that a framework and culture exist within which decision-making processes are clear and effective.

They also have a day-to-day responsibility for guiding the processes used to take major decisions. They have to decide:

- the precise nature of each major decision;
- when the decision should be taken;
- who needs to be involved;
- the period of time over which the decision should be taken.

Chief executives have to decide **how to structure the big decisions**, so as to make it easy to proceed. Structuring decisions in ways that fit with staff and board perceptions makes decisions easier. For example, a decision concerned with improving the quality of a service could be cast as a decision about:

- the need for improved monitoring to pinpoint the problem;
- the need for a new service plan;
- a pilot improvement programme to demonstrate a new approach to quality management;
- an opportunity to raise new funds from a donor who wants the service to be successful;
- firing the manager responsible.

Chief executives have to decide which way to approach the problem in order to achieve the desired results.

Judgements about **whom to involve** in a decision are the next consideration. Consultation is an essential ingredient of the chief executive's job. The problems most organisations have to deal with are highly complex. Expertise and knowledge often reside with many different people whose contribution will often lead to better decisions. Furthermore, their commitment to implementing decisions will be greater if they feel they have been consulted.

Consultation is also essential to hold together the coalition of stakeholders who constitute a third-sector organisation. If funders, board, managers and employees have been consulted, they are more likely to back the decisions the organisation makes, even if the decision is not the one they wanted.

But consultation slows decision-making. When there is too much consultation, people become frustrated at the lack of progress and may feel that the chief executive is abdicating his or her responsibility for taking decisions. So chief executives have to be making a continuous stream of judgements about whom to involve in different types of decisions and when to involve them. They have to **pace decisions**. An attempt to rush key decisions through too quickly can lead to a build-up of opposition. But leaving issues to fester unresolved begins to immobilise organisations. Chief executives have to make frequent judgements about how fast to push people on critically important issues.

Chief executives have to **take decisions**. Although the major decisions are likely to have been widely discussed and are formally taken by the board, chief executives have to make up their own minds at an early stage and drive decisions through the organisation. They have to listen to their colleagues and take advice, but often this will be contradictory. So chief executives have to decide when to listen to advice and when to note it but proceed in order to achieve a desired objective.

Chief executives also have to take critically important decisions about **the amount of work** an organisation should commit itself to achieving. It is always tempting to make more commitments than the organisation can meet. Indeed, a common mistake chief executives make is to take too many management initiatives without taking full account of the limitations on people's time to implement the desired changes. Consequently they are either not done to the required standard or they are so delayed that they lose their impact.

The **timing of initiatives** often rests in the hands of chief executives. It is tempting to concentrate on the substance of a decision and forget that the timing is equally important. Pushing for an urgently needed change (for example, the re-structuring of a team) when no one favours the idea might lead to no change at all. A half-anticipated departure, however, might create circumstances in which the same change is agreed without resistance or difficulty.

Finally, chief executives are responsible for ensuring good **communications** within the organisation. People need information in order to do their jobs effectively and to set their work in the wider context of the organisation. Chief executives have to work to ensure that:

- clear and concise information about why particular decisions have been taken is communicated to managers and staff;
- information reaches everyone who needs to know (including part-time employees, people working away from the head office and people on leave);
- the organisation is not overloaded with news and facts, while failing to communicate the essential information.

Chief executives need to make effective use of a wide range of methods of internal communication, including:

- regular team briefings
- chief executive's newsletters
- managers' meetings and staff conferences
- internal newssheets
- user group meetings
- e-mail and intranets
- telephone conferences
- DVDs.

The people

Building relationships with a wide range of people is a critical part of the chief executive's job. Chief executives have to work particularly closely with board members and the leadership team. They need to form relationships with, and maintain the confidence of the majority of, the individuals in both groups. Chief executives have to **build and develop strong leadership teams**. This is an essential pre-requisite for making a success of the chief executive's job. It requires the chief executive to create good working relationships with each member of the team and with the team as a whole. These are the people who make the organisation work and, without capable directors working as a team, organisations quickly become unmanageable.

Chief executives have to decide on the desirable **structure for the leadership team** and on the **timing of any changes** that need to be made. These are sensitive issues, where support from the chair and the board will often help a chief executive come to the right judgement.

Chief executives have to secure and maintain the confidence of the leadership team. If there are more departures than anticipated or if vacancies are unfilled for too long, chief executives will quickly lose the confidence of their remaining team members and find that the board begins to worry about their competence to lead the organisation.

Sometimes this requires tough judgements to be made about people's suitability for the jobs they are doing. It may be that a role has grown beyond a manager's ability, that an inappropriate appointment has been made or that someone no longer has the ambition and drive needed to deliver the role. In these circumstances, chief executives cannot afford to duck the difficult decision of **moving someone on**, ideally in an honourable and respectful way. That does not mean always moving people on because standards are continually not being met; perhaps in such cases the standards have been set too high. It does mean being bold and decisive when there is a weak link in the top team.

GOOD HABITS

Watching the chief executive of one of Britain's largest third-sector organisations, I noticed that:

- he went out of his way to praise staff for their achievements (both face to face and through personal notes)
- he demonstrated that he had listened to consultation by returning people's comments with his own views annotated in the margin
- he held a conference of all 120 senior managers once or twice a year to share the overall strategy and communicate his view of priorities
- he retained the authority of the position of chief executive by taking decisions when people could not agree
- he worked hard to retain the confidence of his board by keeping them well informed, anticipating difficult decisions and planning how they should be taken, often over a period of many months

These are habits of chief executives who lead their organisations.

Chief executives have to hold members of their team **accountable**. They have to agree objectives with each member of the team and review their performance at regular intervals. This is one of the tougher aspects of chief executives' roles, not least because tough accountability does not always sit comfortably with the caring values espoused by the sector. However, it is vitally important that chief executives are totally clear with each member of the leadership team about the objectives that they are expected to achieve. It is equally important that there is a clear and explicit process for regularly reviewing progress against objectives with each member of the team and that this is carried out rigorously and honestly. It should lead to praise for achievements, challenges to areas where performance is below that expected and constructive learning about what to do differently to improve performance.

Chief executives are also responsible for the **professional development of members of their team**. They can be encouraged to network with similar organisations or to pursue an interest in a field which personally intrigues them. They can be encouraged to take on additional responsibilities or to take time out of work to study. Sometimes chief executives may need to be particularly aware of people's personal circumstances and of stresses in their lives. At other times they may need to give members of their team extra support on an assignment. Chief executives cannot work miracles, but they can hold on to good people if they do all they can to look after the needs of team members.

A particular problem chief executives face is in their relationship with the individual who is responsible for the function that is also the **chief executive's own area of professional expertise**. An example that is known to cause problems is in the relationship with the director of services when the chief executive's background was service management.

Sometimes chief executives are tempted to take the limelight and intervene a great deal in an area because they have specialist knowledge. They feel that they can make a particularly strong contribution here. This can cause problems for the director or manager of that area, who may feel constrained and lacking freedom that is given to the other directors or managers. Conversely, chief executives may realise that this is a sensitive issue and over-compensate by not becoming sufficiently involved in that area. In this circumstance, directors or managers may feel that they are receiving insufficient attention compared to their colleagues. Either way, it is an issue worth bringing to the surface so that both parties come to a mutually satisfactory relationship.

Chief executives also have to form a **close working relationship with their board**. They have to understand their needs and their concerns, and maintain their confidence at all times. This is not straightforward, since chief executives sometimes propose changes that they believe to be essential but which the board does not like. Pushing change too far or too fast carries the risk that members of the board will begin to lose confidence in the chief executive.

AVOIDING BAD HABITS

Working with many chief executives has given me an opportunity to observe some habits that need to be avoided. They include:

- failing to take decisions
- talking too much in meetings
- allowing team members to talk too much
- blaming the board
- failing to hold people to account for their responsibilities
- always seeing people's weaknesses rather than their strengths
- not delivering on tasks they have committed themselves to
- not delegating explicitly
- criticising team members behind their backs
- revealing by their attitude, behaviour and non-verbal communication whom they like and whom they dislike

Everyone makes mistakes. Successful chief executives strive to learn from their errors and to find their own formula for working effectively as a leader.

Alternatively the board may suggest changes that the chief executive considers inappropriate, unworkable, or that managers are unlikely to support. The good relationship that the chief executive has with the board and the trust that they have in his or her judgement will be important in managing such differences of perspective.

To work effectively with the board, chief executives need to **form a particularly strong working relationship with the chair** (see also section 16.2, Managing your boss). This means putting time aside to meet alone with the chair to share concerns, plan board meetings and build and maintain trust in each other. Building this relationship is not always easy, because they have such strangely interlinked and overlapping roles, with the chair usually having ultimate legal responsibility and the chief executive having all the day-to-day executive responsibility. They are very often both busy people and it can be difficult to get space in their schedules for each other. So they absolutely have to make regular time together a priority, whether by phone or in person.

The consequences of a less than ideal working relationship can be very significant for the organisation. The absence of good coordination between the chair and the chief executive can lead to misunderstandings and growing mistrust between the board and the staff. So, even though the two people in these positions may sometimes not be the best of friends, each needs to be able to respect the other and to find the time and motivation to work together as a strong partnership (as discussed in section 4.6, Establishing effective chair–chief executive relationships).

ROLES OF LEADERS

Nanus and Dobbs argue that leaders' attention needs to be focused in four directions:

1. **Inside** the organisation, where the leader interacts with the board, staff and volunteers to inspire, encourage, enthuse and empower them

2. **Outside** the organisation, where the leader seeks assistance or support from donors, grant-makers, potential allies, the media or other leaders in the business or public sectors

3. On **present operations**, where the leader is concerned about the quality of services to clients and the community, and also organisational structures, information systems and other aspects or organisational effectiveness

4. On **future possibilities**, where the leader anticipates trends and developments that are likely to have important implications for the future direction of the organisation

They argue that focusing attention in these four directions requires leaders to deliver six essential roles:

1. **Visionary** – Leaders work with others to scan the realm of future possibilities, seeking clues to a more desirable destination. 'Great leaders have great visions and when they are widely shared they are the principal engines of organisational growth and progress'

2. **Strategist** – Leaders are responsible for ensuring that organisations have strategies that position the organisation to be most effective in meeting present and future challenges. Leaders ensure that their organisations adopt strategies that hold the most promise of fulfilling the vision and achieving the greatest social good

3. **Politician** – Leaders are 'super networkers' who champion the organisation's cause and use their contacts to further the organisation's mission

4. **Fundraiser** – Leaders have an important role in raising funds from the public, foundations and corporations. The authors call this role campaigning, reflecting the common use of the term 'campaigning for funds'

5. **Coach** – Leaders empower and inspire individuals and help them to learn, grow and realise their full potential

6. **Change agent** – Leaders initiate change that positions the organisation for the future, introducing changes externally around the clients, the services offered and the means of financing them, and internally around the organisation's structures and processes

The focus of leaders' attention and the roles they need to perform can be related in the following way:

The roles of nonprofit leaders

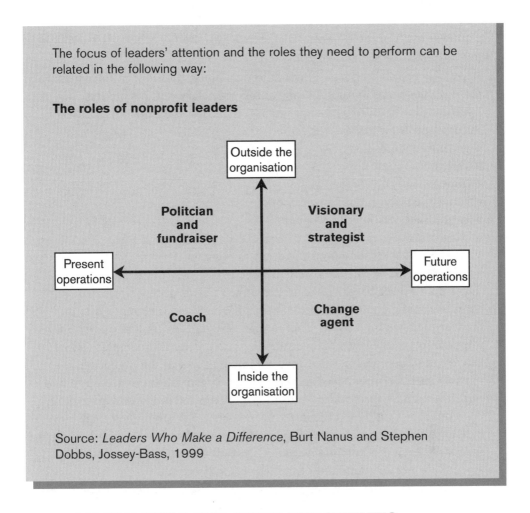

Source: *Leaders Who Make a Difference*, Burt Nanus and Stephen Dobbs, Jossey-Bass, 1999

14.6 MAINTAINING THE CHIEF EXECUTIVE'S AUTHORITY

Effective chief executives carry authority. This authority is earned, and results from the actions they take. Given the extraordinary freedom they have to act, they can do things that increase their authority or they can diminish their authority. This is not to argue that decisions should be taken primarily on the basis of whether they increase or reduce power and influence, but to recognise that authority is a crucial part of being an effective chief executive.

Because the third sector is caring, concerned about equality and values personal relationships, there is danger that chief executives over-emphasise these values in the way they conduct themselves.

The following checklist of ways chief executives should behave is based on 10 points suggested by Richard Lynch:

1. **Recognise people's efforts.** Effective leaders praise the work of their managers, the staff, the board and local branches. As monetary rewards are less significant in the third sector, personal recognition is all the more critical. Recognition is best when it is:
   - given frequently
   - varied
   - honest
   - about the person, not just the work
   - appropriate for the achievement
   - consistent
   - timely – given as soon after the event as possible
   - individualised to suit the recipient's needs.

2. **Develop a power base.** The chief executive's power depends primarily on maintaining the confidence of the board, the staff and, in some cases, the broader membership as well. That implies serving them well and, even more importantly, gaining and maintaining their confidence. This requires chief executives to demonstrate that they are in command of the organisation's affairs. Chief executives need to persuade the organisation to face up to and resolve difficult issues; and they also have to stop the board or staff making decisions that would be difficult to defend. They also strengthen their power base by anticipating divisions of opinion between themselves, their boards and their staff. Each is a potential weakness that others can exploit if the chief executive is not in command of the resolution process.

3. **Use authority effectively.** Chief executives can find it difficult to combine caring values with the need to be tough and decisive when circumstances demand a decision that will not please colleagues. The temptation is to give relationships a higher priority when in practice the long-term interest of the organisation should be paramount. Authority used effectively increases people's respect for the leader.

4. **Use the power of the position.** Recently appointed chief executives often shun the trappings of power. They stress that they are the same as everyone else, and forgo the privileges relevant to the post. This is an understandable reaction, particularly in organisations with a history of equality and consensus decision-making. It can nevertheless be short-sighted because, like it or not, the status attached to the post is one source of the chief executive's influence. Effective chief executives ensure that they retain an appropriate status for the post in the prevailing circumstances. They have an office that gives them an appropriate degree of privacy. They ensure that they have appropriate administrative support. They sit at the head of the table at meetings, giving them maximum access to people's emotional intelligence.

5. **Build a reputation**. Managers respect chief executives who have a reputation in their field of endeavour. Chief executives who have the expertise to make press comments or give speeches strengthen their position within their organisations. They gain a reputation by networking with coordinating groups and by building a profile in their field.

6. **Develop skills and abilities**. Leaders constantly strive to increase their expertise, both as managers and as people who understand the detail of their field of endeavour. When managers know that they can extend their abilities by working with their leader, their respect for the leader grows.

7. **Clarify personal objectives**. Leaders have a burning desire to achieve specific objectives. They are clear about what they want the organisation to accomplish and how they are going to help the organisation to realise it. When this is coupled with a passionate belief in what the organisation can do, it rubs off on everyone else.

8. **Communicate with stakeholders**. Leaders listen to others and the language they use. They put great emphasis on communicating a vision of the future in language that people can understand. They take every opportunity to communicate with as many constituencies as possible.

9. **Develop a positive self-image**. Effective leaders are confident of their abilities. They strive to increase confidence in themselves and in others. They are optimistic. They get into a virtuous circle in which their success feeds their self-image, which in turn leads to further success.

10. **Combine vision with attention to detail**. Leaders judge when to focus on the big picture and when detail has to be given attention.

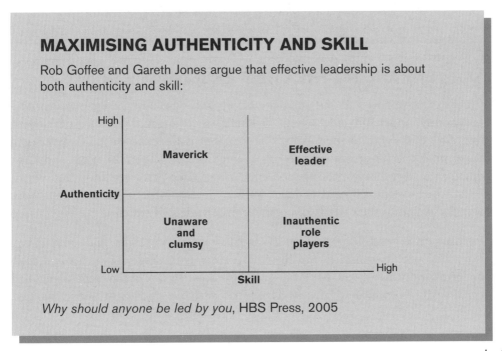

MAXIMISING AUTHENTICITY AND SKILL

Rob Goffee and Gareth Jones argue that effective leadership is about both authenticity and skill:

Why should anyone be led by you, HBS Press, 2005

THE LESSONS OF EXPERIENCE

Douglas McGregor acted as teacher and consultant to many organisations. After being President of Antioch College in the United States, he had the honesty to admit that he had made some wrong assumptions about leadership:

It took the direct experience of becoming a line executive, and meeting personally the problems involved, to teach me what no amount of observation of other people could have taught. I believed, for example, that a leader could operate successfully as a kind of advisor to his organisation. I thought I could avoid being a boss. Unconsciously, I suspect, I hoped to duck the unpleasant necessity of making difficult decisions, of taking the responsibility for one course of action among many uncertain alternatives, of making mistakes and taking the consequences. I thought that maybe I could operate so that everyone would like me – that good human relations would eliminate all discord and disagreement.

I could not have been more wrong. It took a couple of years, but I finally began to realize that a leader cannot avoid the exercise of authority any more than he can avoid responsibility for what happens to his organisation. In fact, it is a major function of the top executive to take on his own shoulders the responsibility for resolving the uncertainties that are always involved in important decisions. Moreover, since no important decision ever pleases everyone in the organisation, he must also absorb the displeasure, and sometimes severe hostility, of those who would have taken a different course.

Source: *Essays of Douglas McGregor,* MIT Press, 1966

14.7 ENHANCING THE CHIEF EXECUTIVE'S SKILLS

Chief executives need to put time and effort into developing their own learning programme and taking the actions required to ensure that they are developing the range and depth of their skills. The first step is to acknowledge that personal development is an essential part of a chief executive's maturation and that, despite the very heavy pressures on their time, it deserves attention and effort. Then, chief executives need to identify their development needs in a systematic way. Insights into their needs can come from a variety of sources.

Psychometric tests help to identify innate personality traits and preferences. They help people to understand their natural strengths and weaknesses and their preferred working styles. They are generally done by an independent, qualified person who is trained to give feedback in a sensitive and constructive manner.

One of the best known is the Myers Briggs Type Indicator, which helps to identify people's psychological preferences.

Competency-based tools help to identify specific skills that leaders deploy in different situations. They help to identify skill gaps by comparing the skills required of a leader with those currently held. The National Occupational Standards for management and leadership are an example.

360° reviews seek feedback from people who report to the post-holder, people the post-holder reports to and the post-holder's peers. The information gathered can be compared with the post-holder's perceptions of his or her own performance, and, if desired they can be benchmarked against the performance of people in similar positions. They generally result in a tailored report and one-to-one feedback from an assessor.

Annual performance reviews are generally undertaken by the chair of the board, to report on achievements, issues that require attention and personal performance. This review should be done against agreed objectives and should be based on evidence gathered by the chair from a range of people and sources of information. The chair may well be assisted by other board members (see section 4.5, Appointing and appraising the chief executive, for further details).

Openly seeking comments from colleagues is another valuable source of insights into development needs. Chief executives can seek ongoing feedback from colleagues. This can come, for example, from reviews of 'things that went wrong', by asking 'what could I have done differently?' Being open to such learning can help to build trusting relationships and indicate that conversations on performance should be part of the culture of the organisation.

Seeking feedback from a coach or mentor can provide further insights into development needs. Coaching and mentoring relationships may be part of the development package that chief executives choose (see below). Both can be used to gain insights into future development needs.

These ways of identifying development needs can be combined, so that evidence, which is always partial and quite judgemental, can be corroborated to give an overall view of the priorities for the leader's development.

There are many options for investing in personal learning. These are described in more detail in section 16.4, Delegating work and empowering people. The points here relate to their use by chief executives.

- **Appointing a coach**. Whilst a chair or a board member can 'coach' a chief executive, there is a danger of muddling different agendas, so some chief executives have an external coach. This means that their most private concerns and issues can be raised in a setting of complete confidentiality. Choice of the coach will depend on the skills the chief executive wishes to develop. The coach could be a past chief executive from the third sector (who, ideally, has gained a coaching qualification) or from the private or public sectors.

- **Finding a mentor**. A mentor is likely to be a chief executive from another organisation who is more experienced or who works for a larger or more developed organisation.
- **Joining an action learning set**. For chief executives these usually work best when they are run by an independent person who can commit the time and effort required to maintain momentum and to plan and prepare meetings. This helps to make best use of chief executives' valuable time.
- **Shadowing another chief executive**. Watching another leadership team in action, attending another organisation's board meeting and taking a structured approach to understanding how another chief executive works are all valuable ways of gaining experience.
- **Undertaking self-directed learning**. Most chief executives read widely and attend learning events. This can be done systematically by analysing needs and then constructing a programme of reading and training that meets those specific needs.
- **Attending courses and gaining a qualification**. Significant numbers of chief executives have an MBA or a qualification from a university that offers post-graduate qualifications, such as the CASS Business School at City University and the Open University.

Many chief executives report that they find coaching and mentoring to be the most valuable and effective methods of delivering leadership development.

SUMMARY OF KEY POINTS

The demanding role of chief executive

- The role of chief executive has changed beyond recognition in the last thirty years
- The job is demanding but can also be immensely satisfying
- The 'leader' is not the only person in the organisation who provides 'leadership'
- Relationships and emotional intelligence are as important as 'technical' skills

Distinguishing management from leadership

- Management is concerned with efficient administration, making processes work, creating structures, developing plans and controlling budgets
- Leadership is concerned with clarifying the mission, motivating people and giving the organisation a sense of purpose

Special characteristics of the chief executive's job

- The chief executive's job is different from all other posts
- It is less structured, highly exposed and lonely. It requires the widest range of abilities, involves the widest range of constituencies and depends on maintaining a reservoir of goodwill

Chief executives need to be genuine and trustworthy

- Chief executives set high expectations of their colleagues and they genuinely appreciate efforts made by other people
- Chief executives are 'servant leaders' who know how to bring the best out of other people
- The best leaders work from a place of integrity in themselves
- Followers expect leaders to be honest, forward-looking, inspiring and competent

Structuring the chief executive's work

- Chief executives can avoid becoming servants of their in-trays by focusing on the five 'Ps':
  - the purpose of the organisation
  - its plans
  - its performance
  - the processes of managing it
  - the people who work closely with them

Maintaining the chief executive's authority

- Chief executives act in a way that enhances their authority
- They systematically develop their leadership skills by recognising people's efforts, developing a power base, using authority effectively, using the power of the position and building a personal reputation
- They also need to develop their skills and abilities, clarify their own objectives, communicate with their followers, develop a positive self-image and combine vision with attention to detail

Enhancing the chief executive's skills

- Chief executives adopt a range of different methods to understand their own development needs
- They use coaches and mentors, they join action learning sets and shadow other chief executives and they invest time in their own learning

FURTHER READING

Learning to Lead – Ten Ways to Develop your Leadership Skills, Third Sector Leadership Centre, 2008

It's Tough at the Top – The No-fibbing Guide to Leadership, Debra Allcock Tyler, DSC, 2006

The Chief Executive's First 100 Days, Fiona Ash, ACEVO, 2007

The Leadership Challenge, 4th Edition, James Kouzes and Barry Posner, Jossey-Bass, 2007

Leaders Who Make A Difference – Essential Strategies for Meeting the Nonprofit Challenge, Burt Nanus and Stephen Dobbs, Jossey-Bass, 1999

More and recent books and reports can be found at www.compasspartnership.co.uk.

15 Directing divisions and managing departments

15.1 MANAGING AT DIFFERENT LEVELS OF THE ORGANISATION

Everyone recognises that managers' jobs differ by function; the director of finance clearly has a very different job from that of the director of services. Equally important, however, is an understanding of how managers' jobs differ by level. It is easy to assume that senior managers have greater responsibility than junior managers, but that the tasks and skills of managing are essentially the same. In practice, nothing could be further from the truth. The roles of chief executives, divisional directors (a level which exists in larger organisations) and managers are fundamentally different.

Chief executives, divisional directors and managers all have to deploy the skills of managing their boss, getting teams to perform, delegating work and encouraging learning. But each has to deploy an additional range of skills.

Chief executives have particular responsibility for leadership of their organisation, for managing the crucial relationships between the board and the staff, and for ensuring that the mission and strategy are clear.

Divisional directors are people who manage a group of services and report to the chief executive. Examples include director of operations and director of fundraising. They have two distinct but related roles. As members of the leadership team, they have to share responsibility with the chief executive for the leadership and management of the enterprise. Within their divisions, they have to be able to build their own team, support and coach their managers, set strategy and hold the managers who report to them accountable.

Managers' jobs are different again. They are responsible for managing people to provide direct services, campaigns or back-office functions (such as finance and

HR). They have a 'small business' within the enterprise and have to develop strategy and deliver services, campaigns and back-office functions that achieve agreed objectives within an agreed budget. In a small organisation they report to the chief executive, and in larger organisations they report to divisional directors.

The skills that need to be deployed at each level are additional. Managers have to be able to use the broad range of skills needed to manage a service. Divisional directors need to apply all these management skills, and in addition they must be able to use the special skills required to manage managers (i.e. directing). Chief executives have to have mastered the art of directing, and they also have to know how to employ the wider range of skills required when leading an organisation.

This short chapter describes the skills of directing and managing and how people acquire them. It sets out:
- the special skills required of divisional directors;
- how directorship skills are learned;
- the core skills of 'front-line' managers.

The term 'director' does not imply any legal responsibility that may be attached to being a director of, say, an organisation which is also a limited liability company.

15.2 **DIVISIONAL DIRECTORS MUST DIRECT**

Divisional directors are people who report to the chief executive and have managers reporting to them. People working at this level are called divisional directors to emphasise the distinction between managers (who are responsible for managing individual services) and divisional directors (whose main task is managing managers).

Directors of effective organisations may spend between a third and a half of their time on their responsibilities as members of the organisation's leadership team. To do this, they have to delegate many of their other responsibilities. The nature of the delegation is different from managerial delegation. When people are first appointed to a management post, they have to learn to delegate work in order to create time to manage. When people are appointed as directors, they have to learn how to delegate management in order to create time to direct. This requires directors to be very clear with everyone who reports to them about what they are responsible for and how they will be held accountable. It needs clarity about objectives to be achieved and arrangements to be put in place for reporting progress and problems.

Skills of effective directors

People generally need to have had substantial management experience before accepting a director-level post. They need to have a functional expertise (for example, service delivery, finance or fundraising) and to have experience in using those skills. They should also have had management experience – perhaps running a unit of an organisation, a geographical territory or an internal service. This will have given them skills in building a team, delegating work and getting performance from people. These will be invaluable when it comes to managing managers and coaching them to perform their tasks.

Once appointed to a director position, they have to develop a new range of skills. First, directors have to learn to see problems from an **organisation-wide perspective.** Each director has to step into the shoes of the chief executive and contribute constructively to the overall management of the organisation. This may mean shaping the development of the organisation's policies, helping to establish organisation-wide priorities or improving processes such as strategic planning, management information, budget-setting and performance review. It may involve chairing a task group or representing the organisation in the media. Whatever the activity, directors need a clear overview of the organisation and its work.

Secondly, directors have to learn to **think at a more strategic level.** This demands the ability to stand back from practical details and take a longer-term and more conceptual view of the organisation and its environment. Directors must allocate significant time to reflecting, talking to other people about strategic issues and building the capacity to contribute constructively to the strategic thinking of the leadership team. This is not easy for managers who are used to being action-orientated, resolving today's crises and taking tomorrow when it comes.

To see the current situation in its correct context, directors need to learn about the organisation's past. They also need to develop a deep understanding of the organisation's present situation and accurately anticipate key elements of the future. This requires an ability to stand back from the detail and summarise the current circumstances into a clear overview. It means talking to people to gain a 'helicopter' view of the organisation. Directors need to make a contribution to the leadership team that moves beyond providing details of their area of work. When they are equipped with this high-level context, directors can discharge their responsibilities for the strategic development of the organisation.

Thirdly, directors have to be much more aware of the changing **social, political and technical environment** around their organisation. Changes in social policy, government policy and party policy are important issues for directors. Such developments require adroit changes to the way the organisation thinks about its work. Directors therefore need to read widely and network extensively to keep abreast of important external trends.

Fourthly, directors need to learn how to **hold managers accountable for their work**. In part, this is achieved by requiring their managers to prepare strategic and operational plans for each service managed by the division. A key role of a divisional director is to support managers in the preparation of their plans, to scrutinise them closely before they are approved and to use them in a regular and systematic way to hold managers accountable for their performance. Divisional directors are discharging their responsibilities most effectively when they keep their eye on the overall performance of each service and avoid the trap of being pulled into the detail.

Finally, directors have to **judge when to intervene** in a situation and when to stand back. Although managerial experience will help here, the task is more complex for directors. They have to judge both when to intervene in managers' work and when to delve one level deeper to have a hands-on involvement in front-line service delivery. Effective directors can use their experience to make a substantial difference at both levels, but they have the time to get involved only in those few decisions where they can make a significant contribution. Examples of circumstances in which directors are likely to have a hands-on involvement include capital investments, exploiting wholly new sources of funds, dismissing people, dealing with abuse and major complaints. It is, however, a mistake to intervene too often. 'He never lets me do my job' is a common cry and one that is often justified.

15.3 **LEARNING DIRECTORSHIP SKILLS**

Ensuring that directors learn directorship skills is a responsibility that is shared by directors and their chief executives. Chief executives help, usually through one-to-one meetings, to identify development needs, to guide directors on changing their priorities and on actions to develop the required skills. As well as helping directors, this also sets an example to directors (and to other managers), who need to pay attention to the development needs of the people who report to them.

The chief executive may be able to help, but the mark of a good director is that he or she is someone who knows their own strengths and weaknesses and who takes action to develop the skills that require attention.

There are a variety of ways of encouraging learning which are similar to those for chief executives and for managers. Directors can:

- **Use a mentor or coach**. Directors can use someone outside the line-management structure as a sounding board or mentor. A trustee with directorship experience, a director of another organisation or a coach can all be used to review experiences and make learning a more systematic process.

- **Use their own teams**. The people who report to you are an important source of learning. By regularly asking for feedback, directors gain important data on their performance and how to improve it.
- **Review learning alone**. Directors can keep a personal record of learning points and routinely update it to build a body of experience and personal learning. They can also read and reflect to consolidate experiences and help to ensure that what is learned is applied in subsequent situations.

CREATING AN ACTION PLAN FOR PERSONAL DEVELOPMENT

Start by thinking back over an issue, a meeting or a decision. Consider what happened and select a part of it that was significant to you:

- Write a detailed account of what happened during that period of activity. Don't at this stage put any effort into deciding what you learned – just concentrate on describing what actually happened
- Then list the conclusions you have reached as a result of the experience. These are, in effect, your learning points. Don't limit the number and don't worry about the practicality or quality of the points
- Finally, decide which learning points you want to implement in the future, and work out an action plan which covers:
  - what you are going to do
  - when you are going to do it
- Spell out your action plan as precisely as possible so that you are clear what you have to do and that it is realistic

Developed by A. Mumford *et al.*

In some organisations, directors are located in different parts of the country (and sometimes in different parts of the world). For these people to work as directors and to be effective members of the leadership team, special attention has to be paid to communication and working together. Extra time has to be given to meetings, because team communication has to be squashed into fewer occasions.

In summary, the work of being a director is very different from that of being a manager. It requires a new layer of skills that can be learned and developed. The task of a director is to understand the differences and to use every means available to acquire the necessary skills. The rewards are potentially high. The divisional director who has mastered the skills and is making a substantial contribution to the overall management of the organisation is well placed to start applying for chief executive positions.

THE EFFECTIVE DIVISIONAL DIRECTOR

Watching the divisional director of a national organisation providing a wide range of services for people with a common disability, I noticed:

- she had reduced the number of managers reporting directly to her to give her time to discharge her director's duties
- she built her managers into a strong team and encouraged them to solve each other's problems
- she took the team out of the office three times a year to plan and monitor progress
- these actions gave her time to think about leadership team meetings, enabling her to have something useful to contribute to each item
- she worked hard to build a network of contacts outside the organisation and used them for advice on organisation-wide issues
- she volunteered to help on strategic problems in leadership team meetings
- she kept abreast of major developments in the disability field so that she could see her organisation in perspective

These are the actions of an effective divisional director.

15.4 MANAGERS MUST MANAGE

Until quite recently, management was not a valued skill in many third-sector organisations. A legacy of this belief is that some managers are expected to learn the skills they need by some mysterious process of osmosis. Some people assume that management is just common sense – something an intelligent person has the innate skills to do. To make matters worse, managers are sometimes managed by people who have been promoted because of their specialist skills and have had little management training. Some chief executives and divisional directors may not have developed the skills of delegating, coaching and holding people accountable.

Faced both with a poor understanding of what being a manager means in practice and with a culture that occasionally does not value management, it is easy to fall into the trap of doing rather than managing. It often appears easier to do a task than to manage someone else to do it, particularly when managers were promoted because they were good at doing that task. Managers feel comfortable when they are busy, and they know that they can usually do the work more quickly than their successors and probably to a better quality. But doing the work is not the job of a manager.

The essential skills of a front-line manager are:

- setting objectives
- building teams
- developing individuals
- taking decisions
- monitoring performance
- resolving problems.

The challenge for managers is that seemingly straightforward tasks are often much more complex in practice. This section explains some of the special characteristics that affect managers in third-sector organisations and suggests ways of becoming a more effective manager in these circumstances. Some of these points are relevant to chief executives and divisional directors as well as to front-line managers. They are grouped together here because they impact most directly on the work of front-line managers.

The task of managing people in this sector has to be seen in the context of the types of people who work in it. The third sector attracts employees with different motives, particularly when compared to the private sector.

Research has shown that they tend to have stronger ideals; they attach greater value to job satisfaction; pay is less important; and job content is seen to be part of the compensation package. People who work in the third sector have been shown to be more caring in spirit, to be more trusting of others and less cynical in their attitude.

The same research also showed that people working in the third sector tend to have higher educational qualifications than people in equivalent jobs in the private and public sectors. They also have greater difficulty balancing their work lives and their private lives. This is hardly surprising: when people live for a cause, the distinction between work and home can become very blurred (*The Quality of Employment in the Nonprofit Sector*, Philip Purvis, Nonprofit Management and Leadership, 1991).

Special challenges for managers

The first challenge managers have to face is that most third-sector organisations have extraordinarily high ambitions. They want to have a significant impact. Objectives such as saving endangered species, discovering a treatment for an incurable disease or alleviating poverty are ambitious, and lack clear boundaries. For front-line managers this means that there is always more they could do. Effective managers consequently have to learn to be realistic about what can be achieved and **ruthless in setting priorities**.

This means that an annual work plan is an essential management tool. It should set out what will be done by whom, and it should leave space every month to deal with unforeseen problems. It also requires managers to check frequently in their own mind what their objectives are, and whether their workload could be reduced by taking out activities that are not top priority.

The second challenge is to **carve out an appropriate role** for the circumstances. Managers can face constraints from their boss not giving them sufficient freedom to get on with their job. The hands-on boss who wants to be involved in all the detail can be a significant impediment to a front-line manager. Managers need to be totally clear about what they are doing and why they are doing it to have the freedom to discharge their managerial duties.

The third challenge is some people's belief that organisations should be managed by consensus. People working on the 'front line' expect to be involved in decision-making, but this expectation can shift subtly from the realistic desire to be consulted on some decisions to the unrealistic demand that all decisions should be taken by consensus. Managers have to **earn their authority** by distinguishing between situations requiring consensus and circumstances in which they should take responsibility, make a decision and be held accountable. Managers consequently need to keep issues which are heading for decisions under constant review and decide when to prolong discussion in order to achieve consensus and when to take command and make decisions.

The fourth challenge is that, in some organisations, the very notion of management sits uncomfortably alongside strongly held values about empowering disadvantaged people. From this perspective, users have rights to define their needs and the way services should be provided. Many no longer want to be given charity; they want to determine what the organisation should be doing for them and not allow management to take decisions, sometimes in a paternalistic way. Managers of these organisations have to combine a strong commitment to **representing users' views** with an ability to make things happen when decisions need to be implemented.

MANAGERS' TASKS ARE EXTRAORDINARILY VARIED

Third-sector managers are expected to perform an extraordinarily wide range of tasks. Leonard Cheshire Disability has 200 homes and services in the UK and a further 250 services in 54 countries around the world. Each home or service has a manager who has to deploy a wide range of skills. A survey identified the following skills which a home manager needs:

- strategic planning
- marketing to purchasing authorities
- negotiating fees and agreeing contracts
- building staff teams
- involving residents/clients in decision-taking
- preparing and monitoring accounts
- budgeting
- training staff
- disciplinary skills
- managing meetings
- dealing with the media
- delegation
- day-to-day management of a home
- interface with volunteers
- purchasing of equipment and services

The fifth challenge is to ensure the department has the resources to meet its commitments. Managers have to **argue for sufficient resources** to do their work.

The sixth challenge is to ensure that, despite time pressures, managers insist that their director or chief executive hold **induction sessions and regular one-to-ones**. When senior managers are overloaded (or unable to establish their priorities), supporting their staff can be the activity that is squeezed out. Holding these sessions is more difficult in geographically spread organisations, where staff work from separate locations. Because of physical separation these are often the very people who ought to get extra support. When managers are not receiving assistance, they have to push for the support they need to do the job effectively.

Finally, managers face particular challenges when it comes to **changing people's roles**. People believe in their jobs; they have often worked tirelessly for the cause, so managers' suggestions for change are sometimes most unwelcome. Redundancies and dismissals are always difficult. Caring organisations are expected to care for their staff – so managers have to be particularly sensitive when they need to adjust the structure or change the membership of their team.

SUMMARY OF KEY POINTS

Managing at different levels of the organisation

- The skills of managing a 'front-line' service, directing a division and leading an organisation are very different
- People at all three levels have to manage their boss, get their teams to perform, delegate work and encourage learning
- Divisional directors have to know about managing services and learn about directing a division. Chief executives (of divisionalised organisations) should know about directing and have to learn how to be a leader

Divisional directors must direct

- Divisional directors have to manage their own department and contribute to the overall management of the organisation
- To become effective, divisional directors have to learn to take an organisation-wide perspective, think at a strategic level, follow trends in the external environment, hold managers accountable for their work and judge when to intervene and when to leave matters alone

Learning directorship skills

- Directors have to take personal responsibility for their own development, though they should expect support from their chief executive
- Ways to support their learning include using a coach or mentor, using their own teams to get feedback and being systematic in embedding their experiences by reflecting, keeping records of learning and applying it in subsequent situations

Managers must manage

- The essential skills for front-line managers are setting objectives, building teams, developing individuals, taking decisions, monitoring performance and resolving problems
- The special challenges of managing third-sector organisations mean that managers have to be ruthless in setting priorities, carve out an appropriate role, earn their authority, represent users' views, argue for sufficient resources and ensure that they are given personal support by their director or chief executive

FURTHER READING

Developing Directors: A Handbook for Building an Effective Boardroom Team, Colin Coulson-Thomas, Policy Publications, 2007

The Fish Rots from the Head, Bob Garratt, Profile Business, 2003

(Note both these books are about directing in a corporate setting rather than in the third sector. I have not come across better books on directing in the third sector, but would welcome readers' suggestions.)

Just about Managing, Sandy Adirondack, LVSC, 2006

16 Managing people and teams

16.1 DEVELOPING PEOPLE AND TEAMS

The ability of third-sector organisations to achieve their objectives depends almost entirely on the skills of their people. Those organisations that have the strongest base of skilled and experienced people are in the best position to raise the largest sums of money and deliver the best-quality services and campaigns. The capacity of their staff and volunteers is determined by the quality of the people who are recruited and by the organisations' investment in developing their expertise.

Investing time and effort in developing the capabilities of managers at all levels of the organisation brings great benefits both to the individuals and to the organisation. It presents people with new challenges to the way they work and consequently makes work more interesting and stimulating. The new skills and abilities they gain make them more rounded and capable individuals. Organisations that strive to develop the capabilities of their staff attract more talented people, who grow personally and perform to higher standards. Organisations that neglect this crucial area have higher staff turnover and a less motivated workforce, and they achieve less with the resources at their disposal.

The potential for increasing the effectiveness of third-sector organisations by developing people's skills is huge. Many managers could improve their delegation skills and give their staff greater responsibility within clearer boundaries. They could also learn more from the people to whom they delegate.

Improving team leadership skills can also yield great benefits. Teams are very sensitive to both good and poor leadership. When they are working at their most effective, they are a powerful means of making things happen. Teams are also a great source of opportunities for managers to learn about themselves, each other and ways of increasing the productivity of the team itself. When they are mismanaged, they are a great obstacle to organisational effectiveness.

There are many ways of encouraging personal development. Coaching, mentoring and shadowing help people to improve their performance. Regular one-to-ones for managers hold them to account, provide support and create opportunities for coaching. Annual reviews present an opportunity for a more thorough appraisal of performance; they also create a situation where managers can learn about their performance from the person they are supervising.

This chapter sets out how to increase the capacity of organisations to be really effective. It describes how to:

- manage your boss;
- get better performance from teams;
- delegate work and empower people;
- supervise, develop and coach people;
- deal with poor performance.

16.2 **MANAGING YOUR BOSS**

Managing your boss (an idea propounded by John Gabarro and John Kotter in *Harvard Business Review*) is a foundation stone of being a good manager. It is possible to be excellent at all the other aspects of management, but fail because people forget to manage this crucial relationship.

Everyone has a boss, from the chief executive who reports to the chair, to front-line staff who report to their supervisors. Some people have two bosses; department, regional and branch managers often report to a line manager as well as to the chair of a committee. These people have the additional challenge of managing two sets of relationships simultaneously.

Managers and staff can do their jobs more effectively if they have a strong and constructive relationship with their boss. Each is dependent on the other: bosses need help, guidance and advice from their manager in order to do their jobs. They need to feel confident that they can depend on their managers. Similarly, managers and staff depend on their bosses for guidance and support. Managers and staff need to understand how their work fits in to the wider context; they need information from their boss and, most of all, they need their boss to help procure the resources required to achieve their objectives.

Poor relationships are often put down to personality conflicts. 'I don't get on with the boss,' is a common sentiment, but one which sometimes conceals simple misunderstandings about the mutual dependencies in the relationship. Managing a boss is a process of working with him or her to obtain the best results for the organisation and using every opportunity to learn from each other.

The first step in managing bosses is to understand their context. This means having a sense of their priorities, their aspirations and the issues that are being addressed at a higher level. It means tapping into their information systems, networking with other managers and asking questions when the broader context is not clear. It requires managers and staff to recognise that their bosses are there not to do everything but to ensure that everything gets done.

The second step is to understand her or his strengths and weaknesses. Successful people recognise that all bosses are different: some are full of creative ideas but need guidance to come to decisions; some are decisive but need to have options developed for consideration. Some are good at networking outside the organisation but need to be briefed on developments within the organisation. People who understand their bosses actively exploit their strengths and support them in their weaker areas. This is particularly important when their boss is the chief executive.

The third step is to understand his or her preferred working methods. This requires watching their behaviour and gaining insights into the way they work. Some people prefer to learn about things on paper; others prefer an oral report. Some like solitary time to think; others prefer to work things out together. Some are lateral thinkers, others are better at making quick judgements. People can get better value from their bosses if they understand their working styles.

TWO MANAGERS AT A HOUSING ASSOCIATION

Jane, the chief executive of a housing association, was formal and well organised. She paid attention to detail and liked to have written reports, and formal meetings with set agendas.

Nick, a flamboyant and creative manager, preferred a more informal and intuitive style. He had great difficulty with the chief executive. Their meetings were always fraught with problems as the chief executive tried to piece together the information she felt she should have had before the meeting. Nick often felt that Jane was meddling in the detail when what he wanted was guidance and support.

Juliet, another manager, worked hard to manage her relationship with the chief executive. She asked what information Jane would like to have before they met. She noticed that the chief executive was most effective when she had time to think about issues before a meeting. Although it took time to prepare the paperwork, Juliet's service grew and flourished because it was able to exploit both her talents and those of her chief executive.

Managers and staff can conceive of their boss as a resource which needs to be used effectively. A boss's time is always limited, so it needs to be used judiciously. Briefing the boss on the issues and action taken is far more helpful than involving them in detail that people ought to resolve on their own. Similarly, judging when an issue needs the boss's attention, preparing thoughts about the problem and knowing what to ask are ways of using the boss's time effectively.

All relationships have frustrations. Successful people learn how to handle them. Those who rebel against their boss or undermine him or her are not creating the conditions for succeeding in their own job. Similarly, people who bottle up all their frustrations and do not share their concerns with their boss are storing up problems for the future. Effective managers and staff work hard to address their frustrations with their boss in constructive ways.

They also seek opportunities to learn from their relationship with their boss. There is a potentially rich resource to mine here, provided both parties are willing to try. Managers and staff can take the initiative by praising their boss when she or he has done things well or has changed their behaviour to improve the relationship. They can offer to support their boss when he or she needs assistance. They should raise anxieties openly and make positive proposals about ways of working together more effectively.

In summary, people who wish to learn should:
- understand the broader context in which their boss is working;
- discover their boss's preferred working style;
- use their boss to help with tasks he or she is good at;
- expect their boss to provide them with support;
- see the relationship as an opportunity for each to learn from the other;
- look elsewhere for the support their boss is unable to provide.

16.3 GETTING PERFORMANCE FROM TEAMS

In addition to creating relationships upwards, managers also have to create relationships with the people who work for them. More than anything, managers need to create and lead a team of people who are dedicated to achieving agreed objectives.

Ultimately, managers' success depends on getting high performance from teams. Their job is to build strong teams, release the potential that is within team members and ensure that the achievements of the team as a whole are much greater than the sum of its parts. Teams are important not only in the line-management structure, but also as an essential integrating mechanism across the departmental structure.

This section covers:
- the characteristics of effective teams
- creating teams
- changing team membership
- developing teams
- leading teams
- adopting different styles for different tasks.

The art of encouraging teams to learn from their experience is described in Chapter 17, Creating a learning organisation.

Characteristics of effective teams

Organisations have different types of team, including:

- **management teams** – consisting of managers and their boss (e.g. the leadership team);
- **staff teams** – consisting of staff and their manager (e.g. the help-line team)
- **project teams** – consisting of a cross-section of managers and their staff (e.g. the lottery project team).

Many of the attributes of effective teams are common to all three types. The important differences are that:

- Management and staff teams have a longer life than project teams, so it is worth investing more effort in ensuring that they work well.
- Management and project teams need to pay close attention to good preparation and paperwork to maximise their effectiveness.
- Project teams have deadlines, so they need to become effective quickly, achieve their objective and dissolve themselves.

When teaching about teams, Ashridge Management College, a research and management school, summarises the characteristics of highly effective teams as groups that are:

- persistent in pursuit of their goals;
- inventive in overcoming obstacles;
- committed to quality in all aspects of teamwork;
- inspired by a vision;
- action-orientated;
- committed to the success of the organisation as a whole;
- able to distinguish the important from the urgent;
- willing to take risks and be innovative and creative;
- always looking for ways to do things better.

This, no doubt, reflects many team leaders' intentions. It is a challenging ideal, but two special characteristics of third-sector organisations have to be overcome in order to attain it. First, the sector attracts an extraordinarily wide range of characters to its organisations, many of whom are intelligent, charismatic and passionate but can be opinionated or even obstinate when it comes to being a team player.

Secondly, managers have to understand that their role is different from that of other members of the team. The democratic values of some organisations and the deeply held desire to represent users' views can spill over into team behaviour. Sometimes managers start from an assumption that their primary duty is to represent the views of their staff or service users. They put their loyalty to their staff or service users ahead of their role as a member of a more senior team where they have to make trade-offs between the interests of different parts of the organisation. They feel more accountable to the people they represent than to the senior team. They find it hard to accept collective responsibility for management decisions and to support those decisions when they have to report back to their own team.

So managers need a repertoire of techniques they can use to create high-performing teams. This section briefly introduces some of the behaviours and actions managers need to have at their fingertips.

LIFE CYCLE OF A TEAM

Groups mature and develop. Like individuals and organisations, they have a fairly well-defined growth cycle. This has been categorised as having four successive stages:

1. **Forming.** The group is a set of individuals. This stage is categorised by talk about the purpose of the group, the definition and the title of the group, its composition, leadership pattern and lifespan. At this stage, each individual tends to want to establish his or her personal identity within the group and make an individual impression.

2. **Storming.** Most groups go through a conflict stage when the preliminary (and often false) consensus on purposes, leadership and other roles, norms of work and behaviour is challenged and re-established. At this stage a lot of personal agendas are revealed and a certain amount of interpersonal hostility is generated. If handled successfully, this period of storming leads to a new and more realistic setting of objectives, procedures and norms. This stage is particularly important for testing the norms of trust in the group.

3. **Norming.** The group needs to establish norms and practices: when and how it should work, how it should take decisions, and what type of behaviour, level of work and degree of openness, trust and confidence are appropriate. At this stage there will be a lot of tentative experimentation by individuals to test the temperature of the group and to measure the appropriate level of commitment.

4. **Performing.** Only when the three previous stages have been successfully completed will the group be at full maturity and fully and sensibly productive.

Some theorists have added two further stages: **re-forming**, to account for changes in the group's membership, and **mourning**, the necessary process of properly marking the end of a group's life.

Source: *Understanding Organisations*, Charles Handy, Penguin, 2005

Creating the team

The first issue to consider is the **size of the team**. Teams that are too small may not contain all the skills required or generate enough variety of thought. Teams that are too large are cumbersome and frustrating for members.

Larger teams are appropriate when:

- some of the posts are similar (for example, managers of similar centres or regions) because they will have common problems;
- members are experienced team players who require less support, one-to-one attention or coaching;
- a wide range of skills is essential to the team's effectiveness (for example, resolving very complex problems).

Smaller teams are appropriate when:

- there is high interdependence between members (for example, an assessment and rehabilitation centre where tight coordination is required) and they need time to work closely together;
- the team works in a rapidly changing environment (for example, a campaign team) where people will need lots of short meetings.

Any rule has exceptions, but for many situations a team of between four and seven people is a common compromise.

RE-ORGANISATION OF A MANAGEMENT TEAM

A British development agency recognised the need for radical change in its management. Senior management team meetings were lengthy and often inconclusive, personal relationships were poor and meeting discipline was deteriorating.

'It's because we can't agree whether our primary objective should be in emergency aid, long-term development, empowerment of local people or institutional change,' said one group within the team. 'If only we could agree upon our fundamental purpose, our problems would be solved.'

'The problem is: we aren't sticking to our strategy,' argued another group. 'We spent a year agreeing a strategic plan, but we never use it to guide our decisions.'

'We can't work together as a team,' claimed a third group. 'We need training in team development and facilitation to help us discover ways of working together.'

In practice, none was right. The central problem was that the team of nine people was too large and too heterogeneous to work together. Too many big personalities, each in charge of a large division, just could not work together.

Re-organised, the team became a group of five people. The creation of a smaller team, three of whose members were recruited from outside the organisation, was enough to break the mould and establish new ways of working together.

The next issue to consider is the **characteristics of team members**. For teams to perform to the highest standard, people have to work closely together, support each other and balance team needs with their own. A compromise has to be found between having people with similar backgrounds and experience who work together well but who see issues only from one perspective, and having a more heterogeneous team drawing on people with different skills. The need for homogeneous teams increases as the tasks they have to undertake become more complex. Heterogeneous teams are more productive when dealing with more straightforward tasks, but they can expect to experience more conflict.

Then there are the issues of **sensitivity and trust**. Groups of people who get along well, who trust each other and are sensitive to each other's needs, are more productive than those where members are suspicious of one another. Sensitivity and trust should grow as the team works together and as members gain deeper insights into their colleagues' strengths and weaknesses.

The fourth crucial issue is creating a group of people who are all able to **communicate and resolve differences**. Effective teams need to consist of people who find it easy to communicate openly and honestly with each other and do not have 'private' agendas. They also need to consist of people who have the capacity to resolve inevitable differences of opinion that emerge. Members need to be able to put their views clearly and effectively, and to negotiate when necessary, and then to support the team's decisions. Teams that have people with these skills are likely to be more successful than those with people who find it hard to compromise.

The final aspect of creating an effective team is allowing **time for people to get to know one another** both professionally and personally. Teams are more effective when people understand one another's personal backgrounds and personalities. They work more efficiently when members have a deep understanding of one another's strengths and weaknesses. This can take many months and often years to assimilate fully. Time for team away days, social events and – particularly in the forming stage – lots of team meetings all help to provide the foundations for a high-performance team.

BELBIN'S TEAM ROLES

Meredith Belbin identified nine roles that are needed for teams to work successfully. These have been tested on thousands of organisations. Managers complete a self-perception questionnaire to identify the roles that people are naturally likely to play in teams. Roles that are over and under-represented can then be identified to help teams understand why they may be having problems and what they might do to improve team working. Each role makes particular contributions to a team, but also displays common weaknesses.

Details of the tests can be found at www.belbin.com.

Team role	Contributions	Allowable weaknesses
Plant	Creative, imaginative, unorthodox. Solves difficult problems	Ignores incidentals. Too pre-occupied to communicate effectively
Coordinator	Mature, confident, a good chair. Clarifies goals, promotes decision-making, delegates well	Can often be seen as manipulative. Off-loads personal work
Monitor evaluator	Sober, strategic and discerning. Sees all options. Judges accurately	Lacks drive and ability to inspire others
Implementer	Disciplined, reliable, efficient. Turns ideas into practical options. Respects established traditions	Somewhat inflexible. Slow to respond to new possibilities
Completer finisher	Painstaking, conscientious, anxious. Searches out errors and omissions. Delivers on time	Inclined to worry unduly. Reluctant to delegate
Resource investigator	Extrovert, enthusiastic, communicative. Explores opportunities. Develops contacts	Over-optimistic. Loses interest once initial enthusiasm has passed
Shaper	Challenging, dynamic, thrives on pressure. Has the drive and courage to overcome obstacles	Prone to provocation. Offends people's feelings
Teamworker	Cooperative, mild, perceptive and diplomatic. Listens, builds, averts friction	Indecisive in crunch situations
Specialist	Single-minded, self-starting, dedicated. Provides knowledge and skills in rare supply	Contributes only on a narrow front. Dwells on technicalities

Changing team membership

Sometimes managers need to change the size, structure or membership of a team in order to improve its performance. Teams can be re-structured as described in Chapter 11. Another option for changing team membership is to make judicious use of opportunities created by people leaving or retiring. A departure gives managers the space to reconsider everyone's responsibilities and either reduce or enlarge the team.

A further, more subtle option is to **change the definition of the team**. Team membership can be adjusted by redefining the scope and purpose of the team and incorporating or excluding people to increase its effectiveness. For example, if a team is too small and the organisation has talented people who are not on the team, it can be expanded for certain types of meeting. A quarterly review of strategy, for example, or a series of planning meetings provide an ideal opportunity to enlarge the team. If the team is too large, it may be necessary to reduce the frequency of meetings and create a smaller group to coordinate activities between meetings.

The right size and composition are both important if a team is to perform. But there is a trap to avoid. Some managers mistakenly assume that getting the right group of people is their single most important task. They continually adjust the structure and the membership of the team – not recognising that **each adjustment is a disruption** to team dynamics. Developing appropriate team behaviour and coaching members so as to help them become better team players can have more effect than adjusting its membership. Each time team membership is adjusted, its behaviour takes a step back in the 'forming, storming model' (see the box on the life cycle of a team, p. 371), a consequence that is sometimes overlooked. In short, oversize or undersize teams with good team behaviour can be more productive than a team with appropriate size and composition and no accepted ways of working.

ADJUSTMENTS TO TEAMS CAUSE DISRUPTION

We trained hard . . . but it seemed that every time we were beginning to form up in teams we would be re-organised. I was to learn later in life that we tend to meet any new situation by re-organising, and a wonderful method it can be for creating the illusion of progress while producing confusion, inefficiency and demoralisation.

Source: attributed to Petronius Arbiter

Developing the team

Five actions are required to develop strong teams.

Teams need objectives. Everyone on the team needs to be totally clear about what the team is trying to achieve. The team needs both to have words that define the objectives and to be clear about the context in which they have to be achieved. The objectives need to be understood from many different perspectives and from the different viewpoints that each team member brings.

Ideally, all team members need to be directly involved in agreeing the objectives. Everyone also needs to believe in them. It is easy to support the words, but the high-performance team needs people who are motivated to realise the objectives, and who demonstrate by their behaviour that they believe in them. This can be achieved only by working on the objectives, taking time away from the office to explore the options and develop the thinking. Objectives can then be tested on other groups (up, down, across and outside the organisation) to make them more robust.

Teams plan together. Successful teams spend time planning their work. Sometimes individual members of sub-groups will prepare plans for achieving a particular objective and bring them to team meetings. In other situations, planning the work will be done in team meetings. If the team has been created to undertake a specific project, it may well identify the factors that are critical to the project's success. Whatever the circumstances, effective teams are clear about how the objectives will be achieved.

Teams need coaching. Managers are responsible for setting the standards for team behaviour. As well as guiding the team in its work, managers encourage members to contribute constructively. They praise good team behaviour, they criticise loose or poor contributions and they help people to improve their work.

Teams need effective meetings. When meetings are carefully prepared and tightly managed they are powerful ways of making things happen. Ill prepared and badly run, they can be an extraordinary waste of people's time. All too often the objectives of items are not clear, agendas are not prioritised and papers are not thought through or not distributed in advance. As a result the work that should have been done in preparing for the meeting ends up being done, a great deal less efficiently, in the meeting.

Managers who prepare well use meetings to debate issues and options and to take clear-cut decisions. The major topics for meetings need to be planned so that papers can be commissioned, reviewed by the manager and distributed in advance. Timing of meetings, appropriate venues and circulation of action notes may all be details, but they are crucial elements of an effective team.

Teams need good administration. Tight administration of teams and frequent communication between meetings are also essential elements of effective teams. A good administrator keeps contact details up to date, knows where team members are and how they can be contacted and can provide a crucial personal touch that makes everyone feel part of the team.

IDENTIFYING CRITICAL SUCCESS FACTORS

Project teams enhance their effectiveness by identifying the factors that are critical to their success. These are the limited number of actions that are both necessary and sufficient to achieve the objective.

Working to identify the actions, boiling them down to a manageable list and checking that they are all both necessary and sufficient provides team members with a deeper understanding of the objectives and how they will be achieved. Descriptions of critical success factors usually begin with the words, 'We must...' or 'We need to...'.

Eastlink Housing Association put together a cross-departmental team to manage a major conversion project. They established the following objectives and critical success factors:

Objective

To convert three old people's homes into local centres for frail elderly people over the next three years.

Critical success factors

- We must raise a total of £3.6 million from statutory and charitable sources to complete the project
- We must create an in-house development team of three people, dedicated to this project alone for at least two years
- We must find superior-quality accommodation for existing tenants and give them a minimum of six months' warning of the move
- We must recruit people with expertise in managing centres for frail elderly people to start work four months before each centre opens
- We need to create new management committees for each centre, incorporating the seven specialist skills identified as critical to their success

Leading teams

Finally, the most effective teams are those that have strong leadership which is sensitive to team members' needs and not dominant or authoritarian. Team leadership is an art. It requires the adroit use of different skills in different circumstances. The critical elements of effective team leadership can be summarised as follows:

Start modestly. Managers should set realistic objectives at the beginning, build the team's confidence in itself and then increase expectations. If leaders are too ambitious, they risk losing credibility when the objectives are not achieved.

Promote the mission. Teams are motivated by missions. They need to feel that their work is vitally important and be able to set it in the broader context of the organisation's overall objectives. Managers should emphasise the value of the work being done and remind people that bureaucracy and management are necessary only in the cause of achieving the mission.

Encourage openness. Teams under-perform when individuals have private agendas or when one group is making different assumptions from those of another. Managers need to tease out private issues and ensure that their own agenda is open and explicit.

Support team members. Members of high-performance teams take particular care to support each other. They build on each other's arguments in meetings, show concern for each other's welfare and assist each other in their work. Managers set the tone by being seen to support team members.

Face up to differences. Managers with strong teams encourage differences of opinion. They expect members to make their differences clear, but to be willing to compromise when decisions are required. They also expect team members to support decisions, once they have been made.

Review performance regularly. Managers set aside time for the team to review its own performance. They identify behaviour that worked well and review situations where improvements could be made. They encourage critical discussion of the team's performance and expect the team to agree actions to improve team performance. They remind the team of agreed actions when behaviour slips below expectations.

Encourage systematic decision-taking. Teams make better decisions if they are systematic about gathering information, diagnosing problems, seeking opinions and evaluating options before taking decisions. Effective leaders encourage a rigorous approach to decision-taking.

Make the team visible. Managers promote their teams both inside and outside the organisation. They communicate up, down and across the organisation, ensuring that their team's work engages with the rest of the organisation.

Encourage action. Managers encourage action. They clarify what needs to be done and ensure that agreed actions are followed through.

Celebrate success. Managers make sure that successes are celebrated. They mark achievements with praise, publicity and parties.

Different styles for different tasks

Leading an effective team also requires the selection of an appropriate style of working for the task at hand. When the team needs to crack through the routine work of communicating with each other, coordinating activities and making regular decisions that do not raise wider issues, it is appropriate that there should be tight chairing, short interventions and timetabled agendas. Where there are disagreements on minor matters, the team leader can impose a decision on the group.

However, where there is a great deal of uncertainty around the issues being addressed and the decisions will have widespread repercussions, an entirely different mode is required. All the skills and all the experience of team members are required to consider the issue. Chairing needs to be more flexible, ownership of the way the discussion is going may move around the team, and timetables need to be less fixed (see also section 17.5, Encouraging teams to learn, for more about 'discussions' and 'dialogues').

The dividing line between different styles is clearly not absolute. Indeed, some issues which may have seemed clear-cut may turn out to raise much wider concerns, and some seemingly open issues may be more clear-cut than anticipated. An experienced team adapts and adjusts its approach according to the circumstances. The more mature a team becomes, the more it will find it can work with sharper differences in style and increase its effectiveness.

STAGES OF DEVELOPMENT OF A TEAM

Characteristic	Undeveloped team	Experimenting team	Consolidating team	Mature team
Atmosphere, feelings and conflict	Tense, individual self-interest; feelings not dealt with; conflicts seen as inappropriate	Dynamic; expressions of mutual interest; feelings begin to be opened up; groups inward-looking	Confident, open approach; resolves interpersonal issues	High commitment to the task and each other; individuals' needs for recognition low
Talking and listening	Very little listening; points of view queuing up	More listening and thinking, less talking in unconnected ways	Listening very good, constructive use of ideas, good balance of agreeing, disagreeing	Careful listening; lots of building and extracting benefits of ideas; summaries stated regularly
Working method	Stick to the established method; scared of changes; time spent considering how to operate	Increasing dissatisfaction with procedures initially established; increased concern with internal processes	Further examination of methods; willingness to change; better understanding of method through discussion	Conscious observation of group process; discussion of its effectiveness; flexible use of procedures and time-keeping
Time management	Ignored; 'speaking clock' tends to operate	Realisation of need to plan and manage time; tentative steps	More realistic time-allocation to the various stages of working	More flexible use of time-allocation and readiness to change to facilitate the task
Understanding the task	Leader's view is often different from the rest; others tend to be confused	Understanding increases through discussion, but little willingness to vary it	Better understood through questioning, leading to group version of the task	Continual monitoring of the task; modification depending on progress and feedback
Decisions	Mostly taken by the leader	Decisions still taken mostly by the leader or by voting	Shared responsibility for decisions; group tries for consensus	Taken by consensus, but leader's role in arbitration is recognised
Using each other's abilities	Individuals keep to narrow roles; low recognition resources available	Increased readiness to deal with quiet members	Clear understanding of strengths and weaknesses	As for consolidating team, but stronger
Personal weaknesses	Covered up; mistakes used to judge people, not to identify learning opportunities	Increased readiness to look at people's preferences and at tasks they feel unhappy with	Now well understood and taken account of in a positive and acceptable way	As for consolidating team
Resilience to the outside	Defensive to outside 'threats'; proposals increase bureaucracy	Increasingly insular and competitive	External demands and conflict handled constructively	Team copes constructively with problems

16.4 DELEGATING WORK AND EMPOWERING PEOPLE

Delegation is the art of sharing work among the team, giving people the freedom to make decisions but retaining responsibility for achievement of the task. Empowerment is a broader concept; it means giving people more latitude around how tasks are completed, and holding them accountable only for the results. It implies less detailed monitoring and an expectation that the delegatee will request assistance when required.

There are many forces that militate against delegation in third-sector organisations. Managers are often highly motivated by the nature of the work they are doing; they believe in the cause they are working for, put in long hours and enjoy the detail. In these circumstances it is very tempting not to delegate enough.

Then there is the problem that delegatees may already feel overloaded. They too are likely to be committed to the cause, and often believe that they could not work harder. So before work can be delegated, managers have to find ways to help their staff review priorities and stop doing some things that they believed were important in order to create the time to do the new work managers wish to delegate to them. The issue is usually not lack of willingness but the ability to set priorities that are consistent with the manager's view of their relative importance.

A frequent obstacle to delegation is the pressure of time. The work needs to be done quickly, so the easiest solution is for managers to do it themselves. It takes time to brief someone, explain what is required and help them to adjust their priorities, so it often appears easier just to do the task. This, however, is a recipe for overload. Effective delegators anticipate the need for the work and decide how it can be done before they become trapped into doing it themselves.

Another obstacle to delegating is the fear that the individual will not be able to do the task. Sometimes this may be entirely justified and the task should not be delegated to that person. But sometimes managers have to take small risks in order to give the person who is delegated the task an opportunity for learning. They can assist in these circumstances by being particularly clear about the objective of the task, its scope and its time-frame, and explicitly checking that the person concerned understands the task.

Successful managers delegate as much as they possibly can. They recognise that their time can be used most effectively when people who are competent are given maximum authority. Often people will rise to the challenge given explicit responsibility and an expectation that their manager will be supportive but not interfering.

Successful managers delegate in stages as people's skill and experience grow; they monitor the individual's performance; and they maintain the level of control needed to ensure a successful outcome. They start by delegating low-risk tasks and, as the person's experience grows, higher-risk tasks are delegated.

To delegate effectively, managers have to trust their staff and be confident that they can do the delegated tasks. Simultaneously, they must reduce the amount of direct control they have over the way the individual does the work. Once the boundaries have been agreed, managers should hand over control. The less control they retain, the more the individual will feel responsible for completing the work to the required standard.

However, delegation is not simply a matter of handing over tasks to another person. It is the skill of giving someone additional responsibilities that are within his or her abilities and providing appropriate advice and support as that person takes greater responsibility for the task. The amount and nature of work that can be delegated depends on the person's experience, the confidence of the manager and the risk attached to the task.

The manager and the person doing the work need to agree the objectives that are to be achieved. Ideally the person who will do the work should propose them and the manager should amend and agree to them. The manager is then in a position to 'manage by objectives' – an adage that is still very pertinent today.

Learning the art of delegating

Becoming an effective delegator requires a particular attitude of mind. Good managers instinctively think ahead and ask themselves how they are going to achieve each task for which they are responsible. Anticipation is the critical ingredient. Managers have to allow time to brief people to whom tasks are delegated, and for those people to fit the work into their already busy schedules. They have to allocate time to review progress, to give advice and to support the delegatee.

Managers also need to clarify why they are delegating tasks. They can delegate:

- **To make better use of time**. Managers are paid to manage, not to do the work. They have to create time to discharge their many managerial responsibilities, and this invariably means delegating as much work as their staff can handle.
- **To give staff development opportunities**. All staff need to develop their skills and abilities. Giving staff responsibility for additional tasks is an ideal way of enabling and encouraging professional development. It provides new challenges within carefully selected boundaries.
- **To use people's skills**. Staff have strengths where managers may have weaknesses. Managers delegate to maximise the use of staff members' skills.

DELEGATING WORK IN A TRADE UNION

'I know I need to delegate more,' the union official told the management consultant. 'I've read all the books on it and even attended a course. It's just not that straightforward.'

'You need to sit down with each member of your team and agree what can be delegated. I'll help by providing an independent perspective,' said the consultant, spotting an opportunity to sell his time.

'That isn't the problem,' said the union official. 'My difficulty is that all the committee members expect me to deal personally with every problem. Committee chairs in particular feel their status is not being recognised if I delegate their problems to my staff. Chairs feel they can do the job they have been elected to do only if they deal with me.'

'Well,' said the consultant, 'we'll have to think about how to persuade them to allow you to delegate.'

Delegation is seldom straightforward.

Some activities cannot be delegated. **People-management responsibilities**, such as one-to-ones, performance reviews, chairing team meetings, discipline, praise and resolution of disputes, are responsibilities that managers should retain in all but the most unusual circumstances. **Policy-making** cannot be delegated. The work of preparing papers, doing research and making proposals can be delegated, but decisions on matters that have widespread repercussions cannot be delegated. **Crisis management** usually requires judgements to be made from a broader perspective; these situations can seldom be delegated. Matters involving **confidential information**, such as sensitive personnel information, cannot be delegated. Finally, the **rituals** of celebrating successes, rewarding long service and representing the organisation or department at major occasions should not be delegated. Position and status both add significantly to the value of rituals.

Improving delegation skills

Good practice in delegation involves:

- Ensuring people understand the broader context into which their work fits. When tasks are delegated, people will understand why the work needs to be done.
- Giving people appropriate information about the task. Hard information about what needs to be achieved is as important as soft data about the people and problems that might be encountered.
- Being clear about the objective but allowing the individual to take the initiative in how it is achieved.

- Being clear about available resources, the milestones that will mark progress, the timescale for achieving the result and the arrangements for reporting on progress.
- Being honest about the task and what it will involve.
- Leaving no confusion about accountability for the work.
- Giving credit for a job well done, and taking responsibility if it does not go well.
- Using mistakes as learning opportunities and not as reasons for allocating blame.

Delegating is a skill that is learned with practice. It is an essential ability that managers need to grasp. Sometimes managers fail to delegate and overload themselves, and sometimes they delegate without providing the support and guidance that are needed to produce the required outcomes. Managers need to practise delegation so that it becomes an instinctive way of working.

Empowering people

Empowering people is a process of giving **greater ownership** of a task or a set of responsibilities to an individual or a group. It is about going one step further than delegation, being very clear about the 'ends' that people are expected to achieve, but allowing them greater freedom in managing the 'means' of achieving the desired end. In an empowered organisation, people are held accountable for their achievements and not for the methods used to accomplish them. Empowering people allows them to take charge of their situation within clearly agreed boundaries and to take more decisions. Empowering people requires that the fundamentals of good management are securely in place. It is appropriate in organisations that already have very clear objectives, strong teams, well-established management processes and good personal relationships.

Initiatives to increase empowerment also require managers to have reached a comparatively experienced stage of their personal development. They should be sufficiently mature to be able to share their anxieties with other people, willing to learn from failures, and able to challenge people confidently, to stand back from detail and to command people's respect.

In its most developed form, the manager is not a 'member' of the empowered group. He or she builds the environment in which the group can do its job, coaches people when support is required and monitors the results.

The most critical judgement that managers have to make is the **extent of empowerment** that is appropriate. On the one hand, managers who hold on to too much power frustrate their staff and do not allow them to perform at the highest level. Staff end up wasting time, working out how to 'get round' the system. On the other hand, managers who expect people to work to very wide briefs when they are not ready to have so much scope run into great difficulties. Activities start to feel less well controlled and staff will begin to express anxieties about managers not discharging their managerial role responsibly.

This is a particular problem in circumstances when it is inherently difficult to set clear and limited objectives, such as in campaigning. At its worst, this leads to an element of organisational anarchy in which everyone is running his or her own initiatives with insufficient coordination to allow a coherent strategy for the department or the organisation as a whole to be constructed.

Attempting to give people power over huge issues with long timescales is just as inappropriate as giving people power over trivial matters. A useful catchphrase is to think about giving people **'freedom within a framework'**, in which the manager is responsible for defining and agreeing realistic conditions within which the empowered person can work.

Empowerment is likely to be appropriate in organisations that are well established and which, over the years, have developed controls and procedures that are now an obstacle to effective entrepreneurial working.

However, care needs to be taken to avoid raising inexperienced managers' expectations that they will suddenly have more power over the organisation and will be participating in all the major decisions. They need to be aware that increased empowerment also means increased responsibility, both for their own work and for their interventions into broader management issues.

Increasing empowerment is a long-term process, requiring changes in the behaviour of board members, managers and employees. It generally requires greater change from managers than from the people they manage. Managers have to put more effort into clarifying objectives and boundaries, coaching staff, giving them links to other people and resources, and encouraging two-way feedback.

Actions to empower people

Managers can take many actions to empower people. Choices will depend on circumstances and on people's views on what will have the greatest impact. The stages of increasing empowerment might include:

- **Involving people in planning** so that they share the ownership of objectives and the means of achieving them. A deep understanding of the purpose and boundaries around the work of an individual is a pre-requisite for devolving power.
- **Communicating extensively with staff** to keep them well informed about the changing context in which they are working and how their work affects the organisation's overall effectiveness. Such communication should be a two-way dialogue that also encourages people to submit new ideas. The best of these can then be fed back in subsequent communications to maintain the dialogue.

- **Removing institutional barriers** that prevent people making changes in their own area of responsibility. Managers should have freedom to make changes that they know are necessary and feasible. Where such changes cross departmental boundaries, set up a 'bureaucracy-busting' task force to find imaginative ways of overcoming obstacles. Examples include forms that gather data that has been collected elsewhere, statistics that hardly anyone uses, onerous authorisation procedures, and requirements to consult committees on matters of detail.
- **Asking staff to keep you appraised** so you get feedback on your performance.
- **Increasing people's spending limits** to indicate confidence in their ability to make good decisions.
- **Requiring reports on results, not activities**, and reducing the formal reporting requirements placed on staff to an absolute minimum.
- **Encouraging people to come with solutions** rather than presenting problems.

Empowering people to take greater responsibility significantly increases an organisation's capability. It releases senior people to put more effort into their critical role of integrating changes in the external environment with the current work of the organisation. But it cannot be done in short timescales. It is achieved over months and years, and results from incremental behaviour changes that become embedded in the organisation's culture.

16.5 DEALING WITH POOR PERFORMANCE

Sometimes, despite managers' best efforts, individual performance does not meet the required standard, and managers have to take actions to resolve the problem. Poor performance can exhibit itself in many different ways, and in managerial positions it can be difficult to pinpoint the problem and its causes because work is often developmental in nature and dependent on other people, and sometimes other organisations.

The problems vary. Work may not be produced to the required quality; there may be complaints from the people who report to the manager; there may be a problem of absenteeism or it may be concerned with other issues such as alcohol or inappropriate behaviour.

In all these circumstances, the person's line manager needs to grasp the situation and deal with it deliberately, objectively and with compassion. These situations can be particularly difficult in third-sector organisations because:

- people believe in the organisation's cause, and sometimes it is the most committed people who have developed their job beyond their ability to manage it;
- people are sometimes renowned leaders in their professional field, but may not be very good at management;
- poor performance is a particularly sensitive issue in organisations whose missions can be about helping less able people.

Nevertheless, most organisations exist to pursue a mission and not to give people employment, so poor performance always requires attention. Furthermore, the impressions that will be given to others if an organisation fails to deal with poor performance are likely to be very damaging to staff commitment and morale.

Organisations with **good supervision systems** in place will find these situations easier to deal with because managers and staff should know what is expected of them and be receiving regular feedback on their performance. Poor performance can be raised early and as part of regular supervisory meetings. Greater problems arise when performance issues are not anticipated by the person concerned or are raised unexpectedly and without a context of performance review.

The starting point for dealing with poor performance is to **establish 'the gap'** between the required standard and what the person is delivering. This can be easier in situations where organisations have established competencies (see section 17.2, Developing individuals), and where the precise performance issues can be pinpointed. In many cases, the issues may not be that clear cut, so effort is required to specify the gap and gather evidence to confirm it exists.

Once the gap has been identified, managers have to **establish reasons** why the person's performance is not meeting the required standard. It could be because:

- expectations have not been clearly established and communicated to the under-performing person, so they are not aware of the problem;
- the person may not agree with the expectations but may not have expressed that disagreement;
- they may not have the skills and experience required;
- circumstances outside their control may be inhibiting them in meeting the requirements;
- there may be unrelated issues concerned with health or a personal predicament that is distracting the individual from their responsibilities.

Whatever the situation, a meeting with the person concerned will be required to describe the manager's perception of the problem and provide the under-performing person with an **opportunity to respond**. This meeting will allow the manager to probe into the circumstances that may have led to the poor performance. The staff member should be given an opportunity to suggest actions that he or she could take to improve their work.

This can lead to the creation of a performance improvement plan setting out the actions the individual proposes to take (with the help of others, not least their manager) to improve their performance. This might also involve finding a mentor or getting some coaching support.

An ideal outcome would be a series of measures to help the person improve their standard of work and some specific targets that the person should meet within an agreed timescale.

If the performance does not improve within the agreed time-frame, then steps may need to be taken to dismiss the person. At the time of writing (March 2008) all dismissals of employees with at least one year's continuous service require a statutory three-stage dismissal procedure to be adopted. The three stages include informing the employee of the reason why dismissal is contemplated, holding a meeting which explores the circumstances before any dismissal and allowing an appeal against dismissal.

This particular regime may be modified or removed in 2009 but even if it is, dismissals will still require employees to be notified that they are at risk and to be considered for suitable alternative employment. Legal advice should always be sought by people who are not experienced in this process.

When a decision is taken to ask someone to change jobs or leave, great care should be taken over the process to ensure that it is seen to be as fair as possible in what are inevitably difficult circumstances. Communication with other people in the organisation needs to be given as much thought as communication with the person concerned. Other people may be expecting a manager to take action over poor performance and the manager may be taking it, but cannot report on progress. All the manager can do is to indicate that he or she hears people's concerns and to ask for their trust whilst action is being taken.

In other circumstances people may be concerned to support someone who is not performing adequately and may feel that the manager is being 'heavy handed'. Again clear communication between the manager and his or her boss and, where possible, with colleagues will be important.

A badly handled departure can have a damaging and long-lasting impact on an organisation's staff and its reputation. Handled professionally, a much-needed departure can enhance a manager's reputation for firm action in what everyone recognises is a difficult situation.

SUMMARY OF KEY POINTS

Developing people and teams

- Investing time and effort in developing the capabilities of managers at all levels of the organisation brings great benefits both to the individuals and to the organisation
- The potential for increasing organisation effectiveness by developing people's skills is huge
- Individuals have to take responsibility for their own learning and development
- Organisations should deploy the full range of methods for encouraging learning to maximise the potential of their people

Managing your boss

- Everyone has a boss. Some people have two bosses
- Managers need to manage their relationships with their bosses
- They need to understand his or her context, strengths and weaknesses and preferred working methods
- Managers should use their boss's strengths and look elsewhere for the support that he or she is unable to provide

Getting performance from teams

- The size of the team needs to be related to the task
- Team membership can be adjusted by including additional people for certain topics or creating sub-groups to address specific issues
- Successful teams need clear objectives, to plan together, coaching from the leader, well-prepared and tightly managed meetings and good team administration
- Team leaders should start modestly, promote the mission, encourage openness, support team members, face up to differences, review performance regularly, encourage systematic decision taking, make the team visible, encourage action and celebrate success
- Teams offer great learning opportunities that should be exploited to maximise organisation learning

Delegating work and empowering people

- Delegation is the art of giving people responsibilities that are within their abilities
- People management, policy-making, crisis management, matters involving confidential information and organisation rituals should not be delegated
- Empowerment is a process of giving people greater responsibilities within clearly defined boundaries

Dealing with poor performance

- Poor performance can exhibit itself in many different ways and in managerial positions it can be difficult to pinpoint the problem
- Line managers needs to grasp the situation and deal with it deliberately, objectively and with compassion
- Evidence of the performance gap should be gathered, and employees should have an opportunity to explain their performance and to suggest how it could be improved
- Dismissals must follow the legally required process, and legal advice should be sought
- Good communication with the person concerned and the rest of the organisation will help to ensure a manager's reputation for firm action in a difficult situation

FURTHER READING

Management Teams – Why they Succeed or Fail, Meredith Belbin, Elsevier, 2004

Managing Performance: Performance Management in Action, Michael Armstrong and Angela Baron, Chartered Institute of Personnel and Development, 2004

More and recent books and reports can be found at www.compasspartnership.co.uk.

17 Creating a learning organisation

17.1 ENCOURAGING LEARNING THROUGHOUT THE ORGANISATION

A learning organisation is 'an organisation which facilitates the learning of all its members and continuously transforms itself' (Bob Garratt) and 'an organisation which harnesses the full brainpower, knowledge and experience available to it, in order to evolve continually for the benefit of all its stakeholders' (Mayo and Lank). The central idea behind the learning organisation is that a high priority is given to learning at all levels of the organisation. This means encouraging:

- **individual learning**, through induction, coaching, one-to-ones, performance reviews, shadowing and mentoring;
- **team learning**, through understanding different team roles, reflecting systematically on the ways teams function and discovering more effective methods of working;
- **organisation-wide learning**, through establishing processes that enable learning to take place and a culture that promotes and is seen to value learning.

Organisations that encourage learning expect people and teams to take responsibility for their own learning and development. They expect people to take every opportunity to enhance their abilities. They encourage people to acknowledge mistakes openly and see them as learning opportunities. They establish systems that require people to see every situation as a learning opportunity and to put that learning into practice. In this way they enhance the abilities of their people and therefore the capability of the organisation itself. When people are learning from each other, the organisation has its own 'brain' and consequently much-increased capacity to change and develop.

Learning is under-valued in third-sector organisations. Surrounded by demands to deliver more services, campaign for change, respond to media opportunities, and resolve the endless stream of short-term crises, the need to invest in learning can be neglected. Yet the benefits are potentially enormous. Increasing the efficiency of the way people work together and of the way work is done can yield benefits that far exceed the time and effort put into learning. For example, in many third-sector organisations huge amounts of time are spent with people working together in meetings. Learning to work more effectively and, for example, saving one hour in an eight-person meeting creates a whole day of time for other activities.

Organisations need to work on the assumption that, if their people are not developing as fast as the changes in their environment, they are losing their capacity to be effective. Organisations have to adapt to changing circumstances, and that depends on people's ability and willingness to learn and then to change their work practices and habits.

The single most critical action in creating a learning organisation is that the chief executive and the directors set an example through their own actions. This means that they are properly inducted, supervised and appraised. They coach, mentor and shadow other people, and they go out of their way to learn from other organisations. They acknowledge that learning is a dialogue in which people are learning from each other in a structured way. They are seen to be using the good practices that they wish other people to adopt.

Learning is a practical process, and it takes time and effort to acquire the necessary skills. In already over-stretched organisations, this can appear an impossible challenge. However, organisations that are too busy to improve themselves will not develop and their abilities will remain fixed at their current level.

This chapter explains how organisations promote learning by:
- developing individuals;
- prioritising one-to-ones and performance reviews;
- encouraging coaching, mentoring and shadowing;
- encouraging teams to learn;
- ensuring organisation-wide learning.

Successful implementation of all of these is dependent on organisations having a culture that encourages, values and gives real priority to everyone's learning. The learning culture is created, not by trying directly to change the culture, but by taking the actions that encourage people to learn, and rewarding those who adopt the new beliefs and values.

17.2 DEVELOPING INDIVIDUALS

Developing individuals means extending their skills and experiences in order to:
- enable them to be more effective in achieving the organisation's goals;
- give them opportunities for personal growth.

Managers can play a significant role in helping individuals to develop. Their enthusiasm, their willingness to think about others' needs, their discipline in holding regular one-to-one sessions, and their ability both to give individuals work that provides development experiences and to help their staff learn from them, are all important ingredients. But the extent to which individuals develop depends ultimately on their motivation and willingness to learn. Their attitudes are, in the end, the crucial determinant of their development.

RECOGNISING DEVELOPMENT NEEDS

By observation, working together and discussion, you will have a sense of someone's strengths and weaknesses; you will also come to know the areas of work that they enjoy, those that they find less satisfying, and their longer-term aspirations. You will also know about the demands and possibilities of the work. In addition, you may have information or ideas about the emerging priorities for the organisation as a whole, and about the prospects and requirements that these may involve. These aspects are represented in the diagram.

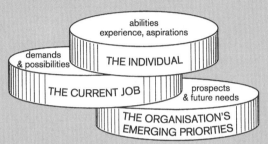

Ideally the three 'discs' would stack neatly on top of each other, meaning that the work being done fitted perfectly with the individual's aspirations and abilities and with the organisation's priorities. Unfortunately, the reality is more complex; the fit is rarely 100% and the 'discs' keep shifting in relation to each other. For example, the work being done may lag behind the latest priorities; or the individual may have to do work that she or he does not feel capable of, nor want to do. Moreover, one 'disc' can cause another to shift with it (as happens when an individual shifts the job to suit her or his abilities, or when an organisation changes its plans in the light of the possibilities revealed by a job). Alternatively, a 'disc' can shift in the opposite direction to the others in reaction to developments (for example, when individuals try to set up a new project to ensure greater opportunities for themselves). So the 'discs' keep moving and your aim can only be to maintain *a reasonable alignment* between them by adjusting the job, by developing the individual, or occasionally by seeking to adjust the organisation's priorities (to take advantage, for example, of under-used skills).

Source: *Managing Voluntary and Non-profit Enterprises,* Book 6, *Choosing and Developing Staff and Volunteers,* Open University Business School

It is sometimes assumed that individual development will somehow happen automatically, and that little more is required of managers than casual enquiries about the progress of team members' work. Nothing could be further from the truth. In practice, promoting learning is a challenging task, and organisations need to set up systems both to ensure that individuals are taking the required actions and to monitor their implementation.

Building a **clear view of an individual's current skills** is the starting point. This can be done by reviewing the person's abilities against a 'ladder' of the skills he or she requires for that job. Reviewing the 'management standards' or 'competencies' required for a job can help to inform the manager and the individual about the skills that are needed, which are present and which have to be developed. This could be done as a joint exercise to pinpoint skills requiring attention or experiences needed to be gained.

MANAGEMENT STANDARDS

Management standards can be used to pinpoint the competencies individuals have and the ones they need to develop. The Management Standards Centre maintains an up-to-date set of standards organised into six groups:

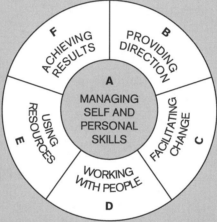

Each group of standards is divided into a series of competencies. For example, the competencies in working with people (Group D) are:

- develop productive working relationships with colleagues
- develop productive working relationships with stakeholders
- recruit, select and keep colleagues
- plan the workforce
- allocate and check work in your team
- allocate and monitor progress and quality of work in your area of responsibility
- provide learning opportunities for colleagues
- help team members address problems affecting their performance
- build and manage teams
- reduce and manage conflict in your team
- lead meetings
- participate in meetings

Managers and their subordinates then need to agree the **next skills or capabilities to be acquired**. The objectives should be highly tailored to the individual's present work situation, the demands that are currently being placed on him or her and the expectations that both the manager and the subordinate have for his or her future development.

Different learning styles

Managers can then play a significant role in helping people to learn. Personal development experiences come from many sources, including:

- the nature of the work that people are doing;
- the teams that people are working with;
- the one-to-ones and performance reviews that people receive;
- the training that people receive;
- the books people read; and most importantly,
- the personal time spent reflecting on performance.

Finally, managers and their staff need to **monitor progress** in using the skills and abilities so that both are aware of improvements. They need to have arrangements to review individuals' development on a regular basis so that the whole approach is embedded in their way of working together.

Managers should recognise that individuals learn in different ways. Alan Mumford has identified four different learning styles:

Activists learn from new experiences and problems and prefer to be involved with other people. They like methods such as role-playing and they dislike solitary work and being asked to review their experiences.

Reflectors like to collect data, to analyse and review. They dislike being thrown into things without thought, being rushed or placed under time pressure.

Theorists learn from models and concepts. They want to question assumptions and logic and be intellectually stretched. They tend to discount methods emphasising emotions and feelings.

Pragmatists want links between the subject matter and their work. They like techniques that provide immediate opportunities for application. They dislike learning concerned with environments quite different from their own.

Managers who want to know more about how their staff learn could suggest that they complete a 'learning styles' questionnaire to identify people's preferences. Free and paid-for questionnaires can be downloaded from websites such as www.peterhoney.com and www.businessballs.com.

HIGH-PERFORMANCE MANAGEMENT COMPETENCIES

A more demanding set of competencies has been developed by academics from London Business School and the University of Florida.

Behavioural definition

THINKING

Information search	Gathers many different kinds of information and uses a wide variety of sources to build a rich information environment in preparation for decision-making in the organisation
Concept formation	Builds frameworks or models or forms concepts, hypotheses or ideas on the basis of information; becomes aware of patterns, trends and cause/effect relations by linking disparate information
Conceptual flexibility	Identifies feasible alternatives or multiple options in planning and decision-making; holds different options in focus simultaneously and evaluates their pros and cons

DEVELOPMENTAL

Interpersonal search	Uses open and probing questions, summaries and paraphrasing to understand the ideas, concepts and feelings of another; can comprehend events, issues, problems, opportunities from the viewpoint of others
Managing interaction	Involves others and is able to build cooperative teams in which group members feel valued and empowered and have shared goals
Developmental orientation	Creates a positive climate in which staff increase the accuracy of their awareness of their own strengths and limitations; provides coaching, training and developmental resources to improve performance

INSPIRATIONAL

Impact	Uses a variety of methods (e.g. persuasive arguments, modelling behaviour, inventing symbols, forming alliances and appealing to the interest of others) to gain support for ideas and strategies and values
Self-confidence	States own 'stand' or position on issues; unhesitatingly takes decisions when required and commits self and others accordingly; expresses confidence in the future success of the actions to be taken
Presentation	Presents ideas clearly, with ease and interest so that the other person (or audience) understands what is being communicated; uses technical, symbolic, non-verbal and visual aids effectively

ACHIEVING

Proactive orientation	Structures the task for the team; implements plans and ideas; takes responsibility for all aspects of the situation even beyond ordinary boundaries – and for the success and failure of the group
Achievement orientation	Possesses high internal work standards and sets ambitious, risky and yet attainable goals; wants to do things better, to improve, to be more effective and efficient; measures progress against targets

Source: John Hunt, (London Business School), and Tony Cockerill, Harry Schroder, (University of Florida)

The learning cycle

The idea of the learning cycle (known as Kolb's learning cycle) is a useful reminder of the necessary steps for effective learning. It suggests that four steps are essential for learning: hands-on experience, reflection, abstract conceptualisation and active experimentation (see the box describing the learning cycle, below). More often than not, busy managers take actions, observe what happens and then take further actions or move on to new projects. This does not allow time to reflect, to learn from successes and failures, to develop models or 'rules of thumb' that can be applied in similar situations in the future, or to communicate that learning to the rest of the organisation.

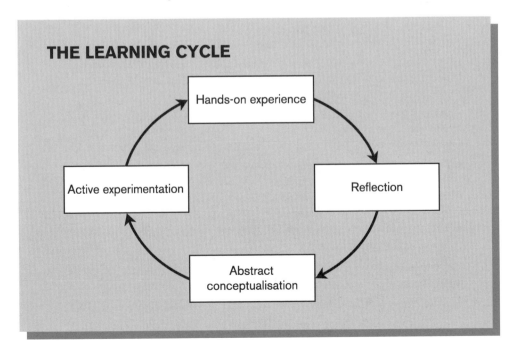

THE LEARNING CYCLE

397

Building a commitment to learning and to continuous personal development begins when potential recruits receive their first communication from the organisation – even when they are sent a recruitment pack. This can stress the organisation's commitment to learning, set out the skills that the potential recruit will be expected to deploy and point to possible development paths within the job or within the organisation.

The induction process needs to ensure that new staff have a learning experience which:

- teaches them how the organisation works;
- communicates the organisation's values;
- clarifies their role in achieving the organisation's mission;
- explains the support and resources that are available to help them achieve their objectives.

The process can stress the importance the organisation attaches to learning by comparing the incumbent's skills with the person specification for the job. This will identify skills that the individual lacks, and so provide the basis for agreeing some initial learning goals.

The importance of using every situation as an opportunity for learning can be instilled at the beginning of new recruits' careers by asking them about their experience of the induction process and what they think could be done to improve it.

THE INCISIVE QUESTION

An incisive question is any question that removes limiting assumptions from your thinking so that you can think again. The incisive question replaces a limiting assumption with a freeing one.

A question works because, unlike a statement, it requires you to think. When you spot an assumption that is limiting someone's thinking, you can remove it with a deft question. Examples of incisive questions include:

- If you were to become chief executive, what problem would you solve first, and how would you do it?
- If you knew that you were vital to this organisation's success, how would you approach your work?
- If things could be exactly right for you in this situation, how would they have to change?

The first part of an incisive question asserts a positive assumption; the second part directs the thinker's attention back to their issue or goal.

Source: *Time to Think*, Nancy Klein, Cassell Illustrated, 1999

17.3 LEARNING FROM ONE-TO-ONES AND PERFORMANCE REVIEWS

This section is about the formal and regular arrangements that organisations should have for managing people and their work on a continuous basis (one-to-ones) and, more thoroughly, at the end of each year (performance reviews).

One-to-ones

The term 'one-to-ones' is used to describe regular meetings between managers and each of their staff. These used to be called supervision meetings, but that word has a top-down connotation that was inappropriate in organisations that are promoting learning and enabling. The term 'supervision' also has a more formal meaning in social work and counselling that is not applicable to one-to-ones.

One-to-ones provide the discipline of thinking about individuals' performance and their development needs on a routine basis. In some organisations, the daily pressures of work conspire against finding time for one-to-one sessions. The latest crisis always seems more important than the one-to-one session, which inevitably has a longer-term pay-back. Discipline in holding the meetings and commitment to preparing for them are needed to ensure development takes place.

One-to-ones follow on directly from delegation. When managers delegate work to individuals, they have a corresponding duty to review progress, help people overcome problems and give constructive feedback.

An individual's objectives and the support the organisation has agreed to give that person set the context for one-to-ones. This should be linked to annual performance reviews, during which objectives will have been agreed. One-to-ones are a structured opportunity to review progress and problems which should:

- review performance against objectives;
- ensure that delegated work is done to the agreed standard and within the agreed timescale;
- check that people have received the resources required to achieve their objectives;
- enable staff to clarify how their work fits in to the broader context;
- enable staff to learn from their work experiences and develop their skills;
- provide a channel for two-way feedback on any other work-related issues (including problems outside work that may affect people's performance);
- allow managers and their staff an opportunity to remind each other of their value to the organisation and that their work is appreciated.

The frequency of one-to-ones depends on both the work that has been delegated and the experience of the person being supervised. When the work is challenging, one-to-ones need to be more frequent and more supportive. Conversely, when the person being supervised is highly experienced or has been in the job for many years, one-to-ones can be less frequent and more consultative in nature. Frequency is likely to vary from weekly (for a new, inexperienced person or someone working in a challenging environment) to quarterly (for an experienced person in a stable environment). For many people, monthly or every other month will be appropriate.

ACTIVITIES IN EFFECTIVE ONE-TO-ONES

Task-related activities

Shaping	structuring the task
Target-setting	setting or agreeing specific goals and deadlines
Explaining	selling policies and plans
Delegating	devolving tasks and responsibilities
Guiding	giving advice, information, being a role model
Limiting	setting boundaries, reining people in
Negotiating	matching individual ideas with organisational policy
Resourcing	arranging back-up, funds, etc.

People-related activities

Coaching	helping people to learn the work
Encouraging	being a sounding board, boosting morale
Facilitating	getting introductions and putting people in touch
Counselling	giving assistance in exploring approaches to situations and dealing with anxieties
Representing	speaking on behalf of individuals
Evaluating	making judgements about achievements and potential

Source: (From: *Managing Voluntary and Non-profit Enterprises*, Book 6, *Choosing and Developing Staff and Volunteers*, Open University Business School)

One-to-one sessions can cover many issues. Most are concerned with either the development of the individual or the work he or she is doing. It is important for managers to ascertain from the people being supervised what they wish to achieve from their one-to-ones. Explicit clarification of the expectations of both parties can lead to much more productive sessions.

Organisations need a system that encourages all staff to meet one-to-one with their line manager at an agreed frequency. Establishing a one-to-one system should involve all the participants, to ensure their active support and commitment to the one-to-one process; this will also help to incorporate it into everyone's work routines. Ideally, it should become part of the accepted culture that everyone expects a one-to-one at an agreed frequency. A series of workshops to tailor a one-to-one process to the organisation's circumstances is a good way to build commitment. This should be followed by management decisions on the frequency of one-to-ones and training requirements to support implementation.

Setting an example from the top is crucial. Chairs are responsible for ensuring that chief executives have one-to-ones, either by doing them themselves or, in exceptional circumstances, by appointing another board member to perform this function. Managers who report to the chief executive should have one-to-one meetings with the chief executive, and the process should cascade down the organisation. Support for people who are anxious about one-to-ones helps to build confidence and commitment to the process. This can take the form of training and opportunities to review progress with senior management.

It takes concentrated effort to build regular one-to-ones into the culture, but they bring huge benefits in focusing people on the organisation's priorities and ensuring that they have the resources and support they require.

Individual performance reviews

Individual performance reviews are regular in-depth reviews of past performance and future expectations of an individual; they used to be called appraisals, another term that has connotations that are inappropriate in organisations committed to learning. Normally carried out annually, they are sometimes done more frequently for a new member of staff or for people whose performance would benefit from more frequent review.

Performance reviews compare an individual's performance with previously agreed objectives. These individual objectives need to tie directly into the objectives of the individual's organisational unit. Performance reviews need to be carried out in a scrupulously professional way. The assessment of an individual's performance must be objective. Areas for improvement should be presented honestly, and the whole process should aim to be a motivating experience.

Performance reviews are a powerful means of assisting individual and organisation learning. By requiring people to stand back and review both their performance and their learning over the previous year, they encourage reflection and help to consolidate experiences at a higher level.

Preparation is critical for a successful performance review. Both parties should agree the broad topics that the performance review will cover before data-gathering commences. In larger organisations, there may be corporately agreed headings or a performance review form to complete. Data for a performance review should be collected by both parties.

A performance review should:
- review achievements, using both quantitative and qualitative criteria;
- reflect on learning and personal development over the past period;
- identify the individual's competencies in relation to the skills required to do the job (these might be National Vocational Qualifications skills set out in a job description, or a set of management competencies);
- identify next steps in the individual's development;
- consider any changes in the way the manager works which might assist the development of the person whose performance is being reviewed;
- lead to agreement on a package of actions (coaching, shadowing, training, reading) to meet the individual's needs;
- consider the next career steps;
- establish objectives and priorities for the next 12 months, usually proposed by the individual and agreed by the manager.

When one-to-ones and regular feedback are working well, there should ideally be no surprises at a performance review. It should be a 'check' on progress and an opportunity to lay plans for the future.

Establishing and refreshing performance review processes

Establishing or reinvigorating an organisation's performance review process is a substantial task that requires significant time. The practical activities are similar to those needed to set up a one-to-one process. A programme of discussions among managers concerning the design or development of the process will help to build commitment and an understanding of the need for change. The scheme should be designed or developed, possibly using specialist external expertise, and subject to widespread consultation to strengthen commitment and support for the initiative.

Once an overall scheme is agreed, tailor-made training designed to suit the specific circumstances of the organisation is essential in order to give people the necessary skills. Everyone should be offered training before being required to carry out a performance review.

The performance review process should roll out, starting with senior management and gradually expanding until it covers all employees. Unequivocal commitment on the part of top management is essential, and should be demonstrated by the chief executive's having a review before reviewing members of the leadership team.

Once established, periodic actions are required to avoid the process becoming a bureaucratic necessity that does not add value to the organisation. Changing the questions on performance review forms, requiring people to link performance reviews explicitly to strategic and operational plans, listing the types of support the organisation can provide and introducing 360° reviews are all examples of ways to give the process renewed life.

Introducing 360° performance reviews

A 360° performance review is a wider and deeper review. It gathers information from a range of people who work with the person being reviewed, to provide the fullest possible picture of his or her performance. Sometimes called a multi-input review, these use information from the person's boss, his or her peers and subordinates and, where appropriate, relevant board members and service users.

This data can be gathered by an independent person or, in organisations with appropriate experience, by the person being reviewed and the person conducting the review. Ideally it should include written feedback from people who work with the person being reviewed so that the person doing the review can draw out common themes.

Some consultancies now offer web-based services that allow everyone involved in 360° reviews to input their feedback and score each individual's performance at their desks. The information is assembled and emailed to the person conducting the review.

These reviews can be both informative and motivating. They give people a more rounded view of their performance, and as a result the approach is becoming increasingly popular. It is particularly suitable for senior managers, because new insights can be gained from seeking the views of all the stakeholders with whom the individual interacts.

LEARNING FROM A 360° PERFORMANCE REVIEW

A charity chief executive wanted to take stock of her own development. Acknowledging that one of the organisation's values was 'to respect and value each other and those for whom we work', she commissioned a 360° review of her own performance.

The consultant she engaged interviewed seven people who knew her work well, including staff, clients and board members. The interviews were anonymous. The consultant reported back to the chief executive that she was seen to be:

- an excellent ambassadorial leader
- persuasive and intellectually consistent
- able to take tough decisions and confront difficult issues
- insistent on quality
- calm and focused
- an accomplished communicator
- an empowering manager for some
- good at giving and receiving feedback

She was advised to focus her development on:

- her speed of decision-making
- appealing to emotion as well as intellect
- taking more risks
- providing more overt direction and consulting less

On receiving this feedback, she was surprised to discover some of her strengths, which had not been apparent to her before. She planned a development programme based on the suggestions.

Fifteen months later, at her regular performance review, her chair told her that he had seen great developments in her skills and performance. She ascribed much of this to the motivation and focus she had gained from learning the combined views of those who knew her work best, through the 360° review.

Specialist expertise may be required to help set up a 360° performance review process, because the procedure of opening up a person's performance for more widespread review can be destructive if not handled well, and, conversely, very motivating and empowering if done in a highly professional way.

17.4   ENCOURAGING COACHING, MENTORING AND SHADOWING

Coaching, mentoring and shadowing are all powerful and comparatively inexpensive ways of encouraging learning and they are all becoming increasingly popular.

Coaching is 'a process that enables learning and development to occur and thus performance to improve. To be a successful coach requires a knowledge and understanding of process as well as the variety of styles, skills and techniques that are appropriate to the context in which the coaching takes place' (Eric Parsloe).

Mentoring is 'off-line help by one person to another in making significant transitions in knowledge, work or thinking' (David Clutterbuck).

There are many similarities between the two. Both:

- understand a manager's situation by questioning and listening;
- help managers to explore problems they are facing;
- are supportive and non-judgemental;
- encourage action and personal growth;
- seek to avoid dependency on the relationship.

The main differences are that:

- coaching aims to improve a particular aspect of an individual's performance whereas mentoring involves giving longer-term support, advice and contacts;
- coaching does not require specialist experience in the field in which the coachee works, whereas mentors are usually experts with experience to share;
- coaches are skilled at questioning, listening and enabling coachees to find answers, whereas mentors give context-specific advice.

Coaching

Coaching has risen up the management development agenda in recent years because it is perceived to be a highly effective and inexpensive way of advancing people's abilities. In its purest form it is done by people with coaching qualifications who are brought into the organisation to support one or more managers. However, the term has also come to describe an approach that line managers can take to support the professional development of their staff.

It generally involves a time-limited series of one-to-one sessions designed to achieve one or more specified objectives.

It can involve:

- exploring particular issues the coachee faces;
- testing ways forward and reflecting on the experience;
- identifying gaps in coachees' skills and experience and agreeing on ways to fill them.

Good coaches will use the following principles:

- Listening is more important than talking.
- What motivates people must be understood.
- Everyone is capable of achieving more.
- A person's past is no indication of their future.
- People's beliefs about what is possible for themselves are their only limits.
- A coach must always provide full support.
- Coaches don't provide the answers.
- Coaching does not include criticising people.
- All coaching is completely confidential.
- Some people's needs cannot be met by coaching, and coaches recognise clients with these needs.

Source: The Coaching Academy

Coaches can be found from one of the many accreditation organisations (such as the European Mentoring and Coaching Council and the Association for Coaching) or through ACEVO, which offers a four-session service for people wanting an introduction to coaching.

Individual coaching can be combined with actions to develop a coaching culture within organisations by encouraging people who have been coached to become internal coaches. They can then demonstrate how enquiring approaches to managing people can be advantageous to the individual and the organisation.

Mentoring

Mentoring is the activity of one person providing individual support to another, to help that person to learn. The mentor is usually a more senior or experienced person who is not the individual's line manager. The mentor may be from the same organisation or from another organisation. A mentor's roles can include:

- acting as a sounding board and an advisor;
- sharing knowledge and experience;
- encouraging individuals to reflect on their decisions and actions;
- supporting an individual's career development.

Mentoring within and across organisations has grown rapidly in recent years because it is seen as a very effective way of helping people to learn in an unthreatening environment.

Mentoring relationships can be short term (to help a manager with a particular problem) or longer term (to help with skill and career development). The relationship typically has a series of stages:

- **Initiation** – when agreement is reached on the nature of the relationship and practical ways of working together.
- **Direction-setting** – when the individual's needs are agreed and objectives are established.
- **Working together** – when they share each other's expertise, review progress and develop their relationship.
- **Moving on** – when the relationship is drawn to a close.

Mentoring is particularly valuable when managers do not have anyone they can turn to for advice. Reasons for this might include:

- the problem is their relationship with their manager (or, in the case of a chief executive, their chair);
- the individual wishes to test out ideas on a third party but does not wish to discuss the issues within the organisation;
- a view that no one within the organisation could provide the required support;
- the individual wishes to discuss career development in private because public discussion might lead to a loss of authority in the organisation;
- the individual needs to adjust his or her relationships with former peers following a promotion.

Mentors need to agree and adhere to strict rules of confidentiality on both professional and personal matters. Generally, they should not mentor more than one person in the same organisation at the same time.

Mentoring can be enhanced if it is combined with being shadowed. When mentoring is done on its own, the mentor often does not see the person 'in action', so the only source of information is the individual himself or herself. When it is combined with shadowing, the mentor gains additional insights into the individual's ways of working that can point to further avenues for enhancing performance.

One danger is that mentoring can also be seen as a criticism of the managers of the people being mentored; managers may feel that they should be providing the support people require. Mentoring can also result in managers feeling threatened when people bring back assumptions and ideas that may conflict with those their managers wish to promote. So it is important to secure the agreement of the mentee's manager before mentoring starts.

Despite these anxieties, mentoring is another method of promoting learning and development that can bring great benefits to people working in the third sector.

Shadowing

Shadowing is a valuable way of giving people learning opportunities. It costs almost nothing and is comparatively easy to organise, but it does require proper preparation if it is to yield the greatest benefits. This takes time for both the shadow and the person being shadowed. However, learning does accrue to both parties. Shadowing can be done within organisations, between organisations in the sector or with people in the public and private sectors.

People who are shadows should specify their learning objectives before deciding whom to shadow. They should be briefed by the person they are shadowing on the situation they will be following before and during the shadowing activity. They should reflect on what they have learned with the person whom they are shadowing. Writing up their learning from the shadowing helps to relate the experience to their work situation.

Shadowing can involve following a manager over a period of days or following a sequence of activities that take place over a number of weeks. Examples of shadowing activities include following:

- a series of strategic planning meetings;
- a board or leadership team meeting;
- a chief executive or divisional director for a period of days;
- a consultant working on a relevant assignment;
- a manager in a similar job in another sector;
- a task group working on a relevant project.

17.5 ENCOURAGING TEAMS TO LEARN

So far this chapter has concentrated on individual learning. The next two sections focus on opportunities for team and organisation-wide learning.

Teams have the potential to generate significant learning for individuals and for the group as a whole. They offer this potential because people see each other working together and inevitably reflect on each other's behaviour. Some of these reflections will contain important insights, if they can be teased out in unthreatening ways.

To learn from the team, members need to be aware of how the team is working at three different levels. Members are usually conscious of how the team is working with the **task**. Comments such as 'We're making good progress' or 'We took a lot of decisions' relate to the task. Team members also need to be conscious of the **processes** of its work, the ways it is tackling its job. Comments such as 'She chaired the meeting well' or 'He brought the best out of her' are indicative of process. Lastly, teams need to be aware of team members' **emotions**. They need to be conscious of how people are feeling about the task, the processes and each other. Comments such as 'I really appreciated his constructive comments on my paper' or 'She was clearly feeling angry about that' relate to the emotions of the team.

Teams need to create opportunities to learn. Rich learning opportunities arise when teams are working in what Peter Senge calls a dialoguing mode. He draws the distinction between **discussions** and **dialogues**. When a team is having a discussion, different views are presented and defended, and the team searches for a solution to a particular problem. This is appropriate at times when a decision is required. A dialogue, on the other hand, is a 'free and creative discussion' of more complex and subtle issues, in which individuals listen closely to one another.

According to Senge, three conditions are necessary for a team to learn from a dialogue:

1. Participants must be willing to expose their assumptions to the team and to have them examined by team members. Questions about what assumptions people are making and why they are making them are encouraged. Team members search for answers in an honest way, and members do not feel threatened by having their assumptions challenged.
2. All team members must regard one another as colleagues and be willing to work on a level field. The benefits of open dialogue must be greater than the privileges that individuals enjoy as a result of their positions.
3. One or more members of the team have to 'facilitate' the dialogue and take responsibility for 'holding the context' and not allow the conversation to drift.

When a team is in dialogue mode, individuals gain insights that they are unlikely to have found on their own or when the team was in discussion mode. The team is likely to get a better understanding of the circumstances outside the team. More importantly, it should get nearer to the truth about what is going on inside the team – and that is really powerful learning.

Organisations that promote learning encourage teams to spend time on dialogue and to maximise the learning that they can generate from themselves.

Another method of learning from the team is to **review and reflect** how it is working. This can happen in many different ways. A good starting point is to spend a few minutes (at the end of each meeting, say) reviewing how the meeting went. A comment from each member of the team can tease out thoughts on:

● What did we do well?
● What did we not do so well?
● What could we do better next time?

These questions can refer to all three levels of team working described above. Reminding people at the beginning of the next meeting what was agreed at the end of the previous meeting is a good way of embedding the required improvements into team behaviour.

Such discussions can go on to consider deeper questions such as:

- What different types of contributions do different team members make?
- What changes are required in the way the team works?
- What changes would I like to see in the ways other team members work in the team?
- What changes would I like to make in the way I contribute to the team?

A thorough review might be combined with the use of one or two of the tests that help people to understand different personalities and the different roles that people play in teams (such as Myers Briggs to identify different personality types) or Belbin (see section 16.3, Getting performance from teams) to identify the different parts that people tend to play. They also help to give a profile of the whole team that can point to gaps in skills or behaviour that need to be filled.

All these actions help teams to become highly sensitive to their own performance. They also make learning an integral part of how the team works. They help teams to understand their strengths and weaknesses and to use the team as a pool of skill and experience that is available to assist all its members.

When these disciplines are adopted and used by the leadership team, it sends powerful messages to the rest of the organisation about the type of learning culture that ought to permeate through the whole organisation.

17.6 ENSURING ORGANISATION-WIDE LEARNING

Organisation-wide learning happens when learning is seen to take place at every level and in every corner of the organisation. While that is easily said, it takes years to create a culture in which people see learning opportunities in everything they do.

There are three elements to creating a learning organisation. It requires:

- **The leadership team to champion learning**. People at the top must be seen to take every opportunity themselves to learn, to encourage learning throughout the organisation and to invest time and resources in learning. Unless they are seen to be putting their commitment to learning into practice, it will be regarded as well-intentioned but not real.
- **Effective communication and education**. People have to understand for themselves why learning is important. They can be helped to do this by extensive communication up and down the organisation that stresses its importance.
- **Effective support systems**. People have to be supported in their learning by a range of systems, including training, facilitation, one-to-ones and team-building sessions.

Many of the management techniques described earlier in this book can also make a huge contribution to learning. Strategic planning is a tool for helping people to learn about their organisation and its external environment. Performance management is a critical element in creating a learning organisation because it establishes a systematic approach to reviewing achievements and feeding back learning into future plans. Management competencies are a means for people to learn how their skills compare with those of others. Investing in people helps them to identify their learning needs. Benchmarking allows people to understand what underlies the differences between their organisation's performance and that of others.

Learning can also come from outside the organisation. Managers can be encouraged to obtain insights from other organisations. This is a rich source of learning, both about different ways of working and about the strengths of one's own organisation. To tap into this learning, managers should be encouraged to attend conferences and workshops, both within the sector and in the public and private sectors. Managers should also become involved in the professional groups that provide development for people in their particular profession.

Organisation-wide learning therefore needs to be seen not as an initiative on its own but as a way of working that permeates all the activities and processes that an organisation undertakes. This will demonstrate to people that the organisation is deeply committed to learning and that it values people who learn.

These actions produce reciprocal commitments from individuals to the organisation. They motivate people to learn and they encourage the openness and information-sharing which is essential to the learning organisation.

SUMMARY OF KEY POINTS

Encouraging learning throughout the organisation

- Organisations enhance their performance by encouraging individual, team and organisation-wide learning
- A structured approach to learning can be under-valued in third-sector organisations
- Senior management has to set an example by being seen to prioritise learning
- A learning organisation requires people to take responsibility for their own learning. The organisation provides support and encouragement to ensure learning opportunities are maximised

Developing individuals

- Managers play a significant role in helping individuals to develop
- Managers should have a clear view of individuals' current skills and the next skills they need to develop
- Personal development experiences come from many sources
- The induction process is an opportunity to stress an organisation's commitment to learning

Learning from one-to-ones and performance reviews

- One-to-ones should:
  - review performance
  - ensure delegated work is done
  - check the required resources were provided
  - enable people to learn from their work
  - remind people that they are valued
- Organisations need systems to ensure that one-to-ones produce real learning opportunities for staff
- Performance reviews should:
  - review achievements
  - reflect on learning and personal development
  - identify current and required competencies
  - agree actions to meet the individual's learning needs
  - establish objectives for the next period
- Individual performance reviews help senior managers in well-developed organisations to get a more rounded view of their performance

Encouraging coaching, mentoring and shadowing

- Coaching and mentoring are increasingly popular ways of learning how to be a better manager
- Coaches help people to improve their performance by questioning, listening and enabling
- Mentors are more experienced people who act as a sounding board, have knowledge and experience and can support career development
- Shadowing enables people to learn from other people's work

Encouraging teams to learn

- Team members need to be conscious of the task, the processes and the emotions
- Teams should distinguish between discussions and dialogues
- Teams need to review and reflect

Ensuring organisation-wide learning

- The essential ingredients of organisation-wide learning include championing learning, effective communication and good support systems
- Managers should encourage people to learn from other organisations

FURTHER READING

Time To Think – Listening to Ignite the Human Mind, Nancy Klein, Cassell Illustrated, 1999

The Fifth Discipline – the Art and Practice of the Learning Organisation, Peter Senge, Doubleday, 2006

More and recent books and reports can be found at www.compasspartnership.co.uk.

18 Managing different types of organisation

18.1 ORGANISATION LIFE CYCLES

The third sector consists of an extraordinarily wide range of organisations. So far this book has concentrated on approaches to management that are common to many organisations. This chapter looks at the management of organisations at different stages of their development and at the management of different types of organisation.

The management of organisations at different stages of development is best understood by considering the notion of their life cycle. This idea was first introduced in Chapter 3 in relation to boards (see section 3.2, The life cycle of boards), but it can also be used to help understand the development of the whole organisation.

The central proposition behind the life cycle is the idea that organisations develop in stages. It was put forward over twenty years ago in a *Harvard Business Review* article entitled 'Evolution and Revolution in Organisations'. It argued that periods of steady evolutionary growth and development are followed by periods of revolutionary development when everything seems to be changing at the same time. This behaviour pattern also occurs in third-sector organisations.

The idea of a life cycle does not imply that all organisations will necessarily move through a pre-determined set of stages. That patently could not be true, because organisations' futures are ultimately determined by governing boards and management taking decisions based on their judgements at particular times. Nevertheless, when one looks at many organisations and summarises their behaviour, a surprisingly large number have a similar evolutionary pattern.

The value of this life cycle idea is that it helps boards and managers to set the opportunities and issues they face in a broader context. It helps people to understand that their problems are not unique or unresolvable. It enables people to explain behaviour in terms of a model that points to actions which need to be taken to help the organisation move on to its next development stage.

ORGANISATION LIFE CYCLE

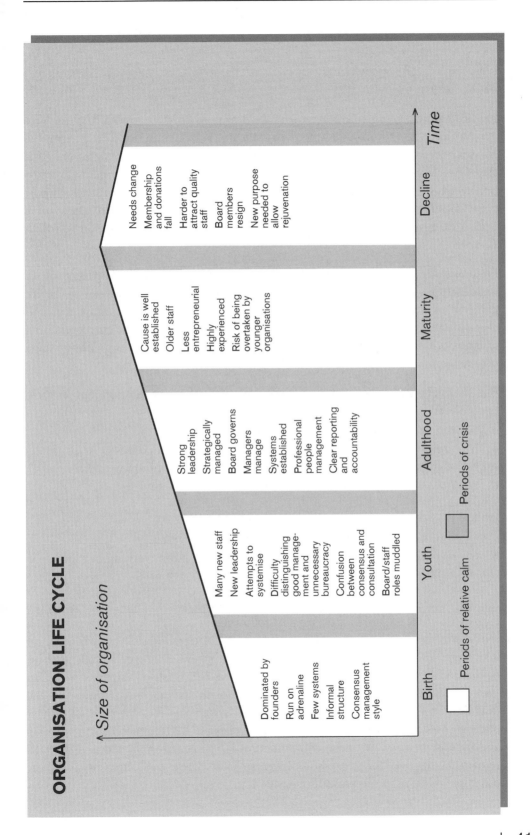

Size of organisation →

Birth
- Dominated by founders
- Run on adrenaline
- Few systems
- Informal structure
- Consensus management style

Youth
- Many new staff
- New leadership
- Attempts to systemise
- Difficulty distinguishing good management and unnecessary bureaucracy
- Confusion between consensus and consultation
- Board/staff roles muddled

Adulthood
- Strong leadership
- Strategically managed
- Board governs
- Managers manage
- Systems established
- Professional people management
- Clear reporting and accountability

Maturity
- Cause is well established
- Older staff
- Less entrepreneurial
- Highly experienced
- Risk of being overtaken by younger organisations

Decline
- Needs change
- Membership and donations fall
- Harder to attract quality staff
- Board members resign
- New purpose needed to allow rejuvenation

Time

☐ Periods of relative calm   ▨ Periods of crisis

There is, it should be emphasised, no one set of characteristics that is 'right' for each stage. Every organisation has its own characteristics and must consequently define its own life cycle.

In the first stage, organisations are often dominated by a founding figure. This person has the vision and energy to create an organisation, to secure the necessary resources and to build a group of people into an organisation. This stage can last from a few years to many decades. Sense (the organisation for people who are both deaf and blind), for example, was a small mutual-support organisation for over thirty years before it embarked in the mid-1980s on a period of explosive growth that took it through the next two stages in less than 10 years.

Founders are critically important in the first stage of the development of an organisation. They have the vision to recognise a social, educational or health problem or an artistic opportunity, and they have the energy, commitment and charisma to create an organisation to address the issue. They are entrepreneurial in approach and are usually unwilling to be stopped by obstacles. Without these people, organisations would never get off the ground.

But founders can be a source of problems once the organisation has become established:
- They can find it difficult to let go of the reins.
- They are often not good at training and coaching their successors.
- They may be unable to adjust to the style and priorities of newcomers.
- They may see the growth of systems and procedures as unnecessary bureaucracy.
- They sometimes plot to overthrow new management in order to put the organisation back on to what they see as the correct track.
- They sometimes leave and establish another organisation working in exactly the same field.

The departure of the founder can be a very difficult period and it can mark the end of the first stage. This is usually followed by a period of upheaval and a move into the second stage. New management brings different approaches and new ideas, and the organisation moves forward. There is, however, still much to be learned in the second stage. Sometimes there is a clash of values between an 'old guard', who see flexibility and opportunism as the very reason for the organisation's success, and the 'new brooms', who see the need for improved planning, more formal decision-making processes, better information systems and more structured management. Sometimes the roles of the board and the staff remain ill defined for a period of years. Until these problems are resolved, organisations stay in the youthful phase.

Eventually organisations grow into adulthood, perhaps following a change of leadership. In their idealised form, adult-stage organisations establish a clear distinction between the roles of governance and management, have a clear purpose and strategy, have effective management information and decision-making systems and develop people to achieve their greatest potential. In practice, not all organisations attain this potential. Changes in board membership, staff and the external environment mean that it is a constant challenge to maintain the highest management standards. Some organisations may slip back into the youthful stage and have to work hard to return to the adult stage of management.

Others move on to maturity. Once the cause is well established, it becomes more difficult to remain 'fired up' about the issues. These organisations probably have good connections with funders and policy-makers, but they may not have the most motivated branches or attract the most ambitious people. They frequently become less entrepreneurial and risk being overtaken by other organisations.

Finally, as needs change, funding, members and donations may start to fall. Unless organisations in this predicament can find a new purpose, they will start to decline. Surprisingly, third-sector organisations seldom die. Some become smaller and less effective and slide into ever-increasing mediocrity; others merge with a larger or newer body that injects new life into the organisation.

The value of the life cycle is that it helps to explain the behaviour of organisations when a number of problems surface simultaneously. This can be a time of great trauma, when different management issues all become entangled with one another. It is frequently a time when management consultants are brought in to help unbundle the problems and create an agenda of actions to move the organisation on to its next stage of development.

18.2 CLASSIFYING ORGANISATIONS

Third-sector organisations can be categorised in many different ways; for example, by size, by geographical scope (international, national, regional or local), by their institutional structure (linear or federal) or by historical stage of development. These are interesting and significant but, for managerial purposes, four types of classification are particularly useful. These are classification by:

- the **type of activities** they pursue (sometimes called sub-sectors);
- the **main source of funds**; (sale of services, grants, donations or membership fees)
- the **composition of the board**; (experts, users or concerned individuals)
- the **approach they take to achieving their mission** (delivering services, offering mutual support or campaigning for change).

417

This section describes these classifications and how different types of organisation fit into each of them. The next section looks at the implications for managing the different types of organisation.

This approach resembles academic analyses of the private sector, in which organisations are divided into categories such as manufacturing and service businesses, capital intensive and non-capital intensive, vertically integrated and horizontally diversified. Such categorisations are valuable because they shed light on common behavioural patterns which cut across industries. The same process leads to a better understanding of the management of different types of third-sector organisations.

Classification by activity

Organisations can be classified according to the activities they undertake: schools provide education, hospitals treat sick people, trade unions represent the workforce and disability organisations represent people with special needs. The International Classification of Non-profit Organisations (see 'Classification by activity' box, opposite) is a good example.

There is a small but growing literature on the special characteristics of the management of different types of organisations. In the UK there are books on the management of international aid organisations, housing organisations, grant-making foundations and religious organisations. In the USA there is also a body of literature on managing independent nonprofit schools and hospitals.

Useful as it is for social research, however, the value of this kind of typology for managers and board members is limited. From their perspective common management and governance characteristics are much more significant.

CLASSIFICATION BY ACTIVITY

The International Classification of Non-profit Organisations categorises organisations by activity:

Group 1: Culture and recreation

Sports, arts and culture, museums, zoos, recreation, social clubs

Group 2: Education and research

School and higher education, vocational training
Medical research, science and technology, policy studies

Group 3: Health

Hospitals, rehabilitation, nursing homes, mental health
Public health, health education

Group 4: Social services

Child welfare, youth services, services for families, elderly and disabled people

Emergency relief, income support, material assistance

Group 5: Environment

Conservation of natural resources, pollution control

Animal protection and welfare, wildlife and countryside preservation

Group 6: Development and housing

Economic, social and community development
Housing, employment and training

Group 7: Law, advocacy and politics

Advocacy organisations, minority groups, civic associations

Legal services, crime prevention, rehabilitation of offenders, victim support

Political parties

Group 8: Philanthropic intermediaries and voluntarism promotion

Grant-making foundations, fundraising organisations

Intermediary organisations

Group 9: International activities

Exchange programmes, development assistance, disaster relief
Human rights and peace organisations

Group 10: Religion Religious organisations

Group 11: Business, professional associations and unions
Employers' organisations, trade unions, professional associations

Group 12: Not elsewhere classified

Source: Johns Hopkins University, Comparative Nonprofit Sector Project, Revised Definitions

Classification by source of funds

A second way of putting some order on the third sector is to classify organisations by source of funds. Organisations are funded from four different sources:

- donations and fundraising activities (including investment and trading income)
- grants
- membership fees.
- direct sale of their services

Although some receive significant funding from more than one of these sources, most organisations receive the greater part of their income from one or two of these sources.

CLASSIFICATION OF CIVIL SOCIETY ORGANISATIONS BY PRIMARY SOURCE OF FUNDS

DONATION FUNDED	GRANT FUNDED
Some voluntary organisations	Quangos
Political parties	Universities
Churches	Foundation schools and academies
Campaigning organisations	Further/higher ed. colleges
	Arts organisations[1]

MEMBER FUNDED	SALES & CONTRACT FUNDED
Trade associations	Housing associations[2]
Trade unions	Independent schools
Professional organisations	Learning & Skills Councils
Employers' organisations	Provident societies[3]
Clubs	Friendly societies[4]
	Some voluntary organisations
	Hospitals[5]
	Social enterprise
	Cooperatives

[1] Also receive significant income from ticket sales.
[2] Also receive significant income from rent (i.e. sales).
[3] Examples include BUPA and Western Provident Society.
[4] After February 1993 no new Friendly societies could be registered.
[5] Located here since the purchaser-provider split was implemented.

The primary source of funding has a significant impact on organisations' strategic freedom. Organisations funded by donations sit at one end of a spectrum. They have great freedom to determine what they will do and how they will do it. Their boards are comparatively unconstrained in how they choose to achieve their objectives. Development agencies, for example, have enormous freedom to determine the activities they will pursue, the parts of the world they work in and the mechanisms they employ for achieving change.

Organisations funded by contracts and, to a lesser extent, those funded by grants are more tightly constrained. Geographical coverage, type of service, qualifications and accreditation may all be fixed. Schools and further education colleges exist at this end of the spectrum. Their users are defined, the curriculum is relatively constrained within fixed national boundaries, staff rewards often follow national schemes, and success is measured by external examination.

In the middle of this spectrum are organisations dependent on a mixture of funding sources. They have some constraints and some freedoms. Arts organisations are a good example; they can choose what to present, when to present it and who will perform, but they are constrained by the requirements of funders and their local catchment area.

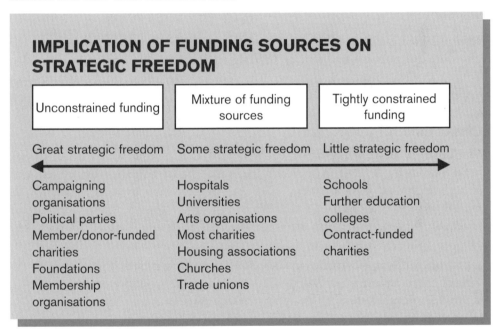

IMPLICATION OF FUNDING SOURCES ON STRATEGIC FREEDOM

Unconstrained funding	Mixture of funding sources	Tightly constrained funding
Great strategic freedom	Some strategic freedom	Little strategic freedom
Campaigning organisations	Hospitals	Schools
Political parties	Universities	Further education colleges
Member/donor-funded charities	Arts organisations	Contract-funded charities
Foundations	Most charities	
Membership organisations	Housing associations	
	Churches	
	Trade unions	

Classification by composition of the board

The third way of classifying organisations is by the motives of the people who are appointed to its board. Organisations attract different types of people to join their boards. These people bring different skills and experiences. Although people do not necessarily fall exclusively into one category or another and many boards consist of a mixture. Three main types can be identified. They are:

- **experts**, who bring knowledge, experience and (usually) specific professional skills to a board;
- **users**, who joined the organisation to benefit from its work or services and who will usually have been elected to the board by the membership;
- **concerned individuals**, who believe in a cause and wish to make their contribution by their voluntary effort as a board member.

421

Each group of people has different expectations of the role of the board and the way it should work.

Experts bring a series of assumptions derived from their work and professional experience. Users bring different assumptions to the board. They have a direct personal interest in the organisation. The services help them as well as other members, sometimes making it difficult to separate the best interests of the organisation from personal preferences and prejudices. Users may bring expertise from a profession as well, but their fundamental motivation for joining the board is different from that of the pure expert. Concerned individuals have another set of motives. They are distinguished by the fact that they feel passionately about an issue and they are willing to give significant amounts of their time to the organisation.

This classification is important because the composition of the board needs to 'fit' with the purpose and source funding of the organisation. As section 18.3, Putting the classifications together, will demonstrate, some combinations work better than others.

Classification by approach

The last way of bringing some coherence to this diverse sector is to classify organisations by the overall approach they take to achieving their objectives. This is a development of a typology that was put forward by Charles Handy in *Understanding Voluntary Organisations.* In this classification, third-sector organisations are divided by their approach to achieving their objectives. They can:

- **provide services** – examples include housing associations, colleges, schools, research organisations, arts organisations and many voluntary organisations;
- **provide mutual support** – examples include trade unions, professional associations, employers' organisations and self-help groups;
- **campaign for change** – examples include campaigning organisations such as Greenpeace, Liberty and Amnesty International.

This simple division into three main approaches is complicated by the fact that some organisations fall into two and some into all three categories. For example, some that began life as mutual-support organisations (say, for parents of children with a disability) start providing services. The services are successful, so they grow and develop. Before long, the organisation is a multi-million-pound service provider. However, it will probably have retained its mutual-support role, so consequently it falls into both categories and has the management issues of both types of organisation.

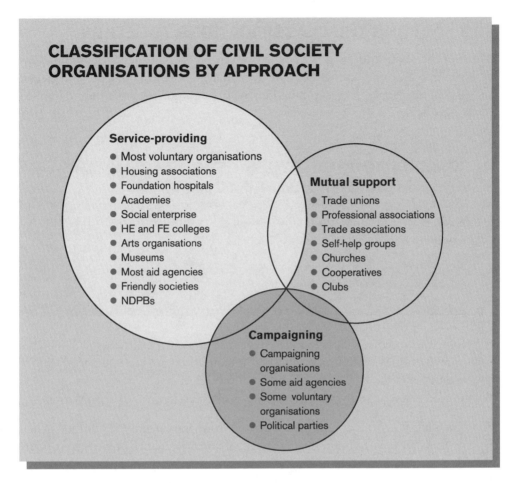

CLASSIFICATION OF CIVIL SOCIETY ORGANISATIONS BY APPROACH

Service-providing
- Most voluntary organisations
- Housing associations
- Foundation hospitals
- Academies
- Social enterprise
- HE and FE colleges
- Arts organisations
- Museums
- Most aid agencies
- Friendly societies
- NDPBs

Mutual support
- Trade unions
- Professional associations
- Trade associations
- Self-help groups
- Churches
- Cooperatives
- Clubs

Campaigning
- Campaigning organisations
- Some aid agencies
- Some voluntary organisations
- Political parties

Similarly, trade unions began as pure mutual-support or solidarity organisations representing the needs of their members. Today, many sell a range of services (such as insurance) to members and non-members alike, as well as campaigning for change.

In summary, the majority of third-sector organisations can be categorised in four dimensions:

- By type of activity:
  - culture
  - education
  - health
  - social services
  - and so on.
- By source of funds:
  - sales and contracts
  - grant funding
  - donations
  - members.
- By composition of the board:
  - experts
  - users
  - concerned individuals.
- By approach:
  - to provide services
  - to give mutual support
  - to campaign for change.

18.3 PUTTING THE CLASSIFICATIONS TOGETHER

Three of the classifications described above can be used to identify combinations of types that are more straightforward to manage and those that present greater managerial challenges. The combinations with a straightforward fit are described in the box below.

COMBINATIONS OF TYPES OF WORK THAT ARE MORE STRAIGHTFORWARD TO MANAGE

Approach	Main sources of funding	Composition of the board
Service	Sales, contracts and grants	Experts
Mutual support	Members	Users
Campaign	Members and donations	Concerned individuals

Although the boundaries between these types are fuzzy, the central logic that drives each combination is straightforward. These organisations are easier and less stressful to manage. Less time is spent resolving conflict, and managers and board members do not need to have a wide range of experience of different types of organisation.

As organisations grow they sometimes expand from one category to another. When they do this they have to build the management and governance capacity to support that change. So when a service-providing organisation starts campaigning it needs to create the capacity to define clear policy objectives, devise strategies to achieve them, raise unrestricted funds (e.g. from donors) and create new structures to manage the work (e.g. policy committees, press officers, lobbying skills). For a period of time, a seemingly small step into the public policy arena can make comparatively large demands on the organisation's management capacity.

Conversely, if an organisation slips into a new type of activity without having meant to, or without building the necessary management capacity, it risks becoming over-stretched and seeing the quality of work deteriorate.

Another example comes from mutual-support organisations that decide to help people outside their membership and start to offer services. At first sight, this is an obvious and sensible decision. The consequences are nevertheless significant. Pure mutual-support organisations have a straightforward logic: members pay fees and the organisation provides them with services in return. When they move into service provision for non-members, they need a different logic, concerned with defining user needs, marketing services and seeking funds to pay for them. Members' needs are no longer the organisation's sole priority. The situation becomes more complicated when, as sometimes happens, the service activities become much larger than the original mutual-support activities. When organisations with an institutional structure suitable for offering mutual support become large service providers, they need very different structures and management processes.

Another consideration is the need for funding sources that fit with the organisation's primary purpose. Combinations in the table above are known to work well. Combinations that cause problems include those shown in the table below.

COMBINATIONS OF TYPES OF WORK THAT CAN BE PROBLEMATIC

Approach	Primary funding source	Potential problems
Service	Donors	Service dependent on continuing support from donors. This works if the organisation has a strong brand (such as NSPCC or RSPCA) but is risky in other circumstances
Mutual support	Grants	Grants are often time-limited, which can lead to constant instability in the organisation
Campaign	Grants	There is a danger that priorities will be inappropriately influenced by the availability or source of funding

The basic message is that an expansion from one fundamental 'type' to two or more is a major strategic decision with wide-ranging consequences. It may require new funding sources, a different management logic and different skills on the board, and is a decision that should be taken with great care.

Having said that, there is evidence to suggest that some of the most effective organisations have achieved their successes by combining different approaches (see 'Forces for good' box overleaf).

FORCES FOR GOOD

Research in the USA asked 2,790 chief executives to nominate up to five nonprofits in their fields that they believed had had the most significant impact in the last 30 years. They enlisted 60 experts to analyse the survey results and narrow this list to 35 organisations. Twelve of these organisations were selected to represent the range of the sector's activity, different business models, geographic distribution and leadership. These were studied for two years to reveal how they made their impact.

The results were surprising. Whilst most of them had 'adequate' management (in terms of 'rigorous strategic plans, brilliant marketing and well-tuned operations') six different characteristics marked out these high-achieving organisations. Their success lay in how they mobilised every sector of society (government, business, nonprofits and the public) to be a force for good.

The six practices were:

1. **Serve and advocate.** High-impact organisations realised that they could not achieve large-scale social change by service delivery alone. They all combined service delivery and campaigning. Some had started as campaigning organisations and developed into service delivery and others had done the opposite

2. **Make markets work.** They learned that tapping into the power of self-interest and the laws of economics was far more effective than appealing to pure altruism

3. **Inspire evangelists.** They built strong communities of supporters who were not only volunteers, donors and advisors but became evangelists for the cause. They created emotional experiences that helped to connect supporters to the organisation's core mission

4. **Nurture nonprofit networks.** These organisations helped their peers to succeed by building networks, sharing wealth, expertise, talent and power with other nonprofits, not because they were saints but because it was in their own interest to do so

5. **Master the art of adaptation.** These organisations were exceptionally adaptive, responding to changing circumstances with many innovations. Not all were successful, but the organisations learned quickly and modified their approaches. They combined creativity with disciplined systems for evaluating, executing and adapting

6. **Share leadership.** The leaders all exhibited charisma, but they did not have oversized egos. They shared power, had strong seconds-in-command, built enduring teams with long tenure and developed large and powerful boards

Source: *Forces for Good,* Leslie Crutchfield and Heather McLeod Grant, Jossey-Bass, 2008

Classification by approach (service providing, mutual support and campaigning) sheds most light on the different methods that should be used to lead, manage and govern different types of organisation, so the next three sections of this chapter explore them in greater detail.

18.4 MANAGING SERVICE-PROVIDING ORGANISATIONS

Service-providing organisations dominate the third sector. Examples from the core of the sector include many voluntary organisations, arts organisations and housing associations. Examples at the periphery of the sector include schools, colleges, hospitals and universities.

These organisations were often founded by an individual or a group of social entrepreneurs. Examples from many years ago include the founding fathers of Oxford University and St Bartholomew's Hospital. Examples from the voluntary sector where the founder's name became enshrined in their organisation's name include Dr Barnardo, Leonard Cheshire, Marie Stopes and Sue Ryder.

The key characteristic of service-providing organisations is that they deliver a range of services to specific groups of service users who are not necessarily members of the organisation. This section describes propositions that are particular to service-providing organisations.

Strategic issues for service-providing organisations

The first strategic question that many service-providing organisations need to answer is: **why are they providing the service?** This is not as straightforward a question as it may appear at first sight. It could be any one, or a combination, of the following:

- meeting users' needs;
- demonstrating the value of the service;
- testing a new approach;
- providing experience to support campaign work;
- making a surplus to invest in other services;
- meeting volunteers' needs.

Answers to this question shed light on the primary objective of the organisation's services. If, for example, the purpose is to test a new approach (e.g. to experiment with a new way of helping single homeless people), then the primary objective might be to monitor how it works, track the outcomes and report on the results.

Alternatively, if the purpose is to support campaign work, the organisation will have to gear itself up to fit the service into its campaign strategy and manage the service, not just for the benefits the service provides, but to demonstrate the results it achieves. The organisation may also want to prove that the state could save money by using the service.

When great efforts are being made to establish or develop a service, it is easy to overlook its fundamental purpose. The service may be excellent but it may not be achieving what it was originally set up to do.

This leads to the second strategic question: **how will the organisation be financed in the long run?** Third-sector organisations are highly innovative when it comes to putting together a range of different sources of funds to finance a service. There are some, however, that do not monitor the extent to which their services are being funded by grants or contracts, subsidised by donors, or paid for by service users. In some cases, services which should be fully funded by the state are being unintentionally subsidised by donors. Managers of service-giving organisations need to be clear about who is funding the service, whether it should be funded in this way and whether the funding is sustainable in the longer term.

The third question is **whether the organisation wishes to go on providing the service in the long term.** In the past, many organisations established services to demonstrate to the state how a particular objective could be achieved. Other organisations have established services with the intention of hiving them off as separate organisations. The National Council for Voluntary Organisations has been particularly successful at that, founding Age Concern, the Charities Aid Foundation, Citizens Advice and many other less well-known organisations. Making each of these initiatives independent has enabled them to grow and become highly successful.

The fourth question is **whether the service should be provided by one organisation alone** or as a partnership between different organisations. Partnerships between third-sector organisations themselves and with businesses are increasingly common (as demonstrated in Chapter 12, Managing strategic partnerships). Further examples include RNIB publishing its electronic newspaper in conjunction with the *Guardian,* housing associations undertaking joint ventures financed partly by city institutions, and Oxfam importing products from small businesses in non-industrialised countries to sell via its mail-order catalogue.

Periodic consideration of these 'meta' issues is an important function for board members and senior managers of service-delivery organisations.

Meeting users' needs

Having established the primary purpose of the service, the central logic that needs to pervade these organisations is that of understanding users' needs and providing services to meet them. This sounds simple in theory; in practice, there are many dimensions to user needs. They include the exact nature of the service, its quality, the way it is delivered, where it is provided, the times it is available, and so on.

In the private sector, these different aspects of the service are bundled together and a price is attached to delivery of the service. When the business is not addressing that bundle of needs, sales fall and everyone knows that action must be taken to pinpoint the problem and make improvements. Many third-sector organisations do not have such a sensitive feedback mechanism, because users seldom pay the full cost of the service. As a result, there are only muted signals about service quality. In some organisations there is virtually no connection between funder and user. Consequently other issues (such as the needs of staff, board politics and policy debates) can creep incrementally up the agenda. There is an ever-present danger that meeting the needs of service users will not be given the attention it requires.

The logic of managing service-providing organisations is therefore dependent on **developing and maintaining a deep understanding of user needs**. This may require research, data-gathering from user groups, focus-group discussions, feedback forms and so on to replace the market mechanism and ensure that managers develop a clear view of user needs. Much has been written about marketing for service-providing organisations (see Further reading), so the concepts are not repeated here.

Having understood user requirements, the whole service delivery system needs **to focus sharply on meeting users' needs**. Objectives should focus on user needs and clarify what the organisation aims to do to meet those needs. The strategy should focus on how the organisation will meet those needs. The performance-monitoring system should gather information on the extent to which users are satisfied with the service.

The people-management process, including induction, supervision and performance review, should also incorporate sections on meeting user needs. Finally, the system for monitoring overall performance of the organisation should provide information on the number of users assisted, the extent of the assistance and its quality.

The effect of not having a direct market mechanism to keep service-giving organisations on their toes cannot be overestimated. Third-sector service providers have to compensate for this by taking every opportunity to ensure that all parts of the organisation are geared up to seek out, listen to and respond to users' needs.

Demand management

In some service-providing organisations, demand for the service exceeds the funds available to pay for it. Economic theory tells us that, as prices for a service fall, demand increases. In some organisations prices are zero – so demand could potentially be infinite.

Organisations therefore have to adopt demand-management techniques that depend on factors other than money. Some organisations allow waiting lists to grow. As they get longer, more and more people will seek the service elsewhere or solve their problem in some other way. Educational organisations have entry qualifications to manage demand. Housing associations measure the extent of people's housing need so that only people with the greatest need are eligible. Some organisations consciously avoid marketing or promoting their service, to avoid being swamped by demand.

Using various mechanisms to control demand is an important task for many service-giving organisations. It may require a balance of:

- qualifying criteria (e.g. degree of disability)
- means testing (e.g. income, savings)
- price (e.g. rents, ticket prices, user charges).

There is often an element of conflict between the need to market services (to ensure that their availability is known to those most in need) and the need to manage demand (to avoid being swamped by people wanting the service). Managers may feel that they are being pulled in two directions simultaneously. It is sometimes necessary to do both in order to concentrate resources on people with the greatest need. Marketing initiatives may need to be focused on particular groups, such as ethnic minorities, to ensure that they have access to the service; simultaneously, opening hours may need to be restricted as a way of controlling availability of the service.

To summarise, trustees and managers of third-sector service-delivery organisations have to ask some fundamental strategic questions about why they are or might be providing the service; they have to orientate all their organisation's systems around meeting users' needs and they often have to market the service and manage demand simultaneously.

18.5 MANAGING MUTUAL-SUPPORT ORGANISATIONS

Mutual-support organisations include many voluntary organisations established and run by members, trade unions, professional associations, employers' organisations and trade associations.

The fundamental difference between service-providing and mutual-support organisations is that members both benefit from and control the management of mutual-support organisations. The special nature of the management of these organisations emanates from this critically important relationship.

Values and management are inseparable

Mutual-support organisations are distinguished more than anything else by the values and beliefs of their members. These organisations usually consist of people who are devoted to the cause that the organisation stands for: people with disabilities, people with health problems, committed trade unionists, enthusiastic members of their profession and hardworking members of trade associations.

In the case of voluntary organisations, many board members may have had a significant life experience that motivated them to join the organisation. Common examples include the birth of a child with disabilities, personal experience as a patient or carer, or the death of a relative as a result of a terminal illness or an accident. Whatever the motive, members of these organisations have something in common. Consequently, the **culture is deeply influenced by members' experience** and the cause they champion.

The impact starts at the top with the board. It is elected by the members to represent their interests and views. Board members are therefore particularly aware of their constituency. They are not only thinking about the best interests of the organisation, its staff and its lobbying actions; they also have to keep their minds clearly fixed on members' views about the decisions and actions they take.

The values and beliefs of members have another – less obvious but nevertheless significant – impact on the way their organisation works. The very **nature of the cause spills over into management**. Take, for example, mutual-support organisations where there is hope for special training for children with disabilities. In these circumstances, members' ambitions and enthusiasm for the cause lead to positive attitudes towards achieving the goals. At the other end of the spectrum, organisations for people with terminal diseases can have a very different atmosphere. Unless values are fully acknowledged, as happens successfully in many hospices, anger, despair and resentment can spill over into the management of the organisation. Members can become angry with staff, and sometimes with each other as well. Debates and decisions become highly politicised and increasingly divorced from the facts.

The point is that values are central in mutual-support organisations, both explicitly and implicitly. Management's task is to make things happen within the framework of the organisation's values. Management may sometimes have to challenge the values, but they must recognise that to achieve significant change they need to bring the members with them.

Tensions between members and staff

Tension between members and staff is seldom far below the surface. There are good reasons why this should be the case, and it is worth acknowledging them explicitly. Members believe, quite rightly, that they own the organisation. They set it up, they pay their membership fees, and they control the governing board. The fact is, though, that their involvement is very much part time, and as the organisation grows they just cannot keep on top of the detail of its activities. They have to delegate to staff, who inevitably begin to feel that they are responsible for the future of the organisation.

This problem becomes more acute when the organisation has hired good-quality staff and has paid less attention to the quality of the organisation's governance. Staff come to feel that they know what is best for the organisation. These tensions should not be allowed to fester, because they de-motivate members and staff alike. The respective roles of the staff and of the board and its committees need to be discussed, clarified and documented.

There is a further complication that affects management. **Tensions are common among members themselves**. Some may have high ambitions for the organisation, some may vigorously argue a particular policy position, and some may have different ideas about the future direction of the organisation. These differences need to be acknowledged. They are all part of the push-and-pull of a diverse group of people who share one common cause. They need to be talked through, and often it will emerge that the views people share outnumber their differences of opinion. In difficult cases, independent third parties may help to resolve the problem. Where differences cannot be resolved, and are incapacitating the organisation, one side or the other should leave. The organisation needs to go one way or the other, not remain in suspended animation without the ability to proceed in any direction.

Employees may include people who are also members of the organisation. Indeed, many organisations go out of their way to recruit people who have had or are having direct experience of the support and services the organisation provides. The advantage of this is that sensitivity to user needs is built into day-to-day management. The disadvantage is that **employees who are personally affected can cause problems**. They do not always have a broad perspective on members' needs. They may hold strong views which can bring them into conflict with staff who are not personally affected by the problem. It requires adroit management and skilled supervision to prevent the views of user-employees from dominating among the staff.

Organisations for people with terminal diseases can be a particularly poignant and difficult case in point. Members with the disease inevitably hold very strong views about priorities, and staff feel they have to be responsive to those views. It is difficult to challenge people when they have all the authority that is provided by their circumstances. But if they hold a minority viewpoint, it has to be done; management has to be seen to be sensitive and yet simultaneously move the organisation forward for the benefit of the majority.

The special case of intermediary organisations

One particular type of membership organisation is the intermediary body. This is an organisation whose members are other organisations. In most fields, such organisations exist to provide an umbrella enabling a number of organisations to work together and speak with a common voice. The National Housing Federation, the National Council for Voluntary Organisations, the Long-term Conditions Alliance, the Confederation of British Industry and the Trades Union Congress are typical examples.

These organisations present a special set of management issues. Many of the people who sit on their boards do so as part of their job rather than as an entirely voluntary activity. Their commitment is consequently very different from that of voluntary board members. Although their primary loyalty should be to the intermediary organisation board, there is an ever-present danger that they will defer to the interests of the organisation they represent (see Conflicts of loyalty in section 3.7, Standards board members should meet). This makes the job of the chairs and chief executives of these organisations significantly more difficult. They have to be consummate politicians as well as effective managers. They have to be able to judge which issue or proposals will command the support of the majority of member organisations and which will not.

Like other membership bodies, these organisations become more complex to manage when they start to offer services to members. The core skills required to manage effective services are very different from those required to represent members. Indeed, the mindset of the service-providing part of the organisation is likely to differ significantly from that of the representative arm. The service provider has a business mentality and is concerned with the market for the service, its quality and its cost. Representation, on the other hand, is concerned with preparing policy, lobbying and the mechanics of political processes.

The issue becomes particularly acute when the service-providing part of the organisation finds itself in competition for contracts with its members. This happens because it is often difficult for intermediary organisations to raise sufficient funds from their members for their representation work, so they start to offer services in order to finance the representation work.

Organisations in this situation may need to review their fundamental purpose, determine whether representation work can become economically viable and, if necessary, float off those services that are competing with members for funds.

18.6 MANAGING CAMPAIGNING ORGANISATIONS

Campaigning organisations form only a tiny proportion of the third sector but they have a disproportionately large impact, despite their small number and comparatively small size. Pure campaigning organisations include Greenpeace, Amnesty International and organisations fighting for minority rights, women's rights and against poverty, prejudice and injustice. There are also many service-giving and membership organisations that run campaigns, so parts of this section are relevant to them too.

Campaigning organisations are particularly difficult to manage. They are often staffed by idealistic and highly articulate people. Many will find themselves with significant management responsibilities when they have had little experience of managing people or working in a team.

The first ingredient of successful campaigning is **leadership**. Successful campaigns depend on individuals who believe passionately in the cause and can argue the case for change to politicians, civil servants and the general public. Campaigning organisations need people who present a cogent case and who can simultaneously champion the cause and sound eminently reasonable.

Second comes the **political acumen** to identify campaigns that can be fought and won. Campaigning organisations need managers who can make judgements about changes that are achievable and who can then galvanise people into action around that change. Campaigns with unrealistic goals soon lose steam. Greenpeace has short-term objectives which it calls 'small wins' – the essential steps in the political process that lead to desired long-term changes.

Campaigning also depends on people with **creative skills** to translate the campaign goals into messages that will work in the media and campaigns that capture the public imagination. This calls for the kind of skills that are found in advertising and public relations agencies: understanding the media, thinking in images and creating new ways of communicating complex messages to the public. Only when the messages are clear can the organisation build a strong constituency of people who support the cause both politically and financially.

These organisations also require **management**. Fired up by the day-to-day tensions of running campaigns, people in these organisations often put insufficient energy into looking after the organisation itself. But organisations do not run on idealism alone; responsibilities need to be divided and individuals made accountable. Teams need to work both in and across the line-management structure; people need to be managed. Campaign managers need to work within budgets and have the information they need to control costs; fundraisers need to be able to compare the cost effectiveness of different fundraising methods. In short, tight management practices are needed to enable people to do the all-important campaigning work.

Boards of campaigning organisations play an important role in getting the right balance between campaign flair and sound management. Although board members will also be dedicated to the cause, they need to be able to stand back from the details of individual campaigns and play a more strategic role. The board's role in securing effective management of the organisation is crucial. Board members need to insist that staff put sufficient attention into looking after the organisation itself, otherwise working for the organisation can become so frustrating that even the motivation of the cause is insufficient to retain good campaigners. Since they are the critical resource, the board needs to ensure that time and money are invested in good administrative systems.

Strategic planning in campaigning organisations has to separate out the strategies of each campaign from **building the capacity of the institution as a whole**. Campaign strategy is concerned with the objectives of the campaign, the strategies that are chosen to achieve the objectives, and the resulting action plans. These are often given close attention; but equally important are the strategies for building a donor base, supporting local groups and creating an organisation that can respond quickly and effectively to campaign opportunities.

A major strategic issue for campaigning organisations is the **choice of campaign priorities**. There are always more issues requiring attention than resources available. Difficult choices have to be made by the board about competing claims for staff time and money. The pressures against setting priorities are often overwhelmingly strong. Board members have their personal – often strongly held – views. Campaign managers inevitably want to champion their own campaigns. Priorities are pushed to the fore by media coverage and public incidents that provide new opportunities to promote a campaign. Shifting government agendas create new chances to achieve a campaign goal.

A logical approach is to tailor-make a set of criteria against which alternative demands for resources can be assessed. Such criteria are likely to include:
• the importance of the issue to the achievement of the overall mission;
• the potential for making significant progress in a reasonable timescale;
• the unique role of the organisation on the issue;
• the scale of resources required to make a significant difference;
• the need to work with other organisations.

When reviewing strategic and operational plans, management and board members can then make the process of choosing priorities more rigorous by giving each campaign that is competing for resources a rating. Such an approach does not obviate the need for the board to use its wisdom to make good judgements. It does help to provide a framework within which these critically important judgements can be made.

SUMMARY OF KEY POINTS

Organisation life cycles

- Organisations develop in stages: periods of stability are followed by revolutionary change
- Founders are critically important in the first stage of an organisation's life because they have the vision and zeal to create it
- The departure of the founder can be one of the most difficult periods for an organisation
- Life cycles for individual organisations differ in detail. The power of the concept is that it helps boards and staff to see their problems in a broader context

Classifying organisations

- Useful ways to classify organisations so as to gain insights into their management are by:
  - the type of activities they pursue
  - the main source of funds
  - the composition of the board
  - the approach they take to achieving their mission
- The purpose of classifying organisations is to determine combinations of approaches, funding sources and board membership that fit together well and to identify combinations that cause problems

Putting the classifications together

- Combinations which are comparatively straightforward to manage include:
  - service organisations funded by sales, contracts or grants and managed by experts
  - mutual-support organisations funded by members and managed by users
  - campaign organisations funded by donations and managed by concerned individuals
- Recent research from the USA shows that some of the most successful organisations:
  - provide services and campaign
  - make markets and self-interest work in their favour
  - inspire supporters to evangelise about their cause
  - build and support networks of like-minded organisations
  - are highly creative and adaptive
  - build strong teams with long tenure and powerful boards
- Some organisations have combinations of approaches, sources of funding and board compositions that are much more challenging to manage

Managing different types of organisation

- Special characteristics of the management of **service-delivery** organisations include:
  - clarifying the fundamental purpose
  - orientating systems around meeting users' needs
  - marketing the service and simultaneously managing demand
- Managers of **mutual-support** organisations have to work with the values associated with the cause. There can be tensions between members and staff and they need to be addressed openly
- Successful **campaigning organisations** require strong leadership, creative skills and political acumen. They need to avoid the pitfall of paying insufficient attention to the practicalities of management and they need to be ruthless in setting campaign priorities

FURTHER READING

Forces for Good, The Six Practices of High-Impact Nonprofits, Leslie Crutchfield and Heather McLeod Grant, Jossey-Bass, 2008

Charity Marketing: Meeting Need Through Customer Focus, Ian Bruce, ICSA, 2005

Strategic Marketing for Nonprofit Organizations, Philip Kotler and Alan Andreasen, Prentice Hall, 2002

Understanding Voluntary Organisations, Charles Handy, Penguin Business, 1990

More and recent books and reports can be found at www.compasspartnership.co.uk.

19 Glimpsing into the future

From the turn of the nineteenth century to the end of the Second World War, the third sector was in decline. Ideas and services that emanated mainly from charitable initiatives were gradually being taken over by the state. Provision of housing, schools and health care was increasingly seen as a government responsibility. Many services that historically had been provided or supported by charitable institutions were slowly being incorporated into the public sector. From the end of the Second World War to the early 1970s, the charities that remained in the core of the third sector were seen as playing only a minor and secondary role to the new and rapidly growing public services.

During the early 1970s that situation began to change. It started when charitable organisations began to reassert their influence, often driven by idealistic people who were determined to take action to address the pressing social, health, environmental and educational problems that society faced. A combination of imaginative new ideas and increased funding from donors and the state led to the beginning of a period of explosive growth.

From the mid-1980s, there was a more fundamental change. The assumption that large public-sector organisations, funded and managed by the state, were the best way to provide public services began to be challenged. The separation of 'purchasers' and 'providers' had a dramatic impact on the third sector as organisations began to compete for work that had previously been undertaken by the public sector. At the same time, a number of public-sector services, such as local authority housing departments and residential homes, left the public sector and became independent third-sector organisations. Despite the misgivings many people had about separating purchasers and providers and making charities compete against one another for contracts, they have undoubtedly led to better services and have become an accepted way of working.

From the 1990s social enterprise, organisations that work primarily on a business model but generate a profit to further their social and environmental objectives, grew exponentially. They include cooperatives, housing associations, social firms, leisure trusts, furniture recycling organisations and development trusts. They now account for 5% of all businesses with employees. Well-known examples include the Eden Project, the Fairtrade Foundation and *The Big Issue*. They will continue to grow rapidly as more people who are motivated by social and environmental concerns establish organisations that sell products and services and re-invest their profits in the community.

More recently, the agenda for many third-sector organisations has moved on again, as government has indicated that it sees partnerships between the public, private and third sectors as another important development in the provision of more comprehensive and better-integrated services. Joint ventures, loose networks and strategic alliances are becoming the way to take new initiatives and achieve results quickly.

This final chapter takes a glimpse at the future of the third sector. It is a personal view, derived from my experience of working in the sector. It contains a mixture of some predictions and some aspirations for a sector of the economy that I believe will be an increasingly powerful force in years to come.

The sector will continue to grow and diversify

Until comparatively recently, the third sector was not recognised as a sector at all. It was a group of disparate and unconnected organisations that championed good causes but were often seen as inefficient and badly managed. Today it is seen as an essential part of the fabric of society, because people need organisations that are neither profit-seeking nor part of the public sector. Slowly but steadily, all these organisations are being acknowledged as one group that has a common cause: to take independent action to make the world a better place without excessive personal gain.

In the foreseeable future the third sector will become fully established as a group of organisations that are as essential to post-industrial, democratic and caring societies as the private and public sectors. This will be underpinned by the strong support that the sector now has from the three main political parties. Although it will remain smaller in economic terms than the private and public sectors, it will continue to have disproportionate influence because it champions justice, fairness and morality.

The sector will continue to grow because:
- Public-sector organisations that are on the boundary of both sectors (such as colleges, schools and the health service) will increasingly become part of the third sector as they diversify their income sources and their independence grows.
- More social enterprises will be established by people who are motivated to run business organisations with social and environmental purposes.
- Ever-more sophisticated ways of raising new funds will be created, with a much higher proportion coming from the internet.

- More charities will establish business subsidiaries. It is already possible to buy environmentally friendly washing machines and fridges from Friends of the Earth, furniture from Oxfam, insurance from RSPB, clothes from amnesty.org.uk, and gifts from most major charities. These opportunities will grow as third-sector organisations realise that the 'feel-good' factor associated with purchasing a product or service is a competitive advantage that can be exploited to raise unrestricted funds.
- A new generation of mega-philanthropists who have accumulated great wealth will want to give their money away during their lifetimes rather than as a legacy when they die.

These trends will combine to create a stronger, more vibrant and more effective third sector. That expansion will be driven by internal growth of the sector and by the coalescence of a wider range of organisations into a more broadly based civil society sector. That sector may already account for almost 12% of GDP (using 2008 figures from National Council for Voluntary Organisations and the Office for National Statistics). It could grow considerably larger in the coming years.

Accountability will continue to increase

When the sector was smaller, expectations for it to be accountable were low. That is now changing, with a growing requirement that these organisations should be much more transparent about what they do, what it costs and what they achieve. There are now higher standards for reporting (for example in annual reports) and there is more independent scrutiny (for example by organisations like Intelligent Giving). These requirements will continue to grow.

People will increasingly expect to be able to click on to the internet and quickly discover where organisations get their money from, who runs them, what they have done and whether they are having a significant impact.

Organisations will be judged by their results

Organisations will increasingly be expected to both report on what they have done and to show the difference they have made. They will need to demonstrate the improvements they have made to people's lives and the policy changes that have resulted from their campaigns. Those organisations that are seen to deliver the most impact will command greatest public respect and receive a larger share of the available funds. Those that are less able to demonstrate their impact will grow more slowly than the leaders.

Management attention will therefore have to focus much more sharply on demonstrating tangible results. Objectives, strategies and plans will have to be based on demonstrating positive outcomes for services and campaigns. Funders will set performance standards, and organisations will need to find ways to measure results and report on the impact of their services.

This will require significant investment in systems that allow organisations to track their performance and to follow users up, months (and sometimes years) after the service was provided, in order to pinpoint the difference that the service made. Boards and managers will then be able to adjust their services to focus on approaches that have been shown to have the greatest long-term impact.

Cost effectiveness will be the primary measure of success

The prevalent assumption that reducing costs automatically leads to a reduction in quality will be challenged, as innovative organisations discover imaginative ways of achieving the desired outcomes with fewer material and human inputs. The private sector has demonstrated conclusively that, with effective management, services can be improved and costs reduced at the same time. At present third-sector organisations find it difficult to see how these seemingly contradictory objectives can be achieved.

However, pressure to compete successfully for contracts and to deliver quality services to users will drive organisations to discover ways of increasing their productivity. Managers will increasingly be expected to demonstrate how every person and every item of expenditure contributes directly to the delivery of a cost-effective service. Activities that do not make a cost-effective contribution will be cut.

Missions will have to motivate people

As more people look for greater meaning in life, and in particular for purposes beyond meeting their own needs, third-sector organisations will provide more opportunities for them to contribute to society in meaningful ways. Younger people will increasingly see the sector as a positive career choice and older people will see it as providing new opportunities for voluntary work in retirement.

There will be much greater competition for people. Board members, staff and volunteers will have to be inspired to volunteer and work for these organisations. Those that promote their missions powerfully will have motivated people who have the energy and commitment required to deliver top-quality services.

In his book *The Hungry Spirit,* Charles Handy talks about accepting responsibility for making the most of oneself by finding a purpose beyond oneself. He calls this being 'properly selfish'. Third-sector organisations offer just that opportunity, provided management ensures that their missions are strongly promoted and are at the heart of all their work.

Specialisation will increase

Competition for contracts, donors and sales will force organisations to specialise in those services in which they have most expertise and to withdraw from services in which they have fewer skills. Niche providers will grow faster than generalist organisations that diversify into many services and inevitably develop cumbersome management overheads.

As organisations are driven to focus on those activities in which they have the greatest expertise, they will need to adjust the portfolio of services they manage. Broadly based 'conglomerate' organisations will be driven to pursue more focused strategies as they face stronger competition from more specialised organisations. This will mean more movement of services between organisations as they acquire, dispose of and exchange services with other organisations. This will happen mainly within the sector, but there will also be more movement between all three sectors.

Strategic partnerships will become more prevalent

There will be more strategic partnerships as organisations seek to find ways to increase their impact. There will be a wide range of relationships ranging from loose alliances to long-term strategic partnerships. More organisations will share back-office services and more will move into the same premises as another way of increasing cooperation and joint working.

There will also be many more mergers as the sector matures and coalesces and as organisations seek to benefit from economies of scale.

Organisations will use a wider range of methods of finance

Organisations have traditionally relied on membership fees, donations, grants and earned income to finance activities, to build their organisation and to raise working capital. They have been reticent to borrow money and growth has sometimes been constrained by a conservative approach to finance. In future they will access a much wider range of financial instruments including loans, loan guarantees, quasi-equity (where the investor and the organisation share the risks and rewards) and equity investments (where the investor takes more risk and can get higher rewards).

There will be more investors who want to help organisations expand but also want a financial return on their investments. As this book goes to press plans for the establishment of a social stock exchange are well advanced and I anticipate that it will quickly become an accepted method of financing third-sector organisations that operate on a business model.

Third-sector organisations will also accelerate their growth and impact by fitting activities and their sources of finance much more strategically. In the past they have focused most of their attention on improving the delivery of services and little on how they are financed. Business has given much more attention to the finance side of the equation. Third-sector organisations are now recognising that they may be able to accelerate their growth by using different sources of finance to grow different types of activities. In future they will only use their most valuable 'unrestricted' funds where there is no other suitable source of finance.

In doing so, they will have to become much more sophisticated in understanding and managing risk. In the past they have taken virtually risk-free financing strategies, usually waiting for funds to be raised before embarking on new initiatives. Being bolder will require organisations to learn how to manage and mitigate risk.

New technology will transform the way organisations work

The impact of ICT – and, in particular, communications technology – will dramatically change the way third-sector organisations work. Many organisations are spread around the country and the globe. Until now, their centre or headquarters has been the hub of the organisation and of its communications. Teleconferencing and video conferencing will change all that. The furthest parts of the organisation will be able to communicate with each other easily and cheaply. This will drive the centres of organisations to define their unique contribution more precisely and give the outposts more freedom to do their work within agreed boundaries.

Management and governance will be streamlined

Internally, organisations with cumbersome management structures, boards and committees will streamline themselves to increase their effectiveness. Management structures will become flatter as managers and their staff discover more effective ways of working together. Boards will continue to grow smaller and at the same time more accountable. More of the largest and most complex organisations will find that the time required from board members to provide fast, effective and engaged governance will mean that they have to pay board members to recruit people with the required skills and experience.

The notion that committees automatically add value will be challenged. The governance of large organisations will be much more concerned with holding management to account, so large and complex committee structures may no longer be necessary.

All this will require greatly increased effort to be put into governance and management development. Training courses, mentoring, shadowing and coaching will all play a greater role in the daily lives of managers. Skill-acquisition will become a major objective of ambitious managers. Organisations will have to respond by making time and resources available for board members and managers to become more capable.

Managers will face many contradictory pressures

Managers will be expected to work with many contradictory pressures. They will be expected to:

- give the organisation a strong sense of direction *and* adapt quickly to changing circumstances;
- have long-term objectives and strategies *and* meet short-term performance targets;
- devolve power to the field *and* maintain a common purpose throughout the organisation;
- streamline management and governance *and* maintain people's motivation;
- expect massive commitment from people *and* offer them less job security;
- invest in organisational learning *and* work with fewer spare resources.

These will provide challenges for managers throughout the sector.

Characteristics of successful organisations

To meet these challenges, organisations will need to exhibit many characteristics. They will require:

- **leadership from visionary individuals**
  - ensuring that a clear mission pervades all parts of the organisation
  - communicating effectively with all stakeholders;
- **a sharp focus on results**
  - understanding what users want
  - providing services that exceed users' expectations
  - continuously monitoring service quality
  - benchmarking against the best in the world;
- **investment in people**
  - empowering them to deliver results
  - learning continuously from each other
  - encouraging innovation in all aspects of their work;
- **enthusiasm for change**
  - embracing new opportunities and ways of working
  - relishing the chance to be more effective.

An ambitious list, you may say. But most third-sector organisations want to make a significant impact on the world in which we live. To achieve that ambition will require excellence in all aspects of management.

Appendix 1

ORGANISATION EXPERIENCE INFORMING THIS BOOK

This appendix sets out some of the organisations that the author has worked with and that have provided the practical experience which has informed the advice set out in this book. (Organisations' names at the time of publication are used.)

Arts
Arnolfini
Arts Council England
Association of British Orchestras
Bristol Old Vic
Britten-Pears Foundation
English National Ballet
National Theatre
Opera North
Scottish Chamber Orchestra
Wordsworth Trust
Youth Music

Consumer and human rights
Amnesty International
Equality and Human Rights
Commission
Liberty
National Consumer Council
Scottish Consumer Council

Education and training
CfBT Education Trust
Girls' Day School Trust
Office of the Independent Adjudicator
for Higher Education
Thames Valley University
Universities UK

Environment
Council for the Protection of Rural
England
Durrell Wildlife Conservation Trust
Environment Agency

Environmental Partnership for Central
Europe
Friends of the Earth
Greenpeace
Groundwork
Institute for European Environmental
Policy
International Union for the
Conservation of Nature
National Energy Action
Natural England
Plantlife International
Woodland Trust
WWF-UK

Foundations and funders
Association of London Government
Big Lottery Fund
Futurebuilders
Impetus Trust
Joseph Rowntree Charitable Trust
Laing Family Trusts
Lloyds TSB Foundation for England
and Wales
Nationwide Foundation
Norwich Consolidated Charities
Nuffield Foundation

Health and disability
Alcohol Concern
Arthritis Research Campaign
Association for Real Change
Asthma UK

Benenden Healthcare
Breakthrough Breast Cancer
Breast Cancer Care
British Deaf Association
British Diabetic Association
British Stammering Association
Brook
Cancerlink (now part of Macmillan Cancer Support)
CLIC Sargent
Communications Forum
Connect
Department of Health
Diabetes UK
Digestive Disorders Foundation
Disabled Living Foundation
Equinox
Guide Dogs
Guy's and St Thomas' Charity
Health Foundation
Homerton Hospital NHS Trust
I CAN
International Guide Dog Federation
Leonard Cheshire Disability
Liverpool Drug Prevention Team
Liverpool Social Partnership
Macmillan Cancer Support
Mencap
Mental Health Providers Forum
Mind
Motability
Motor Neurone Disease Association
Multiple Sclerosis Society
National AIDS Trust
National Autistic Society
National Eczema Society
National Library for the Blind (now part of RNIB)
National Association for Colitis & Crohn's Disease
Order of St John Care Trust
Parkinson's Disease Society
Prostate Cancer Care
Rethink

Royal National Institute of Blind People
Royal National Institute for Deaf People
Scope
Spurgeons
St Andrew's Group of Hospitals
St Dunstan's
Terrence Higgins Trust
Turning Point
Twins and Multiple Births Association
United Response
Vision 2020 UK
Whizz-Kidz

Housing and care
Advance Housing and Support
The Big Issue
Guinness Trust
Homeless Network
Housing 21
Housing Corporation
Methodist Homes
Methodist Ministers' Housing Society
National Housing Federation
Officers' Association
Shelter
St Mungo's

International development
ActionAid
British Red Cross
Christian Aid
Disasters Emergency Committee
East European Partnership
Health Unlimited
Hope and Homes for Children
International Institute for Environment and Development
International Planned Parenthood Federation
Oxfam
Save the Children
Uganda Society for Disabled Children
UNICEF

United Nations Association – UK
VSO
WaterAid
World Population Foundation
World Vision

Professional and trade associations
Association of Chief Executives of
Voluntary Organisations
British Marine Federation
British Printing Industries Federation
Chartered Society of Designers
Confederation of British Industry
Environmental Services Association
Institute of Chartered Accountants in
England and Wales
International Water Association
National Association of Head Teachers
National Association of Steel
Stockholders
Picon
Railway Industry Association
Royal College of Nursing

Sector infrastructure
Brent Council
Capacitybuilders
Carmichael Centre – Dublin
Charities Aid Foundation
Charity Commission
Community Foundation Network
Department for Business, Enterprise
and Regulatory Reform
Development Trust Association
Governance Hub
Greater Manchester Council for
Voluntary Organisations
Hampshire County Council
Home Office
Infrastructure National Partnership
Kent County Council
National Association for Voluntary
and Community Action
National Council for Voluntary
Organisations

New Philanthropy Capital
Office of the Third Sector
Third Sector Leadership Centre
Volunteering England
VONNE

Social Welfare
Age Concern England
Apex Trust
Carers UK
The Children's Trust
Citizens Advice
The Fostering Network
Jewish Community Centre
National Consumer Council
National Council of Voluntary Child
Care Organisations
NSPCC
Outward Bound
Prince's Trust
Refugee Council
Relate
The Royal British Legion
Royal Philanthropic Society
The Royal Society for the Prevention
of Accidents
Samaritans
ScotsCare
TLC Care Services
UNISON
Victim Support
Vitalise
wpf Counselling and Psychotherapy
WRVS
YMCA

Welfare of animals
Bat Conservation Trust
Battersea Dogs and Cats Home
Farm Animal Welfare Forum
RSPCA

Appendix 2

ORGANISATION DEVELOPMENT DIAGNOSTIC TOOL

This tool is designed to help nonprofit organisations make a preliminary diagnosis of the development needs of their organisation.

Compass Partnership	ORGANISATION DEVELOPMENT DIAGNOSTIC TOOL				

Part A Governance	Very	Quite	Not very	Not at all	Don't know
1. How clear is the board's view of the organisation's mission, objectives and strategic direction?	☐	☐	☐	☐	☐
2. How well do board members understand the distinctive roles of governance and management?	☐	☐	☐	☐	☐
3. How clear are board members about their responsibilities?	☐	☐	☐	☐	☐
4. How appropriate is board members' mix of skills and experience for the challenges it faces in the future?	☐	☐	☐	☐	☐
5. How well do board members work as a team?	☐	☐	☐	☐	☐
6. How effective is the organisation's chair?	☐	☐	☐	☐	☐
7. How clear is the delegation of authority to the chief executive?	☐	☐	☐	☐	☐
8. How effective is the board's process for monitoring the performance of the chief executive?	☐	☐	☐	☐	☐
9. How good is the relationship between the chair and the chief executive?	☐	☐	☐	☐	☐

Part A Governance	Very	Quite	Not very	Not at all	Don't know
10. How systematically does the board review its own performance?	☐	☐	☐	☐	☐
11. What changes would you propose to give the organisation clearer objectives?					

Part B Mission, objectives and strategy	Very	Quite	Not very	Not at all	Don't know
12. How clear is the organisation's mission?	☐	☐	☐	☐	☐
13. How clear are the organisation's strategic objectives for achieving the mission?	☐	☐	☐	☐	☐
14. How clear are the strategies for achieving the objectives?	☐	☐	☐	☐	☐
15. How well understood are the mission, objectives and strategies by all staff?	☐	☐	☐	☐	☐
16. How specific are the annual objectives for the organisation as a whole?	☐	☐	☐	☐	☐
17. How clear are the longer-term objectives for individual services and campaigns?	☐	☐	☐	☐	☐
18. How specific are the annual objectives for individual services and campaigns?	☐	☐	☐	☐	☐
19. What changes do you think need to be made to strengthen the organisation's mission, objectives and strategies?					

Part C Management and staff	Very	Quite	Not very	Not at all	Don't know
20. Overall, how strong are the individuals on the senior management team?	☐	☐	☐	☐	☐
21. How appropriate is the management structure to meet the future demands of the organisation?	☐	☐	☐	☐	☐
22. How effective are meetings of the leadership team?	☐	☐	☐	☐	☐
23. How open are personal relationships on the leadership team?	☐	☐	☐	☐	☐
24. How creative is the leadership team?	☐	☐	☐	☐	☐
25. How skilled are staff for the roles they are expected to perform?	☐	☐	☐	☐	☐
26. How effective are the processes for recruiting, retaining and rewarding staff?	☐	☐	☐	☐	☐
27. How often do staff feel they are 'overloaded' with work?	☐	☐	☐	☐	☐

28. What changes do you think are required to strengthen management and the staff?

Part D Management processes	Very	Quite	Not very	Not at all	Don't know
29. How effective is the organisation's strategic planning process?	☐	☐	☐	☐	☐
30. How effective is the process for monitoring progress in achieving strategic objectives?	☐	☐	☐	☐	☐
31. How clear are individuals about their objectives?	☐	☐	☐	☐	☐
32. How well developed are processes for setting and monitoring budgets?	☐	☐	☐	☐	☐

Part D Management processes	Very	Quite	Not very	Not at all	Don't know
33. How well does the organisation promote its achievements?	☐	☐	☐	☐	☐
34. What changes would you recommend to strengthen the organisation's management processes?					

Part E Infrastructure	Very	Quite	Not very	Not at all	Don't know
35. How appropriate is the organisation's accommodation to meet future requirements?	☐	☐	☐	☐	☐
36. How appropriate are the organisation's electronic systems (website, intranet, communications) to meet future requirements?	☐	☐	☐	☐	☐
37. What changes would you recommend to strengthen the organisation's infrastructure?					

Part F Income and expenditure	Very	Quite	Not very	Not at all	Don't know
38. How effective is the organisation's fundraising strategy?	❏	❏	❏	❏	❏
39. How effective is the organisation at selling its services to public authorities or end users?	❏	❏	❏	❏	❏
40. How well is the organisation able to balance income and expenditure?	❏	❏	❏	❏	❏

41. What changes would you recommend to strengthen the organisation's capacity to raise income?

Part G   Overview

42. Overall, what are the three top organisation development issues your organisation needs to address? Please list in order of priority.

Appendix 3

COMPASS PARTNERSHIP

Compass Partnership is a management consultancy that works exclusively with 'civil society' organisations. It provides consultancy services to chairs, chief executives and senior managers. We help organisations and their funders with:

Strategic planning

We work with boards and senior managers to:
- revitalise and re-frame their mission
- create inspiring strategies to achieve their mission
- establish ambitious and realistic business and operational plans to achieve the organisation's strategic objectives.

Performance management

We work with chief executives and senior managers to:
- shout about success by articulating their achievements in compelling ways.
- strengthen systems for monitoring and managing strategic performance
- benchmark performance and processes.

Management development

We work with chief executives and senior managers to:
- renew management structures and processes
- develop high performance teams
- deliver complex change management projects

Governance development

We work with chairs to:
- re-structure boards and committees
- review the performance of board and committee members
- clarify board and management relationships

Research

We work with managers at all levels to:
- design and deliver policy, market and social research

Compass works with all types of organisation, including voluntary organisations, housing organisations, social enterprise, development agencies, arts organisations, professional associations and the organisations that fund them, including government departments, non-departmental public bodies and foundations.

If you would like assistance, please do not hesitate to contact our Business Manager at demerson@compassnet.co.uk or on +44 (0)1628 478561 or visit our website www.compasspartnership.co.uk.

Author Index

Organisations Index

Subject Index